Voting and Democratic Citizenship in Africa

The Global Barometers Series

The Global Barometers Series publishes work that draws on the Global Barometers Surveys. For information on the surveys, see http://www.globalbarometers.org.

Voting and Democratic Citizenship in Africa

EDITED BY
Michael Bratton

LYNNE
RIENNER
PUBLISHERS

BOULDER
LONDON

Published in the United States of America in 2013 by
Lynne Rienner Publishers, Inc.
1800 30th Street, Boulder, Colorado 80301
www.rienner.com

and in the United Kingdom by
Lynne Rienner Publishers, Inc.
3 Henrietta Street, Covent Garden, London WC2E 8LU

Library of Congress Cataloging-in-Publication Data
Voting and democratic citizenship in Africa / edited by Michael Bratton.
    p. cm. — (The global barometers series)
    Includes bibliographical references and index.
    ISBN 978-1-58826-894-5 (alk. paper)
    1. Voting—Africa. 2. Political participation—Africa. 3. Elections—
Africa. 4. Africa—Politics and government—1960–   I. Bratton,
Michael. II. Series: Global barometers series.
    JQ1879.A5V686 2013
    324.65096—dc23

                                                          2012035208

British Cataloguing in Publication Data
A Cataloguing in Publication record for this book
is available from the British Library.

Printed and bound in the United States of America

∞   The paper used in this publication meets the requirements
       of the American National Standard for Permanence of
       Paper for Printed Library Materials Z39.48-1992.

5 4 3 2 1

Contents

Preface

Over a long career studying politics in Africa, I have had the privilege of many memorable experiences. These include formal meetings with African presidents, emotional interviews with human rights victims, and the charms and challenges of living for a spell in a rural village.

But one encounter was especially vivid. During the historic multiparty elections of 1991 in Zambia—which brought an end to the one-party rule of nationalist founding father Kenneth Kaunda—I was assigned by the Carter Center to lead a small election observer team to Kalabo district in the country's distant Western province. Our first foray into the area to check on election preparations had been by canoe across the Zambezi; but this time, for the election itself, we were dropped off in style by a small charter airplane. We rose early on election day to watch the opening of polls in the district capital, traveled to several outlying polling stations near the Angolan border, and, on our return journey, stopped at a rural school to observe the closing of the polls. It was here, in the fading light that followed a brilliant African sunset, that the deeper meaning of the day's events began to hit home.

Crowded into a dingy schoolroom, voters—men and women, old and young—declined to leave after casting a ballot. Even though they had queued for hours to wait for a late-opening poll, they insisted on remaining in place to ensure the integrity of their vote. Denied the opportunity to have votes counted and announced at the polling station itself, voters—along with party agents and nonpartisan monitors—were allowed to observe the sealing of the ballot box and its transportation to a counting center. In the gathering gloom, candles were lit to melt red-wax seals. All eyes, reflecting the flickering flames, were focused on the ballot box as if it were a sacred reliquary. In the eerie silence of the ceremony, one felt that it contained all the hopes and aspirations of the assembled people. Only when polling officials hoisted the box aloft and moved toward the door did the throng burst into a round of cheers and ululations.

I learned that day that vote choice matters. It matters most deeply to people long denied the right. The act of casting a ballot in a meaningful election signifies more than the chance to participate in choosing a head of state or a representative to parliament. The voting act conveys human dignity by symbolizing that every participating individual is an equal and respected member of a political community. As such, voting is a meaningful step on the road to democratic citizenship.

This book reports on how individuals in Africa regard elections, how they vote, and whether and how they try to make themselves heard between elections. Ultimately it is about the political role of the individual citizen in Africa's would-be democracies.

The contents of the book summarize a decade's worth of research on voting and democratic citizenship by investigators in the United States and Africa connected by a cross-national survey project known as the Afrobarometer. This network of researchers is united by a shared concern with the micropolitics of democracy building. All of the contributors base their analyses on Afrobarometer survey data. Together, the contributions represent a collective effort to cast light on the features, origins, and mechanisms underlying popular participation in Africa's new democracies.

*   *   *

In the course of assembling this volume, the contributors and I accumulated many debts. At the risk of overlooking key colleagues, I mention just a few of the people who helped to bring our project to fruition.

For helping to design research studies and to raise research funds, I thank my collaborators in the executive leadership of the Afrobarometer Network: Emmanuel Gyimah-Boadi, Robert Mattes, Carolyn Logan, Leonard Wantchekon, and Paul Graham. The capable staffs at the Afrobarometer's core partner institutions carried much of the load in research administration, especially Daniel Armah-Attoh at the Center for Democratic Development in Ghana, the late Gregoire Kpekpede at the Institute for Empirical Research in Political Economy in Benin, and Zenobia Ismail at the Institute for Democracy in South Africa.

We could not have implemented surveys or understood results without the efforts of the research teams led by national investigators in every Afrobarometer country. Through the first four rounds of surveys, these investigators included Mogopodi Lekorwe (Botswana), Augustin Loada (Burkina Faso), Francisco Rodrigues, Jose Semedo, and Deolinda Reis (Cape Verde),

Winnie Mitullah (Kenya), John Gay (Lesotho), Dan Saryee and Alaric Topka (Liberia), Mireille Razafindrakoto and Desiré Razafindrazaka (Madagascar), Blessings Chinsinga and Maxton Tsoka (Malawi), Massa Coulibaly (Mali), Carlos Shenga (Mozambique), Bill Lindeke and Andrew Niikondo (Namibia), Innocent Chukwuma and Taofeeq Akinremi (Nigeria), Babaly Sall and Ibrahim Gaye (Senegal), Lucas Katera (Tanzania), Robert Sentamu (Uganda), Peter Lolojih (Zambia), and Eldred Masunungure (Zimbabwe).

Although African institutions lead the Afrobarometer, support units provide analytic services, quality assurance, and capacity building. At Michigan State University, Rhonda Burns and Kelly Fenn kept the wheels of the project turning. And Libby Downes and Kimberly Smiddy did the same at the University of Cape Town. Also at MSU, the following individuals provided research assistance, managed datasets, or operated publication and website programs: Paloma Bauer, Virginia Beard, Danielle Carter, Tse-Hsin Chen, Wonbin Cho, Tetsuya Fujiwara, Matthew Kirwin, Eric Little, and Fabiana Machado.

We also received insightful comments on draft papers from Yun-han Chu, Jeffrey Conroy-Krutz, Larry Diamond, Boniface Dulani, Nicholas Kerr, Adrienne LeBas, Marta Lagos, Ellen M. Lust, Stephen N. Ndegwa, Muna Ndulo, Nicolas van de Walle, and several anonymous reviewers. The papers on which the chapters are based were road-tested at various professional conferences, university seminars, and public gatherings. Too numerous to mention individually, these events provided audience reactions that helped us with revisions. For sharing his dataset on elections in Africa, I thank Staffan Lindberg.

Several contributions were prepared expressly for this volume (Chapters 1, 2, 13, and 15). Early versions of most of the other chapters first appeared in the Afrobarometer Working Papers series at www.afrobarometer.org. Some were subsequently edited for inclusion in published volumes: Chapter 11 is a revised version of "Voters but Not Yet Citizens: Democratization and Development Aid" in *Smart Aid for African Development,* edited by Richard Joseph and Alexandra Gillies (Boulder: Lynne Rienner, 2009); and Chapter 14 is a revised version of "The Democracy-Governance Connection" in *Governing Africa's Changing Societies: Dynamics of Reform,* edited by Ellen M. Lust and Stephen N. Ndegwa (Boulder: Lynne Rienner, 2012). Other working papers were revised for publication in scholarly journals and are included here in further revised form with the permission of the authors and publishers: Chapter 4 is drawn from the *American Journal of Political Science* (54, no. 2, April 2010, pp. 494–510), Chapter 5 from *Commonwealth and Comparative Politics* (50, no. 1, February 2012, pp. 27–52), Chapter 7 from *Electoral Studies* (27, 2008, pp. 621–632), Chapter 8 from the *Journal of Modern African Studies* (50, no. 2, pp. 625–655, December 2012), Chapter 10 from *Governance* (25, no. 4, September 2012, pp. 617–637), and Chapter 12 from the *British Journal of Political Science* (39, no. 2, 2009, pp. 345–366).

Finally, but importantly, acknowledgment is due to the various agencies that provided resources for the first four rounds of the Afrobarometer. Major sustained contributions were made by, among others, the Swedish International Development Cooperation Agency, the US Agency for International Development, the Department for International Development (UK), the Canadian International Development Agency, the Royal Danish Ministry of Foreign Affairs, the Netherlands Ministry of Foreign Affairs, Michigan State University, and the World Bank. The National Science Foundation provided seed money for the Afrobarometer and funded the panel study mentioned in Chapter 8. Without the support of these institutions, my colleagues and I would not have been able to do our work.

No organization or contributor, however, should be held responsible for the contents of this book. All errors of fact and interpretation are the editor's alone.

—*Michael Bratton*

1

Voting and Democratic Citizenship in Africa: An Overview

Michael Bratton

Politics in Africa are commonly viewed from the top down. Journalists and social scientists alike tend to focus on the deeds—and misdeeds of African presidents and the coterie that surrounds them. The mixed political history of postcolonial Africa, for example, is often written in terms of the leadership of exceptional individuals like Mandela, Mugabe, and Museveni. And political developments are often summarized with reference to distinctive national institutions like dominant ruling parties or interventionist armed forces. Ordinary people, who initially embraced one-party and military rule, are conventionally portrayed in the literature on African politics as mere bit players in supporting roles to centralized institutions or influential "big men."

This imbalance in the coverage of elite and mass politics was disrupted when political openings began across sub-Saharan Africa some thirty years after independence. In the 1990s—foreshadowing the Arab Spring of 2011—citizens in many African countries took advantage of the end of superpower support for ailing dictators to demand civil and political rights. Analysts took note by paying greater attention to civic associations, the informal economy, street protest, and the emergence of opposition political parties. Some of these popular initiatives contributed to a groundswell of constitutional and political reforms, to the convocation of multiparty elections, and occasionally even to transitions to fragile or hybrid forms of democracy. The advent of a measure of democratization seemed, for the first time since the struggle for independence, to hold out the promise of a greater measure in African politics of "rule by the people."

But by the first decade of the twenty-first century, political elites had learned to adapt to new expectations. Leaders had little choice but to

1

recognize that political legitimacy required a popular vote in multiparty elections. Thus some African presidents bowed to democratic institutions, for example by peacefully accepting a loss at the ballot box or refraining from running again for office when they encountered term limits. But other leaders chose a different path, which encouraged analysts to return attention to elite behavior and institutional rules. The current literature on African politics features accounts of efforts by political incumbents to manipulate electoral laws, evade formal accountability, employ patronage and violence for political ends, and revive and maintain dominant party institutions. Emblematic of this new form of top-down politics are attempts by long-serving presidents to bypass constitutional restrictions on the number of terms in office that they are allowed to serve.

While acknowledging that political elites and dominant institutions retain the upper hand in African politics, I argue that ordinary people are not powerless. Nor should their political attitudes and behavior be overlooked. By voting in competitive elections, for example, they hold within their purview the power to bestow political legitimacy on—or withhold it from—leaders, institutions, and regimes. And by developing other attributes of democratic citizenship between elections—such as engaging in public events, joining others to address collective problems, and contacting political leaders—individuals can enhance the likelihood of holding leaders accountable.

Purpose

This book draws attention to recent research on voting and democratic citizenship in Africa. It seeks to offset the neglect of mass politics in the recent literature on African politics by posing a set of interrelated research questions. How do ordinary Africans view competitive elections? How do they behave at election time? In particular, do they vote for incumbents or opposition? What motivates their vote choice? How do people react to electoral malpractice? How do they participate in politics between elections? What are the implications of new forms of participation for democratic citizenship? And what are the implications of competitive elections for democracy?

In the past, it was difficult to offer convincing answers to any of these questions. Not only were elections uncompetitive in one-party and military regimes, but few other prospects were available to ordinary Africans for meaningful political participation. Moreover, data on voting and citizenship were often unreliable because official turnout rates or presidential victory margins were manufactured to favor incumbents. And the content of public opinion remained unknown because entrenched authoritarian rulers forbade national probability sample surveys on mass political attitudes and behavior.

In the absence of systematic empirical evidence, analysts had little choice but to make inferences about voting patterns, popular participation, and citizen preferences from small sets of qualitative interviews or narrowly drawn case studies.

The Afrobarometer has created opportunities for a much more rigorous research agenda. The Afrobarometer is a cross-national survey research project that measures a country's social, economic, and political atmosphere as seen by a representative sample of its adult population. Launched in 1999 as a response to a liberalizing political environment on the African continent, the project had conducted five rounds of surveys by 2012. The resulting Afrobarometer database contains well over 100,000 interviews with everyday people on subjects ranging from democracy and governance to social identity and economic well-being.

This volume assembles between two covers a selection of analyses on voting and citizenship by scholars who have made use of this unique empirical resource. As such, *Voting and Democratic Citizenship in Africa* represents the culmination of a focused and collective research effort by scholars on several continents over the course of at least a decade. It aims to move discussion of these topics forward by granting long-overdue attention to the attitudes and behaviors of ordinary people.

Approach

When analysts focus at the macro level, they are inclined to study large structures and whole systems. The literature on democratization, for example, tends to devote attention to relationships between national political institutions and political regimes writ large. For example, considerable ink has been spilled debating the exact nature of the relationship between elections and democracy. Most analysts take to heart Terry Karl's (1986) warning about "the electoral fallacy," namely that elections alone—however free and fair they may be—do not a democracy make (see also Diamond and Plattner 2010; Birch 2011). Instead, other institutions such as a constitutional rule of law, an independent legislature and judiciary, civilian control of the military, and a functioning civil society (including free mass media) are deemed also to be necessary. Indeed, policymakers and practitioners now commonly see the challenge of democracy building—not to mention economic development—in terms of "getting the institutions right" (Rodrik 2004; Bjornlund 2004; Carothers 2006; USAID 2010).

I do not deny the formative influence of a polity's institutional framework on regime outcomes. Nor do I question the centrality of the rule of law to the consolidation of democracy. But political institutions are more than formal-legal structures. They only come alive when political actors breathe life into them. We need to know what people actually think and do when they inhabit political roles and embrace political rules—in short, when they make institutions their own. Do they attach political value to constitutional norms and allow institutional routines to regulate and shape their behavior? In turn, do they express opinions and exert influences that endow political institutions with indigenous legitimacy? In my opinion, political institutions and political culture tend to coevolve, with the most legitimate institutions being those to which the largest numbers of people voluntarily grant consent. For this reason alone, any account of regime consolidation must attend to the micropolitics of individual attitudes and behavior.

This book puts the spotlight on micropolitics. The unit of analysis in all the chapters that follow is the individual, whether as voter or citizen. A distinction is drawn between voting behavior and democratic citizenship, though each complements the other. Voting behavior is a set of personal electoral activities, including participation in electoral campaigns, turnout at the polls, and choosing for whom to vote. Democratic citizenship is defined here as participation in popular collective action and engagement with political leaders and institutions, including between elections and within a rule of law. This broad notion of citizenship goes well beyond the formal attributes of legal citizenship—such as birth, marriage, or naturalization—that entitle an individual to hold a passport or national identity card. Rather, it refers to a political understanding of citizenship based on civic engagement and participation. It is consistent with the contrasts made in the literature between citizens, on the one hand, and "parochials" (who are disengaged from the political system) and "subjects" (who passively defer to authority) on the other (Almond and Verba 1963; Mamdani 1996). Citizens are also distinguished from "clients," understood as those who simply seek patronage rather than a role in political decisionmaking (Fox 1994; Bratton 2008).

The authors of the chapters that follow employ Afrobarometer survey data to measure both voting behavior and democratic citizenship. They make reference to individuals' turnout at the polls, choice of election candidates, mass engagement with political institutions, and popular affect for political regimes. By viewing politics from below, the aim is to draw a much more complete picture of the range of actors (common as well as elite) who shape political institutions. And by bringing considerations of mass political culture into the picture—usually by means of cross-national analysis—the goal is to improve understanding of the conditions under which political regimes (whether democratic, hybrid, or authoritarian) survive and consolidate.

Take the foundational issue of the connection between elections and democracy. Operating from a holistic perspective, most analysts would probably agree that elections are the sine qua non of democracy, but not its be-all and end-all. One can certainly find empirical cases of elections in the absence of democracy (see Chapter 2). But the converse is not true: one never finds democracy without elections. Stated succinctly, elections are a necessary condition for democracy, even if not a sufficient one.

But does this relationship hold at the micro level as well as at the macro level? In determining whether people regard elections as essential to democracy, we need in the first instance to know whether ordinary people value electoral institutions. And we must ascertain whether they connect their evaluations of the quality of elections to judgments about the establishment of democracy. Also, we must study whether popular electoral behavior reinforces any such cultural attachment. Finally, we would be interested to know whether individuals follow through after elections to supplement voting with autonomous efforts to seek responsiveness, representation, and accountability from political leaders.

After all, there may be a micro-level analog to the macro-level "electoral fallacy." One might think of it as the "voting fallacy." In this construct, people may minimally meet the necessary condition of turning out at the polls and casting a ballot. But they may also fail to fulfill the much more demanding requirements of active citizenship during the long periods between elections. As a working hypothesis, one should expect that, just as elections do not a democracy make, so voting does not a citizen make. On its own, the act of voting may not be enough to create democratic political orientations or stimulate a full range of democratic behaviors. Rather, other values, attitudes, and activities are required for voters to become well-rounded and effective participants in a democratic regime. Together, these attributes amount to the sufficient condition for citizenship.

The prevailing institutional framework for African politics obviously poses formidable barriers to active citizenship. Many residents of sub-Saharan countries—especially the poor—are citizens in name only, since they enjoy few meaningful channels of political participation. Elections tend to be contests between corrupt and clientelistic elites who stand ready to resort to vote buying, even violence. Far from providing a two-way linkage between citizens and the political center, African political parties are usually personalistic, elite-dominated, and internally undemocratic. As a result, elections often produce national assemblies and local governments that remain unrepresentative of broad-based constituencies and unresponsive to popular demands.

Moreover, shortcomings in democratic development may emanate from the individual level as well as the institutional level. One would expect, for example, that if people in Africa vote reflexively along lines of ethnic identity, then they forego opportunities to appraise incumbent governments on the basis of policy performance. Or, if voters tend to sell their votes to the highest bidder, then it is questionable whether they have a full appreciation of citizen rights and obligations. Alternatively, if individuals are partly responsible for a "representation gap" between themselves and their elected representatives, then they are unable to participate fully in the democratic policy process. In sum, if people in Africa are voters but not citizens (see Chapter 11), or if they are "uncritical" citizens (see Chapters 9 and 12), then one would expect negative consequences for the consolidation of democracy.

Method

Since the Afrobarometer provides the empirical foundation for this book, a brief review of the project's main organizational features and research protocols is in order. By summarizing this material here, it becomes possible to reduce the amount of methodological justification offered in each chapter. In describing the Afrobarometer method, I make explicit a few technical caveats.

The Afrobarometer is an independent, nonpartisan, social science research project. It is dedicated to three main objectives: to produce scientifically reliable data on public opinion in Africa; to strengthen capacity for survey research in African institutions; and to broadly disseminate and apply survey results. Because of its ambitious scope, the project is organized as an African-led international collaboration. The Afrobarometer Network is managed by core partner institutions: the Center for Democratic Development in Ghana, the Institute for Democracy in South Africa, the Institute for Empirical Research in Political Economy in Benin, and, as of 2011, the Institute for Development Studies at the University of Nairobi in Kenya. Analytic and support services are provided by the University of Cape Town and Michigan State University. The network also includes national partner institutions—such as university-based research groups, independent think tanks, and private polling firms—that conduct surveys and compile raw results in each participating country.

Surveys are conducted in multiple countries—starting with twelve in 1999 and growing to more than thirty in 2012—and are repeated on a regular cycle. Five rounds of surveys had been completed or were under way at the time of writing. The thrust of the Afrobarometer questionnaire concerns democracy and governance. What do ordinary people think about a democratic form of government and alternative regimes? And to what extent do they participate in decisionmaking and policy implementation? Because the instrument asks a standard set of questions, countries can be systematically compared and trends in attitudes and behaviors can be tracked over time. Each round of surveys also includes an in-depth, specialized module on a selected subject like ethnic identity, economic reform, political leadership, local government, or the use of information and communication technology.

This book draws mainly on the Round 3 Afrobarometer survey, conducted in eighteen countries in 2005, which features the project's most comprehensive data module on elections, voting behavior, and political participation between elections.

A multinational committee from within the Afrobarometer Network develops the questionnaire for each round of surveys. The items in the instrument are indigenized to reflect local institutional nomenclature, translated into major native languages, and then blindly translated back into the original national language. Refinements to ensure consistency in question wording are made at every stage. Within each country, interviewers are trained to administer the questionnaire in a weeklong preparatory program that involves interview simulations and field tests. Once deployed to the field, teams of four interviewers travel together to selected research sites and are constantly monitored by survey supervisors. It is the interviewers' job to seek each respondent's informed consent to participate in the survey, to administer the questions in the language of the respondent's choice, and to record responses, usually by selecting a precoded numerical score. On occasion, interviewers also record open-ended verbatim statements in the respondent's own words. Supervisors make follow-up visits to randomly selected households as well as checking every completed survey before teams leave the field.

In each country, the Afrobarometer covers a representative sample of the adult population—that is, those who are over eighteen years old and eligible to vote. Individuals are selected using a multistage, stratified, clustered area design that is randomized at every stage. The stratification ensures that all main administrative regions (and cultural groups) are included in the sample and that urban and rural populations are represented in correct relative proportions. The latest national census, updated with projections where necessary, is used as a sampling frame to randomly choose primary sampling units with probability proportional to population size. If household lists are unavailable within the primary sampling units, which is often the case, then households are selected using a random walk pattern from geographical start points chosen by chance. Within the household, respondents are picked by a blind drawing of names from a list of household members, but with the proviso that interviews are alternated between men and women. This multistage sampling design produces not only equal numbers by gender but also a cross-section of the eligible electorate.

The target sample size for any survey in any country is a minimum of 1,200 respondents. For descriptive statistics, this sample size is sufficient to yield a confidence interval of plus or minus 3 percentage points (actually 2.8 percentage points) at a confidence level of 95 percent. In countries that are especially culturally diverse, a larger sample size of 2,400 respondents is employed, the better to reduce sampling error and to allow enough cases to enable generalization about minority subpopulations. If minorities are purposely oversampled within a country (like Coloureds and Indians in South Africa, or Delta-region ethnic groups in Nigeria), then data are corrected by weights. Similarly, when data are pooled across countries, an additional weight is applied to standardize all countries at the same sample size ($n = 1,200$) regardless of total population. Frequency distributions record proportions of valid responses (including "don't know") and are rounded to the nearest whole percentage point. Readers should bear these rounding rules, confidence intervals, and weighting effects in mind when interpreting particular data points.

Special care is required when making inferences from aggregate cross-national statistics that purport to represent an Afrobarometer "mean." For one reason, average scores can be misleading because they smooth out and cover up some of the most interesting variations between countries and among individuals. In addition, it is essential to note that, while the countries included in Afrobarometer surveys do not differ significantly from sub-Saharan averages on selected socioeconomic indicators, they are not fully representative of Africa as a whole. Having undergone a measure of political and economic reform, they are among the continent's most open regimes. However, the inclusion of countries with past or present internal conflicts—like Liberia, Nigeria, Sierra Leone, Uganda, and Zimbabwe—helps to make the country sample more representative of the subcontinent. But considerable caution is nonetheless warranted when projecting Afrobarometer results to all "Africans."

Many of the analyses that follow reflect a growing methodological sophistication in the comparative analysis of African politics. Most of the authors of this volume employ regression analysis, usually based on Round 3 data pooled across eighteen countries ($n = 21,351$). For purposes of inferential statistics, weights are always turned off. In some chapters, authors employ multiple-imputation software to infer values for missing cases; in other chapters, they drop those cases from analysis. Where the possible effects of these alternate data management methods are explicitly tested, results remain robust (e.g., Chapter 5). Several chapters focus on political objects of interest that have a discontinuous, binary form: voters either turn out at the polls or they do not; they vote for the incumbent or they do not. Accordingly, authors choose forms of regression (logit or probit) that are suited to analyzing dependent variables of this kind (e.g., Chapters 3 and 6). Moreover, several authors acknowledge the nested structure of Afrobarometer data in which cases are clustered rather than independent, for example within the distinctive settings of particular countries. To address these systematic patterns, they opt to supplement the Afrobarometer with national-level data from independent sources and to apply multilevel hierarchical regression techniques (e.g., Chapters 4, 5, and 10).

Methodological rigor brings both advantages and disadvantages. While strict adherence to statistical procedures can increase confidence in research outcomes, too much attention to method can obscure the substance—and thus diminish the interest and importance—of results. I have tried to strike a happy medium in this book. In order to focus on tangible outcomes, to allow access for the general reader, and to keep the book to manageable length, I have edited out some of the supporting technical matter that usually appears in journal articles in the scientific literature. Wherever possible, detailed methodological discussions and technical footnotes have been removed. Readers who wish information on the nuts and bolts of survey and statistical analyses may visit the Afrobarometer website (www.afrobarometer.org), consult unedited versions of those papers previously published in scientific journals, or contact the authors directly.

One last point. How valid and reliable are the subjective views of ordinary citizens? On a continent where most people live in rural areas and where a good education is hard to find, individuals may not be well enough informed to offer dependable opinions. Or so goes the argument. While education clearly improves a respondent's comprehension of survey questions and adds sophistication to answers, my colleagues and I nevertheless resist concluding that nonliterate or locally oriented respondents lack the capacity to form opinions. On the contrary, we have found that, as long as questions are stated plainly and concretely (question wordings are provided in the text and tables that follow), Africans can express clear opinions on subjects like voting behavior, electoral choice, and political authority.

Indeed, I would argue that in the realm of politics, perceptions matter just as much—if not more—than reality. That which people think to be true—including judgments about the quality of elections and the perfor-mance of regimes—is a central motivation for behavior. Perceptions are paramount, not only in the interest-driven realm of the marketplace, but also in the ideological realm of politics. Whether or not attitudes exactly mirror exterior circumstances, an individual's interior perspective forms the basis of any bottom-up calculus for action. And, consistent with my instinct that all people, whatever their material circumstances, are capable of acute observation and rational thought, the contributors to this book find that public opinion is not only a useful predictor of mass political behavior, but also an essential element in the consolidation of political institutions and regimes.

Results

This book describes and analyzes voting and interelectoral behavior across a range of Africa's new democratic regimes. And it evaluates the contributions of individual citizens, and the limitations they face, in contributing to the consolidation of democracy. Among the main results are the following:

- In all countries selected for study, Africans consider elections as the best means of forming a government, and they judge the quality of democracy accordingly.
- When choosing candidates in elections, African voters are motivated by social identity, but they also consider partisan loyalty and especially economic performance.
- Vote buying appears to increase voter turnout, but violence depresses it.
- When deciding how to cast a vote, Africans are usually able to sidestep unwanted inducements and pressures (like vote buying and violence) and to vote mainly according to their own preferences.
- In certain countries, many Africans display uncritical citizenship as characterized by low levels of political knowledge and unreflective political evaluations.
- After elections, voters in many African countries commonly fail to demand vertical accountability; they do not always see themselves as responsible for holding leaders in check.
- Free and fair elections build popular demand for democracy, but more so among election "losers" than election "winners."
- High-quality elections give citizens confidence that abuse of public office will be reined in (control of corruption) and that official policy directives ought to be obeyed (legitimacy of the state).

Outline of the Book

Expanding on the themes of this introduction, Chapter 2 asks, Where do elections lead in Africa? At issue is whether competitive voting contests help to foster democracy or whether they serve as a smokescreen for the persistence of authoritarian forms of government. I examine this foundational issue with reference to recent theoretical debates and to sources of both macro- and micro-level data. The evidence from both levels strongly suggests that regime outcomes depend on the quality of elections: only free and fair contests foster democratization, whereas elections on an unlevel playing field are an institutional recipe for disguised autocracy. Moreover, only in Africa's more open societies do citizens react against poor-quality elections by organizing collectively to demand greater accountability.

Thereafter, the volume is divided into five parts. Part 1 deals with vote choice. Whom do Africans vote for and why? In Chapter 3, Pippa Norris and Robert Mattes ask whether Africans vote along ethnic lines. Their seminal, ground-clearing analysis finds evidence to both confirm and undermine this commonplace assumption. On one hand, they report that ethnic-group membership is a significant predictor of partisan attachments in most of Africa's plural societies. On the other hand, the observed ethnic effect on party preferences is relatively small, does not always accrue to the advantage of sitting leaders, and is sometimes eclipsed by popular evaluations of incumbent performance. In other words, ethnic identity seems to matter to voting in Africa, but only as part of a more complex set of considerations that includes citizens' instrumental appraisals of the track record of the party in government. Following Norris and Mattes, analysts have since concluded that voting behavior must be modeled in multivariate terms and that election outcomes can no longer be reduced to a simple "ethnic census."

In Chapter 4, Benn Eifert, Edward Miguel, and Daniel Posner reverse the causal arrow. They investigate whether exposure to political competition during elections inclines voters to identify in ethnic terms. They show that "close" elections, which combine proximity in time with a tight race, are associated with an increase in the salience of ethnicity. While voters are not innately predisposed to identify in ethnic terms—in fact, more Africans self-define in occupational or other terms—they incline toward ethnic reasoning in the heat of approaching political contests. This original insight is consistent with both a theory of political entrepreneurship in which politicians play an "ethnic card" in order to mobilize support and a theory of political motivation in which voters seek to associate themselves with candidates deemed likely to distribute patronage. Most important, these authors provide evidence that modern ethnic identities in Africa are fluid, situational, and constructed, including from an explicitly political source: competitive elections.

In Chapter 5, my colleagues Ravi Bhavnani and Tse-Hsin Chen and I offer a comprehensive account of popular voting intentions. In an effort to arbitrate a debate between advocates of ethnic and economic voting, we show that competitive elections in Africa are more than mere ethnic censuses or simple economic referenda. Instead, Africans engage in both ethnic and economic voting. Not surprisingly, people who belong to the ethnic group in power intend to support the ruling party, in contrast to those who feel a sense of discrimination against their cultural group. But, to an even greater extent, would-be voters in Africa consider policy performance, especially the government's perceived handling of unemployment, inflation, and income distribution. We reconcile the coexistence of different types of voting by suggesting that ethnic voting is rooted in an economic logic. Moreover, a full account of the intention to vote in Africa also requires recognition that citizens are motivated—sincerely or strategically—by partisan considerations; they vote for established ruling parties because they expect that incumbents will win. We show that voters attempt to associate themselves with prospective winners because they wish to gain access to patronage benefits and to avoid retribution after the election. These dynamics are most evident in African countries where dominant parties restrict the range of electoral choice.

Part 2 of the book deals with electoral malpractices, particularly the influence of political money. What effects, if any, does vote buying have on voter turnout and partisan choice? In Chapter 6, Eric Kramon studies the relationship between an individual's exposure to material inducements and his or her subsequent turnout at the polls during an election in Kenya. He finds that vote buying, which politicians target disproportionately at people without formal education, has a discernible positive effect on voter turnout. This effect is especially pronounced in districts where elections are closely fought and where outcomes are most uncertain. In seeking to explain the link between vote buying and voter turnout, Kramon finds suggestive evidence for at least two mechanisms, both expressed in terms of citizen perceptions. First, vote buying "works" best among citizens who believe that political parties are capable of monitoring turnout at the polls and punishing those who abstain from voting. And second, vote buying induces participation among clients who regard it as a signal of a patron's credibility to keep campaign promises once the election is over.

Vote buying and violence in election campaigns in Nigeria are the subject of Chapter 7. I report that both sorts of malpractice were important, if epiphenomenal, dimensions of a 2007 national election campaign. According to survey-based estimates, fewer than one out of five Nigerians was personally exposed to vote buying and fewer than one in ten experienced threats of electoral violence. But when, as commonly happens, campaign irregularities are targeted at the rural poor, effects are concentrated: violence reduces turnout, and vote buying enhances partisan loyalty. But, perhaps because most citizens condemn campaign manipulation as wrong, compliance with the wishes of politicians is not ensured. Defection from threats and agreements is more common than compliance, especially where voters are cross-pressured from both sides of the partisan divide.

Chapter 8 turns from Nigeria to Uganda. Jeffrey Conroy-Krutz and Carolyn Logan delve in depth into the determinants of incumbent Yoweri Museveni's victory in the 2011 presidential election. The authors question a conventional storyline that attributes the election outcome to the power of political money—that is, that the incumbent bought the election through massive spending. They demonstrate that Ugandans who were exposed to vote buying, or who benefited from political goods distribution and the creation of new rural districts, were hardly more likely than their fellow citizens to vote for the incumbent. Instead, the authors trace Museveni's electoral success to an uninspiring slate of opposition candidates, a growing economy, and an improved security situation, particularly in the northern part of the country. In so doing, the authors perform a useful service in situating vote buying and related inducements in a broader context of policy performance.

Part 3 examines the aftermath of voting. Do voters become democratic citizens in the sense of seeking to hold political leaders accountable between elections? In Chapter 9, Robert Mattes and Carlos Shenga introduce the concept of "uncritical citizenship." In the context of Mozambique, high levels of poverty along with underdeveloped infrastructure greatly inhibit citizens' ability to participate in politics. Moreover, low rates of formal education, high levels of illiteracy, and limited access to news media reduce the flow of political information that would allow citizens to develop informed opinions. Many Mozambicans are unable to answer questions pertaining to the performance of government or to offer preferences about what kind of regime Mozambique ought to have. And those who are able to offer answers often uncritically overrate regime performance. Perhaps because of high levels of popular satisfaction with the supply of democracy, Mozambicans express low levels of demand for the further deepening of democracy. The authors argue that this sort of "uncritical citizenship" is a function of living in a "low-information society."

Wonbin Cho's contribution in Chapter 10 draws an important distinction about the perceived functions of competitive elections: Are these institutions seen to produce accountability or representation? As measured in the Afrobarometer, the former refers to leadership turnover at the polls, the latter to leadership responsiveness in office. Utilizing this distinction, the author traces citizen confidence in legislative institutions to the nature of electoral systems under which African legislatures are chosen. Majoritarian electoral systems promote a sense of citizen control over policymakers (that is, accountability), whereas proportional representation systems increase the perception of inclusion across a society's factions (that is, representation). Because sub-Saharan African citizens typically prioritize representation rather than accountability when evaluating their legislative institutions, proportional representation systems are found to have an advantage in boosting public trust in political institutions in the region.

In Chapter 11, my colleague Carolyn Logan and I ask why multiparty elections have so far failed to secure greater political accountability. One answer concerns how Africans themselves understand the contours of new political regimes and, in particular, their own roles in a democracy. Afrobarometer respondents do not believe that elections have been particularly effective at securing political accountability. And when it comes to asserting control over elected leaders in the long intervals between elections, a substantial number of Africans do not see any role for themselves. Even while becoming active voters, they do not appear to assert political rights as citizens, notably to regularly demand accountability from leaders. As such, most African political regimes have yet to meet the minimum requirements of participatory democracy and instead share characteristics with Latin America's "delegative" democracies. But the problem for many new democracies in Africa is not so much that citizens knowingly delegate authority to strong presidents, but that democracy remains unclaimed by mere voters.

In Part 4, the scope of the analysis widens to consider the effects of voting and citizenship on prospects for democratic development. In Chapter 12, Devra Moehler examines the consequences of elections for popular perceptions of political legitimacy. She finds that, in multiparty regimes in sub-Saharan Africa, where elections are often imperfect, supporters of losing political parties express much less support for political institutions than do winners. The so-called losers—who tend to judge the quality of elections more harshly than do the winners—are less inclined to trust national political institutions, to consent voluntarily to the commands of the governing authority, and to feel that voting matters. Contrary to initial expectations, however, losers are more willing than winners to defend democracy against official manipulation. Losers are critical of prevailing proto-democratic institutions, but nonetheless are willing to protect them. By contrast, winners tend to be submissive subjects, granting unconditional support to current leaders. Finally, Moehler notes that divergent evaluations of electoral fairness are responsible for only a small portion of winner-loser gaps in legitimacy. Losers are much more likely than winners to denounce flawed elections, but losers have additional reasons to doubt the legitimacy of the current structure of political institutions.

Chapter 13 returns to a question first raised in Chapter 2: Does the quality of elections matter for the subsequent consolidation of democracy? Ari Greenberg and Robert Mattes provide additional statistical evidence for an answer in the positive. They show, first, that international election observers and ordinary Africans are in general agreement about the quality of particular electoral contests in Africa. In places and times where elections are deemed free, people subsequently judge that political elites are supplying democracy. But wherever elections are flawed, people tend to conclude that democracy is not being delivered. To tease out the causality in this relationship, the authors compare free and flawed elections that occur between rounds of Afrobarometer surveys, tracing impacts on changes in public opinion. Accordingly, they make a case that the relationship between election quality and the supply of democracy is a causal one, with the former shaping the latter. Finally, they note that, while election quality shapes perceptions of the supply of democracy, it has little influence on popular demand for democracy. One possible reason is that flawed elections encourage democrats in the general populace to redouble their commitments to installing or reinstating their preferred political regime.

Chapter 14 peers further into the future. Using macro-level, micro-level, and trend data, it asks: Does democratization lead to improved governance? I find an elective affinity between free elections, democracy, and improved governance, at least as these concepts are seen and understood by ordinary Africans. But the democracy advantage is more apparent in relation to some dimensions of public governance than others. For example, while Africans apparently think that elections boost the rule of law and control of corruption, they also seem to worry that democracy undercuts the transparency of government procedures and the responsiveness of elected officials. To address the debate on causality, I compare governance performance before and after electoral alternations, finding a positive effect. Accordingly, I conclude that—as a rule of thumb for policy sequencing—democracy promotion need not await the prior establishment of rule of law.

Finally, in Part 5 in Chapter 15, building on the collective enterprise contained within these pages, I conclude the book with a few reflections on lessons learned about mass political behavior and propose an agenda for future research on voting and democratic citizenship.

2

Where Do Elections Lead in Africa?

Michael Bratton

Where do competitive elections lead in Africa? Do these institutions reinforce democracy or contribute to the durability of authoritarian rule? Some scholars argue that repetitive elections, even when flawed, chart a path toward democracy. In his causal theory of "democratization by elections," Staffan Lindberg proposes that an uninterrupted series of elections has "self-reinforcing power" to imbue society with democratic attributes (2006: 2; see also 2009: 25–46). These qualities include political competition, popular participation, and broad acceptance that electoral rules are legitimate. He conceives of regular elections as a "new mode of transition" that, cumulatively over time, precipitates regime change (2009: 2). In the later versions of his theory, Lindberg acknowledges the reality that elections can sometimes foster "autocratization" as well as democratization (2009: 13). But he continues to insist that "the link between elections and democratization is not theoretically tied to freedom and fairness of elections" (2009: 328). In short, it is the frequency of elections that supposedly creates democratic change; the quality of these contests is apparently less important.

Other scholars disagree. Steven Levitsky and Lucan Way (2010) take note of the spread of "competitive authoritarian" regimes in the post–Cold War world (see also Schedler 2006; Gandhi and Lust-Okar 2009). These hybrid systems combine electoral competition with new forms of autocratic rule. A defining characteristic of competitive authoritarianism is low-quality elections: competition is "real but unfair" because it is never played out on "a reasonably level playing field" (Levitsky and Way 2010: 5, 7). The electoral terrain is uneven because incumbents take advantage of access to state resources for partisan campaigns while systematically blocking opposition forces from organizing a winning challenge. Under these circumstances, multiparty elections do not necessarily herald the arrival of democracy. Instead, autocrats learn how to control a seemingly democratic process with vote buying, ballot stuffing, and manipulation of the vote count, and also, if necessary, by resorting to repression and violence. In these ways, competitive elections contribute not so much to democratization as to the longevity and respectability of authoritarian rule.

In this chapter, I seek empirical resolution of the debate about the consequences of competitive elections for African political regimes. My main premise is that the role of elections in political development depends critically on their quality. High-quality elections contribute to the deepening of democracy, but poor-quality elections enable the durability of autocracy. I find Levitsky and Way's argument about competitive authoritarianism generally persuasive for regime developments in Africa, where recent elections are marked by a downturn in quality. I also note that, among individual Africans, popular judgments about the quality of elections strongly predict whether people think they are living in a democratic or nondemocratic regime. Finally, there is some evidence to support Lindberg's observation about a linkage between elections and democracy—as well as evidence of emerging democratic citizenship beyond elections—but only in those politically open African countries that have managed to maintain relatively high standards of electoral quality.

Political Trends in Africa, 1990–2011

Trends in Democracy

The wave of democratization that followed the end of the Cold War began to ebb in the first decade of the twenty-first century. As dictators learned to live with competitive elections, democracy retreated around the globe (Economist Intelligence Unit 2010). Larry Diamond was among the first to note that "the democratic wave has been slowed by a powerful authoritarian undertow, and the world has slipped into a democratic recession" (2008a: 36). By the end of 2011, Freedom House reported that civil liberties and political rights had suffered an overall net decline in every year since 2006, with more countries around the world displaying setbacks than gains (Puddington 2012). Notwithstanding popular uprisings and the departure of dictators in Tunisia, Egypt, Libya, and Yemen in 2011, the Arab Spring could not offset the global slump in democratization. If anything, dramatic political events in North Africa and the Middle East prompted reactive or preemptive crackdowns by authoritarian regimes in Syria, Bahrain, Russia, and China.

Sub-Saharan Africa was not spared from this backwash of political retrenchment. Figure 2.1 shows that an inflection occurred in democratic

Figure 2.1 Trends in Democracy in Sub-Saharan Africa, 1990–2011

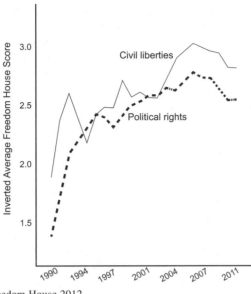

Source: Freedom House 2012.

development on the continent around 2006. Prior to that time, and as a result of political openings and regime changes during the 1990s, political rights and civil liberties in African countries were steadily rising (Freedom House 2012). In the early years of democratization, Africans gained access to the political rights associated with multiparty electoral competition—to join organizations, to vote, and to hold leaders accountable—in a positive trend that gradually gained strength. Africans also came to enjoy greater civil liberties such as personal autonomy, freedom of expression, and access to the law. Overall, this set of personal freedoms was usually even more readily available than political rights.

By 2006, however, the wave of democratization crested, and then retreated. In 2011, political rights and civil rights across African countries had dropped to average levels of a decade earlier, though, importantly, they remained markedly higher than in 1990. Together, these indicators signaled a partial reversal of the democratic impulse in Africa. While the glass remained more than half full, there was a hole at the bottom.

It is important to remember, however, that continent-wide averages of democracy mask major differences across countries. Of the forty-three African countries tracked on a standard democracy index between 2006 and 2010, more than half (twenty-four) registered declines, but a significant proportion (seventeen) registered improvements (Economist Intelligence

Unit 2010: 14–15). According to Freedom House, Gambia, Madagascar, and Mauritania were the worst backsliders in the world between 2007 and 2011, and Ethiopia and Burundi ranked in the top ten (Puddington 2012: 8). At the same time, however, other countries such as Sierra Leone and Guinea emerged from civil conflict or military rule via reasonably open multiparty elections that installed civilian governments. For the most part, democratic gains in Africa accumulated in small countries, including island states, that had limited land areas and tiny populations. Many of the continent's largest countries, like Sudan and the Democratic Republic of the Congo (DRC), remained mired in authoritarian rule and political instability. And the two most strategically important states in Africa moved on opposite trajectories. Nigeria's shaky democratic regime was buttressed to a welcome degree by relatively peaceful and honest elections in April 2011. But South Africa's impressive democratic credentials were called into question as evidence began to emerge of pervasive elite corruption and government pressure on judges and journalists.

What explains these divergent trends toward and away from democracy? Much depends on the governance choices made by political leaders. As Goran Hyden (2012) proposes, governance can be understood as the politics of rules. Do leaders voluntarily abide by a constitutional rule of law even if it entails constraints on their power? Or do they manipulate the rules of the political game—including electoral rules—in order to retain political control at all costs?

Once in office, leaders face daily choices between good and bad governance over myriad political and policy issues. I would argue that the tone for normal, day-to-day administration is set by the initial posture of political elites over the conduct of elections. If leaders choose to respect formal rules—ranging from constitutional term limits on the presidency to detailed regulations over the counting of votes and the announcement of results—then a foundation is laid for later improved governance. But if political elites—especially incumbent office holders—intentionally create an uneven playing field that tilts the rules of electoral competition in their own favor, then it is very likely that they will go on to govern in an opaque, illegal, and unaccountable fashion. In short, electoral conduct is a both a bellwether for the subsequent political regime and a key mechanism by which democracy is either built or broken.

The tension between the rule of law and rule by men is nicely illustrated by political struggles over presidential tenure. Transitions from military and one-party rule in Africa in the early 1990s were accompanied by a flowering of constitutional reforms that sought to limit executive powers. Central to the reform effort were rules designed to prevent the old men in top leadership positions from overstaying their welcome; new constitutional provisions required national presidents to step down from office after a proscribed period, commonly two five-year terms (Posner and Young 2007). Of the sixty-four constitutions newly enacted in African countries between 1990 and 2009, forty-nine contained presidential term limits (Dulani 2011: 136). The question then became: Would incumbents respect the new rules?

On the one hand, the rate of alternation of African presidents increased: between 1990 and 2009, some fifteen sitting heads of state left office upon the expiry of constitutionally mandated terms. This number includes two presidents each in Ghana (Rawlings and Kufuor) and Tanzania (Mwinyi and Mkapa), but excludes Mandela in South Africa, who chose to serve for only one term voluntarily. Sometimes the alternation was a mere rotation of leaders within the same ruling party, as in Tanzania and South Africa. But in about half the cases—including Benin, Kenya, and Sierra Leone—there was a complete turnover of power to an opposition party, a standard some consider essential for establishing democracy (Przeworski et al. 2000). In Cape Verde and Ghana, this full form of electoral alternation occurred twice, a criterion others find adequate for designating a country as a consolidated democracy (Huntington 1991). Either way, the average tenure of an African president dropped by almost half, from thirteen years before 1990 to seven years thereafter (Dulani 2011: 141).

On the other hand, term limits failed to fully eradicate the intense personalization of power in African politics (van de Walle 2007; Villalón and von Doepp 2005). Skillful authoritarians devised schemes to circumvent the formal strictures of the rule of law. For example, Presidents Wade (Senegal) and Campaoré (Burkina Faso) argued that constitutional reforms should only apply prospectively and not to current terms. Other leaders sought to amend constitutions by abolishing or loosening new restrictions, and succeeded in securing bids for a third term more often than they failed. Of fifteen cases in which presidents launched legislative initiatives to remove term limits, they were successful on twelve occasions and were blocked only three times (in Malawi, Nigeria, and Zambia) (Dulani 2011: 147).

Moreover, unconstitutional transfers of power did not disappear from the African political scene. While the rate of military coups dropped precipitously after 1990, these events still occurred sporadically, as in Mauritania in 2008 (followed by the fraudulent election of the coup leader) and Niger in 2010 (where the military allowed a smooth electoral alternation to a new ruling party). In Guinea-Bissau in 2009, soldiers assassinated the president (followed by the return of the presidency to the country's party of independence). And dynastic successions—as occurred in Equatorial Guinea, Togo, and Gabon, where the presidency was passed on from father to son —did not technically violate the letter of the electoral law, but certainly contravened the spirit of open political competition.

Even where office holders attained power by reasonably free and fair means, unchecked super-presidents continued to benefit from the concentration of executive authority at the pinnacle of the state. Larry Diamond states the problem well: electoral democracy is "a superficial phenomenon, blighted by multiple forms of bad governance: abusive police and security forces, domineering local oligarchies, incompetent and indifferent state bureaucracies, corrupt and inaccessible judiciaries, and venal ruling elites who are . . . accountable to no one but themselves" (2008a: 38). It may go too far, however, to declare that freedom in sub-Saharan Africa is in a "perilous state" and that the continent "will continue to slip back toward where it started in the early 1970s" (Petrovic 2012: 4). On the contrary, civil liberties and political rights are now more readily available to African citizens than in 1990, let alone in the 1970s. But the quality of African democracy is strained—and its development has stalled or reversed—in far too many countries.

Trends in Elections

To further set the context, I briefly summarize here a few key trends in African elections. Beyond description, my purpose is to explore whether the evolution of elections in Africa mirrors the continent's evolving landscape of political regimes. After all, if one believes that elections and democracy are joined at the hip, then one would expect that indicators of the frequency, competitiveness, and quality of elections would reflect the trajectory already seen for democracy. In order to track election trends, I extend and update to 2011 a dataset first constructed to analyze African elections in the period 1989–2006 (Lindberg 2007).

Over the past two decades, competitive elections became a commonplace feature of African politics. Political leaders—democratic and authoritarian alike—had little choice but to regularly expose themselves to some sort of a popular vote. To win domestic and international legitimacy, any such electoral contest had to allow a semblance of opposition competition. Between 1990 and 2011, the forty-eight sub-Saharan African countries convened 344 competitive elections for the national presidency or lower house of the national assembly. As Table 2.1 shows, the annual frequency of elections gradually increased, from 13.5 per year at the beginning of the period to 17.4 per year by the end. Since the number of countries did not change (new nations like Eritrea and South Sudan were excluded from the calculation), this increase reflected a gradual spread over time in the practice of competitive elections.

Moreover, the regularity of electoral cycles strongly suggests that elections were becoming institutionalized. In places like Botswana and Mauritius, the latest legislative contest was the ninth in an uninterrupted sequence stretching back to independence. By 2011, countries that had led the wave of democratic transitions in the early 1990s—like Benin and Zambia—completed a continuous succession of six elections (legislative and presidential respectively). Even postconflict countries that were latecomers to

Table 2.1 Trends in Elections in Sub-Saharan Africa, 1990–2011

	1990–1995	1996–2000	2001–2006	2007–2011
Number of elections	81	81	95	87
Number of elections, annual average	13.5	16.2	15.8	17.4
Average competitiveness of elections[a]	0.591	0.537	0.621	0.593
Quality of elections[b]	61.7%	54.3%	67.4%	64.4%

Source: Data set on African elections (Lindberg 2007; updated to 2011 by author).

Notes: a. Average competitiveness is calculated for either presidential votes or legislative seats as [100 – (winner's percentage – 2nd-place percentage)]/100. On a scale of 0 to 1, 0 indicates a perfectly uncompetitive election and 1 indicates a perfectly competitive election. For two-round elections, the competitiveness score is calculated on the distribution of votes in the first round.

b. Estimated percentage of elections that were substantially free and fair and/or that met minimal international standards. Any irregularities did not affect the overall election outcome.

the democratization wave—like Liberia, Sierra Leone, and the Democratic Republic of the Congo—managed to stage a second election by 2011, even though, in the DRC case, the exercise was badly bungled. Only where military or palace coups caused interruptions—for example in Burundi and Comoros—was the chain of successive contests broken.

For the most part, elections also took place roughly on time—that is, according to a constitutionally mandated schedule. This punctuality reflected not only growing experience and capacity on the part of electoral management bodies but also, and even more importantly, a mounting consensus among political contenders about adherence to agreed-upon electoral rules. True, there were minor logistical delays in places like Sierra Leone in 2007 and Benin in 2011, and military coups disrupted incipient elections in Mali and Guinea-Bissau in early 2012. Moreover, a couple of countries remain stubbornly outside the electoral fold: Eritrea has failed to hold general elections since independence in 1993 and Somalia had not voted since the election of a transitional president in 2004; Angola last held a presidential election in 1992 and, at the time of writing, a contest planned for 2009 remained indefinitely postponed. In addition, numerous African countries—including Angola, the Central African Republic, Côte d'Ivoire, Malawi, and Sudan—repeatedly pushed back local government elections, either because they lacked the financial or administrative wherewithal to run local contests or for more dubious partisan motives (EISA 2012).

But how meaningful were voting contests in the growing number of African countries that held regular elections? Did these events represent genuine competition between multiple political parties in which there was a measure of uncertainty over who would win? Or did politicians and voters simply go through the motions of convening a ballot in the full knowledge that incumbents controlled the process, including the outcome?

Data on election tallies over time suggest that African elections reflect real, but unequal, political rivalries. A standard formula for political competitiveness takes the winner's percentage of presidential votes or legislative seats, subtracts the second-place finisher's percentage, and then subtracts the result from 100. The product can be converted to a 0–1 scale in which 0 represents a perfectly uncompetitive election (winner = 100 percent, loser = 0 percent) and 1 represents a perfectly competitive election (50 percent to 50 percent). Table 2.1 shows that on average, African elections since 1990 have been only somewhat competitive, with an average competitiveness score of about 0.60 over the past two decades representing a winner's margin of some 40 percentage points over the second-place finisher. In other words, losers have usually been able to establish a presence among the voters at election time, but winners have usually won comfortably. An optimistic interpretation sees no drop-off in competitiveness over time: elections in the period 2007–2011 were no less spirited than during 1990–1995, when democratization in Africa was just getting under way. And one can always find particular contests—like the presidential election in Ghana in 2008—where the race was so close that the winner in the first round lost in the second round. But overall, the level of competitiveness in Africa's multiparty elections remains roughly constant, with a low overall average.

The quality of African elections is mixed, and increasingly difficult to determine. Analysts usually rely on the judgments of international election observers for measuring the achievement of elusive "free and fair" norms (Birch 2011; Hyde and Marinov 2011; Kelley 2010; Laakso 2002). But as the wave of initial regime transitions recedes and the number of competitive elections increases, international actors mount fewer oversight missions. African regional organizations—like the African Union, the Arab League, the Economic Community of West African States (ECOWAS), and the Southern African Development Community (SADC)—now vie for the lead in election observation. These organizations reach conclusions about election quality that often clash with the verdicts of Western observers, not to mention with the beliefs of losing political parties (Kelley 2012). For example, the African Union and the Arab League pronounced themselves "satisfied" with Djibouti's 2008 one-party legislative elections that were boycotted by the opposition. Moreover, incumbent autocrats have become skilled at fixing election outcomes through compliant election commissions and by using techniques of media control, vote buying, and violence well before international observers arrive in the country.

I estimated election quality for Africa's most recent elections by supplementing election observer reports (where available) with a systematic search of news and professional archives (Inter-Parliamentary Union at www.ipu.org/parline-e/parlinesearch.asp; All-Africa at www.allafrica.com/ search). Table 2.1 shows that the majority of African elections (some 61 percent on average) met minimal international standards over the two decades between 1990 and 2011. To be judged acceptable, an election does not have to be entirely free of irregularities; rather, the results should reflect the general will of the electorate (measured here as either fully or substantially free and fair). Although the quality of African contests declined for late-transition and early-second elections in the late 1990s, standards rose in the 2000s, peaking around 2006. As with democratization, the main trend in electoral quality has been upward, at least until a partial decline set in during the period from 2007 onward. Indeed, one would expect a connection between levels of democracy (Figure 2.1) and the quality of elections (Table 2.1), not least because expert judgments on the availability of civil liberties and political rights derive in part from observations of a country's performance at conducting elections.

The overall slippage in electoral quality that is evident on the continent is driven by several high-profile failures. The 2007 general elections in Nigeria, for example, saw intimidation of voters, exchange of money for votes, and manipulation of the vote count, a combination of irregularities that momentarily set back the country's political progress. The disputed results of Kenya's 2007 presidential election sparked a paroxysm of political violence in early 2008 that damaged interethnic relations and undercut growth in the economy. And the second-round runoff election for the presidency in Zimbabwe in June 2008 was so seriously marred by state-sponsored terror that the opposition candidate, who came out ahead in the first round, felt compelled to drop out of the race. The year 2010 proved particularly bad for the quality of African elections, featuring more flawed contests than acceptable ones. Whether due to the arrest of journalists in Ethiopia, the assassination of opposition figures in Rwanda, or allegations of ballot stuffing in Sudan, none of these processes could be counted as free and fair.

In a related development, some rulers sought to cling to power even after they lost elections. In Kenya, the 2007 presidential vote was so close— and the count so compromised by deceit on both sides—that a true winner could not be discerned. In response, international negotiators recommended a coalition government as the only way forward. The 2008 presidential vote in Zimbabwe was much less close and much more fraudulent, but the incumbent, backed domestically by the military and internationally within the region, was able to survive by agreeing in principle (but not in practice) to also share power. Perhaps learning from these precedents, international actors (in this case the United Nations, France, and ECOWAS) refused to extend the lifeline of a power-sharing deal to the sitting president of Côte d'Ivoire, who was defeated in elections in 2010. Instead, he was removed by force and the rightful winner was installed in power. But leadership transitions driven from abroad through power sharing or armed interventions do not deepen democracy. Instead, they signal that the electoral process has broken down.

Figure 2.2 summarizes results so far. By displaying the data from Table 2.1 in graphical form, it confirms that the quantity of elections in Africa is rising, but also that this quality—always mixed—has begun to decline. By juxtaposing these trends on regime outcomes (as first displayed in Figure 2.1), we can cast light on the debate about the role of elections in regime change and consolidation.

To begin, I see little connection between the annual frequency of elections (which has increased) and the overall level of democracy in sub-Saharan Africa (which has recently turned down). This disjunction suggests that there is no automatic linkage between the amount of electoral activity and the deepening of democracy. We must therefore question the logic of the "democratization by elections" argument, which holds that any sort of

Figure 2.2 Trends in Democracy and Quality of Elections in Sub-Saharan Africa, 1990-2011

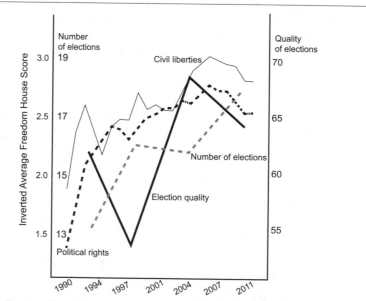

Sources: Freedom House 2012; Lindberg 2007, updated to 2011 by author from observer and press reports.

Notes: Number of elections is the annual average by period; quality of elections is the average percentage of free and fair elections by period. For periods covered see Table 2.1.

election, even if dubiously conducted, is on balance positive for democracy building. On the contrary, it seems likely that, in many places in Africa, authoritarian elites are manipulating electoral mechanisms to legitimize their own preferred form of political regime. They may even find the competitive presence of a weak opposition that always loses elections to be a useful smokescreen to disguise their own determination to dominate. Moreover, authoritarian rulers have learned to tolerate a managed degree of political competition. As evidence, I note the lack of isomorphism between the competitiveness of elections in Africa, which has stayed relatively constant at low levels, and the rising and then falling trend in democracy.

Rather, the score of election freedom and fairness more closely approximates the trend line of democratization (see Figure 2.2). This conjunction strongly suggests that the quality of elections matters for the institutionalization of civil and political rights, and thus of democracy. Otherwise, the mere repetitive conduct of low-quality elections in Africa—what Joel Barkan (2008) calls "C-minus" elections (see also Bovcon 2012)—appears to be quite compatible with the consolidation of "competitive authoritarianism." At the time that Lindberg was first writing, it may have been plausible to propose that low-quality elections could precipitate democracy; until 1998 there was little connection between the falling quality of African elections and a cresting wave of democracy. Thereafter, however, election quality and democratic outcomes tended to move in lockstep, rising until 2006 but falling after that. This relationship is explored statistically in Chapter 13.

Trends in Voting

Until now, little has been said about the key actors in democratic elections in Africa: the voters. To what extent have eligible citizens taken advantage of new opportunities for political participation in competitive elections by registering to vote, turning out for elections, and choosing who will govern them? Moreover, can we discern changes in aggregate patterns of political behavior over time?

A basic requirement is voter registration; individuals may cast a ballot only if their names appear on an official voter's roll. But comprehensive registration—and with it the realization of a genuinely universal franchise—has proven difficult in many African countries (International IDEA 2002). By 2000, barely half of the voting-age population was registered to vote in countries like Chad, Sudan, and Zambia, perhaps in part because populations were scattered across extensive land areas. At the other end of the scale, Cape Verde, Comoros, and Malawi possessed inflated registers in which the number of listed voters exceeded the total size of the voting-age population, thus creating opportunities for electoral fraud. Only a handful of countries appeared to have achieved near-universal registration (up to 98 percent), either because electoral management bodies were administratively capable (as, for example, in Mauritius and Namibia) or because they massaged official figures (as, perhaps, in Angola, Guinea, and Niger). The capacity of electoral management bodies to produce reliable registers has improved of late, especially where modern electronic tools—including biometric voter identification—have been introduced, as in Mozambique, Nigeria, and the DRC. But questions remain about the sustainability of these expensive technologies, their applicability to all countries, and the political acceptability of the resulting rolls (Evrensel 2010).

Growing popular access to the vote is reflected in a shrinking share of respondents to Afrobarometer surveys—dropping from 20 percent to 12 percent across eighteen countries between 2005 and 2008—who report abstaining from their country's last election *because* they were not registered. Ideally, the registration process should be physically reachable, as well as readily understandable, by all qualified persons. But the need to travel long distances to registration centers disenfranchises vulnerable populations, including the infirm and disabled. In 2005, women were significantly less likely than men (by 5 percentage points) to report being registered. And young people, defined as those under thirty years old, found themselves severely disadvantaged (by 30 percentage points compared to those aged forty-five and older). Similar gender and age gaps were therefore evident at the time of actual voting.

This brings us to voter turnout, measured here as total votes cast as a proportion of registered voters. By world standards, voter turnout in sub-Saharan Africa is relatively low, averaging 65 percent in the second half of the twentieth century compared with 72 percent in Latin America, 74 percent in Asia, and 83 percent in Western Europe (International IDEA 2002; see also Bratton, Chu, and Lagos 2010). But voter turnout in established democracies has been in gradual decline and, following the excitement of transitional or "founding" elections, has also dropped off in many new democracies (Franklin 2004; Norris 2002). Not so in sub-Saharan Africa. As Table 2.2 shows, the average voter turnout rate has held steady between 1990 and 2011 at approximately the same level as in the pre-democracy period. In other words, democratization has apparently neither encouraged nor discouraged political engagement at the polls by African voters. In contrast to other world regions, there is also no evidence that voter turnout is in decline in Africa, for example as a result disillusionment with democracy.

As always, aggregate averages conceal vast variation. Official turnout statistics for parliamentary elections range from a dismal 21 percent reported for Mali in 2002 to the improbable 99 percent claimed in 2008 by the government of Rwanda. What explains this disparity? Institutional factors have little effect. In the period 1990–2011, voter turnout was virtually

Table 2.2 Trends in Voting in Sub-Saharan Africa, 1990–2011

	1990–1995	1996–2000	2001–2006	2007–2011
Average voter turnout[a]	63.5%	63.2%	67.1%	64.6%
Number of electoral alternations	20	14	18	12
Rate of alternation[b]	24.7%	17.3%	21.2%	13.8%

Source: Data set on African elections (Lindberg 2007; updated to 2011 by author).
Notes: a. Calculated as percentage of registered voters.
b. Calculated as percentage of elections during each period.

identical for presidential and parliamentary elections, despite the high stakes in the former contests (65 versus 63 percent, a statistically insignificant difference). Turnout was significantly higher in countries with electoral systems based on proportional rather than plurality rules (69 versus 62 percent), probably because the former allow broader representation for minority groups (see Chapter 10). Most interesting are regime effects. I find a propensity for voter turnout to be just as high, if not slightly higher, in countries classified by Freedom House as "not free" as in those deemed "free" (66 versus 64 percent). This result reminds us that voter turnout in many African countries remains a function of authoritarian mass mobilization efforts—including the positive inducements of patronage and the negative sanctions of coercion—by one-party-dominant regimes.

Once voters arrive at the polls, which candidates do they support? At the core of an individual's vote choice is a decision about whether to back an incumbent or a challenger. Over time, as presidential term limits began to take effect, fewer incumbents participated in African elections: whereas 66 percent ran for reelection in the period 1990–2000, just 57 percent did so in 2001–2011. Moreover, as voters began to assert the right of free choice, incumbents were sometimes defeated and challengers from other political parties acceded to office. Out of the 344 elections conducted in sub-Saharan Africa since 1990, an alternation of power occurred in the presidency or national assembly on sixty-four occasions (see Table 2.2). The average rate of electoral alternation (18 percent) in the period 1990–2011 stands in stark contrast to the near absence of such turnovers before 1990 (which occurred only once, in the 1982 parliamentary election in Mauritius).

Yet African voters still regularly ally themselves with incumbent rulers. Since the reintroduction of competitive elections across the continent, the *rate* of electoral alternation dropped by almost half (from 25 percent to 14 percent of all elections). These data suggest one of two possibilities. Either voters are expressing satisfaction with the performance of incumbent governments, which is possible in places where economic growth is taking place. Or rulers are finding ways to command the electoral playing field in order to renew a token popular mandate. In my opinion, the latter interpretation is more often correct in a context where, as we have seen, the quality of African elections has begun to decline.

Values, Attitudes, and Behavior

In testing the effects of elections on democracy in Africa, I have so far referred to data on regimes, institutions, and voting in the aggregate. At the level of whole countries, it seems that high-quality elections are associated with democratization but that elections of low quality are compatible with protracted autocracy. But do these results hold up when we move to the individual level of African voters and citizens? I turn here to Afrobarometer surveys in order to ask whether popular attitudes, values, and behavior reinforce the emerging link between the quality of elections and regime outcomes.

Attitudes to Voting

There is little doubt that Africans welcome the advent of open voting and competitive elections. More than three-quarters of respondents to Afrobarometer surveys (77 percent) agreed that "we should choose our leaders in this country through regular, open, and honest elections." Just one in five (20 percent) disagreed: "since elections sometimes produce bad results, we should adopt other measures for choosing this country's leaders." Strong majorities favor an open vote for leaders in all countries surveyed, peaking at 88 percent in Botswana and 85 percent in Ghana. Thus, like democracy, the institution of free elections has become widely regarded—almost universally in some places—as a desirable public good.

But how deep are mass commitments to open elections? Can popular support for elections withstand the negative side effects that sometimes accompany multiparty competition? After all, some analysts argue that the mobilization of competing political forces in a context of low national income and weak political institutions is an invitation to violence and instability (Collier 2009; Snyder 2000; Wilkinson 2006).

On the one hand, Africans clearly reject political violence. The 2005 Afrobarometer survey found that more than three-quarters of respondents thought that "the use of violence is never justified in politics"; only 17 percent considered that "it is sometimes necessary to use violence in support of a just cause." Comparing the present to the past, most people saw greater freedom to vote as they wish (70 percent), presumably due to reduced levels of campaign strife. Nevertheless, by 2009, about one-third of all respondents across twenty countries (32 percent) still indicated that they "feared political intimidation and violence," especially during election campaigns, either "somewhat" or "a lot." And more than half (58 percent, but rising to 83 percent in Zimbabwe) felt they must "be careful what they say about politics."

On the other hand, and despite the assumption by some analysts that rivalry between political parties in Africa leads to disorder, I detect a rising trend of popular acceptance of multiparty competition. All measurements are for the twelve countries for which Afrobarometer possesses data over four rounds of surveys, 1999–2009. Figure 2.3 shows a steadily increasing popular acceptance of the idea that "many political parties are needed to make sure that [Africans] have real choices in who governs them." This sentiment has grown even in the face of the opposing idea that "political parties create division and confusion; it is therefore unnecessary to have many political parties in [our country]." While a bare majority supported multiparty competition in 2002, almost two-thirds did so just seven years later. I interpret this upsurge of support for political competition to mean that, even though the quality of elections is deteriorating and fears of intimidation persist, Africans increasingly prefer genuinely open voting to

Figure 2.3 Trends in Attitudes to Elections in Sub-Saharan Africa, 1999–2009

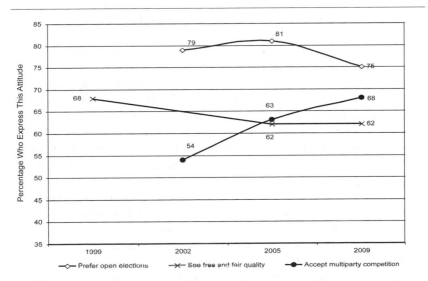

Sources: Afrobarometer surveys, 1990–2009.

Notes: Percentage of survey respondents who express this attitude in twelve countries: Botswana, Ghana, Lesotho, Malawi, Mali, Namibia, Nigeria, South Africa, Tanzania, Uganda, Zambia, and Zimbabwe. Dates are approximate.

stage-managed one-party elections. Especially in places like Zimbabwe, where a de facto one-party regime uses manipulation and violence to "win" elections, fully three-quarters of all adults now call for "real choice" among multiple political parties.

But there may be a wide gap between what the electorate wants and what political leaders deliver. Asked directly in 2009 about the quality of the last elections in their countries, six in ten Africans interviewed (62 percent) reported that, in their opinion, these contests were either "completely free and fair" or "free and fair, but with minor problems." Respondents offered positive assessments of the voting process in countries like Benin, Botswana, Ghana, and Namibia, where more than four out of five voting-age adults saw free and fair elections. But offsetting majorities in Kenya, Nigeria, and Zimbabwe saw either "major problems" with the conduct of the polls or election procedures that were "not free and fair." Figure 2.3 shows that popular perceptions of the quality of elections are in gradual secular decline (from 68 percent in 1999). Moreover, popular support for voting in elections as the preferred method of choosing leaders dropped by 6 percentage points (from 81 to 75 percent) between 2005 and 2009. Both of these indicators of individual opinion are consistent with the recent decline in electoral quality noted earlier at the aggregate level.

Attitudes to Citizenship

As argued in Chapter 1, democracy requires more than the mere convocation of elections. There is an analogue at the individual level to this truism about political regimes: for individuals, the development of democratic citizenship involves more than mere voting. Citizenship, as understood here, is an array of political rights and responsibilities through which ordinary people partake in many stages of the political process. A democratic form of citizenship involves civic engagement around claims for inclusion, responsiveness, and representation. In short, democratic citizens demand political accountability. Active participation in voting is an essential building block of democratic citizenship, especially where it results in a peaceful alternation of power.

But the critical test for democratic citizenship concerns individual orientations and behaviors *between* elections. How do ordinary individuals see their political roles during the long intervals of normal politics that transpire between intermittent episodes of voting? And what do citizens actually do in trying to obtain accountability?

Clearly, Africans are not yet convinced that competitive elections guarantee the accountability of leaders. Asked to consider "how elections work in practice in your country," fewer than half think they work well. In 2008–2009, only 47 percent thought that elections "ensure that members of parliament reflect the views of voters" and only 45 percent reported that elections "enable voters to remove from office leaders who do not do what the people want." People also expressed considerable uncertainty about the purpose of elections; on each of these items, 12 percent said they "didn't know" whether these institutions were intended to secure political representation or leadership alternation. As always, average figures conceal considerable cross-national variation: whereas, in 2009, more than two-thirds of Ghanaians and Malawians saw elections as a reliable means of replacing unresponsive political leaders, less than one-quarter of Nigerians and Senegalese shared the same conviction. These divergent public views probably reflect popular judgments about the variant quality of the last national election in different countries. Unless well conducted, elections can hardly be expected to establish a precedent for accountability.

In a common interpretation of accountability, Africans insist that political representatives should respond to popular needs. Participants to the 2005 Afrobarometer survey believed by a margin of almost six to one that "elected officials should listen to constituents' views and do what they demand" (82 percent). This sample of respondents roundly rejected the proposition that "elected leaders should follow their own ideas in deciding what is best for the country" (14 percent). In other words, people do not regard elections as a blank check that permits political representatives to exercise wide discretion. Indeed, instead of passively "respecting authority," a clear majority (58 percent) thought that "citizens should be more active in questioning the actions of leaders." And reflecting this emergent demand for accountability, fully 69 percent favored limiting the occupants of the presidency to no more than two terms in office.

In practice, however, Africans feel that they cannot make their voices heard between elections. By 2009, more than six in ten (62 percent) reported that it was "somewhat difficult" or "very difficult" for ordinary people to achieve this goal. Much depends on the types of leaders concerned: members of parliament or assembly deputies were widely seen as deaf to popular demands (by 72 percent of respondents), in contrast to traditional chiefs and village heads, who were seen as more responsive (only 39 percent of respondents said they "don't listen"). And while local government councilors were also accused of not listening (by 62 percent), a majority of respondents (57 percent) expressed confidence that they could get together with others in the community to draw the attention of this group of leaders to popular concerns.

This brings us to citizenship behaviors beyond voting. On the one hand, Table 2.3 shows positive developments in the extent to which individuals reported engaging in collective political action at the grassroots level. Comparing 2009 to 1999, more people said that they discussed political affairs with family and friends (71 percent, up from 63 percent). Reported attendance at community meetings rose even higher (64 percent, up from 50 percent). And the proportion of survey respondents who claimed that they joined

Table 2.3 Trends in Democratic Citizenship in Sub-Saharan Africa, 1999–2009

	1999	2002	2005	2009
Collective Action				
Discussed political affairs	63	62	70	71
Attended community meetings	50	67	68	64
Joined others to raise issue	44	52	51	54
Contacting Leaders				
Contacted local government councilor	n/a	29	26	29
Contacted member of parliament	n/a	12	12	14
Contacted civil servant	14	14	12	14

Sources: Afrobarometer surveys, 1999–2009. Dates are approximate.

Notes: The table shows percentages of survey respondents who say they took these actions in twelve countries: Botswana, Ghana, Lesotho, Malawi, Mali, Namibia, Nigeria, South Africa, Tanzania, Uganda, Zambia, and Zimbabwe.

n/a = data not available.

with others in the locality to address an issue of common concern also registered a solid gain (54 percent, up from 44 percent). Taken together, these upbeat trends imply that Africans are taking responsibility for political action into their own hands. In other words, there is evidence that a measure of autonomous democratic citizenship is emerging at the community level at moments beyond elections (Gyimah-Boadi and Attoh 2009).

On the other hand, would-be citizens continue to encounter difficulty in attracting the attention of political leaders. Table 2.3 traces linkages with three types of leaders: local government councilors, members of parliament, and civil servants in government ministries. Strikingly, "contacting"—an activity always limited to a small proportion of adults—neither rose nor fell over the 1999–2009 period. In this regard, I find little evidence that, despite electoral democratization, ordinary Africans are gaining access to routine procedures of decisionmaking within the formal institutions of a broader political system. True, people report some success at reaching local government councilors (29 percent), but the leaders of central government institutions, both legislative and executive, remain well beyond their grasp (14 percent). For this reason, Africans continue to address their search for solutions to quotidian problems more often to traditional, religious, and informal leaders outside of the official structures of the state.

Attitudes to Democracy

What are the implications for democracy of popular frustrations with poor-quality elections and unaccountable leaders? One might expect, for example, negative effects on mass support for democracy and on popular satisfaction with its operation in practice.

Figure 2.4 shows average trends in popular attitudes to democracy for the twelve countries for which the Afrobarometer has complete time-series data. At first, and as expected, newly formed democratic regimes apparently lost adherents, but an upswing in both support and satisfaction evidently occurred after 2005. The reasons for the changing direction of opinion remain unclear: "Perhaps economic recovery spurred by a commodity price boom has encouraged growing faith in the political regime. . . . More likely, citizens perceive that political reforms are taking root; after three or four rounds of competitive elections, including several cases of turnover of ruling parties, they are gaining confidence in the institutionalization of their right to choose leaders" (Afrobarometer 2009).

Over time, however, the gap between support and satisfaction diverged. Barely half of the Africans interviewed by 2009 were satisfied with the way democracy works in their country (53 percent), a level distinctly lower than in 1999 (61 percent). A long-term drop-off in regime satisfaction is consistent with previous observations about declining election quality and blocked access to citizen participation. But an overall rise in the level of expressed popular support for democracy between 1999 and 2009 suggests an alternative

Figure 2.4 Trends in Attitudes to Democracy in Sub-Saharan Africa, 1999–2009

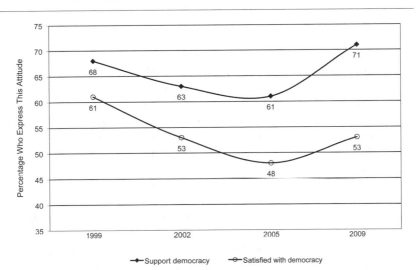

Sources: Afrobarometer surveys, 1990–2009.

Notes: Percentage of survey respondents who express this attitude in twelve countries: Botswana, Ghana, Lesotho, Malawi, Mali, Namibia, Nigeria, South Africa, Tanzania, Uganda, Zambia, and Zimbabwe. Dates are approximate.

dynamic. Rather than encouraging citizens to accept the inferior standards of authoritarian rule, perhaps a political environment of poor-quality elections and few opportunities for citizenship induces people to redouble their search for a democratic ideal.

Certainly, it is important to acknowledge the discrepancy between macro- and micro-level measurements of trends in democracy. Figure 2.1 shows a recent decay in the actual level of democracy whereas Figure 2.4 shows a recent climb in popular democratic attitudes. This difference provides leverage in understanding the diversity of regime trajectories in sub-Saharan Africa. On the one hand, Figure 2.1 represents the continent as a whole, including all of its most untransformed and retrograde autocracies. Figure 2.4 represents a smaller sample that includes most of the continent's open political systems, many with a long history of high-quality elections, some leading to electoral alternation. It should not be surprising, therefore, that the effects of voting and elections on regime consolidation are different in these two groups of countries.

Indeed, this observation reinforces my key argument: the quality of elections is associated with regime outcomes. Popular judgments about the quality of elections are excellent predictors of democratic values and attitudes. Across four rounds of Afrobarometer surveys, people who see their country's elections as free and fair are more likely to say they are satisfied with "the way democracy actually works" ($r = 0.374$, $p < 0.001$). The perceived quality of elections is even connected to voting behavior, since voter turnout is lower among citizens who see the last election as failing to meet free and fair standards ($r = 0.106$, $p < 0.001$). These insights strengthen the argument that the quality of elections matters for democratization, in this case because low-quality elections do not nurture democratic values, attitudes, or behavior. (For fuller analysis, see Chapter 13.)

Stated differently, results of micro-level analysis of public opinion data reinforce an earlier finding at the macro level: low-quality competitive elections undermine democracy. Even across a dozen of the most politically open African countries, ordinary people perceive a gradual decline in the quality of elections. Perhaps as a result, a growing minority has begun to lose faith in elections as the best method for choosing leaders. Fewer than half of all persons interviewed now think that elections work well at securing popular representation and leadership accountability. In particular, people find it hard to gain access to elected leaders and to have their voices heard in decisionmaking. Coincident with these trends, they report declining levels of satisfaction with democracy ($r = 0.168$, $p < 0.001$).

On the other side of the coin, high-quality elections help to build popular legitimacy for a democratic regime. Despite overall declines in the quality of elections, a majority of Africans interviewed still regard their country's latest election as free and fair. This group is likely to suppose that elections enable the formation of a legislative body that is representative of the electorate at large. They are also inclined to believe that elections enable voters to remove unpopular politicians, including entrenched office holders who lead long-standing ruling parties. Finally, the beneficiaries of free and fair elections consider with a high degree of probability that their country has achieved the status of a full (or almost full) democracy. By way of confirmation, a growing proportion of African interviewees say they favor open political competition among multiple political parties—a hallmark of democracy. And the tendency to support multiparty competition is strongest among those who perceive high-quality elections.

Conclusion

In this chapter I have entered a debate between the proponents of "democratization by elections" and witnesses to the spread of "competitive authoritarianism." At issue is an institutional dilemma. Do the rules of competitive elections bring about regime change—that is, toward democracy? Or, alternatively, does periodic voting ensure regime continuity that is, by lending legitimacy to dictatorship?

My contribution to the debate is to draw attention to the intervening factor of the quality of elections. I conclude that elections lead in multiple directions depending on their quality. While a string of well-conducted free elections may indeed be vital to the institutional consolidation of democracy, low-quality elections are entirely compatible with the survival and strengthening of autocratic forms of rule.

On the one hand, it is inadequate to assume that the mere convocation of some sort of vote, regardless of probity, will inevitably contribute to a process of democratization. In recent years in sub-Saharan Africa, we have seen numerous imperfect, violent, and disputed elections that have ensured authoritarian continuity or led to military or external intervention. We have also observed—even in previously democratic countries—novel power-sharing deals that allowed defeated incumbents to remain in office. It is therefore difficult to sustain an argument for a one-to-one relationship between the frequency of elections and the emergence of democracy.

To explore the links between electoral quality and regime outcomes, I have undertaken an empirical examination. I have done so from both a macro perspective, using data on African countries and elections, and a micro perspective, using public opinion data. I find certain consistencies across levels of analysis—for example, regarding recent declines in the quality of African elections. I also discover connections between low-quality elections, on the one hand, and shortfalls in objective ratings of civil and political rights and in subjective citizen perceptions of satisfaction with democracy, on the other. These results lend credence to Levitsky and Way's argument that stage-managed electoral competition on an uneven playing field is compatible with the survival of authoritarian regimes.

But I also discover anomalies that are more challenging to interpret. For example, even as the quality of elections has recently turned down in Africa, popular support for democracy has turned up. This result lends support to the argument about democratization via elections, at least in a subset of African countries where the quality of elections is above the norm. The micro-level investigation also adds insight into a possible mechanism by which low-quality elections can sometimes stimulate democratic action. Over time, Africans in the continent's most open societies report becoming active citizens; they claim to engage in political discussions, attend community meetings, and join others to raise issues of common concern. Note, however, that these forms of civic activism are most common among those who perceive their country's last election to be *less than free and fair*. In this case, therefore, emerging citizenship appears to be a corrective response to a low-quality poll rather than a natural extension of a voter's participation in a well-run election. This is consistent with Lindberg's observation that "bad experience with electoral practices . . . may stimulate activism in society even more than free elections do" (2009: 328; see also Chapter 12 in this volume).

But this exceptional result runs against the grain. Generally speaking, the nature of the political regimes hinges on the quality of elections. Autocracies are vulnerable to citizen mobilization in genuine elections conducted under free and fair rules. And democratic regimes are undermined by a stolen election or a string of low-quality contests.

Part 1

Vote Choice

3

Does Ethnicity Determine Support for the Governing Party?

Pippa Norris and Robert Mattes

A classic issue in electoral behavior concerns the relative strength of social groups and political issues in structuring vote choice and party identification. Following the seminal structural theories of Seymour Martin Lipset and Stein Rokkan (1967), much of this literature has focused on the cleavages of social class, religion, and center-periphery that have long divided established democracies. Debate has centered on whether the strength of these social cues on electoral behavior has weakened in postindustrial societies during recent decades, with commentators emphasizing the process of partisan dealignment and the rise of issue voting among more cognitively skilled citizens (Dalton, Flanagan, and Beck 1984; Crewe and Denver 1985; Franklin, Mackie, and Valen 1992; Evans 1999; Norris 2003).

An important related question, although one that has received less systematic attention, concerns the strength of social cleavages in developing societies, and in particular whether ethnicity determines stable patterns of party support and electoral behavior in these countries, analogous to the anchor of social class in industrialized nations. This question is most relevant for electoral democracies in sub-Saharan Africa, where ethnic ties based on kinship and family, language and dialect, tribal customs and local communities, as well as shared religious faiths, have long been regarded as playing a critical role in party politics (Horowitz 1985; Salih and Markakis 1998; Palmberg 1999; Bekker, Dodds, and Khosa 2001; Daddieh and Fair 2002). Structural theories predict that the cues of social identity, particularly ethnicity, should exert a strong influence on voting choices and party support in developing societies, which are characterized by low levels of education and minimal access to the news media. This phenomenon is important, not

41

just for understanding the basis of electoral behavior, but also because of its potential consequences for the process of democratization.

Few commentators doubt that ethnicity exerts *some* influence upon party politics in Africa. But the relevant question is: *How much* influence can be attributed to ethnic cues when compared with other structural factors (such as urbanization, age, and education) and political attitudes (such as evaluations of government performance)?

To explore these issues, this chapter analyzes the influence of ethnolinguistic and ethnoracial characteristics on identification with the governing party in a dozen African states, compared with other structural and attitudinal factors commonly used to explain patterns of party support. It draws upon the first round of the Afrobarometer, a cross-national representative survey of political and social values conducted in 1999–2001 in twelve nations in sub-Saharan Africa. This comparative framework has the advantage of including many countries from one continent that share similar developing economies, cultural traditions, colonial histories, and social structures, yet have widely differing degrees of ethnolinguistic and ethnoracial fractionalization, types of party systems, and levels of democracy.

The research design uses binary logistic regression analysis with hierarchical blockwise entry, using both pooled and national samples, with identification with the governing party (coded as a dummy) as the dependent variable. The first model examines the direct effects of ethnolinguistic and ethnoracial cleavages upon partisan attachments, without any controls. The second model adds controls for other standard social characteristics associated with party identification in many previous studies, including age, gender, urbanization, class, education, and also "lived poverty" as an indicator of severe economic deprivation. The third model then adds blocks of variables measuring political attitudes, including retrospective evaluations of the government's policy performance, economic evaluations, the legislature's performance, and left-right economic ideology.

Our study establishes three main findings. First, we confirm that, as expected and even with social and attitudinal controls, ethnolinguistic cleavages are a significant predictor of support for the governing party in most, although not all, of the African societies under comparison. Second, the strength of this association varies cross-nationally, with the linkages strongest in societies fragmented by many languages, such as Nigeria and South Africa, while weakest in countries where the ethnolinguistic landscape is more homogeneous, including Lesotho and Botswana. We therefore need to qualify theoretical claims by Donald Horowitz (1985), as well as widespread popular perceptions that ethnolinguistic cleavages inevitably determine party politics across all African societies. Third and finally, structural explanations based on ethnicity are limited: evaluations of the policy performance of the party in government also shape patterns of support for the governing party in many countries, even with prior social controls. The conclusion summarizes the results and considers their broader implications for understanding the role of ethnicity in elections within plural societies.

Theories of Voting Behavior

The classic structural theory of voting behavior developed during the 1960s by Lipset and Rokkan (1967) emphasized that social identities formed the basic building blocks of party support in Western Europe. For Lipset and Rokkan, European nation-states were stamped by social divisions established decades earlier. They highlighted the regional cleavages of center-periphery, the class inequalities of workers-owners, and sectarian cleavages over church and state that split Christendom between Catholics and Protestants. These traditional cleavages were thought powerful in Western Europe for several reasons. First, they reflected major ideological fissions in party politics. Social class mirrored the basic schism between the left, favoring a strong role for the state through egalitarian welfare policies, fiscal redistribution, and interventionist economic management, and the right preferring a more limited role for government and laissez-faire market economics. The religious division reflected conservative and liberal moral debates, such as those surrounding the role of women, marriage, and the family. Differences between core and periphery concerned how far the nation-state should be centralized or how far power should be devolved downward to the regions. Lipset and Rokkan theorized that organizational linkages arose when the mass franchise was expanded to most citizens and gradually strengthened over the years, as party systems "froze." In Western Europe, stable patterns of party competition revolved around the salient primary cleavages dividing each society, as exemplified by the role of class in Britain (Butler and Stokes 1974), religion in France (Lewis-Beck and Skalaban 1992), and language in Belgium (Mughan 1983).

The structural theory provided by Lipset and Rokkan became widely influential as the established orthodoxy in understanding voting behavior and party competition in Western Europe, as well as in many other established democracies such as Australia and Canada (Alford 1967; Rose 1974). Nevertheless these accounts came under increasing challenge from the mid-1960s onward as newer minor parties started to gain electoral momentum and a foothold of parliamentary representation (Rose and Urwin 1970; Daalder and Mair 1985; Pederson 1979). Many observers now suggested that the process of societal modernization was eroding the "traditional" social identities of class and religion that had predicted the mass basis of party support in established democracies during earlier decades (Crewe, Alt, and Sarlvik 1977; Nie, Verba, and Petrocik 1976; Crewe and Denver 1985; Franklin,

Mackie, and Valen 1992; Dalton, Flanagan, and Beck 1984; Evans 1999; Manza and Brooks 1999; Clark and Lipset 2001). If class and religion no longer anchored voters to parties in postindustrial societies, then significant consequences could be expected: growing volatility in electoral behavior and party competition; split-ticket voting across different levels; the occasional sudden rise of protest parties; vote switching within and across the left-right blocks of party families; and the growing influence of short-term events, party strategy, candidates and leaders, and media coverage in determining the outcome of election campaigns.

Can the structural theory be extended to provide insights into party support and voting behavior in developing societies such as those in sub-Saharan Africa? These societies have predominantly agrarian populations characterized by subsistence livelihoods largely based on farming, fishing, and unskilled work, with low levels of literacy and education, minimum standards of living, and restricted social and geographic mobility. Citizens are commonly believed to be strongly rooted to local communities through primary ties of "blood and belonging," including those of kinship, family, ethnicity, and religion, as well as long-standing cultural bonds (Salih and Markakis 1998; Palmberg 1999; Bekker, Dodds, and Khosa 2001; Daddieh and Fair 2002). Structural theories suggest that within this context, in electoral democracies, the basic cleavages within each society should provide cues linking voters to parties representing each major social sector, whether divisions of ethnicity, region, class, or religion.

Donald Horowitz (1985, 1991, 1993) offers an influential theory about the relationship between ethnicity, party systems, and voting behavior in developing societies. For Horowitz, ethnicity exerts a strong direct impact on electoral behavior in ethnically segmented societies, through generating a long-term psychological sense of party loyalty that anchors citizens to parties, whereby casting a vote becomes an expression of group identity. By implication, other social divisions become subsumed as secondary to ethnicity. Horowitz defines ethnic parties as those that derive their support from an identifiable ethnic group and serve the interests of that group. "To be an ethnic party, a party does not have to command an exclusive hold on the allegiance of group members. It is how that party's support is distributed, not how the ethnic group's support is distributed, that is decisive" (1985: 293). Horowitz quotes the examples of Guyana, Trinidad, and Ghana, where surveys during the 1960s found that parties often received 80–90 percent of their votes from one ethnic group. Those voters who crossed ethnic-party lines were subject not just to the usual group pressures, but also to actual intimidation and even physical violence. Where ethnic parties predominate, Horowitz suggests that an election essentially becomes an "ethnic census."

Party systems are defined as ethnic if all parties are ethnically based, as exemplified for Horowitz in the mid-1980s by Sudan, Sri Lanka, Chad,

Benin, Kenya, and Nigeria. Such party systems are prone to conflict, exacerbating existing ethnic divisions, Horowitz argues, because holding the reins of power in state office is often seen as a zero-sum game, rather than a process of accommodation. Where party systems in Africa are divided by more than one predominant issue cleavage, for example over issues of economic redistribution, then Horowitz suggests that the system can become multiethnic or nonethnic, although he regards such cases as relatively rare. Unlike other social cues, Horowitz regards ethnicity as a particular problem for the usual process of bargaining and compromise that characterizes normal politics in representative democracies, because he sees ethnicity as ascriptive, and therefore more segmented and rigid than social identities that are more flexible and fluid, or even self-selected, such as those based on class or shared ideological beliefs. In the distinction drawn by Pippa Norris (2003), ethnic parties are regarded in this theory as essentially "bonding" and not "bridging" types.

Yet as societies develop further, theories of partisan dealignment suggest that economic shifts in the mode of production—from agriculture toward heavy industry and then the service economy—erode traditional social identities. Theories suggest that higher levels of literacy, education, geographic mobility, and access to the news media, associated with human development and societal modernization, lay the social foundations for greater partisan fluidity and issue voting (Dalton, Flanagan, and Beck 1984; Crewe and Denver 1985; Norris 2003). Better-educated and more cognitively sophisticated citizens, it is argued, have less need to rely upon the traditional social cues of ethnicity in electoral choices. The mass media allow citizens to compare a range of parties, leaders, and public policy issues, potentially exposing them to many dissonant values beyond those shared with family and neighbors in their local community.

In Africa, geographic mobility and urbanization generate crosscutting cleavages based on location, occupation, and communication, weakening linkages with local communities, extended family networks, and tribal groups. In this context, issue voting based on retrospective evaluations of the performance of the governing parties, the role of party leaders, and the prospective policy platforms offered by each party, could all be expected to become a more important component of voting decisions. If the structural thesis is correct, then the strength of cleavage and issue politics can be expected to vary systematically among nations at different levels of development. In particular, where free and fair democratic elections are held in Africa, traditional ethnic identities based on language, region, tribe, or religion are expected to exert a strong influence on party support and voting behavior. But where societies are experiencing the process of human development, these traditional cues are expected gradually to weaken, and "bonding" parties will be displaced by "bridging" parties that appeal to multiple overlapping social groups.

What evidence would allow us to test these important claims? The strength of linkages between ethnicity and party voting has been studied in African societies by qualitative examination of particular election campaigns, and by comparing aggregate election results at the district level (see, for example, Ojo 1981; Reynolds 1994; Christopher 1996; Ake 1996; Eldridge and Seekings 1996; Takougang 1996; Ayee 1997; Mozaffar 1997; Burnell 2002; Smith 2002). Research has also focused upon how far plurality, majoritarian, or proportional electoral arrangements can best accommodate ethnic parties (Rabushka and Shepsle 1972; Lijphart 1978, 1994, 1999; Barkan 1998; Reynolds and Reilly 1997; Sisk and Reynolds 1998; Reilly and Reynolds 1998; Scarritt, McMillan, and Mozaffar 2001), as well as upon longitudinal trends in ethnic conflict in Africa and around the world (Gurr 1993, 2000; Saideman et al. 2002). These surveys are sometimes out of date, given the transformation of the continent in recent years and powerful cycles of democratization (Bratton and van de Walle 1997). So far, however, little systematic cross-national survey evidence has been available for use in analyzing and exploring the underlying reasons for electoral behavior and party support based on representative samples of the general electorate covering a wide range of African societies, with the notable exception of South Africa (Mattes and Gouws 1999; Mattes, Taylor, and Africa 1999; Mattes and Piombo 2001). Comparative surveys of many countries and multivariate analysis are both essential to establishing the relative influence of ethnicity today when compared with other structural and attitudinal factors potentially shaping electoral behavior and party support.

Framework, Indicators, and Hypotheses

Selection of Cases

To examine this issue, we analyze the impact of ethnolinguistic and ethnoracial characteristics on support for the governing party in a dozen African states, based on the first round of the Afrobarometer survey (1999–2001). The comparative framework used in this study provides the advantages of the "maximum similarity" strategy (Landman 2000), which compares countries sharing similar cultural traditions within one world region while varying in their social structure and party systems in important ways. The cases under comparison range from newer democracies such as Botswana, characterized by effective multiparty competition, political stability, and a positive record on human rights, through systems struggling in the transition to stable democracy, to corrupt presidential dictatorships that are predominantly one-party states with rigged elections and weak opposition movements, exemplified by Mugabe's Zimbabwe (Bratton and van de Walle 1997; Laakso 2002; Taylor 2002). The levels of ethnic fractionalization also vary: some societies, such as Botswana, contain relatively homogeneous populations, while others are divided by multiple divisions of language, religion, or region, as exemplified by increasing religious tensions, communal violence, and separatist conflict evident within Nigeria. The party systems in these nations also differ in their degree of political institutionalization, meaning the regularity of party competition, the extent of parties' roots in society, the extent to which winning parties assume government office, and the structure of party organizations (Kuenzi and Lambright 2001).

Over 258 million people live in the countries under comparison, accounting for about one-third of all sub-Saharan Africans. The geographic distribution of countries covers mainly southern and western Africa, excluding areas north of the Sahara. All are former British colonies with the exceptions of Mali (France) and Namibia (granted independence in 1990 from South Africa). The countries vary systematically in their level of democratic consolidation and party institutionalization, which has the advantage of allowing us to monitor African attitudes and behavior under very different political contexts. Botswana, South Africa, and Namibia are currently classified by the Freedom House index as newer democracies, characterized by extensive political rights and civil liberties and multiparty competition. All the African societies under comparison are defined by the United Nations Development Programme as relatively impoverished, with an average per capita income of around US$1,000 per annum, but it is notable that the most democratic countries in the survey have a per capita gross national product about ten times higher than that of the other nations. Both South Africa and Namibia have a proportional representation electoral system for national parliaments, yet they also continue to have one-party-dominant systems, facing a fragmented and weak opposition (Giliomee 1998; Lanegran 2001). Botswana and South Africa are also the most urbanized societies under comparison. Another seven of the countries under comparison can be classified according to Freedom House as "partly free" or "semidemocratic" states, with more limited political rights and civil liberties. Some of these have a checkered history of interrupted electoral democracy since the era of decolonization, including Nigeria (Koehn 1989), while others such as Mali have held more open and competitive multiparty elections only during the past decade (Gibson 2002; Ndegwa 2001). Last, two societies, Zimbabwe and Uganda, currently have the greatest restrictions on democracy. Uganda has introduced several Western-style reforms in restructuring the economy, as well as strengthening human rights, but at the time of writing the government prevented multiparty elections (Nohlen, Krennerich, and Thibaut 1999).

The Afrobarometer survey, with the first round conducted in a dozen societies from 1999 to 2001, was carried out with at least 1,200 respondents of voting age drawn from each nation, including double this sample size in South Africa, Nigeria, and Tanzania, producing a total random sample of 21,531 respondents. The surveys used a standard multistage probability sample, and weights were used both within and across countries so that each country sample size was equal in the pooled data.

Measures of Ethnic Cleavage

Ethnic identities are complex phenomena, understood in this study as social constructs with deep cultural and psychological roots based on national, linguistic, racial, or religious backgrounds (Anderson 1996; Billig 1995; Gellner 1983; Brown et al. 1997; Taras and Ganguly 1998). They provide an affective sense of belonging and are socially defined in terms of their meaning for the actors, representing ties of blood, soil, faith, and community. No single demographic category can define ethnic identities in every society; ethnoreligious cleavages are believed to be important in some, such as conflict within Nigeria between the Christian south and Muslim north, while tribal clans located in particular regions provide close kinship and family ties in others, and ethnolinguistic divisions play the more important role in still others, such as South Africa. In the literature there is considerable debate about the nature of ethnic identities, and whether these should be regarded as largely innate, ascribed, and unchangeable, or alternatively as socially learned, acquired, and plastic, or possibly as some mix (Anderson 1996). Without wading into this controversy, we assume without further argument that the social meaning of ethnicity is largely socially derived, and that the political relevance of these identities can be exacerbated or mitigated by political parties depending upon whether they emphasize "bridging" or "bonding" appeals (Norris 2003).

This study is limited in certain important ways. First, we only examine the impact of language and race for ethnic identity, leaving aside alternative important types of ethnic identities, including region and religion. We acknowledge that other factors might well play an important role in ethnic identities, but their analysis requires a different approach focused on provincial- or regional-level comparisons. For example, in Rwanda, Kinyarwanda is the universal official vernacular language, yet this did not prevent deep-rooted conflict between majority Hutus and minority Tutsis. Second, we focus upon analyzing support for the party in government, as the most important party for the working of the political system, without examining support for all other parties. It could well be that minor parties serve particular ethnic communities, but in some cases we are limited by sample size. This study is therefore restricted to analyzing only some important aspects of ethnic cleavages in African party politics, but we recognize that it is far from the complete story.

Linguistic cleavages are widely regarded as important in African societies for ethnic identities, and language represents one of the indicators of ethnic fractionalization that has been most widely used in the literature (Ordeshook and Shvetsova 1994; Neto and Cox 1997; Alesina et al. 2002). In this study we assume that the ethnolinguistic identities under comparison are acquired through the socialization process in early childhood, based on the primary language spoken at home, at school, and within the local community. Obviously, multilingual and bilingual households, and the acquisition of languages through schooling, may dilute or even transform linguistic identities, for example among émigrés. The distribution of ethnolinguistic cleavages, shown in Table 3.1, is measured in each country by the language spoken in the home. We exclude minor groups where languages are spoken by less than 2 percent of respondents and any reliable analysis is limited by the size of the sample. Largely homogeneous societies are exemplified by the ubiquitous use of Sesotho in Lesotho and of Setswana in Botswana, where almost everyone shares the same language. By contrast, considerable linguistic fractionalization is evident in Nigeria, Uganda, Zambia, and South Africa, where seven or more languages are spoken. The number of groups, their size, and particularly the degree of linguistic fractionalization—which can range from none in the case of one predominant language group, to minor in the case of two equally balanced groups, to moderate in the case of three to five groups, to extreme in the case of more than five groups—are expected to be important for patterns of competition in the party system. The ethnolinguistic fractionalization index in Table 3.1 summarizes the degree of heterogeneity, ranging from 0.026 in Lesotho to 0.886 in Uganda.

Alternatively for comparison we also analyze racial ethnic identities, based on the physical characteristics of skin color, dividing the populations into "black" and "others." We assume that racial characteristics are primarily the product of biological inheritance, although the meaning, interpretation, and relevance of physical characteristics, and how they lead toward group identities, are also socially constructed. In all the countries under comparison, 96 percent of respondents were classified as black, 2 percent were white, and the remainder were categorized as "colored" or "Asian." In some nations, such as Ghana, Tanzania, and Uganda, 100 percent of respondents were defined as "black," limiting our ability to examine other more subtle types of racial characteristics. While many other ethnic characteristics may well overlap with language and race, especially at the regional level, this study is restricted to the analysis of ethnolinguistic and ethnoracial cleavages at the national level.

Table 3.1 Distribution of Ethnolinguistic Groups in Sub-Saharan Africa by Size, 1999–2001 (percentages)

	Largest Group		2nd Largest		3rd Largest		4th Largest		5th Largest	
Lesotho	Sesotho	98.7								
Botswana	Setswana	97.1	English	1.3						
Zimbabwe	Shona	78.5	Ndebele	15.3	Sepedi	2.1	English	1.6		
Malawi	Chewa	70.8	Tumbuka	9.6	Yao	5.2	Chisena	3.7	Nyanja	3.6
Ghana	Akan	60.1	Ewe	11.8	Ga	5.9	Dangbane	2.4	Frafra	2.3
Tanzania	Swahili	57.5	Sukuma	11.7	Haya	4.6	Nyakyusa	4.0	Nyamwezi	2.9
Namibia	Oshiwambo	50.0	Afrikaans	11.3	Otjiherero	8.1	Damara	7.0	Nama	6.6
Mali	Bambara	48.4	Somrhai	7.9	Fulfulde/Peul	7.7	Dogon	6.1	Tamasheq	6.0
Zambia	Bemba	40.0	Nyanja	23.3	Tonga	13.1	Silozi	11.8	English	4.1
Nigeria	Hausa	31.5	Yoruba	25.5	Ibo	16.7	Edo	3.6	Kanuri	3.4
South Africa	Zulu	22.5	Afrikaans	17.4	Xhosa	16.6	English	11.7	Setswana	9.7
Uganda	Luganda	25.4	Luo	12.9	Rutooro	11.9	Lusoga	9.9	Rukiga	6.4

(continues)

Table 3.1 Continued

	6th Largest		7th Largest		All Others		Ethnolinguistic Fractionalization Index
Lesotho					All others	1.3	0.026
Botswana					All others	1.6	0.057
Zimbabwe					All others	2.5	0.360
Malawi	Tonga	2.5	Lomwe	1.4	All others	3.2	0.483
Ghana	Hausa	2.0	Dangaare	1.4	All others	14.4	0.630
Tanzania	Chagga	2.5	Pare	2.5	All others	14.3	0.650
Namibia	Silozi	5.2	English	3.2	All others	8.6	0.718
Mali	Soninke	6.0	Malinke	4.4	All others	13.5	0.741
Zambia	Luvale	4.0	Kaonde	2.7	All others	1.0	0.751
Nigeria	Tiv	2.2	Ibibio-Efik	2.2	All others	14.9	0.804
South Africa	Sesotho	8.5	Sepedi	7.3	All others	6.3	0.856
Uganda	Lumasaba	5.2	Ateso	4.8	All others	23.5	0.886

Source: Afrobarometer survey, 1999–2000.

Notes: The Afrobarometer asks: "Let's think for a moment about the languages that you use. What language do you speak most at home?" Note that dialects within languages are not counted separately in this classification, hence "Sesotho" includes Sotho and Southern Sotho, and "Setswana" includes Tswana. Groups comprising less than 1 percent of the sample are excluded.

Measures of Partisan Identification

Many studies focus upon understanding patterns of voter choice. In the absence of direct measures of voting behavior, this study examines party identification as the key dependent variable. Not only is party identification usually closely related to voting choice, so that many argue that these two indicators vary systematically in tandem (Thomassen 1976; Holmberg 1994; Brynin and Sanders 1997), but ever since the classic studies of *The American Voter* by Angus Campbell and colleagues (1960) it has also been widely regarded as theoretically important as an anchor of voting behavior in its own right. The measure of partisan identification was gauged by the question: "Do you usually think of yourself as close to any particular political party?" If the respondent answered yes, this was followed by the question: "Which party is that?" For the dependent variable, patterns of partisanship were dichotomized into identification with the party in government or not. As shown in Table 3.2, the largest parties identified with ranged from the Movement for Multiparty Democracy in Zambia (85 percent support) and the National Resistance Movement in Uganda (82 percent), where other Ugandan parties could not legally contest elections, to the more moderate lead over the opposition enjoyed by the Democratic Party in Botswana (59 percent) and the National Democratic Congress in Ghana (57 percent). Support in some countries, such as Lesotho and Botswana, was divided between two major parties and one minor party, while in others, support was highly fragmented across multiple contestants. In this study, we make no assumptions about the psychological nature of partisan identification nor its longevity but rather use it, in the absence of voting choice, as an indirect measure of party preferences.

Analysis of Results

To examine the basis of party identification, our research design employs multivariate modeling using binary logistic regression with blockwise entry. The models are first applied to the pooled sample and then to each nation. The dependent variable is partisan identification, measured by the attachment to the main party in government. As mentioned earlier, the first model examines the direct effects of belonging to the largest ethnolinguistic group and to racial characteristics (black versus all other) upon partisan attachments without any controls. The second model then adds controls for other standard social characteristics that studies have commonly found to influence patterns of partisanship, including age (in years), gender (male), urbanization (rural residency), social class (middle), and education (a four-category scale). Given the existence of extreme social deprivation in Africa,

Table 3.2 Distribution of Party Identification in Sub-Saharan Africa, 1999–2001 (percentages)

	Largest Party		2nd Largest		3rd Largest		4th Largest		5th Largest		All Others	
Lesotho	Congress for Democracy	66.5	Basotho National	21.7	Basutoland Congress	8.9					All others	2.9
Botswana	Democratic Party	59.0	National Front	29.5	Congress Party	6.0					All others	5.5
Zimbabwe	Zimbabwe African National Union–Patriotic Front	72.5	Movement for Democratic Change	13.1	African People's Union	4.8	Integrated Party	1.7	Democratic Party	1.5	All others	6.4
Malawi	United Democratic Front	59.0	Malawi Congress	31.0	Alliance for Democracy	9.2					All others	0.8
Ghana	National Democratic Congress	56.9	New Patriotic Party	37.6	People's National Convention	2.2	Convention Party	1.9			All others	3.3
Namibia	South West African Peoples' Organization	80.1	Democratic Turnhalle Alliance	9.8	Congress of Democrats	5.6					All others	4.5
Mali	Alliance for Democracy in Mali	72.4	Party for National Rebirth	6.5	Union for Democracy and Development	4.2	Congres National d'Initiative Démocratique	3.1	Union Soudanais/ Rassemblement Démocratique Africain	3.0	All others	10.8
Tanzania	Chama cha Mapinduzi	78.7	Civic United Front	10.2	Tanzanian Labor Party	6.6	Chama cha Demokrasia na Maendeleo	2.4			All others	2.1
Nigeria	Peoples' Democratic Party	64.3	All Peoples' Party	19.9	Alliance for Democracy	15.8					All others	0.0
Zambia	Movement for Multiparty Democracy	85.0	United National Independence Party	8.5	United Party for National Development	3.7					All others	2.8
Uganda	National Resistance Movement	81.9	Democratic Party	8.3	Uganda Peoples' Congress	6.6	Uganda Young Democrats	1.8			All others	1.4
South Africa	African National Congress	75.4	Democratic Party	6.8	New National Party	5.7	Inkatha Freedom Party	4.3	Pan Africanist Congress	2.5	All others	5.3

Source: Afrobarometer survey, 1999–2001.

Notes: The Afrobarometer asks: "Do you usually think of yourself as close to any particular political party?" and (if yes) "Which party is that?" This table examines the distribution of support among those who express a party identification. Fringe parties (those with less than 1 percent support) are grouped under "all others." More details about these parties are available from Nohlen, Krennerich, and Thibaut 1999.

we also include a measure of "lived poverty," indicating reported shortages of food, health care, and water at home.

The final model then examines the indirect effect of ethnolinguistic cleavages after we add blocks of variables measuring political attitudes. Factor analysis (with details not reported here) was used for the construction of the attitudinal scales. The models included a scale measuring retrospective evaluations of the government's performance on six issues such as health care, education, and employment, as well as evaluations of the performance of the legislature. We monitored attitudes toward left-right ideology, with a 28-point scale measured by summing agreement with a series of seven items gauging support for the free market economy versus the state, such as "The private sector should build houses," "The private sector should fight crime," and "The private sector should provide schools." The economic satisfaction scale was constructed from three items concerning satisfaction with the present state of the national economy, satisfaction with the national economy during the past year, and expectations that the national economy would improve during the next year. Full details of the questions and coding are given in Table 3.3. It should be noted that in these models we are essentially concerned with testing the strength and significance of the relationship between the independent variables and party identification, not the direction. The structural theory makes no predictions about the positive or negative sign of the coefficients for social structure, which can be expected to vary in different countries depending upon the nature of the governing party and the type of campaign appeals that they make when seeking support from the electorate, for example whether they seek to build support among urban or rural constituents, or among younger or older voters.

The baseline models presented in Table 3.3 summarize the results for the pooled sample across twelve African countries. There are three main findings evident from the analysis. First, ethnicity does matter for partisan identification in African societies, as many commonly claim. The results in model 1 confirm that both language and race are significant predictors of support for the governing party, although these two factors alone fail to explain a great deal of variance in party attachments. Model 2 adds a variety of social controls to see whether this reduces the power of ethnicity. The results demonstrate that language and race remain significant, so that their impact cannot be interpreted as simply the by-product of other structural cleavages in society. Moreover, all the standard structural factors that are most commonly used to explain partisan identification in many other countries are also significant in African societies, with the governing parties getting slightly stronger support among men, older citizens, the less educated, rural populations, and the poorer classes. The overall fit of the model strengthens slightly, although it remains modest. Model 3 adds the attitudinal indicators, and the evaluations of the government's policy record, approval of

Table 3.3 Baseline Model, Identification with the Governing Party, in Sub-Saharan Africa, 1999–2001

	Model 1: Ethnicity Without Any Controls			Model 2: Ethnicity + Social Background +			Model 3: Ethnicity + Social Background Political Attitudes		
	B	S.E.	Sig.	B	S.E.	Sig.	B	S.E.	Sig.
Ethnicity									
Language (belongs to largest linguistic group)	0.171	0.041	***	0.160	0.042	***	0.196	0.045	***
Race (African black = 1, else = 0)	0.752	0.110	***	0.639	0.119	***	0.588	0.123	***
Social structure									
Gender (male = 1, female = 0)				0.006	0.003	*	0.004	0.003	
Age (years)				0.008	0.002	***	0.011	0.002	***
Education (4-point categorization)				-0.162	0.025	***	-0.106	0.026	***
Urbanization (rural = 1, urban = 0)				0.436	0.044	***	0.545	0.048	***
Social class (middle = 1, else = 0)				-0.113	0.046	**	-0.120	0.048	**
Political attitudes									
Government policy performance scale							0.079	0.006	***
Approve of legislative performance							0.287	0.024	***
Economic satisfaction scale							0.041	0.008	***
Left-right attitudes toward market vs. state							-0.002	0.000	***
Constant	-1.26			-1.88			-3.98		
Nagelkerke R^2	0.010			0.048			0.137		
Percentage correctly predicted	61.1			62.0			65.9		

Source: Afrobarometer survey, 1999–2001.

Notes: Data compiled for twelve countries: Botswana, Ghana, Lesotho, Malawi, Mali, Namibia, Nigeria, South Africa, Tanzania, Uganda, Zambia, and Zimbabwe. The models represent the result of binary logistic multiple regression including unstandardized regression coefficients (B), standardized error (S.E.), and their significance (Sig.). The dependent variable is identification with the governing party. The data were weighted by across-country and within-country weights so that each country sample was equal. In total, 15,783 cases were included in the pooled sample.

*** $p < 0.001$, ** $p < 0.01$, * $p < 0.05$.

the performance of the legislature, economic satisfaction, and left-right ideology are, as expected, strongly related to support for the governing party. Even after the addition of all the other social background and attitudinal measures, the measures of ethnolinguistic and racial characteristics remain strongly significant predictors of support for the governing party, despite our most rigorous tests.

Are similar patterns evident if the sample is broken down by country? Table 3.4 explores this by replicating model 3 in each nation. Here interpretation of the results is more complex, as both the significance and the direction of the regression coefficients vary from one country to another. In part, as mentioned earlier, this can be explained by the particular characteristics of the governing party and the type of linkages it develops with the electorate through its campaign appeals.

The second major finding is that, even with the range of social and attitudinal controls, belonging to the largest ethnolinguistic group is a significant predictor of attachment to the governing party in most, but not all, of the African nations under comparison. Exceptions are found in two of the most homogeneous linguistic societies, Lesotho and Botswana. Language also fails to prove significant in Mali and Tanzania, although these are more linguistically fragmented. Moreover, in some states where there is a significant relationship, the linkage is positive, including in Malawi, Namibia, Nigeria, and Zambia, indicating that the predominant linguistic group is strongly associated with the governing party. This is shown further in Table 3.5, indicating the proportion of the largest linguistic group identifying with the governing party. In others the relationship proves negative, including in Ghana, South Africa, and Uganda. For example, in South Africa, the African National Congress draws more support from Xhosas than from Zulus, although the latter are marginally larger in size. The relationship between language and party support also proves strongest in Namibia and Nigeria, indicating deep ethnolinguistic political cleavages in these states.

Yet the explanatory power of ethnicity remains limited, since approval of the government's policy performance on the provision of basic services such as health care, education, and employment is also significantly related to identification with the governing party. This pattern is evident in all nations except for Nigeria and Uganda. Approval of the performance of the legislature was also significantly associated with party identification in many nations. Although structural explanations receive further confirmation from the analysis, thus explaining party support in African nations in a way similar to the pattern found in many established democracies, nevertheless the role of ethnicity should not be exaggerated. A more rational calculation of how well the government and the legislature perform is also part of the reason for patterns of support for the governing party, beyond any traditional group loyalties.

Table 3.4 National Models Explaining Identification with the Governing Party in Sub-Saharan Africa, 1999–2001

Social Structure

	Language		Race (black)		Gender (male)		Age (years)		Education		Rural-Urban (rural)		Class (middle)		Lived Poverty	
	B	Sig.	B	Sig.	B	Sig.	B	Sig.	B	Sig.	B	Sig.	B	Sig.	B	Sig.
Botswana	0.669		-0.175		0.000		0.023	***	-0.130		0.536	***	0.252		-0.207	
Ghana	-0.595	***			0.009		0.004		-0.213	***	0.392	**	-0.504	**	0.086	
Lesotho	-1.580				0.001		0.018	**	-0.422	**	-0.362		0.057		-0.334	*
Malawi	0.628	***	6.400		-0.225	*	-0.006		-0.194		0.147		0.061		-0.584	***
Mali	-0.214				-0.238		-0.001		-0.065		0.566	**	0.080		-0.046	
Namibia	1.720	***	0.166		-0.010		0.010		-0.146		0.841	***	-0.194		0.448	*
Nigeria	0.835	***			-0.568	***	0.008		0.180	x	0.345	*	-0.090		0.180	
South Africa	-0.499	***	2.170	***	-0.255		0.002		0.003		-0.028		-0.327	*	-0.042	
Tanzania	-0.247				0.604	***	0.036	***	-0.223		0.333		-0.114		0.060	
Uganda	-0.627	*			-0.239		-0.001		-0.018		0.274		0.323			
Zambia	0.427	**	-0.044		-0.001		0.031	***	-0.036		0.149		-0.238		0.036	
Zimbabwe	0.423	*	5.880		0.012		0.029	***	-0.228	*	0.858	***	-0.473	**	0.119	

(continues)

Table 3.4 Continued

| | Political Attitudes | | | | | | | | | |
| | Approve of Policy Performance | | Approve of Parliamentary Performance | | Left-Right Ideology | | Economic Satisfaction | | R^2 | % |
	B	Sig.	B	Sig.	B	Sig.	B	Sig.		
Botswana	0.135	***	0.598	***	0.001		0.093	**	0.206	67.7
Ghana	0.108	***	-0.111		-0.013		0.145	***	0.229	69.4
Lesotho	0.136	***	0.231	**	0.001		-0.035		0.179	67.9
Malawi	0.240	***	0.458	***	-0.038	**	0.004		0.299	69.4
Mali	0.038	*	0.371	***	0.032		0.055		0.120	63.0
Namibia	0.122	***	0.514	***	0.001		0.048		0.388	75.1
Nigeria	0.008		0.236	**	-0.007		0.049		0.106	74.2
South Africa	0.047	*	0.438	***	0.029	*	0.067	*	0.254	70.3
Tanzania	0.076	***	0.378	***	0.022		0.039		0.173	67.4
Uganda	0.032		-0.062				0.056		0.032	78.7
Zambia	0.123	***	0.181		0.001		0.010		0.101	69.6
Zimbabwe	0.070	*	0.123		-0.001		0.005		0.188	73.2

Source: Afrobarometer survey, 1999–2001.

Notes: The models represent the result of binary logistic multiple regression including unstandardized regression coefficients (B), and their significance (Sig.). The total number of cases is 15,783. The dependent variable is partisan identification with the governing party. The final two columns summarize the overall fit of the model provided by the Nagelkerke R^2 and the percentage of cases correctly predicted. Race data are unavailable in countries where 100 percent of respondents were coded as "black." Lived poverty and left-right ideology also are unavailable in the Ugandan survey.

*** $p < 0.001$, ** $p < 0.01$, * $p < 0.05$.

Table 3.5 Largest Language Group Identifying with the Governing Party in Sub-Saharan Africa, 1999–2001

	Largest Language Group	Percentage of This Group Who Identify with the Governing Party
Namibia	Oshiwambo	71.4
Tanzania	Swahili	56.1
Malawi	Chewa	49.6
Botswana	Setswana	45.5
Nigeria	Hausa	35.2
Lesotho	Sesotho	34.5
Zambia	Bemba	34.2
Mali	Bambara	33.7
Zimbabwe	Shona	31.3
South Africa	Zulu	29.8
Ghana	Akan	29.3
Uganda	Luganda	13.4
Average		38.7

Source: Afrobarometer survey, 1999–2001.

Conclusion

Structural theories have long dominated explanations of party support and voting behavior in established democracies. If these accounts are extended to elections in African societies, they suggest that ethnic identities can be expected to strongly orient citizens toward the party system by providing a simple, low-cost guide to voting decisions, enabling information shortcuts that allow people to decide which politicians and parties to support over successive contests. These cognitive shortcuts are predicted to be particularly useful for the least-sophisticated citizens, especially those with minimal literacy and schooling, and with limited access to independent political information available from the mass media. These party attachments are predicted to gradually weaken and erode through socioeconomic development, particularly rising levels of education and cognitive skills that can help individuals to master understanding of the complexities of public affairs and the policymaking process.

The results of the analysis of systematic survey evidence serve to confirm the common assumption that ethnolinguistic cleavages do indeed structure party identification in many, although not all, of the African societies under comparison. In the national models, ethnicity remained significant in eight out of twelve countries. Yet ethnicity was not necessarily the primary cleavage, as other structural factors were also important for partisanship, if less consistent across all societies under comparison. These factors include the rural-urban cleavage dividing cities, towns, and villages in Mali, Namibia, and Tanzania, the role of age and generation in Botswana, Tanzania, and Zambia, and the impact of education in Ghana, Nigeria, and Zimbabwe. Moreover, far from support being an automatic expression of group loyalties, judgments contingent upon how well the government delivered services to its citizens were also related to their patterns of party support in most countries.

Further analysis is required to explore the role of ethnicity in African electoral politics in greater depth, and subsequent research should analyze a range of alternative indicators of ethnic identity, including religious faiths, adherence to shared histories and customs, and tribal identities within particular regional communities. Ethnicity is a complex phenomenon and the impact of single indicators can be expected to vary among different societies. The geographic distribution of ethnic identities must also be explored at the subnational or provincial level, since this is critical to political representation and the role of ethnic parties, especially in majoritarian electoral systems. Moreover, we also need to test the impact of ethnicity on many other factors beyond party support, including on voting choice and electoral turnout, as well as on broader attitudes toward a broad range of social and political values, such as support for democracy and satisfaction with the workings of the political system. Although the first round of the Afrobarometer covers a wide range of countries on the continent, subsequent surveys will expand coverage to additional African states, facilitating broader generalizations, such as among a range of Muslim and non-Muslim societies, as well as among countries with different colonial histories and transitions since independence. Nevertheless, the results of this analysis serve to confirm that, far from reflecting any "African exceptionalism," often stressed by area specialists and students of ethnic conflict, structural and attitudinal factors explaining partisan identification in Africa are similar to the explanatory factors found in many other countries, in both established and newer democracies worldwide.

4

Political Competition and Ethnic Identification in Africa

Benn Eifert, Edward Miguel,
and Daniel Posner

Ethnic identities are believed to be powerful motivators of behavior in Africa, but the source of their salience in political and social affairs remains debated. One perspective holds that ethnic identities are salient in Africa because they reflect traditional loyalties to kith and kin. By this view, ethnic identities are hardwired—intrinsically part of who people are—and their salience follows directly from their link to people's natural makeup. A contrary perspective argues that ethnicity is salient because it is functional. The world is a competitive place, proponents of this position hold, and in that world ethnicity serves as a useful tool for mobilizing people, policing boundaries, and building coalitions that can be deployed in the struggle for power and scarce resources. By this view, the salience of ethnicity is intrinsically bound up in political competition.

In keeping with the conventional wisdom in the scholarly literature (e.g., Bates 1983; Horowitz 1985; Young 1976), we find strong evidence in favor of the latter perspective. In departure from that literature, however, we draw our conclusions from cross-national survey data rather than case studies and anecdotal evidence. This approach permits us to generalize across settings and puts us in a much stronger position to rule out competing explanations for the patterns we find. Our results therefore rest on much firmer empirical foundations than prior research on the political sources of ethnic identification.

In generating our findings, we take advantage of two clear implications of the political logic of ethnic identification. First, if ethnic identities are tools that people use to obtain access to political power, then they are likely to be rendered most salient when political power is at stake—that is, during the periods around national elections. Second, if the role that ethnicity plays is to secure an advantage in the competition for power, then it is likely to be most useful, and to become most salient as a social identity, during elections that are closely fought.

61

We would therefore expect ethnic attachments to be strongest not just when elections are proximate but when they are also highly competitive.

We test these expectations using survey data on the primary social identity of more than 35,000 respondents in twenty-two Afrobarometer survey rounds across ten African countries. We find evidence that the strength of ethnic identification—which we operationalize as the likelihood that a respondent names a tribal- or language-group membership in response to a question about the social group to which they feel they belong first and foremost—changes dramatically within African countries over time. We also find strong and robust evidence that these changes are associated with how close in time the survey is to a presidential election and that this proximity effect is conditional on the competitiveness of that election (which we define in terms of the margin of victory between the election's winner and that winner's closest challenger). When the most proximate presidential election is very competitive (i.e., when the margin of victory is near zero), we find that the likelihood that a survey respondent will identify him- or herself in ethnic terms rises by 1.8 percentage points with every month closer the survey is to the election. But as the competitiveness of the election falls, the impact of electoral proximity diminishes, reaching zero in landslide elections where the margin of victory exceeds roughly 40 percentage points. These are exactly the patterns we would expect to observe if ethnic identities in Africa are strengthened by political competition—and *not* the patterns we would expect to see if, as journalistic accounts of Africa imply, ethnic attachments are simply "in the blood."

Having demonstrated that exposure to electoral competition is associated with a strengthening of ethnic identity, we then examine which other identities are displaced when people identify more closely with their ethnic groups. Individuals have identities rooted not just in their ethnicity but also in their membership in religious communities, occupation or class groups, and gender categories, among other social affiliations. To explore the impact of elections on these other dimensions of social identification, we employ a multinomial discrete choice (logit) framework to estimate simultaneously the effects of electoral proximity and competitiveness on four different categories of social identity: ethnicity, class/occupation, religion, and gender. Our main finding is that the increasing salience of ethnic identification that occurs in proximity to competitive presidential elections corresponds with a decreasing salience of class/occupational identities. For every additional month closer a survey respondent is to a competitive presidential election, the salience of his or her class/occupational identity decreases by 1 percentage point—an effect that diminishes (as with the corresponding increased salience of ethnicity) with the declining competitiveness of the election. In keeping with case study findings (e.g., Melson 1971), our results thus imply that electoral competition causes ethnic identities to displace class/occupational identities.

Apart from these empirical findings, this chapter also makes three important methodological contributions. First, along with Michael Bratton and colleagues

(2005) and in keeping with the literature that stresses the multidimensional nature of social identities (Chandra 2004; Horowitz 1985; McLaughlin 2008; Posner 2005; Scarritt and Mozaffar 1999), we define our main dependent variable in terms of the social group to which respondents feel they belong first and foremost from among multiple categories of social identity. Thus, while our main interest is in the political sources of *ethnic* identification, the multinomial logit empirical methodology we adopt permits us to make inferences about the impact of political competition on other kinds of social identification as well, and about the kinds of identities that individuals *switch out of* when attachments to their ethnic groups move to the forefront of their identity repertoires. The use of this statistical technique represents the first attempt of which we are aware to simultaneously generate estimates of the factors associated with the salience of multiple dimensions of social identity.

A second methodological contribution is our use of repeated country-level observations with micro-level individual survey data. One of the difficulties with isolating the sources of ethnic identification among survey respondents sampled from multiple countries is that the importance that a respondent attaches to his or her ethnicity is likely to be affected by the characteristics of the broader political and social environment in which he or she lives. For example, factors such as a country's level of economic development (Bates 1983; Melson and Wolpe 1970), its electoral institutions (Reilly 2001; Reynolds 2002), its ethnic diversity (Collier 2001; Bates 2000), its colonial heritage, and the nation-building emphasis of its leaders (Miguel 2004) have all been argued to affect the importance that citizens attach to their ethnic identities. While it is fairly straightforward to control for many of these factors, others are either very difficult to operationalize (for example, "leadership") or are colinear with the country-level political variables whose impact on ethnic identification we seek to estimate. A major advantage of the data we employ in this study is that it has been collected not just across multiple countries but also at multiple points in time for the same countries. This permits us to employ country fixed effects that control for country-level features, including unobservable characteristics that we cannot measure. This, in turn, permits us to focus attention on factors that vary within countries across survey rounds, such as the proximity of the survey to the nearest presidential election and the competitiveness of that contest.

Finally, the measure of ethnic salience we adopt in this chapter represents a significant advance over measures employed in earlier studies, almost none of which quantify ethnic salience directly. Most studies that deal with this issue rely on inferences based on the presumed effects of ethnic salience. In effect, they reason that, because there is ethnic violence in the country in question or because voting patterns or the distribution of patronage appears to follow ethnic lines, ethnicity must be a salient motivating factor in people's behavior. Others rely on assumptions about what the diversity of ethnic groups in a society implies about the salience of ethnicity in that society's politics (e.g., Alesina, Baqir, and Easterly 1999)—a relationship that finds little support in the empirical literature. Neither approach is as defensible as the one pursued here, which bases its assessment of ethnic salience on the self-reported identities of individuals as collected in nationally representative sample surveys.

Data and Methodology

To investigate the sources of ethnic identification in Africa, we employ data collected in Rounds 1, 1.5, and 2 of the Afrobarometer, which were administered between 1999 and 2004. These are the only rounds that included the key question from which we construct our dependent variable. Nationally representative samples were drawn through a multistage stratified, clustered sampling procedure, with sample sizes sufficient to yield a margin of sampling error of plus or minus 3 percentage points at the 95 percent confidence level. Our data consist of 35,505 responses from twenty-two separate survey rounds conducted in ten countries: Botswana, Malawi, Mali, Namibia, Nigeria, South Africa, Tanzania, Uganda, Zambia, and Zimbabwe. To make possible the inclusion of country fixed effects, we limit our analysis to countries for which more than one survey round of data is available.

The main dependent variable we employ comes from a question designed to gauge the salience for respondents of different group identifications. The question wording is: "We have spoken to many [people in this country] and they have all described themselves in different ways. Some people describe themselves in terms of their language, religion, race, and others describe themselves in economic terms, such as working class, middle class, or a farmer. Besides being [a national of this country], which specific group do you feel you belong to first and foremost?" As noted, a major advantage of the way this question was constructed is that it allows multiple answers and thus permits us to isolate the factors that are associated with attachments to different dimensions of social identity. We group respondents' answers into five categories: ethnic, religion, class/occupation, gender, and "other."

Before we turn to the findings, several methodological issues bear mentioning. First, as we have stressed, the salience of any social identification—be it ethnic or otherwise—is necessarily context-specific, and the Afrobarometer data only permit us to ascertain the way respondents identified themselves in the specific context in which they were surveyed. Our task is to use what we know about that context to make inferences about the factors that determine when ethnic-group memberships become most salient. The context-specificity of respondents' answers is central to our research design. Since our main focus is on the timing of the survey vis-à-vis the most proximate presidential election, we report coefficient estimates only on the election-related variables. However, all of our analyses are robust to the inclusion of controls for other contextual factors, including the characteristics of the interview (whether people other than the respondent were present, whether the respondent consulted other people while answering, whether, in the interviewer's judgment, other people influenced the respondent's answers, and whether the respondent seemed engaged, at ease, suspicious, or threatening) and the characteristics of the interviewer (his or her age, gender, urban-rural background, and education). The country fixed-effect framework we adopt also automatically controls for many other aspects of context that are correlated with the country in which the survey is taking place—its history, its diversity, its colonial heritage, its level of economic development, and the like.

Second, quite apart from the issue of the reliability of responses across contexts, the use of self-reported identities introduces the possibility of bias. Respondents in countries where the social norm is not to talk openly about ethnicity might be less likely to confess that their most important social affiliation is with their ethnic community, which would generate a downward bias in measured ethnic salience in that country. This may be particularly likely in a context where open confessions of ethnic solidarity are frowned upon by the regime and where survey interviewers are suspected of being affiliated with the government. While this concern cannot be ruled out, it is dampened by the way the Afrobarometer survey was conducted—confidentially and in private by interviewers who were not affiliated with the government or any political party.

Also, the Afrobarometer survey is not primarily about ethnicity or social identity. The question we use to construct our measure of ethnic salience is just one out of more than 175 questions asked in the standard Afrobarometer questionnaire, only a handful of which make any mention of ethnicity or social identity. Respondents are thus likely to have treated the "with which group do you identify" question as a background query rather than as the central issue around which the survey revolved. Indeed, questions about ethnic background, religious-group membership, and language use are standard background questions included in most surveys conducted in Africa. We therefore expect that respondents were probably less guarded in their responses about their ethnic identities than might otherwise have been the case. In addition, to the extent that social norms against confessing the strength of one's ethnic identification vary by country, the country fixed-effect framework that we employ should control for these differences. Similarly, to the extent that a respondent's willingness to speak freely about his or her ethnic identity depends on the characteristics of the person who is asking the questions, the robustness of our findings to the inclusion of controls for the age, gender, urban/rural background, and education of the interviewer, as well as for the presence of other people at the survey location at the time of the survey, should minimize concerns about this possible source of bias.

Two additional potential concerns stem from the way the survey question was structured. A first issue is that the question explicitly bars respondents from describing themselves in terms of nationality: it asks *"Besides being* [your nationality (e.g., Namibian, Zambian, etc.)], which specific group do you feel you belong to first and foremost?" We therefore cannot rule out the possibility that respondents might consider national identity as more important to them than all of the identity categories recorded in our data. This said, to the extent that the patterns of ethnic identification we observe are due to unobserved variation in levels of national identification, these levels plausibly vary across countries more than within them over time and, as such, should be controlled for by our inclusion of country fixed effects.

A related issue is that the survey question provides information about the salience of the reported group membership in relative, not absolute, terms. All we are able to infer from respondents' answers is the identity that they rank first from among those identity categories explicitly mentioned in the question (and, as noted, excluding national identity). We have no way of knowing how much absolute importance respondents attach to their first-ranked (or second- or third-ranked) group memberships. To conclude on the basis of our data that ethnicity is more salient in one country compared to another because a larger share of survey respondents in the former country ranked ethnicity first is therefore not quite right. It is conceivable, though we think unlikely, that ethnicity might be more salient in absolute terms to people in the latter country, even though a larger share of them ranked some other category of identity as even more important than ethnicity.

Finally, legitimate questions can be raised about the generalizability of our findings. Although broadly representative of Africa as a whole, the ten countries included in our study are not a substitute for a continentwide sample. Our sample includes just one francophone country (Mali), no countries that have failed to introduce at least some democratic or market reforms (a precondition for an Afrobarometer survey) over the past decade, and, with the exception of Uganda, no countries involved in civil wars at the time the survey data were collected. As Table 4.1 indicates, per capita income in the ten countries is about 75 percent higher than the African average (though this is mainly driven by the southern African cases of Botswana, Namibia, and South Africa—the other seven countries are actually poorer than the sub-Saharan Africa average) and rates of under-five child mortality in our sample are slightly lower than in Africa as a whole. Rates of urbanization are roughly comparable to the regional average. Presidential elections appear to be similarly uncompetitive in our ten sample countries as in Africa as a whole (the average margin of victory in presidential contests is 32 and 34 percentage points, respectively), but citizens in our sample enjoy slightly more extensive political rights than in the average African country (note that on the Freedom House scale, which runs from 1 to 7, lower numbers indicate greater rights).

Our findings therefore must be interpreted with the caveat that they may not be entirely representative of Africa as a whole. This said, the fact that Thomas Bossuroy (2011) reports results similar to ours in a parallel study using comprehensive survey data from a quite different set of African countries lends confidence to the generalizability of our findings.

Table 4.1 Economic and Political Characteristics of Sample Countries in Sub-Saharan Africa, 1999–2004

Country and Survey Round	Economic Characteristics			Political Characteristics		
	Per Capita Income (US$)	Under-Five Mortality	Percentage Urban	Political Rights Rating	Months to Election	Vote Margin
Botswana, 1999	7,122	101	52	2	−1	0.30
Botswana, 2003	8,725	116	56	2	16	0.26
Malawi, 1999	594	188	15	3	−5	0.07
Malawi, 2003	569	175	16	3	12.5	0.09
Mali, 2001	894	224	27	2	15.5	0.07
Mali, 2002	913	224	28	2	−6.5	0.07
Namibia, 1999	6,074	69	32	2	−2	0.66
Namibia, 2002	6,389	65	33	2	−28	0.66
Namibia, 2003	6,274	64	34	2	14.5	0.69
Nigeria, 2000	882	207	44	4	−11	0.26
Nigeria, 2001	875	205	45	4	19.5	0.30
Nigeria, 2003	1,000	199	46	4	−6	0.30
South Africa, 2000	9,488	63	57	1	−13.5	0.57
South Africa, 2002	9,819	65	58	1	18.5	0.57
Tanzania, 2001	541	137	22	4	−5	0.55
Tanzania, 2003	593	129	23	4	29	0.69
Uganda, 2000	1,249	145	12	6	9.5	0.42
Uganda, 2002	1,301	141	12	6	−18.5	0.42
Zambia, 1999	764	182	35	5	25	0.02
Zambia, 2003	823	182	35	5	−16.5	0.02
Zimbabwe, 1999	2,759	117	35	6	8.5	0.02
Zimbabwe, 2004	1,832	129	36	7	−26	0.14
Average for sample countries	3,185	142	34	3.5	14.1[a]	0.32
Average for sub-Saharan Africa, 2004	1,803	168	35	4.3	[b]	0.34

Sources: World Bank 2008; Freedom House 2006; African Elections DataBase 2006.

Notes: Per capita incomes are adjusted for purchasing power parity. Under-five mortality is the number of infant deaths per 1,000 live births. Months to election is the number of months to the nearest national election, with negative numbers signaling that the nearest election is in the past. Electoral margin is defined as the gap in the vote share between the winner and the runner-up in the most recent presidential election; if no presidential elections were held within five years (e.g., if the president is elected by the legislature), then the most recent legislative election is used.

a. Average electoral proximity for Afrobarometer countries corresponds to the average of the absolute values.

b. Average for sub-Saharan Africa is not meaningful, as not all countries hold regular elections.

The Salience of Ethnic (and Other) Identities

Table 4.2 reports the frequency distribution of responses to the identity question ("which specific group do you feel you belong to first and foremost?") for all twenty-two surveys in our sample. Contrary to the stereotype that Africans are unidimensionally ethnic in their self-identifications, a minority of 31 percent of respondents identify themselves first and foremost in ethnic terms. Indeed, fewer respondents choose ethnic identities than class/occupation identities, which are chosen by 36 percent of respondents. In addition, responses vary tremendously across countries and, perhaps even more strikingly, within countries over time—a finding consistent with theories of ethnic identification that

Table 4.2 Social Identities Ranked "First and Foremost" in Sample Countries, 1999–2004

Country and Survey Round	Ethnic	Occupation/ Class	Religion	Gender	Other	No Answer
Botswana, 1999	0.44	0.09	0.05	0.00	0.35	0.07
Botswana, 2003	0.28	0.12	0.08	0.02	0.45	0.06
Malawi, 1999	0.37	0.25	0.24	0.00	0.07	0.08
Malawi, 2003	0.20	0.58	0.08	0.04	0.08	0.02
Mali, 2001	0.40	0.23	0.23	0.04	0.11	0.00
Mali, 2002	0.37	0.36	0.24	0.03	0.01	0.00
Namibia, 1999	0.52	0.32	0.05	0.00	0.01	0.10
Namibia, 2002	0.62	0.17	0.06	0.02	0.09	0.04
Namibia, 2003	0.25	0.24	0.03	0.29	0.17	0.03
Nigeria, 2000	0.48	0.29	0.21	0.00	0.02	0.00
Nigeria, 2001	0.31	0.41	0.21	0.04	0.03	0.00
Nigeria, 2003	0.49	0.20	0.19	0.03	0.07	0.01
South Africa, 2000	0.42	0.15	0.18	0.00	0.24	0.02
South Africa, 2002	0.22	0.42	0.06	0.05	0.23	0.01
Tanzania, 2001	0.03	0.79	0.05	0.09	0.04	0.00
Tanzania, 2003	0.17	0.38	0.07	0.02	0.27	0.08
Uganda, 2000	0.13	0.66	0.09	0.06	0.05	0.01
Uganda, 2002	0.18	0.59	0.08	0.06	0.07	0.01
Zambia, 1999	0.12	0.46	0.34	0.00	0.04	0.04
Zambia, 2003	0.11	0.44	0.18	0.02	0.04	0.23
Zimbabwe, 1999	0.47	0.37	0.08	0.00	0.06	0.02
Zimbabwe, 2004	0.19	0.29	0.20	0.12	0.25	0.02
Average	0.31	0.36	0.14	0.04	0.12	0.04

Source: Afrobarometer surveys, 1999–2004.
Note: Average values for each column weight each survey round equally, so respondents from countries with larger sample sizes are weighted less.

stress contextual variability. The variation we observe across countries confirms the necessity of adopting an estimation framework that controls for country-specific factors. The variation within countries over time is, of course, central to our identification strategy: our main interest is in ascertaining whether (or what share of) that variation can be explained by the proximity and competitiveness of the nearest presidential election.

Since the surveys are repeated cross-sections rather than panels of individuals, we cannot reject completely the possibility that sampling variation is behind some of the changes that we observe within countries across survey rounds. However, since the Afrobarometer employs the same sampling methodology in all survey rounds, and given the large, nationally representative sample of individuals included in each survey, we can be fairly certain that sampling variation is not primarily behind these shifts. The robustness of our findings to dropping countries one at a time also allays fears that sampling variation in a single country might be driving our results.

A crucial, and slightly different, question relates to the timing of the Afrobarometer surveys, which provides the source of variation in our key proximity variable. One concern is that surveys might have been deliberately scheduled close to exciting, hotly contested elections, perhaps because they represent moments when political attitudes are particularly interesting and worth surveying. Fortunately, there is little evidence that the timing of surveys was in any way related to electoral cycles, in part because the enormous logistical task of selecting interview sites and setting up field teams requires that preparations be made many months or even years in advance. Moreover, this timing would not account for the strong interaction effects between election proximity and competitiveness that we document later.

To the extent that survey timing was in any way endogenous to election timing, it was through what appears to have been a conscious decision by the Afrobarometer organizers after Round 1 not to schedule surveys right near elections. While this would have been a uniform (and thus unproblematic) policy change, the worry is that such a change in the timing of surveys (away from elections) might have combined with a downward secular trend in the salience of ethnic identities to produce a spurious correlation between electoral proximity and ethnic identity salience. We deal with this possible confounding story, as well as the possibility that changes in survey implementation might have generated changes in reported levels of ethnic identification across survey rounds, by including fixed effects in our regressions for each survey round (1, 1.5, 2) as well as a linear time trend.

The Political Sources of Ethnic Identification

What, then, accounts for the variation we observe in the tendency of survey respondents to identify in ethnic terms? To answer this question, we model the salience that each individual respondent attaches to his or her ethnic identity as a function of his or her observable individual characteristics and his or her country's political environment (recall that "salience" is operationalized as the likelihood that a respondent answers the "with which group do you identify first and foremost" question in terms of his or her membership in a tribe or language group). The particular country characteristics in which we are most interested are the proximity in months between the nearest presidential election and the administration of the given survey (as captured by –1 multiplied by the absolute value of months) and the competitiveness of the same election (as measured by –1 multiplied by the vote-share margin between the winner and the runner-up). Country-level values for these variables are provided for each survey round in Table 4.1.

Table 4.3 presents the results of four regressions of ethnic identification on our main independent variables: proximity, competitiveness, and proximity multiplied by competitiveness. All four specifications include country fixed-effects and weight each observation by 1 divided by the number of observations

Table 4.3 Political Determinants of Ethnic Identification in Sample Countries, 1999–2004

	Logit			Ordinary Least Squares (country level)
	(1)	(2)	(3)	(4)
Electoral proximity	0.003	0.018	0.018	0.018
	(0.003)	(0.003)***	(0.002)***	(0.008)**
Electoral competitiveness	–0.387	–0.285	–0.304	0.246
	(1.490)	(0.553)	(0.721)	(1.290)
Proximity × competitiveness	—	0.044	0.045	0.041
	—	(0.007)***	(0.007)***	(0.014)***
Individual-level covariates	No	No	Yes	n/a
Number of country rounds	22	22	22	22
Observations	35,505	35,505	35,505	22
R^2	0.09	0.09	0.10	0.53

Source: Afrobarometer surveys, 1999–2004.

Notes: Coefficients reported are marginal effects dP(ethnic)/dX. Standard errors (clustered at the country level) appear in parentheses. All logit specifications include country fixed effects and trend and survey-round controls; ordinary least squares country-level regression includes country fixed effects only. Observations are weighted by 1 divided by the number of observations from that country, in order to weight each country survey round equally.

***$p < 0.01$, **$p < 0.05$, *$p < 0.10$.

n/a = not applicable.

from that country in order to weight each country survey equally. The first three columns are logit models with standard errors clustered at the country level to account for the hierarchical nature of the data. These three regressions also include the survey-round controls and time trend discussed earlier. Clustering error terms at the country level should deal appropriately with the dependence of the key independent variables for individuals in the same country and the same survey round. Nonetheless, as a robustness check, in the fourth column of the table we revisit the analysis in an ordinary least squares regression with data aggregated to the country-round level ($n = 22$; here the dependent variable is the share of respondents in the country survey round who identified in ethnic terms, as in Table 4.2). The fact that all three versions of our main specification (the second, third, and fourth columns) generate almost identical results speaks to the robustness of the relationship between ethnic identification and the political factors we are investigating.

The results reported in the first column of Table 4.3 suggest that, on average, neither the proximity of the survey to a presidential election (in months, absolute value) nor the competitiveness of that election (the margin of victory, in percentage points) has any independent impact on the likelihood that a survey respondent will identify him- or herself in ethnic terms. Some caution must be taken, however, in interpreting the "electoral competitiveness" term given the relatively small degree of within-country variation we observe in our data on this variable (see the "vote margin" column in Table 4.1). Indeed, in four of our ten countries, the same election serves as the most proximate contest to the two country surveys we use, so there is no variation on this term. Since all of the explanatory leverage in our specification comes from within-country comparisons, the coefficient estimates on the "competitiveness" variable are being produced by only a subset of our (already small) set of country cases. This problem is compounded by the fact that the within-country variation we do observe is based on relatively small differences in the margin of victory between the winning presidential candidate and the runner-up—differences that are likely a product as much of measurement error or electoral fraud or both as of true changes in the underlying competitiveness of the contests. Given these considerations, we do not put much weight on our rather imprecise estimates on the "competitiveness" variable.

Rather, we focus on the interaction term between proximity and competitiveness, and it is the substantial cross-country variation in electoral competitiveness that allows us to estimate this effect. When we add such an interaction term to our initial specification (the second column of Table 4.3), we find that the coefficients on proximity and the interaction term are statistically significant. Taken together, the interpretation of the point estimates in the second column is that the likelihood that a person will identify him- or herself in ethnic terms increases by 1.8 percentage points (standard error of 0.3 percentage points) for each month closer to an election the survey is administered, *but* that this effect falls as the competitiveness of the election decreases, dropping all the way to zero for landslide elections with a margin between the winner and runner-up of roughly 40 percentage points. Thus a survey respondent, asked within a month of a closely fought presidential election how she or he self-identifies would be nearly 22 percentage points (standard error of 3.6 percentage points) more likely to respond in ethnic terms than if she were asked a year earlier or a year later. However, if the election was won in a landslide, her answer would be unaffected by the proximity of the election. Given that the baseline likelihood of ethnic identification in our sample is 31 percent, a predicted change of 22 percentage points over the course of twelve months is a very large effect indeed.

These results are confirmed in the third column of Table 4.3, which adds a host of individual-level controls for respondents' age, gender, occupation, education, media exposure, and urban or rural residence (coefficients not shown), and the fourth column, which replicates the analysis at the country level. The fact that the findings are highly statistically significant using the conservative country-round level approach in the fourth column, with only twenty-two observations, indicates that the results in the first through third columns are not simply an artifact of using large samples of individual-level data. The findings are nearly identical across all three specifications; moreover, as noted, all results are robust to dropping countries one at a time.

The main results are presented graphically in Figure 4.1, where the proximity to the closest country election is presented on the horizontal axis (de-meaned by

Figure 4.1 Ethnic Identification and Electoral Proximity in Sub-Saharan Africa by Competitiveness of National Elections, 1999–2004

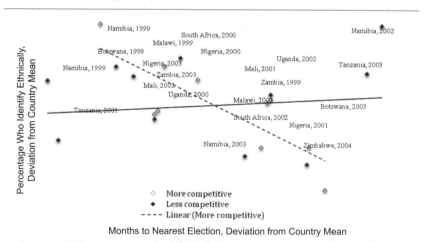

Sources: Afrobarometer surveys, 1990–2005.

Note: "More competitive" elections are defined as those in which the electoral margin is less than 29.5 percent, the median in our sample.

country, which is equivalent to our country fixed-effects regression specification), and the extent of ethnic identification is on the vertical axis (also de-meaned by country). Two plots are presented: one pattern for relatively competitive elections (cases where the electoral margin is less than the sample median of 29.5 percentage points), and one for landslide elections (when the margin is greater than the median), although the results are nearly unchanged using a lower competitive election threshold of 10 percentage points (not shown). The relationships come through clearly: the plot is strongly negative for competitive elections (meaning that ethnic identification falls sharply when surveys are conducted further away in time from competitive elections) but is nearly flat for landslide elections. All of this is consistent with a story whereby the salience of ethnic identities is correlated with the electoral cycle, but only in settings where elections constitute meaningful contests for political power.

Political Competition and Other Social Identities

Our main dependent variable (based on the question: "which group do you feel you belong to first and foremost") permitted multiple responses. This makes it a natural fit for a multinomial discrete choice empirical framework, which can be used to explore the social identities that individuals switch out of when, in proximity to competitive elections, they embrace their ethnic identities above others. To model this process, we modify slightly the framework we introduced earlier. Instead of attaching salience just to their ethnic identity, we now conceive of individuals as having multiple dimensions to their identities—ethnic, religious, occupation/class-based, gender, and so forth—and attach a different salience to each of these identity dimensions. When asked to report the group with which they identify first and foremost, respondents choose the identity dimension with the highest salience.

Two important aspects of this analysis bear mentioning. First, the choices we observe only contain information about *relative* preferences. We therefore cannot estimate the impact of electoral proximity or competitiveness on the absolute level of identity strength, only on the degree to which they make a respondent more or less likely to say that one identity is the one they identify with first and foremost.

Second, the probabilities that particular social identities are chosen are not independent of one another. As the probability rises that a particular social identity is chosen, the probability of others being chosen necessarily falls, since only one identity can be indicated in the interview. In particular, the marginal effects must mechanically sum to 0, because probabilities must always sum to 1. As we have stressed, a major advantage of our multinomial approach is that, if the salience of one dimension of social identification increases in response to a particular explanatory variable, we can simultaneously estimate which identity dimensions are becoming less salient. That is, our method estimates substitution patterns among social identities in response to changes in the characteristics of individuals and in their political environment.

In Table 4.4, we present our estimates for the impact of proximity, competitiveness, and proximity multiplied by competitiveness on the salience respondents attach to their ethnic, class/occupational, religious, gender, and other identities. The results in the first column (ethnicity) are nearly identical to those reported in Table 4.3: the salience of ethnicity increases by 2 percentage points for every month closer a respondent is to a presidential election, with the effect declining as the election becomes less competitive. Reading across the first row of Table 4.4 allows us to discover which identity dimensions lose salience as elections come closer. More than half of the increased salience of ethnicity comes from substitution away from class/occupation identities, though some of it appears to come from the gender and "other" categories. The interpretation of the estimated electoral proximity coefficient in the class/occupation column is that the likelihood that a respondent will identify him- or herself in class/occupational terms decreases by 1.2 percentage points for every month closer he or she is to a presidential election. Effects for gender identity are also statistically significant and go in the same direction (i.e., substituting for ethnic identity), but are less than a third as large.

For reasons described earlier, while we do not read too much into the lower-order coefficient estimates on the competitiveness variable, the interactive effect of competitiveness and electoral proximity is informative. The negative signs on the proximity multiplied by competitiveness coefficients in the second

Table 4.4 Determinants of Ethnic and Other Social Identities in Sample Countries, 1999–2004

	Ethnicity	Class/ Occupation	Religion	Gender	Other
Electoral proximity	0.020	−0.012	0.001	−0.003	−0.006
	(0.002)***	(0.005)**	(0.003)	(0.001)**	(0.002)**
Electoral	0.117	2.154	−2.025	0.073	−0.173
competitiveness	(0.548)	(0.907)**	(0.475)***	(0.178)	(0.449)
Proximity ×	0.049	−0.044	−0.001	−0.008	0.004
competitiveness	(0.007)***	(0.009)***	(0.010)	(0.002)***	(0.004)

Sources: Afrobarometer surveys, 1999–2004.

Notes: Multinomial logit. Coefficients reported are marginal effects dP(identity)/dX. Standard errors (clustered at the country level) appear in parentheses. All specifications include country fixed effects, individual-level covariates, and trend and survey-round controls. Observations are weighted by 1 divided by the number of observations from that country, to weight each country survey round equally.

***$p < 0.01$, **$p < 0.05$, *$p < 0.10$.

(class/occupation) and fourth (gender) columns of Table 4.4 suggest that the movement out of class/occupational (and, to a lesser extent, gender) identities is heightened when elections are not just proximate but also highly competitive—a finding consistent with the increased likelihood of ethnic identification as competitiveness increases.

Discussion

The robust relationship we find between ethnic salience and exposure to political competition provides strong support for instrumental understandings of ethnicity. The fact that ethnic identities become systematically more important to people at the time that competitive elections are being held suggests that ethnicity plays a role in the struggle for political power. But exactly what role does ethnicity play? And for whom?

One prominent answer in the African politics literature emphasizes the role of political elites. By this account, politicians find it advantageous to "play the ethnic card" as a means of mobilizing supporters to acquire or retain political power (e.g., Bates 1983; Ferree 2006; Posner 2005; Young 1965, 1976). Since elections provide the principal occasion for political power to change hands, politicians' efforts at ethnic mobilization are especially likely to take place during the period immediately preceding elections. These efforts are also likely to be particularly vigorous when the elections are close and the advantage to be gained by mobilizing supporters will be greatest. Thus, to the extent that politicians' ethnic appeals make ethnicity more salient for voters, and to the extent that, once made salient, ethnic identities take some time to return to baseline levels, we would expect to find exactly the pattern that we do: stronger ethnic attachments during the periods preceding and following competitive national elections than at other times.

An alternative explanation for the link between political competition and ethnic identification focuses not on elites but on regular citizens—specifically, on their beliefs that jobs, favors, and public goods will be channeled disproportionately to coethnics of the person who is in a position to allocate them (Barkan 1979; Posner 2005; Throup and Hornsby 1998; van de Walle 2007; Wantchekon 2003). Since elections are the moment when the people who will control the allocation of resources are chosen, they are also the occasion when people should be most mindful of their ethnic identities and of the match between their own identity and that of the candidates vying for power. The association we find between ethnic identification and the electoral cycle is, again, consistent with this story.

Unfortunately, our data do not permit us to adjudicate between these two explanations. To do so would require systematic information collected at different points in each country's electoral cycle about the kinds of ethnic appeals politicians make—data that the Afrobarometer surveys do not collect (and that are difficult to gather systematically in a single country, let alone in ten). Yet even if we had such data, it is not clear that it would make sense to test one explanation against the other, for the two accounts are less competing than complementary. When politicians in the run-up to Sierra Leone's 2007 presidential election promised that "if you help your kinsmen you will survive; we will give you jobs, opportunities and education" (Manson 2007), were they manipulating voters or simply playing to their expectations? When voters in recent elections in Kenya (Gibson and Long 2008), Malawi (Posner 1995), or South Africa (Ferree 2006) overwhelmingly supported presidential candidates from their own ethnic or racial groups, were they responding to the candidates' ethnic appeals or simply channeling their votes to the politicians who they thought would best look out for their interests? The answer is almost certainly "both." Politicians will only invoke the need for voters to support members of their ethnic groups if they believe that such appeals will resonate, which in turn will depend on voters' beliefs about how patronage is channeled in Africa. Similarly, although most citizens do not need to be reminded that their ethnic connection with the election's winner is likely to affect the level of resources they will receive in the election's aftermath, politicians' ethnic appeals almost certainly reinforce such expectations. The result is an equilibrium in which expectations of ethnic favoritism by voters generate ethnic appeals by politicians that, in turn, reinforce voters' expectations of ethnic favoritism. Because this mutually reinforcing process is driven by the competition for political power, it makes perfect sense that it should cause ethnicity to become more salient in proximity to competitive elections, since this is the time when political power is most clearly at stake.

Conclusion

Our central result is that exposure to political competition powerfully affects whether or not survey respondents identify themselves in ethnic terms. The finding—based on precisely the kind of cross-national data that have hitherto been lacking—provides strong confirmation for situational understandings of ethnicity and for theories that link the salience of particular social identities to instrumental political mobilization. Beyond their relevance for this academic literature, these results also have important implications for policymakers and researchers interested in elections and ethnicity.

It might be tempting to interpret our findings as suggesting that, by heightening the salience of ethnic identities, the reintroduction of multiparty elections in Africa in the 1990s—widely celebrated as a positive development—may have a conflict-inducing downside. Kenya's 2007 presidential contest, which triggered weeks of violence that left more than 1,000 people dead and 300,000 displaced (International Crisis Group 2008), would seem to provide strong support for this thesis. Yet it would be wrong to construe our results as endorsing this position. While we do find strong evidence that ethnic identities are heightened by exposure to political mobilization, our findings do not support the proposition that political competition accounts for the baseline levels of ethnic salience that make mobilizing ethnicity so politically useful in many African countries—indeed, our fixed-effect estimation strategy makes it impossible for us to test such a claim. Nor do our results suggest that the increasing competitiveness of African elections (Diamond 2008b) will necessarily instigate ethnic violence. Our findings suggest that countries with periodic competitive elections should experience *fluctuations* in ethnic salience that are correlated with their electoral cycle, not that they will exhibit higher levels of ethnic identification, on average, than countries without competitive elections. The relationships we uncover would be consistent with such a pattern, but establishing such a relationship would require a different research design than the one we adopt here.

Yet the fact that elections make ethnicity (even momentarily) more salient does suggest the need for African governments to develop policies and institutional mechanisms that are capable of dealing with ethnic divisions. Policies and institutions such as those in place in Tanzania—a country known for its efforts at nation building through the promotion of Swahili as a national language, civic education, and institutional reforms like the abolition of chiefs, as described by Edward Miguel (2004)—might serve as a model for how Kenya and other African countries might dampen destructive ethnic divisions. Perhaps due in part to these policies, Tanzania has among the lowest degree of ethnic identity salience in one of the Afrobarometer survey rounds, at just 3 percent.

5

Voting Intentions in Africa: Ethnic, Economic, or Partisan?

*Michael Bratton, Ravi Bhavnani,
and Tse-Hsin Chen*

When Africans consider their voting choices, do they do so on ethnic or economic grounds? On the one hand, advocates of identity voting draw attention to a citizen's sense of belonging to cultural collectivities— like ethnic and linguistic groups—that aggregate individual choices into blocs of votes. Studies in Zambia and Kenya find that the structure of ethnic groups in society is the predominant influence on vote choice (Posner and Simon 2002; Erdmann 2007; Bratton and Kimenyi 2008). On the other hand, backers of interest-based accounts of voting argue that citizens use the opportunity of periodic elections to punish or reward incumbents based on economic performance. Evidence from Ghana, for example, suggests that economic evaluations drive vote choice (Jeffries 1998; Bawumia 1998; Youde 2005; Fridy 2007; Lindberg and Morrison 2008).

In the new electoral democracies of sub-Saharan Africa, voting motivations may not be quite so clear-cut. For if Africans vote ethnically, why do so many African presidents hail from minority ethnic groups? And if Africans vote economically, why are incumbents routinely reelected even when economic conditions are bad? The literature on voting behavior in Africa is therefore divided: some country studies report that ethnic attachments trump economic calculations, whereas, in other analyses, popular evaluations of government performance overshadow attachments to language and tribe. A definitive arbitration of this debate is long overdue.

In this chapter, we present systematic, cross-national evidence to the effect that, alongside ethnic identities, economic interests play a larger role in African elections than has hitherto been recognized. We also consider alternative formulations. Perhaps voting intentions in new African democracies are driven by other factors, such as the partisan calculations made by clients in search of patronage. If so, then voters will seek to gain access to the positive benefits that ruling parties can bestow and to avoid the negative sanctions that can follow from supporting opposition groups. When voters express close identification with the ruling party, they may be either sincere or strategic. But either way, they epitomize a widespread popular recognition that incumbents at the helm of dominant parties are most likely to win in African elections.

The chapter proceeds in three steps. First, we present theories of ethnic, economic, and partisan voting. Second, we describe operational indicators to distinguish voters' intentions along these lines, as well as relevant controls. Third, we present logistic regression models that explain why African voters say they plan to support ruling parties. In specifying these models, we compare the effects of ethnic and economic motivations while, at the same time, considering other voting rationales and the effects of country contexts. As previously stated, we find evidence to support a thesis of economic voting in a context of dominant patronage parties. A concluding section draws out the implications of the evidence from Africa for the further development of theories of voting behavior.

Theories

Ethnic Voting

In Africa, ethnic identity—that is, the inclination of individuals to define themselves and others in terms of cultural origins—is widely perceived to be the predominant organizing principle of society and politics (Olorunsola 1972; Horowitz 1991; Berman, Eyoh, and Kymlicka 2004). Most thoughtful analysts agree, however, that, far from being primordial or atavistic, ethnic identity is constructed, fluid, and one among multiple identities that actors can adopt depending on the situations in which they find themselves (see Chapter 4). Importantly, however, "identities . . . constitute distinct social roles and are not simply surrogates of nascent social classes; cultural pluralism is more than simply 'false consciousness'" (Young 1976: 65). In short, from the subjective perspective of individual African citizens, feelings of ethnic identity are sufficiently concrete to constitute a basis for forming political opinion and stimulating political action.

Ethnic voting occurs whenever members of a cultural group show a disproportionate affinity at the polls for a particular political party (Wolfinger 1965). In short, they tend to vote as a bloc. The logic of ethnic voting is as follows: by expressing solidarity, subnational groups seek to elevate leaders from their own cultural background into positions of power, especially the top executive spot, thereby gaining collective representation (Posner 2005). In extreme manifestations, this form of identity-based voting can lead to outcomes that are mere head counts of ethnic groups. If voter turnout is high, and if all voters choose parties associated with their own communal identities, then an election can even resemble an ethnic "census" (Lever 1979; Horowitz 1985; Ferree 2006; McLaughlin 2008). Under these circumstances, cultural demography is the principal determinant of the distribution of votes.

Economic Voting

The voluminous literature on economic voting posits a powerful alternative explanation. At its heart is a simple proposition: citizens vote for the incumbent government if economic times are good; otherwise they vote against it (Key 1964; Tufte 1978; Lewis-Beck and Stegmaier 2000). Concisely stated, elections are won or lost on the economy. Moreover, voters punish governments for poor economic performance but do not necessarily reward success. Some even argue that "economic conditions may be far more important determinants of the vote in developing countries than in the West, at least when times are bad" (Pacek and Radcliff 1995: 756–757; see also Lewis-Beck and Stegmaier 2008).

In recent years, analyses of aggregate patterns of economic voting have taken an institutional turn. At issue is whether institutional arrangements clarify or obscure the ruling party's responsibility for economic conditions (Anderson 2000, 2007). Although the effects of formal political institutions are evident across Western democracies, it remains to be seen whether these are also manifest in new multiparty political systems in Africa. Other generalizations have emerged from survey research at the individual level: that, when estimating economic interests, voters more commonly refer "sociotropically" to the condition of the economy as a whole rather than "egotistically" to their own living standards (Kinder and Kiewiet 1981; Lewis-Beck 1988), and that prospective expectations of personal well-being are more determinative than retrospective evaluations of government popularity, at least in Britain and Russia (Price and Sanders 1995; Hesli and Bashkirova 2001). We have yet to learn whether voters in Africa make the same sorts of economic calculations at election time.

Problematically, however, models of economic voting may suffer from circularity. We know that vote choice and partisan identification are closely related, not least because some studies use the latter as a proxy for the former. But partisan identification may also color economic perceptions: supporters of the incumbent party are often too generous in their evaluations of the government's economic performance, while opponents are overly critical. At issue, therefore, is whether economic perceptions are sufficiently independent of vote preference to serve as the foundation of a theory of economic voting (Evans and Andersen 2006; Lewis-Beck, Nadeau, and Elias 2008). At minimum, party identification must be included in any multivariate explanation, preferably in an operational form that strictly distinguishes partisanship from considerations of economic performance.

A Reinterpretation

On the basis of cross-national research in Africa, we argue that the distinction between ethnic and economic voting is overdrawn. Both patterns of voting behavior are evident in African elections. These complex contests cannot be reduced to a one-dimensional construct, for example as an ethnic census or an economic referendum. It remains to be seen whether ethnic or economic considerations—or some other influences—are paramount in driving a multivariate explanation. But, at minimum, we argue that African voting intentions do not adhere to media stereotypes of Africans as exclusively ethnic voters, nor to the popular assumption that elections always and everywhere are about "the economy, stupid."

The present study departs from previous efforts in several important ways. First, the scope of the study is not limited to one election in one country, which has been a hallmark of the literature on Africa to date. Instead, we employ a large cross-national set of Afrobarometer survey data with identical indicators for 23,093 adult citizens in sixteen countries in 2005–2006. Popular preferences about vote choice were standardized with a hypothetical ballot at the time of the survey.

Second, the object of explanation is a citizen's *intended vote choice* rather than proxies like presidential popularity, which were too often used in prior research. The main advantage is that voting intentions are a better guide to actual voting behavior, though obviously the reliability of this indicator decreases with temporal distance from the next election.

Third, we recognize that rival concepts—ethnic identity and economic interest—are multidimensional and that their various aspects may have differential explanatory power. We therefore seek to capture the richness of each concept by measuring several facets with alternative indicators. By decomposing the broad concepts of ethnic identity and economic interest, we hope to cast light on the mechanisms that lead our respondents to arrive at an intended vote choice.

Fourth, we propose a multilevel explanatory model in a bid to account for variance in intended voting behavior across countries as well as among individuals. Guided by prevailing theoretical debates, we explore the influence of relevant social, economic, and political differences at the country level using data gleaned from standard sources of aggregate data.

Finally, we emphasize that the candidate preferences of African voters may be driven by political considerations rather than by ethnic or economic factors. Analysts have long recognized that *partisan identification*—a voter's underlying allegiance to a political party—explains a great deal about individual attitudes and actions (Campbell et al. 1960; see also Shively 1980;

Lewis-Beck et al. 2008). Indeed, recent studies of electoral participation in African countries have confirmed the central mobilizing role of political parties (Bratton 1999; Kuenzi and Lambright 2007) and the stability of partisan alignments (Lindberg and Morrison 2005; Young 2009).

Thus, one would expect voters to plan to vote for the party to which they say they feel closest. To avoid the obvious circularity in this relationship, we refine the concept of partisan identification in this study by distinguishing sincere and strategic voting. *Sincere partisans* are individuals who intend to vote for a party out of deep attachment or ingrained habit; they express partisan loyalty without reference (sometimes even in direct contradiction) to the party's actual performance. We expect to find many such "uncritical citizens" among the adherents of the long-standing ruling groups in one-party-dominant regimes (see Chapter 9).

Alternatively, the structure of incentives in Africa's neopatrimonial regimes (Clapham 1982; Nugent 1995; Bratton 1997a; Wantchekon 2003; Kitschelt and Wilkinson 2007; Erdmann and Engel 2007) also gives rise to strategic voting. In Africa's "winner take all" politics—where electoral victory conveys political control over state-dominated economies—the credibility of patronage parties depends on their ability to actually attain, hold, and exercise power. Since opposition parties are novel and weak, an incumbent ruling party can make the most credible patronage commitments. Under these circumstances, an individual's expressed preference of "closeness" to a ruling party may therefore be deeply instrumental, reflecting a calculation that incumbents will routinely win. Regardless of real preferences, *strategic partisans* will also associate themselves with the ruling party in the hope that they will be rewarded—or at least not punished—after the election.

If these accounts are correct, then we would expect three important outcomes. First, a large portion of intended voting behavior should be explicable in terms of expressed partisan identification—whether sincere or strategic, or whether motivated by positive or negative incentives. Second, the greater the dominance of the ruling party over opposition parties—and thus the firmer the former's control of material and coercive resources—the greater the likelihood that voters will signal an intention to vote for the ruling party. And third, ethnic identities and economic interests, far from being rival sources of intended vote choice, would both matter. Table 5.1 presents a full set of independent variables plus associated hypotheses.

Measurement and Hypotheses

Intended Vote Choice

This study seeks to explain an African citizen's intended vote choice. The survey asks, "If a presidential election were held tomorrow, which party's

84

Table 5.1 Voting Intentions in Sub-Saharan Africa: Hypotheses

Other things being equal, we expect to find that an intention to vote for the ruling party is positively related to indicators of an individual as follows:

Hypothesis	Concept	Indicator
	Ethnic identities	
H1A	Nominal ethnic identity	Membership in the largest ethnic group
H1B	Ethnic group in power	Shared ethnicity with the head of government
H1C	Salience of ethnicity	Preference for ethnic over national identity[a]
H1D	Interethnic distrust	Distrust in members of other ethnic groups[a]
H1E	Ethnic discrimination	Perception of unfair group treatment (negative relationship)
	Economic interests	
H2A	Retrospective, sociotropic assessments	Positive evaluation of past economic conditions
H2B	Retrospective, egocentric assessments	Positive evaluation of one's own past living standards
H2C	Prospective, sociotropic assessments	Positive evaluation of future economic conditions
H2D	Prospective, egocentric assessments	Positive evaluation of one's own future living standards
H2E	Attitude to economic policy performance	Positive evaluation of government handling of economic policies
	Political considerations	
H3A	Partisan identification (sincere + strategic)	Remains "close" to ruling party, even if president has underperformed
H3B	Expectation of patronage	Perception that politicians will deliver development after election
H3C	Expectation of compulsion	Perception of survey as government-sponsored (proxy)
	Demographic characteristics	
H4A	Gender	Female
H4B	Age	Years since birth
H4C	Education	Years of schooling
H4D	Poverty	Lack of access to basic human needs (negative relationship)
H4E	Residential location	Rural
	Country contexts	
H5A	a. Ethnic fragmentation b. Ethnic polarization	Contexts where one ethnic group is dominant, (a) demographically or (b) politically

(continues)

Table 5.1 Continued

Hypothesis	Concept	Indicator
H5B	a. GDP growth rate b. Inflation rate	Contexts where (a) the macroeconomy is expanding and (b) consumer price rises are moderate
H5C	a. Presidential constitutions b. Effective number of parliamentary parties c. Level of democracy	Contexts of (a) institutional clarity of political responsibility, (b) limited vote choice, and (c) inverted 2005 Freedom House 14-point scale

Note: a. We expect the sign to depend on whether the respondent belongs to the ethnic group in power—positive if yes, negative if no.

candidate would you vote for?" Because the stakes in African elections are high—winners control state resources in a context where private economies are weak—election campaigns often have the tenor of life-or-death struggles. On this uneven playing field (Schedler 2006; Levitsky and Way 2010), elites do not hesitate to manipulate electoral rules and offer patronage inducements; for their part, voters commonly feel exposed to surveillance, monitoring, and intimidation. Thus we wondered if people would volunteer honest answers.

Results are reassuring. Only 6 percent of respondents refused to divulge their voting intentions, for example by invoking ballot secrecy, and just 13 percent said that they "didn't know" how they would vote. The remaining respondents were scored 1 if they intended to vote for the ruling party or 0 if they planned to support a ruling party.

Overall, the distributions of intended vote choice revealed by the survey enjoy face validity since they conform to known patterns, such as official results of previous or subsequent elections (*African Elections Database* at http://africanelections.tripod.com). On average, 60 percent of eligible voters reported an intention to vote for the presidential candidate of the ruling party in 2005, with the remainder saying they intended to vote for opposition candidates (33 percent) or to abstain (7 percent). Yet the strength of support for the ruling party varies considerably across African countries, from a high of 88 percent in Tanzania to a low of 30 percent in Benin (see Figure 5.1). Hence an intention to vote for the political status quo depends not only on the attributes of individual citizens, but also on national contexts, thus requiring multilevel analysis.

Measuring Ethnic Identities

Turning to explanatory factors, we measure nominal ethnic identity in terms of an individual's answer to the blunt question, "What is your tribe?" The

Figure 5.1 Intended Vote for Ruling Party in Sub-Saharan Africa, 2005

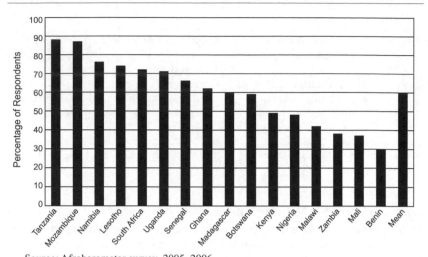

Source: Afrobarometer survey, 2005–2006.
Notes: Afrobarometer question: "If a presidential election were held tomorrow, which party's candidate would you vote for?" Survey size of 23,093 respondents.

controversial term "tribe" is part of the everyday lexicon in African countries and never evoked resistance from Afrobarometer respondents. From the 319 groups named in the survey, we classify four comparable types: (1) *majority* ethnic groups, which constitute 50 percent or more of the national population; (2) *plurality* ethnic groups, which are the largest group in the country, but constitute less than 50 percent of the population; (3) *secondary* ethnic groups, which constitute more than 10 percent of the population; and (4) *minority* ethnic groups, which constitute 10 percent or less of the population. Either a majority or a plurality group constitutes each country's *largest ethnic group,* whose sheer demographic weight might be expected to convey political ascendancy in a mass democracy (hypothesis H1A in Table 5.1).

Because ethnicity becomes politically germane via a group's access to governmental authority, we also measure whether an individual is a member of the *ethnic group in power.* Ideally, one would take account of a range of top officeholders in determining which group (or groups) is actually in charge. Absent comprehensive data on the social backgrounds of cabinet ministers or permanent secretaries in African countries, however, we resort to a conventional indicator: the ethnicity of the head of government. This operational pointer does "an excellent job of picking out the group locally regarded as most powerful . . . [because] the president's ethnic group is the most favored and politically dominant" (Fearon, Kasara, and Laitin 2007: 190). Individuals with the same nominal ethnic identity as the incumbent head of government are scored as members of the ethnic group in power, which should predict their support for the ruling party (hypothesis H1B). Interestingly, however, there are few places in Africa where one group constitutes half the population or more; a majority ethnolinguistic group holds power in only three countries: Lesotho, Botswana, and Namibia. And the largest ethnic group rules in fewer than half the countries studied.

But demographic distributions and power positions do not exhaust the complexity of ethnicity. Three other dimensions are plausibly important to a voter's intended choice. First is the *salience of ethnicity,* or the weight that individuals place on ethnicity as a core identity, for example in comparison to other available identities (Bhavnani and Miodownick 2009). We measure ethnic salience by asking respondents to choose between nominal ethnic identity and national identity, a critical cultural tension. Across sixteen African countries, some 40 percent of survey respondents claim to value national above ethnic identity, with some 15 percent taking the opposite view (42 percent value both equally). If these voters are genuinely nationalistic rather than sectarian, we would expect them to spurn ethnic identity as a basis for voting for the ruling party (hypothesis H1C).

Second is *interethnic distrust.* Voters are guided at the polls not only by self-described cultural attachments, but also by expectations about the political behavior of others. To get at this reactive dimension of ethnic voting, the survey asks about an individual's trust in a range of other social actors: family members, neighbors, members of one's own ethnic group, and most importantly, members of other ethnic groups within the country. Whereas 43 percent say they trust people from other ethnic groups "somewhat" or a "lot," 55 percent do so "just a little" or "not at all." If a vote for the ruling party is to any degree a rejoinder to expected bloc voting by ethnic rivals, we would expect it to be captured by this indicator (hypothesis H1D).

Third, the expression of ethnic identity in the voting booth may be triggered by an individual's sense of collective grievance. To measure perceived *ethnic discrimination,* the survey asks, "How often is [your named ethnic group] treated unfairly by the government?" Almost half say "never" (49 percent) and a further quarter say just "sometimes" (24 percent). Across the sixteen countries, a relatively small proportion of the adult population, averaging only 18 percent, reports unfair treatment "often" or "always." Minority ethnic groups are more prone than others to perceive ethnic discrimination. Furthermore, we expect a sense of ethnic discrimination to undermine citizens' willingness to return the sitting government back to power (hypothesis H1E).

Measuring Economic Interests

Several standard indicators capture economic influences on voting intentions. For popular views of *past economic conditions*—whether sociotropic or egocentric—the survey asks, "Looking back, how would you rate economic conditions in this country [or your living conditions] compared to twelve months ago?" And for *future economic conditions* the question is, "Looking ahead, do you expect economic conditions in this country [or your living conditions] to be better or worse in twelve months time?" In all cases, responses are scored on a 5-point scale ranging from "much worse" to "much better."

The Africans surveyed apparently harbor mixed feelings about past economic performance. On average, 37 percent see the economy getting worse, but 34 percent see it getting better (with considerable cross-national variation). And when asked about personal living conditions over the last year, the number of respondents who feel their conditions are worsening (35 percent) is similar to the number who feel their conditions are improving (34 percent). However, when asked about their opinion of future economic conditions in their country, roughly twice as many individuals think performance will be better (56 percent) as think it will be worse (25 percent). And citizens everywhere harbor high hopes for future personal living standards; only 18 percent see life getting worse, with 49 percent seeing it getting better. Whether looking forward or back, and regardless of referent—national or personal—we expect voters to lean toward incumbents if they see life getting better economically (hypotheses H2A–H2D).

In addition, we introduce an original indicator of policy perceptions. *Economic policy performance* is a valid and reliable 4-point index of how well or badly the incumbent government is seen to handle economic management, job creation, control of inflation, and income distribution. Respondents generally resent the prevailing policy regime, which usually features austerity measures to reduce state spending. Two-thirds think that governments are managing the economy badly (66 percent). Other things being equal, one would expect these negative sentiments to reduce electoral support for the ruling party (hypothesis H2E).

Measuring Political Considerations

Among individuals, the main political considerations measured in this study are partisanship, patronage, and compulsion. As discussed, we expect that clients who seek patronage (or wish to avoid exclusion and compulsion) will be inclined to express partisan identification with the ruling faction. To stiffen the criterion for partisanship, we consider only those individuals who *disapprove* of the incumbent president's performance in office yet *still* say that they feel "close" to the current ruling party. Some of these self-described partisans will vote for continuity out of party loyalty (the *sincere* partisans), but others will do so because they know that their preferred candidate cannot win (the *strategic* partisans). Either way, we expect that ruling-party identification (strictly defined) will strongly bolster incumbents' chances of retaining office (hypothesis H3A).

For at least some voters, however, overt expressions of partisanship are instrumental: they want to reap the benefits of associating with prospective winners and to avoid the costs of attachment to likely losers. To test this conjecture, we add independent variables that directly measure the costs and benefits of neopatrimonial rule. On the positive side, we measure citizen expectations of future patronage rewards with a question about the credibility of politicians: how often do they "deliver development" after elections? On an average 4-point scale ranging from "never" to "always," some 40 percent of respondents say "never" and 15 percent say "often" or "always." We anticipate that the minority of voters who find promises of patronage rewards to be credible will be inclined to vote for the ruling party (hypothesis H3B).

On the negative side, we test for compulsion-driven voting with a specification about political monitoring. As a parting question, the Afrobarometer asks, "Who do you think sent us to do this interview?" Even though interviewers introduce themselves as affiliated with "an independent research organization" that does not "represent the government or any political party," only 31 percent of respondents see the survey as autonomous. The remainder either "don't know" (17 percent) or see the survey as sponsored by an agency of the incumbent government (52 percent). Under these circumstances, it is essential to consider the possibility that people might censor their stated vote choices according to misperceptions about who is asking politically sensitive questions. Because perceptions of official sponsorship are higher in less democratic countries and among more evasive respondents, we regard this indicator as a viable proxy for the costliness of political dissent. We expect it to be positively related to an intended vote for the ruling party (hypothesis H3C).

Measuring Contextual Effects

Voting behavior is guided not only by political "nurture"—an individual's learned political attitudes—but also by the "nature"—the country context in which voters find themselves. These contextual factors may be economic, social, or political. For simplicity's sake, we take account of only two relevant country-level indicators of each type (see Table 5.2). To capture *economic context*, we consider average growth of gross domestic product (GDP) and average inflation rates for the five-year period up to 2005. To capture *social context*, we measure the fractionalization of "politically relevant ethnic groups" (Posner 2004) and the degree of ethnic polarization, that is, fractionalization weighted by relative group size (Montalvo and Reynal-Querol 2005). The *political context* is represented by three institutional

Table 5.2 Country-Level Contextual Factors in Sub-Saharan Africa, 2005

	GDP Growth (%), Average Annual (2000–2005)	Inflation (%), Average Annual (2000–2005)	Ethnic Fractionalization (politically relevant ethnic groups)	Ethnic Polarization	Constitutional Form (1 = presidential, 0 = parliamentary)	Effective Number of Parliamentary Parties	Level of Democracy[a]
Benin	4.2	09.5	0.30	0.44	1	4.95	10
Botswana	5.9	11.7	0.00	0.65	0	1.56	10
Ghana	4.8	89.8	0.44	0.66	1	2.10	11
Kenya	3.1	08.6	0.57	0.38	1	2.21	8
Lesotho	2.8	18.7	0.00	0.34	0	2.16	9
Madagascar	3.0	29.2	0.00	0.02	1	2.31	8
Malawi	2.6	53.1	0.55	0.74	1	4.22	6
Mali	5.9	11.4	0.13	0.42	1	4.61	10
Mozambique	7.5	39.9	0.36	0.50	1	1.85	7
Namibia	4.4	21.8	0.55	0.72	0	1.68	9
Nigeria	5.5	40.1	0.66	0.40	1	2.15	6
Senegal	4.4	05.0	0.14	0.56	1	1.76	9
South Africa	3.9	20.2	0.49	0.72	0	1.94	11
Tanzania	6.3	19.7	0.59	0.27	1	1.30	7
Uganda	5.6	11.6	0.63	0.28	1	2.04	5
Zambia	4.6	70.2	0.71	0.61	1	2.99	6

Sources: World Bank, 2008; Posner 2004; Montalvo and Reynal-Querol 2005; Laakso and Taagepera 1979; Freedom House 2006.
Note: a. Inverted 2005 Freedom House scale, civil liberties + political rights.

variables: (1) the constitutional form, whether presidential or parliamentary; (2) the party system, measured as the effective number of parliamentary parties in 2005 (Laakso and Taagepera 1979); and (3) the level of democracy, measured as a country's combined inverted Freedom House score in 2005.

Analysis and Results

A multilevel model allows us to examine how covariates measured at each of two levels—individual (level 1) and country (level 2)—affect a respondent's stated intention to vote for the ruling party, our outcome of interest (Raudenbusch and Bryk 2002; Steenbergen and Jones 2002). Specifically, Table 5.3 presents a logistic random-effects model that provides a maximum-likelihood estimation of vote choice using adaptive quadrature to approximate integrals (Rabe-Hesketh and Skrondal 2008). We start by estimating the combined effects of individual-level variables on vote choice in model 1, controlling for standard demographic influences. We then specify model 2 in an effort to test whether the inclusion of country-level indicators improves the estimation of intended vote choice. Given the difficulty associated with a direct interpretation of multilevel logistic coefficients, we end our discussion by reporting predicted probabilities. A number of interesting insights arise.

Ethnic Identities

Model 1 suggests that ethnic identities do indeed affect voters' intentions, albeit with some dimensions of ethnicity pushing in unexpected directions. For example, being a member of the largest ethnic group (hypothesis H1A) is no guarantee that voters will express intent to support the party in power. This result calls into question the assumption that, in African countries, the largest ethnic group is always able to attain political dominance. Instead, what really matters is an individual's relationship to the ethnic group—regardless of size—that currently controls executive power. An individual who belongs to the same ethnic group as that of the incumbent president (the ethnic group in power) is far more likely to express an intention to vote for the ruling party (hypothesis H1B). This strong and significant result lends credence to the interpretation that people expect leaders to treat co-ethnics more favorably than others when exercising public power.

On the other hand, we find that the salience of ethnicity—measured as the tendency to self-define in terms of ethnic rather than national identity—reduces a voter's intention to support incumbents (hypothesis H1C). And interethnic distrust (hypothesis H1D), which fails to reach statistical significance, also disinclines a voter to back the ruling party. Two caveats are in

Table 5.3 Multilevel Logistic Regression: Intention to Vote for Ruling Party in Sub-Saharan Africa, 2005

	Model 1		Model 2	
	Coefficient	Standard Error	Coefficient	Standard Error
Level 1 (individual)				
Constant	−1.766***	(0.241)	−0.230	(0.617)
Ethnic identities				
Member of largest ethnic group	−0.006	(0.090)	−0.019	(0.096)
Member of ethnic group in power	0.462***	(0.134)	0.478***	(0.142)
Salience of ethnicity	−0.067**	(0.023)	−0.067**	(0.024)
Interethnic distrust	−0.023	(0.018)	−0.025	(0.019)
Ethnic discrimination	−0.202***	(0.041)	−0.210***	(0.046)
Economic interests				
Retrospective sociotropic	0.048	(0.025)	0.049	(0.027)
Retrospective egocentric	−0.015	(0.022)	−0.015	(0.024)
Prospective sociotropic	0.125***	(0.029)	0.129***	(0.031)
Prospective egocentric	0.014	(0.024)	0.016	(0.026)
Economic policy performance	0.551***	(0.069)	0.579***	(0.068)
Political considerations				
Partisan identification	1.946***	(0.336)	1.972***	(0.333)
Expectation of patronage	0.058*	(0.029)	0.061*	(0.031)
Expectation of compulsion	0.228***	(0.044)	0.243***	(0.045)
Demographic controls				
Female	0.086*	(0.038)	0.091*	(0.041)
Age	−0.001	(0.002)	−0.001	(0.002)
Education	−0.024	(0.022)	−0.026	(0.024)
Poverty	0.042	(0.040)	0.042	(0.043)
Rural	0.230***	(0.056)	0.243***	(0.058)
Level 2 (country)				
Ethnic fragmentation			0.495	(0.826)
Ethnic polarization			−0.725	(0.966)
GDP growth rate			0.038	(0.118)
Inflation rate			0.003	(0.004)
Presidential constitution			−0.409	(0.339)
Effective number of parliamentary parties			−0.359***	(0.077)
Level of democracy			−0.083	(0.055)
Variance components				
Intercept	0.518[a]		0.383[b]	

(continues)

Table 5.3 Continued

	Model 1		Model 2	
	Coefficient	Standard Error	Coefficient	Standard Error
–2 × log-likelihood	63,235.32		64,834.46	
Number of level-1 units	23,093		23,093	
Number of level-2 units	16		16	

Source: Afrobarometer survey, 2005–2006. See also sources for Table 5.2.
Notes: Coefficients are maximum-likelihood multilevel logit estimates, with country specified as random intercept.
 a. $\chi 2$, 15df = 37.6, p < 0.001.
 b. $\chi 2$, 8df = 23.6.
***p < 0.001, **p < 0.01, *p < 0.05.

order. First, the way in which these ethnic traits affect vote choice hinges essentially on the relationship of the voter to power holders. Depending on whether the voter belongs to the same ethnic group as that of the sitting president (i.e., the ethnic group in power), ethnic salience and distrust have divergent effects for intended vote choice: positive if voters are coethnics and negative otherwise. But since interactive terms do not reach statistical significance, neither is reported.

Much more influential is a citizen's sense that his or her group suffers ethnic discrimination at the hands of the state authorities (hypothesis H1E*).* As expected, a sense of political grievance—namely that the government has meted out unfair treatment to one's cultural group—helps to shape the voting calculus. Unlike people who belong to the ethnic group in power, however, individuals who perceive ethnic discrimination are strongly and significantly inclined to vote *against* the ruling party.

Economic Interests

Turning to economic interests, model 1 in Table 5.3 confirms that Africans also express intentions to vote economically, with two of the five indicators of economic interests being statistically significant. A voter's views about the past condition of the economy-at-large (hypothesis H2A) appear slightly more formative for voting decisions than views about past personal living standards (hypothesis H2B), though neither is statistically significant. Instead, a voter's expectation about the future condition of the economy has an important influence (hypothesis H2C), more so than views about future personal living standards (hypothesis H2D). Most important, however, an individual's assessment of the government's performance (hypothesis H2E) at implementing a range of macroeconomic policies—managing the economy, creating jobs, controlling inflation, and closing income gaps—is a major economic influence on intended vote choice.

As such, we infer that Africans in the countries surveyed take economic considerations into account as they form their voting intentions. Like voters elsewhere in the world, they calculate their economic interests with greater reference to the condition of the national economy than to the state of their family finances. And, contrary to the easy view that Africans think fatalistically, we find that they place greater weight on hopes of future economic prosperity than on evidence of past economic performance.

Political Considerations

As a final contender among rival explanations, we confront the possibility that voters fall back on partisan feelings of closeness to the ruling party. To repeat, we do not take reports of "party identification" at face value. Instead we consider only those voters who claim affinity to the incumbent's party while also judging that, as national president, he has performed poorly and does not deserve reelection. We surmise that some of these partisans are sincerely motivated by party loyalty, while others are positioning themselves strategically behind the party most likely to win. In one of the strongest results in the study, we discover that partisan identification, even when defined narrowly and instrumentally, is powerfully associated with intended vote choice (hypothesis H3A).

Consistent with this outcome, popular anticipation of future patronage rewards adds extra impetus to a voter's intention to choose the ruling party (hypothesis H3B). Some voters apparently calculate that incumbents are more credible than opposition politicians in promising the delivery of development after the election. At the same time, other voters are strongly motivated by concern about potential negative sanctions. People who (wrongly) suspect government involvement in the Afrobarometer survey are likely to say that they will vote for the ruling party (hypothesis H3C). We interpret this result as fear of political surveillance and monitoring. Being seen by the ruling party to have voted the "wrong" way exposes individuals to the risk of postelection retribution. Not wanting to be excluded from official patronage networks or exposed to coercive state sanctions, some individuals opt for the safe strategy of voting for the ruling party.

Demographic Controls

It may be tempting to regard African voting intentions as a direct function of an individual's place in the social structure. To be sure, women and rural dwellers are more likely than other voters to say they will cast a ballot for the ruling party (hypotheses H4A and H4E). But other demographic controls, including age, education, and poverty, remain insignificant.

Country Contexts

Past analysis has paid scant attention to the distinctive social structures, economic conditions, and political institutions prevailing in particular countries. We therefore take account of social, economic, and political factors at the country level. Model 2 in Table 5.3 reveals that only one contextual factor is important: the effective number of parliamentary parties. As expected, the larger the number of political parties that secure seats in the national legislature, the less likely voters are to opt for the presidential candidate of the ruling party (hypothesis H5Cb). We interpret this result to mean that some voters feel that they have little choice but to vote for the incumbent in one-party-dominant systems. By contrast, as multiparty competition increases, so voters are better able to express their identities and interests when choosing who will rule.

Marginal Effects

The concrete implications of this study are best expressed as the marginal effects of independent variables on the likelihood of an individual's intent to vote for the ruling party. These effects are computed as the differences in predicted probabilities from the lowest to the highest response category on each independent variable (not shown). The point of reference is a rural female voter who does not belong to the ethnic group in power, who evaluates the government as performing badly on economic policy performance, and who does not identify with the ruling party.

With respect to ethnicity, membership in the ethnic group in power increases this sort of voter's intention to cast a ballot for the ruling party by a margin of 11 percentage points. But if she feels the sting of ethnic discrimination, then the outcome is a reduction of 15 percentage points. Thus the negative consequence of felt group discrimination outweighs the positive inducement of belonging to the most powerful ethnic group.

With regard to economic factors, faith in the economic future (prospective sociotropic voting) increases support for the ruling party by 13 percentage points. And a favorable evaluation of the government's policy performance increases support by 37 percentage points. This hefty individual-level effect is the largest in the model, suggesting that a voter's overall response to public provision of job opportunities, low prices, and income distribution is the prime mover of voting intentions. Indeed, this performance-based economic interest has at least twice as large an impact as any aspect of ethnic identity.

With regard to political factors, partisan identification increases support for the ruling party by 32 percentage points, also a large effect. In
weighing incentives for voting for the incumbent, the lure of patronage rewards has the expected positive effect (of 4 percentage points), but expectations of compulsion are even more influential (at 6 percentage points). Finally, at the country level, a shift from a party system in which one party is
dominant to a system fragmented by multiple parties reduces intended support for the ruling party by a margin of 31 percentage points. In other
words, the pattern of voting intentions reported here is most common in
country contexts where a dominant incumbent party commonly wins.

Conclusion

This chapter confirms that conventional theories of voting behavior provide
leverage as starting points for understanding the outcomes of multiparty
elections in sub-Saharan Africa. Using survey and aggregate data, we have
shown that, to measurable degrees, Africans seek to engage in both ethnic
and economic voting.

Thus elections in Africa are much more than mere ethnic censuses or
straightforward economic referenda. The complexity of voting motivations
is evidenced by unforeseen facts: contrary to the stereotype of ethnic voting, many African heads of government hail from secondary or minority
ethnic groups; and converse to the economic voting thesis, incumbent presidents often gain reelection despite the poor performance of African economies. It is therefore necessary to move beyond confirmatory results about
single-factor explanations in order to make several original claims.

First, our cross-national test yields an unexpected result. Regardless of
the commonplace trope that African voters are motivated mainly by ethnic
solidarities, we find that economic interests are uppermost. Without deny-
ing that ethnic sentiments play a role in shaping vote choice, we note that
rational calculations about material welfare are apparently at the forefront
of voters' minds. We take this observation as a positive sign that African
politicians cannot count indefinitely on cultural appeals to kith and kin but,
in order to be consistently reelected, must also establish a track record of
social and economic delivery.

Second, by distinguishing various dimensions of economic interest and
ethnic identity, we cast light on the mechanisms that drive the formation of
voting preferences. As for economic interests, we note that voter expectations about the future health of the economy outweigh any other past, present, or future evaluation, especially of personal living standards. Thus,
while we have confirmed that Africans resemble the sociotropic voters so
common in other parts of the world, we also find that they think about the

economy more like future-oriented "bankers" than backward-looking "peasants" (MacKuen, Erikson, and Stimson 1992; Erikson, MacKuen, and Stimson 2000). Moreover, for the Africans we interviewed, rational assessment of actual government performance at macroeconomic policy management is the principal economic influence on intended vote choice.

Regarding ethnic identity, an individual's connection to the largest ethnic group and distrust of ethnic strangers play almost no role in shaping a vote for the political status quo. What matters instead is membership in the ethnic group that currently holds political power. Conversely, an intention vote for the opposition is driven mainly by whether an individual partakes in a collective sense of ethnic discrimination. In this regard, the principal line of ethnic cleavage in the context of electoral competition is whether individuals are "insiders" or "outsiders" to the prevailing distribution of political power.

How might parallel manifestations of economic and ethnic voting be reconciled? We propose that voters arrive at political loyalty to an ethnic group as a rational calculation that, if one's group can capture state power, group members will reap economic dividends. In this regard, ethnic voting is economically instrumental (rather than merely culturally expressive) as well as being forward-looking (hinging as it does on the expectation of future rewards). Thus, building on the findings presented in Chapter 4, we regard ethnic voting as not only constructed and situational, but also rooted in a solid economic logic.

A related third point is that an individual's partisan attachments have instrumental underpinnings. Because the distribution of development resources in a winner-take-all system depends upon political connections, voters have a strong incentive to declare fealty to the incumbent, including by saying they will vote for him. Their hope is that, by overtly (but not necessarily sincerely) demonstrating political loyalty, material rewards will follow. Especially where one party is dominant and opposition parties are weak—the only contextual factor that we have found to be important—it is sometimes too risky to come out openly and express an intention to vote against an incumbent.

The incentives for reelecting incumbents turn out to be positive as well as negative. On the positive side, the perception that incumbent politicians are able to make credible campaign promises to deliver patronage after elections leads to a measurable increase in ruling-party support. On the negative side, some would-be voters state an intention to back the ruling party because they worry about harmful political and economic repercussions from agents of the state. For reasons of self-protection, some unknown but probably substantial proportion of these citizens therefore follow through with actual votes for the party in power.

Fourth and finally, we have traced voting intentions to a feature of African political institutions at the country level. Our multilevel model suggests that African citizens are much more likely to vote for incumbents in places where there is a low effective number of parliamentary parties—that is, where dominant parties continue to stride the political stage. In places with weak oppositions—such as Tanzania, Namibia, Mozambique, and even Botswana and South Africa—voters have a restricted range of political choice; they essentially face the narrow option of endorsing or rejecting some form of de facto single-party rule. It is for this reason that instrumental expressions of partisanship are so widespread among African electorates. Thus, even as African voters increasingly seek to hold political leaders accountable for economic performance, they encounter the institutional constraints of party systems inherited from a postcolonial past.

Part 2

Vote Buying

VOTING AND DEMOCRATIC CITIZENSHIP IN AFRICA; ED.
BY MICHAEL BRATTON.
                              Cloth   323 P.
BOULDER: LYNNE RIENNER, 2013
SER: GLOBAL BAROMETERS SERIES.

ED: MICHIGAN STATE UNIVERSITY. PREVIOUSLY
PUBLISHED PAPERS. NEW SERIES.
LCCN 2012-35208
  ISBN 1588268942   Library PO# GENERAL APPROVAL

	List	65.00	USD
5461 UNIV OF TEXAS/SAN ANTONIO	Disc	17.0%	
App. Date 3/13/13 POL.APR 6108-11	Net	53.95	USD

SUBJ: 1. VOTING--AFRICA. 2. POLITICAL
PARTICIPATION--AFRICA.

CLASS JQ1879   DEWEY# 324.65096   LEVEL ADV-AC

YBP Library Services

VOTING AND DEMOCRATIC CITIZENSHIP IN AFRICA; ED.
BY MICHAEL BRATTON.
                              Cloth   323 P.
BOULDER: LYNNE RIENNER, 2013
SER: GLOBAL BAROMETERS SERIES.

ED: MICHIGAN STATE UNIVERSITY. PREVIOUSLY
PUBLISHED PAPERS. NEW SERIES.
 LCCN 2012-35208
  ISBN 1588268942   Library PO# GENERAL APPROVAL

	List	65.00	USD
5461 UNIV OF TEXAS/SAN ANTONIO	Disc	17.0%	
App. Date 3/13/13 POL.APR 6108-11	Net	53.95	USD

SUBJ: 1. VOTING--AFRICA. 2. POLITICAL
PARTICIPATION--AFRICA.

CLASS JQ1879   DEWEY# 324.65096   LEVEL ADV-AC

6

Vote Buying and Electoral Turnout in Kenya

Eric Kramon

Wherever people vote, the phenomenon of vote buying tends to follow. From the Roman republic (Yakobson 1995), to nineteenth-century Britain (O'Leary 1962) and the United States (Anderson and Tollison 1990), to newer democracies in the Philippines (Schaffer 2007) and Argentina (Stokes 2005; Brusco, Nazareno, and Stokes 2004), and to African countries like São Tomé and Príncipe and Nigeria (Vicente 2008; Chapter 7 in this volume), the practice of vote buying has been commonplace in political campaigns.

Yet despite the persistence of vote buying, its relationship to citizen voting behavior, particularly in the context of the secret ballot, has puzzled both the political elites who integrate vote buying into their electoral strategies as well as the scholars who seek to study those elites. First, if privacy of voting is protected and politicians cannot ensure that targeted citizens will vote for them, why does vote buying occur? Where the vote is secret, politicians lack mechanisms to ensure voter compliance, while citizens cannot credibly commit to providing their vote after a gift or bribe is received. As such, we should expect to see the practice of vote buying disappear as the secrecy of the vote increases, and in fact there is evidence to believe that nineteenth-century laws providing for the secret ballot in both the United States and Great Britain were in large part responsible for the decline of vote buying in those countries (O'Leary 1962; Anderson and Tollison 1990). A second puzzle relates to the relationship between vote buying and the behavior of voters. If citizens can accept a preelection gift but are free to vote as they please and are not even required to turn out at the polls, why might vote buying have an effect on voter behavior?

This chapter seeks to shed light on these questions by examining the effect of vote buying on individual voter turnout in Kenya, a country where vote buying is pervasive in election campaigns. Kenya's 2002 presidential and parliamentary elections serve as a good case for the study of vote buying and political behavior, as vote buying was widespread during the election campaign but the polls themselves were relatively free of meddling and distortion.

That vote buying is a strategic rather than a random act on the part of political parties and their allies poses a challenge to estimating its causal effect (Morgan and Winship 2007). This challenge is compounded by the fact that the theoretical literature produces a number of conflicting predictions regarding the strategies that parties are likely to employ when they select vote-buying targets. This lack of theoretical (and empirical) convergence renders it impossible to make *a priori* assumptions about the strategies of Kenyan vote buyers that could then be accounted for in the estimation procedure. As such, this chapter also analyzes strategies of vote buying in Kenya. Results suggest that individuals in more politically competitive areas and those who support relatively weak political parties are most likely to be targeted by a vote buyer. Using these results about vote-buying strategy, I apply statistical techniques to account for them in the estimation strategy.

The statistical results are robust and substantively strong, with individuals in Kenya who have been approached by a vote buyer being about 15 percentage points more likely to vote than those who have not been approached. This suggests that, in Kenya, preelection resource transfers are an important driver of voter turnout. I also find evidence that the least-educated citizens are those whose decision to vote is most influenced by vote buying, while I estimate that vote buying has no effect on the likelihood that a highly educated person will vote. These results suggest that education and learning might mediate the impact of vote buying on individual behavior.

That vote buying has such a strong effect on voter turnout is puzzling. If voters incur costs to go to the polls, as the rational choice voting model suggests (Downs 1957; Tullock 1967), then they should, in the context of secret and voluntary voting, be better off accepting the bribe or gift but remaining home on election day. Drawing ideas from the literature on turnout and clientelism, I suggest that vote buying might influence an individual's decision to vote through two channels: on the one hand through a monitoring and punishment mechanism, and on the other through a credibility-signaling mechanism (Keefer and Vlaicu 2008; Robinson and Verdier 2002). The latter part of the chapter tests empirical implications of these arguments, with results lending support to the monitoring and punishment hypothesis. This suggests that vote buying influences individual perceptions of a political party's monitoring capacity, including its potential for retaliation and punishment. The analysis also provides support for the credibility-signaling mechanism. Individuals approached by a vote buyer are more likely to believe in the credibility of politician campaign promises than are those not approached. Vote buying thus may help to convey credibility to potential voters and illustrate the willingness and capability of the vote-buying politician to distribute resources to supporters.

The Literature

Voter Turnout

The rational choice voting model suggests that people will only vote when the expected benefits of voting outweigh the costs (Downs 1957; Tullock 1967). The act of voting thus appears paradoxical, as the probability of being a pivotal voter in any election, but particularly a national election, is so small as to essentially be zero, ensuring that any cost to voting will exceed the act's expected benefit. That rational choice approaches have had difficulty explaining one of the most fundamental acts in democratic societies has led to a number of attempts to alter the original model in order to "rationalize" voting behavior. For instance, the rational choice voting model has been expanded by including an additional parameter, such as the felt duty to vote, social pressure, or the value citizens attach to having democracy continue (Riker and Ordeshook 1968; Gerber, Green, and Larimer 2008). According to John Aldrich (1993), the costs of voting are not particularly high, helping to explain high turnout rates.

Still others have looked to empirical data to determine the structural and institutional determinants of turnout. Mijeong Baek (2009) finds that where information costs are low, turnout tends to be higher. G. Bingham Powell (1980) argues that turnout is higher in proportional representation electoral systems (see also Blais and Carty 1990), and Robert Jackman (1987) argues that nationally competitive electoral districts tend to promote higher turnout.

Fewer studies have examined turnout outside the advanced democracies. In a cross-national study of turnout in Africa, Michelle Kuenzi and Gina Lambright (2007) find that the electoral system and the concurrency of presidential and parliamentary elections are predictors of turnout. Regarding China's local government elections, Jie Chen and Yang Zhong (2002) report that those who support the regime are the individuals most likely to vote, whereas Tianjian Shi (1999) finds that individuals vote in order to punish corrupt officials and facilitate political change. Regarding Eastern Europe and Latin America, Tatiana Kostadinova and Timothy Power (2007) find that turnout decreases rapidly following founding elections. In a study of political participation in Zambia, Michael Bratton (1999) finds that participation, which includes but is not exclusive to voting, is in large part determined by institutional linkages between individuals and the state, an argument confirmed by Kuenzi and Lambright (2007) across several African countries.

Vote Buying and Clientelism

Another branch of literature links vote buying and clientelism. Focusing on the strategic logic of vote buying, Gary Cox and Mathew McCubbins (1986) predict that political parties will target efforts on "core" supporters with whom they have informational advantages. Susan Stokes (2005) extends this logic with a model that predicts that vote buying will occur only in the context of machine politics, meaning institutionalized patronage. Because citizens have incentives to accept inducements but then vote as they please, vote buying is only effective in situations where political regimes have the capacity to monitor individuals and ensure their compliance. Simeon Nichter (2008) argues that vote buying is targeted at regime supporters not because of the monitoring abilities of political regimes, but rather because parties seek to buy turnout through the mobilization of previously inert party supporters. With reference to Mexico, Alberto Diaz-Cayeros, Federico Estevez, and Beatriz Magaloni (2007) argue that politicians are more likely to invest in clientelistic distribution in the most electorally risky areas of the country.

Despite the purported pervasiveness of clientelism in Africa, the evidence is mixed on its effectiveness as a political strategy in the electoral context. In an experimental study conducted in Benin, Leonard Wantchekon (2003) finds evidence that voters are more responsive to clientelistic rather than universal appeals. In a randomized field experiment in São Tomé, Pedro Vicente (2008) argues that vote buying increases voter turnout by "energizing" potential voters. Other empirical studies contradict these results. Regarding Ghana, Staffan Lindberg and Minion Morrison (2008) find that voters evaluate candidates based on policy prescriptions rather than on ethnic or clientelist bases. Similarly, Daniel Young (2008) finds no evidence in Kenya and Zambia that clientelism has improved the vote share of incumbent members of parliament.

The 2002 Elections in Kenya

Kenya's 2002 presidential and parliamentary elections were the third since the country's transition to multiparty politics in 1991. These polls marked the first peaceful turnover of executive power since the transition, with Mwai Kibaki of the National Rainbow Coalition (NARC) defeating the candidate of the long-ruling Kenyan African National Union (KANU), Uhuru Kenyatta. The latter was appointed by Daniel Arap Moi, the outgoing president, who conceded to abide by constitutionally mandated term limits. Also, in contrast to elections in 1992 and 1997, once fragmented opposition groups overcame historical divisions and united under the umbrella of the NARC and its presidential candidate, Kibaki.

The elections also marked a newfound independence and assertiveness for Kenya's national electoral commission. The counting of votes and the verification of ballots was conducted at polling places and overseen by observers from the parties and the international community, which thus hampered any attempts by parties to steal the election, as many suspect had been done in the past (Ndegwa 2003).

Nevertheless, political parties and their supporters still worked to influence—sometimes illegally—the outcomes of the election before the day of the polls. Incidents of violence occurred in the period preceding the election and many Kenyans claim to have been prevented from registering. Political-party operatives were also reported to have offered small amounts of cash in exchange for votes. John Githongo (2007)—the now exiled former permanent secretary for governance and ethics in the office of the president—recalls observing "offerings of cash, T-shirts, and food in exchange for votes."

Data and Indicators

Data are taken from Round 3 of the Afrobarometer survey, which was conducted among a nationally representative sample of 1,278 individuals in Kenya in 2005. The object of explanation is voter turnout, operationalized as a dichotomous indicator taking on a value of 1 if the individual voted in the 2002 elections and 0 if the person did not vote in the election. I generate this variable from a survey question that asks the following: "With regard to the most recent, 2002 national elections, which statement is true for you?" The allowed responses are: "You voted in the elections," "You decided not to vote," "You could not find the polling station," "You were prevented from voting," "You did not have time to vote," "You did not vote for some other reason," and "You were not registered."

Sixty-three percent of Kenyan survey respondents reported voting in the 2002 elections. The International Foundation for Electoral Systems reports that national turnout for the 2002 elections was about 57 percent (IFES 2012). Voter turnout is therefore comparatively higher in my sample, but not substantially so. One respondent could not find the polling place, another eight claim to have been prevented from voting, 144 were too young, five could not remember whether or not they voted, and for two individuals the data are missing. Because these individuals may have wanted to vote or claim to have tried to vote, I drop them from the data, leaving a sample size of 1,118.

The explanatory variable of greatest interest is exposure to vote buying. It is also a dichotomous variable, measuring whether or not an individual had been approached by a political-party representative and offered a material reward in exchange for a vote in the 2002 election campaign. I generate this variable from an Afrobarometer question that asks: "And during the 2002 elections, how often [if ever] did a candidate or someone from a political party offer you something, like food or a gift, in return for your vote?" Respondents could answer "never," "once or twice," "a few times," "often," or "don't know." Just over half of those surveyed (about 56 percent) report that they had never been approached by a candidate, about 15 percent report having been approached "once or twice," 14 percent report having been approached "a few times," and 12 percent report having been approached "often." About 40 percent of respondents therefore claim to have been approached at least once. Such individuals are assigned a value of 1 on the vote-buying variable, while all others are assigned a value of 0.

It is important to note that respondents do not report whether they accepted the bribe or gift. The data also contain no information about the magnitude of the gift. Rather, we only know that a party representative or supporter with an offer to exchange money or resources for a vote approached them. As such, it is perhaps best to interpret the treatment as exposure to a vote-buying offer.

The survey question also does not provide information about the precise timing of the offer. If vote buyers targeted voters while they were on the way to the polls (having already decided and made the effort to vote), then the statistical results will overstate vote buying's influence on voter behavior. Yet the fact that about two-thirds of those exposed to vote buying claim to have been approached "a few times" (14 percent of all respondents) or "often" (12 percent) illustrates that much vote buying occurs before election day. Moreover, anecdotal evidence from the 2002 election as well as other elections in Kenya suggests that a great deal of vote buying occurs in the days and weeks leading up to elections. In an interview with a *New York Times* correspondent in the period before the 2002 elections, one citizen reported: "A NARC agent stopped me at a bus stop and asked me who I was voting for. When I said KANU, he offered me 500 shillings [about US$6] for my vote" (Lacey 2002). Another Kenyan described his vote-buying experience before election day as follows: "A man approached me in Naivasha at a bar and asked me what party I'm from. He said he's an agent for KANU and would buy my vote for 700 shillings" (Lacey 2002). A study conducted by a Kenyan anticorruption organization on the 2007 elections estimates that in the two weeks leading up to the elections, "candidates [spent] about 60 to 80 thousand shillings per day on distribution of money and other benefits to voters" (CAPF 2007).

There are potential sources of bias in survey data. People tend to respond to surveys in ways that they believe are socially acceptable. Kenyans are exposed to normative discourses that suggest that voting is the right thing to do but that vote buying is not. Thus, alongside the slight overreporting already noted for voter turnout, we might expect underreporting of a socially disapproved activity like vote buying.

The extent to which these potential tendencies for over- and underreporting damage the inferences drawn in the study depends on their direction. In this regard, the results are relatively safe from major distortions due to misreporting. Figure 6.1 presents four different types of individuals labeled by combinations of their actions or experiences. First, for individuals who were exposed to vote buying and turned out to vote, we might logically expect them not to report this exposure, which would bias the results toward a null result. It is possible that these individuals would report not having voted, which in combination with a failure to report having been approached by a vote buyer could be problematic, but such a situation is unlikely, as respondents are far more likely to over- rather than underreport their voting history. Second, for those who were not exposed to vote buying and did vote, we would not expect them to misrepresent their histories given their behavior. Third, for those who were not exposed to vote buying and did not vote, this combination would again bias the results toward a null result. Finally, and representing the only behavior combination that poses a potential problem, are those individuals who were exposed to vote buying and did not vote; these individuals might misrepresent their voting history, potentially inflating our estimate of the effect of vote buying. Yet this potential bias is attenuated by the fact that those who feel socially pressured to say that they voted in the last election are also likely those that feel socially pressured to say that they did not interact with vote buyers. Individuals who misrepresent their voting history are likely to answer both questions falsely, giving the impression that they were not exposed to vote buying but that they did vote. As before, these responses would bias the estimated effect of vote buying toward zero.

The statistical models that follow also include a number of control variables. An individual's level of education, for instance, may positively predict likelihood of voting. But Lisa Blaydes (2006) suggests that in Egypt, where vote buying is prevalent, those with lower education levels are likely to vote. Similarly, poorer voters might be more susceptible to vote buying because they attach value even to small transfers. To test for

Figure 6.1 Potential Sources of Bias

Approached and voted	Approached and did not vote
Not approached and voted	Not approached and did not vote

this possibility, I use several measures of an individual's economic condition, including cash income and access to food.

Because the decision to vote might quite reasonably be related to one's political allegiance, I also include control variables indicating the political-party preference of the individual. I approximate an individual's intrinsic benefit from voting by using their opinion about democracy as the best form of government. And because an individual's belief in her or his ability to influence politicians might reasonably have an effect on their decision to participate in politics, I include this variable as a control in several of the statistical models. As is conventional, I also include controls for the age and gender of the respondent, as well as for whether the respondent lives in an urban or rural area.

Finally, the competitiveness of the election may also be relevant to potential voters. We might speculate that the closer the outcome of the election, the greater the perceived probability of being the pivotal voter. As the perceived probability of being pivotal increases, so too does the expected benefit of voting. Moreover, the competitiveness of a district might matter for vote buyers. Kenya has a peculiar system for the election of the president that requires the winner to win at least 25 percent of the vote in five of the country's seven provinces. Political parties therefore have incentive to target their campaigns to broad sections of the country and to win votes from areas outside their strongholds. To control for these factors, I include election-outcome margin as a variable, which is simply the percentage-point difference between the proportion of votes won by the winner in a district and the proportion of votes won by the runner-up. I assume that potential voters can estimate how close the outcome of an upcoming election might be and use results from the 2002 presidential elections to create the variable. I aggregate constituency-level presidential election data up to the district level and integrate the variable of election-outcome margin into the individual-level dataset.

Who Voted? Whose Votes Were Being Bought?

Vote-buying attempts are fundamentally strategic acts on the part of political parties. Estimating their causal effects on voter turnout therefore requires a systematic analysis of the vote-buying assignment mechanism. I therefore first describe the data with a particular focus on characteristics of voters and nonvoters, as well as those who were approached by vote buyers. This section ends with a statistical analysis designed to identify the strategic logic of vote buying from the perspective of vote-buying parties.

About 33 percent of Kenyans claimed the NARC as their party of choice, 12 percent support the Liberal Democratic Party (LDP), 10 percent support KANU, and about 36 percent claim no attachment. The turnout rate during the 2002 elections was highest for supporters of the NARC, which was perhaps due to excitement about its potential to defeat KANU. Yet vote buyers targeted only 30 percent of NARC supporters, well below the national rate of over 40 percent, while they targeted about 60 percent of LDP supporters.

Table 6.1 presents results from probit analyses conducted to answer the question of who gets targeted by vote buyers. Those who claim to have

Table 6.1 Probit Analyses of Vote Buying's Determinants in Kenya, 2002

	Model 1	Model 2	Model 3	Model 4	Model 5
Intercept	−0.29*	−0.25*	−0.13	−0.12*	−0.32*
	(0.07)	(0.06)	(0.09)	(0.06)	(0.16)
Cash income	−0.06				−0.02
	(0.08)				(0.10)
Insufficient food	0.32*				0.37*
	(0.08)				(0.09)
Male		0.20*			0.20*
		(0.08)			(0.09)
Urban		0.12			0.14
		(0.08)			(0.11)
Age		−0.00			−0.00
		(0.00)			(0.00)
No education			−0.02		−0.06
			(0.15)		(0.20)
Primary education			−0.02		−0.04
			(0.11)		(0.15)
Secondary education			0.02		0.12
			(0.11)		(0.14)
KANU supporter				−0.02	−0.13
				(0.13)	(0.15)
NARC supporter				−0.20*	−0.22*
				(0.09)	(0.10)
LDP supporter				0.46*	0.46*
				(0.12)	(0.15)
Vote margin					−0.27*
					(0.12)
N	1,118	1,118	1,118	1,118	838
Log L	−752.99	−753.58	−758.17	−744.10	−512.220

Source: Afrobarometer survey, 2005.
Notes: Dependent variable is a dichotomous measure indicating whether an individual was approached by a vote buyer. Standard errors appear in parentheses.
*$p < 0.05$.

gone without sufficient food in a recent period—a reasonable measure of poverty—are more likely to be targeted by a vote buyer. Men are also far more likely to be targeted than women. The education-level variables are not, however, statistically significant, nor are the coefficients substantively large. Thus an individual's education level is not a strong predictor that she or he will be targeted by vote buyers.

The results concerning the political variables are illuminating. While being a supporter of KANU is not a significant predictor, supporters of the opposition NARC are far less likely to be targeted than are the supporters of other parties or those who claim no allegiance. LDP supporters, on the other hand, are substantially more likely to be vote-buying targets, perhaps because in 2002 the LDP was not considered a serious contender, and so its supporters may have been perceived to be attractable "swing" voters. Finally, the political competitiveness of an individual's electoral district is statistically and substantively predictive of an increase in the probability that a vote buyer will target that individual. These results suggest that politically parties are more likely to engage in vote buying in the most politically competitive districts. This finding runs contrary to a number of influential theoretical predictions, including those of Cox and McCubbins (1986), who argue that private goods (like bribes or gifts) are more likely to be targeted toward core supporters; Stokes (2005), who argues that vote buying will only occur where political machines are strong enough to monitor voters and ensure compliance; and Nichter (2008), who argues that parties do not buy votes but rather turnout, and seek to do so in places where they have the most unmobilized support.

Model Estimation and Results

What, then, is the effect of vote buying on an individual's decision to vote? In Table 6.2, I present a number of probit models using different covariate combinations. The estimated effect of having been offered a bribe or a gift in exchange for a vote, on the probability that an individual does vote, is positive and significant in each specification. Moreover, the magnitude of the coefficient is stable across the specifications. To estimate the substantive effect of a vote-buying attempt on the probability that an individual votes, I simulate predicted probabilities of voting for "treated" and "untreated" individuals (Imai, King, and Lau 2007). The estimates suggest that a vote-buying attempt increases the probability of voting by about 10 percentage points (the 95 percent confidence interval spans the interval from about 5 percent to about 15 percent).

The results also suggest that one's assessment of the intrinsic value of democracy plays a role in determining his or her decision to vote. In all

Table 6.2 Probit Analyses of Individual Voter Turnout in Kenya, 2002

	Model 1	Model 2	Model 3	Model 4	Model 5
Intercept	0.48*	0.25*	0.25*	0.10	−0.24
	(0.05)	(0.09)	(0.12)	(0.13)	(0.20)
Vote buy	0.31*	0.30*	0.29*	0.27*	0.34*
	(0.08)	(0.08)	(0.08)	(0.08)	(0.10)
Democratic belief		0.30*	0.30*	0.20*	0.26*
		(0.09)	(0.09)	(0.10)	(0.12)
No political efficacy		0.03	0.02	0.01	−0.01
		(0.08)	(0.08)	(0.09)	(0.10)
Cash income			−0.13	−0.10	−0.18
			(0.08)	(0.09)	(0.11)
Insufficient food			0.15	0.12	0.01
			(0.08)	(0.09)	(0.10)
Male				0.50*	0.42*
				(0.09)	(0.10)
Urban				−0.14	−0.03
				(0.09)	(0.11)
Age				0.00	0.00
				(0.00)	(0.00)
No education					0.27
					(0.21)
Primary education					0.14
					(0.16)
Secondary education					0.17
					(0.15)
KANU supporter					0.41*
					(0.17)
NARC supporter					0.40*
					(0.11)
LDP supporter					0.21
					(0.16)
Vote margin					0.01
					(0.13)
N	1,118	1,118	1,118	1,118	838
Log L	−640.68	−629.31	−620.76	−591.25	−411.59

Source: Afrobarometer survey, 2005.
Notes: Dependent variable is a dichotomous measure indicating whether an individual voted in the 2002 elections. Standard errors appear in parentheses.
*$p < 0.05$.

specifications, the democratic-belief variable is statistically significant and positive, and its magnitude is generally similar to that of the vote-buying variable. Those who believe democracy is always the best form of government are therefore about 10 percentage points more likely to vote than those who do not. The data also illustrate that individuals who associate themselves with the two most competitive parties are substantially more likely to vote than their counterparts who do not associate strongly with a political party. In particular, association with the main opposition coalition, the NARC, is strongly predictive of turnout. This finding is consistent with studies that link party identification to voting in Africa (Bratton 1999; Kuenzi and Lambright 2007).

To test whether vote buying has a greater impact on poorer individuals, I test how the vote-buying variable interacts with two indicators of material wealth: cash income and access to food. The analysis suggests no meaningful difference in the effect of vote buying for poorer or richer individuals (not shown). The same is true for primary and secondary education, though an interaction term suggests that there is a statistically significant effect of vote buying on turnout for persons with no formal education (not shown).

Estimating the Causal Effect of Vote Buying

A key hurdle one faces in estimating the causal effect of vote buying on voter turnout arises from the fact that political parties do not buy votes randomly, but rather strategically. If vote buyers target those who are also more likely to turn out—perhaps because they know the returns to their investment are likely highest among such people—then a standard statistical analysis will tend to overestimate vote buying's influence. A solution to this inferential problem lies in preprocessing the data using a method of propensity-score matching that links the pretreatment covariates to vote-buying strategies (Rosenbaum and Rubin 1985; Ho et al. 2006).

I use the method of exact matching, using the following pretreatment covariates: education, political-party affiliation, economic indicators (cash income and insufficient food), as well as gender, urban residence, and age. The process discards 364 individuals who cannot be matched using each of the control variables from the probit models, leaving a sample of 756 individuals in the preprocessed data. Probit analyses run on the preprocessed data indicate that the initial findings are robust to reductions in model dependency (not shown). Moreover, they suggest that the results from the initial analyses may *underestimate* the causal effect of vote buying on turnout. I now estimate that individuals approached by a vote buyer are about 14 percentage points more likely to vote (the 95 percent confidence interval runs from about 8 percent to about 20 percent).

But a puzzle remains. Where the ballot is secret and voting is voluntary, a preelection material transfer should not on its own influence the probability that the expected benefits to voting might exceed the costs. As long as the probability of being a pivotal voter remains low and the costs to voting remain fixed, no preelection bribe should influence a voter's decisionmaking calculus. Yet this study illustrates that in Kenya such transfers do have a sizable impact. Here I present potential explanations linking vote buying and turnout, and explore their empirical implications.

Monitoring and Punishment Mechanism

For political parties, monitoring turnout is an easier task than monitoring vote choice (Nichter 2008). If parties can credibly threaten to check the presence at the polls of those whose votes they have purchased, then potential voters are likely to alter their decisionmaking calculus. Specifically, a party's capacity to monitor and punish increases the costs to citizens for noncompliance.

Reports from election observers suggest that Kenyan parties systematically monitored turnout (and attempted to monitor vote choice) during the 2002 elections. Political-party agents were present in most, if not all, polling stations on election day. Often these party representatives were members of the communities in which the polling stations were located, providing them with local knowledge with which to effectively monitor voter behavior. Kenyan parties also took advantage of legal provisions allowing for "assisted voting." According to Kenyan electoral law, those individuals who feel they cannot properly vote by themselves are permitted to bring into the voting booth an individual of voting age to assist them. According to election reports:

> It was not uncommon to see several party agents as well as the presiding officer crowding around the voting booth to observe the voting process. In one polling station . . . nearly all women voters claimed illiteracy, requested assistance, and received assistance from the presiding officer. . . . It appears that the provision of assisted voting for illiterate voters may have been abused, with an unusually high number of voters demanding such assistance in some stations. (Carter Center 2003: 29–33; see also Lehoucq 2007)

These observations suggest that less educated people—as the most likely to be illiterate or require voting assistance—may be the easiest voters to monitor. Party agents are able to closely monitor not only whether they vote, but potentially even *how* they vote. Thus people with the lowest levels of education might be influenced by vote buying not so much because their circumstances render them "easier to buy," but rather because they are easiest for vote purchasers to monitor.

Moreover, Kenyan citizens had legitimate reasons to fear retaliation and punishment on the part of parties and their allies. During the 1992 and 1997 elections, militant youth organizations that were both formally and informally affiliated with KANU were active during the campaigns, while ethnic-cleansing attempts occurred in some areas of the country (Anderson 2002; Laakso 2007). Though the 2002 elections were far more peaceful than the previous two contests, sporadic incidents of election-related violence—for instance in the Rift Valley, where youth groups threatened individuals with homemade weapons—still weighed heavily on the minds of many Kenyans. And the involvement in politics of criminal groups like Mungiki rendered the threat of violence palpable. As such, the potential costs of violating, or being perceived to have violated, a vote-buying bargain could have been considerable.

How does vote buying relate to individual perceptions of a party's monitoring capacity and the possibility of violent punishment? To examine individual perceptions of these issues, I take advantage of two Afrobarometer questions. First, do respondents think the "freedom to choose who to vote for without feeling pressured" is better, worse, or about the same as in years past? And second, how often do they think that "competition between political parties leads to violent conflict": always, often, rarely, or never?

Ordered probit analyses reveal that vote buying has a substantial and statistically significant effect on respondents' perceptions of their freedom from pressure as well as on their perceptions of electoral violence (not shown). Figure 6.2 illustrates that those who are approached by a vote buyer are about 10 percentage points more likely to believe that freedom from political-party pressure on vote choice is either the same or worse, and almost 15 percentage points less likely to believe that it has improved. Figure 6.3 illustrates that those who are approached by a vote buyer are between 10 and 15 percentage points more likely to believe that political-party competition always leads to violence, while the same individuals are about 15 percentage points less likely to believe that such competition rarely or never leads to violence.

Credibility-Signaling Mechanism

An alternative explanation features the signals that vote buying sends to potential voters. In low-information environments, information about politician performance, behavior, and credibility is difficult for voters to obtain. Vote buying provides politicians and parties with a method to convey signals about their capacity in these areas. A preelection gift can signal to voters the politician's willingness to distribute resources to supporters, and his credibility for doing so. Vote buying thus creates the expectation that compliant

Figure 6.2 Estimated Effect of Vote Buying on Perception of Political-Party Pressure on Vote Choice in Kenya, 2002

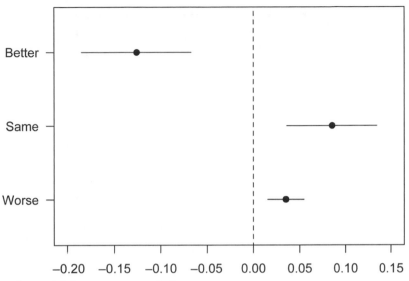

Source: Afrobarometer survey, 2005.

Notes: Afrobarometer question: "Is freedom to choose who to vote for without feeling pressured better, worse, or the same as a few years ago?" Those who were approached by a vote buyer were far less likely to report that freedom to vote without pressure had improved.

voters might likely receive future benefits, contingent on the electoral success of the gift giver.

Scholars have suggested that vote buying is a credibility-signaling mechanism. Nicolas van de Walle (2007), for instance, questions the extent to which parties in Africa have the capacity to monitor voter compliance, suggesting instead that preelection transfers in Benin and Nigeria are symbolic and ritualistic. Frederic Schaffer (2007) finds support in ethnographic studies of the Philippines and Taiwan that clientelism is more than an economic relationship and that vote buying is a ritual signaling a more fulsome social commitment to the recipient. These findings resonate with a formal model by Philip Keefer and Razvan Vlaicu (2008) that characterizes clientelism as a cost-effective method by which politicians can build credibility. Similarly, James Robinson and Thierry Verdier (2002) argue that clientelism is the cheapest way to signal credible commitment in weakly institutionalized systems, and Pierre Englebert (2002) argues that patronage provides an effective way of building legitimacy in weak states.

**Figure 6.3 Estimated Effect of Vote Buying on Perception of
Electoral Violence in Kenya, 2002**

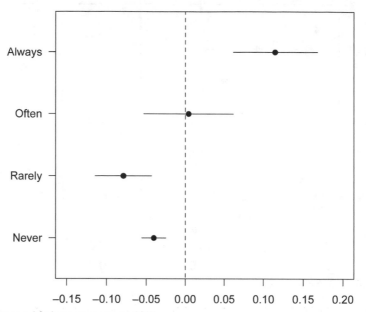

Source: Afrobarometer survey, 2005.
Notes: Afrobarometer question: "Does competition between political parties lead to violent conflict?" The figure illustrates that those who were approached by a vote buyer were far more likely to believe that competition between political parties always leads to violence.

To test whether vote buying influences voter perceptions of politician credibility, I use an Afrobarometer survey item that asks: "In your opinion, how often do politicians keep their campaign promises after elections?" I create a dichotomous measure of politician credibility perception by coding those who believe that politicians always or often keep their campaign promises as having positive perceptions of credibility, while those who believe that politicians rarely or never keep their promises are coded as having negative perceptions.

Table 6.3 presents results from probit analyses designed to identify the relationship of vote buying to individual perceptions of politician credibility. As expected, the coefficient on the vote-buying variable is positive and statistically significant, albeit at the 0.10 level. In other words, the probability that an individual believes that politicians fulfill campaign promises increases with exposure to vote buying. The evidence is therefore consistent with the notion that vote buying signals politician credibility and commitment to potential voters.

Table 6.3 Probit Models of Vote Buying and Perceptions of Politician Credibility in Kenya, 2002

	Model 1	Model 2
Intercept	−0.15**	−0.15
	(0.05)	(0.20)
Vote buy	0.12^	0.14^
	(0.08)	(0.08)
Urban		0.04
		(0.09)
No education		−0.40*
		(0.16)
Primary education		−0.19
		(0.12)
Secondary education		−0.04
		(0.12)
Cash income		0.15^
		(0.08)
Democratic belief		−0.00
		(0.10)
Interest in politics		0.03
		(0.04)
Male		−0.19*
		(0.08)
NARC supporter		−0.01
		(0.09)
KANU supporter		0.19
		(0.13)
LDP supporter		0.03
		(0.13)
N	1,118	1,118
Log L	−765.50	−722.5

Source: Afrobarometer survey, 2005.
Notes: Dependent variable is an indicator of whether an individual perceives that politicians' campaign promises are credible. Standard errors appear in parentheses.
**$p < 0.01$, *$p < 0.05$, ^$p < 0.10$.

Conclusion

In this chapter I have attempted to identify and explain the relationship of vote buying to individual voting behavior in Kenya. I find that the distribution of material benefits by political parties to prospective voters in the pre-election period is important to understanding why people vote in Kenya. I estimate that Kenyans who have been approached by a vote buyer are up to 14 percentage points more likely to vote than those who have not. And this effect is most likely among the least-educated citizens.

Above the individual level, I find strong evidence that vote buying is most likely to occur in electorally competitive locations and that male supporters of a somewhat marginal party are most likely to be targeted. Supporters of the strongest opposition coalition, on the other hand, are systematically less likely to be targeted. These results have implications for our understanding of the distributive strategies of political parties. While some models predict that private transfers will be targeted toward core supporters, among whom monitoring is easier and compliance is more likely, these findings suggest that vote buyers may reach outside of their core constituencies to attract new voters. In Kenya, supporters of the LDP were most likely to be approached, which suggests that vote buyers view potential "swing" voters as the most attractive targets.

I have also endeavored to solve a puzzle about why people are more likely to vote after being offered a bribe when they could simply accept the gift and stay home on election day. I propose two possible answers: a monitoring and punishment mechanism, and a credibility-signaling mechanism. I find statistical evidence for both mechanisms. Exposure to vote buying is positively associated with an increase in the perceived ability of political parties to exert pressure on vote choice, and an increase in the perception that parties are involved in retaliation and punishment. Exposure to vote buying is also positively associated with an increase in perceived credibility of politicians, suggesting that preelection gifts serve as instruments through which politicians signal commitment to distributing resources to supporters after the election.

Both mechanisms seem more likely to work among the least-educated citizens. First, these voters are likely easier for political parties to monitor: they are most likely to request assistance in registering to vote, getting to the polls, and even voting. Thus there are multiple opportunities in the voting process for party officials to monitor turnout, and potentially even vote choice. Second, less educated individuals may lack information about the past behavior and future credibility of politicians. For such citizens, the signals conveyed by vote buying will weigh more heavily in the decisionmaking process than they will for individuals with more education or access to a wider range of information sources (Grossman and Helpman 1996).

What does democracy mean when less educated voters are induced to participate by preelection monetary and other rewards? Are such practices harmless "warts" on democracy's surface, or substantial threats to the principles of accountability, responsiveness, and "rule by the people"? If Kenyan anticorruption activist John Githongo (2007) is correct when he argues that, "if you are a politician in Kenya today, people will line up and

take your money, your T-shirts, and your food, but they will vote their con-
sciences," then perhaps we should not be too troubled. If he is right, vote
buying is simply a form of political mobilization, and one that we might expect to slowly disappear as parties realize its futility in attracting votes. But
if Githongo is wrong and vote buying affects both turnout and vote choice,
then the political equality of voters and the political accountability of leaders are surely at risk. This is particularly the case given the disproportionate influence of vote buying on the least-educated members of society.

7

Vote Buying and Violence in Nigerian Election Campaigns

Michael Bratton

Elections in Africa often resemble bitter struggles over access to the resources controlled by the state, which are the biggest prize in society. Given these high stakes, politicians resort to a variety of means—whether fair or foul—to attain public office. To be sure, candidates go through the motions of presenting programmatic promises. But the pledges of politicians commonly lack credibility, are virtually identical across contending parties, or quickly dissolve into personal attacks (Keefer 2004; Salih and Nordlund 2007; van de Walle 2003). In this context, voters choose among candidates less on the basis of distinctive policy positions than on the candidates' assumed trustworthiness and reliability as prospective patrons (Kitschelt and Wilkinson 2007; Bratton and Lewis 2007; Bratton 2007a).

Instead of providing opportunity for public deliberation, African election campaigns often feature material inducement and political intimidation. In extreme forms, unconventional modes of electoral practice are manifest in explicit acts of vote buying (Schaffer 2007; Lindberg 2003) and electoral violence (LeBas 2006; Wilkinson 2006). Both kinds of activity, which aim to deny citizens the freedom to express their electoral preferences, are incontrovertibly illegal. But because persuasion alone seldom generates enough support, candidates nonetheless regularly attempt to purchase or compel votes.

This chapter explores the nature, extent, and effectiveness of irregular modes of electioneering. What form—in cash or kind—does vote buying take? What sorts of practices—of threats or action—characterize election violence? How frequently do these departures from democratic procedure occur? Who are the victims? And most important, do inducements and compulsions

121

work? If they do, which are more effective: the carrots of vote buying or the sticks of political violence?

In order to estimate the effectiveness of different sorts of electoral malpractice, I distinguish three alternative courses of action for citizens: to refuse, to defect, or to comply. First, the voter can "refuse." With reference to vote buying, the individual can decline to enter into an agreement to trade his vote. Or she can seek to avoid violence, for example by publicly shaming the perpetrator or, more likely, exiting the electoral arena. Second, the individual can enter a vote-buying agreement or shoulder a threat of intimidation with no intention of complying. When the time comes to cast a ballot, the individual instead "defects" by failing to vote at all or by voting as he or she pleases. Finally, the citizen can "comply" with inducement or intimidation by turning out to vote and voting the "right" way, meaning in accordance with the instructions of the vote buyer or political persecutor. These three possible responses—which echo Albert Hirschmann's (1970) alternatives of exit, voice, and loyalty—represent an ascending scale of popular submission to elite efforts to manipulate elections.

Based on survey materials from Nigeria, I show that citizens in one African country clearly regard vote buying and electoral violence as infractions of public morality. Most ordinary people resist efforts of political elites to illegally influence voter behavior. But some individuals—especially society's poorest and most vulnerable members—have little choice except to comply. Their only other viable option is to feign compliance while refusing in practice—a strategy I call defection—which is a commonplace "weapon of the weak" (Scott 1985).

Importantly, evidence suggests that vote buying and political intimidation are ineffective campaign practices. In reality, people who are paid or threatened during the election campaign are actually less likely to turn out to vote. Moreover, while voters may be willing to cast their ballots for parties whose candidates have broken electoral laws, many would have done so anyway—that is, without extralegal incentives or punishments. Most important, many who enter vote-buying agreements say they will ultimately defect—that is, by taking the money but voting as they please. Defection is especially likely when voters are cross-pressured from both sides of a partisan divide or when exposed to both vote buying and violence.

I conclude the chapter by exploring the implications of campaign malpractices for the health of democracy. One particularly interesting result, which deserves further exploration, is that vote-buying behavior is determined collectively. People are most likely to defect if they think that others will do so too, thus availing themselves of the protections provided by collective defense. But if collective action also shapes norms—that is, if people justify wrongful behavior for themselves because everyone else is doing it—then campaign irregularities can corrode the quality of democratic citizenship.

The Campaign Context: Nigeria 2007

Nigeria's general elections of April 2007—which featured contests for the federal presidency, state governorships, and legislative assemblies—promised a political watershed (Mustapha 2006; Ibrahim 2007; Rotberg 2007). For the first time since independence in 1960, a third sequence of regular elections would be held under a civilian regime, and one elected president would succeed another. If peacefully and honestly implemented, these elections promised to legitimize and strengthen Nigeria's fragile new democracy. But the serious misconduct in the prior polls of 1999 and 2003 had cast doubt on whether Nigeria would easily attain a free and fair election.

In the event, the 2007 elections were deeply flawed (Human Rights Watch 2007). Seasoned observers predicted that, as "various powerful figures calculate their best interests and shift their factional alignments . . . tremendous amounts of largesse will change hands and some of the players will likely resort to force" (Sklar, Onwudiwe, and Kew 2006: 108). A bitter feud between outgoing president Olusegun Obasanjo and his vice president Atiku Abubakar, an aspirant successor, dominated the election season. Dueling lawsuits, boycott threats, and shifting alliances between opportunistic political parties and factions created a chaotic atmosphere of uncertainty. Election preparations—such as a delayed voter registration exercise—were woefully inadequate and questions soon arose about the impartiality and competence of the national election commission (Transition Monitoring Group 2007).

These concerns were borne out on the days of the election. Voting for president and the national assembly failed to take place in certain polling stations in half a dozen Nigerian states in the southeast and northeast due to the nondelivery of electoral materials. In numerous locations across the country, ballot papers were misprinted or arrived late. In the Niger Delta zone, armed militias brazenly stole ballot boxes or substituted prestuffed containers of their own. Despite guarantees from the inspector-general of police that public security would be ensured, opposition candidates were harassed or arrested, voters were turned away from polling places by gangs of young thugs, ballot secrecy was violated by party workers and police, and some 300 persons were killed in election-related violence. The national election commission announced an overwhelming victory for the ruling People's Democratic Party (PDP), but polling-station results often bore little resemblance to actual turnout or voter intentions. All told, the fraudulent election left Nigeria's voters feeling frustrated and disenfranchised.

This chapter documents neglected aspects of an election campaign awash with oil money and marred by escalating violence. I focus on ordinary citizens rather than political elites by looking at campaign abuses at the individual level, one citizen at a time. Who was affected, and how did they respond? Data are drawn from a preelection Afrobarometer survey conducted in Nigeria in January and February 2007 with questions about the previous 2003 and forthcoming 2007 general elections. Given a representative national sample of 2,410 adult respondents, inferences can be made to the Nigerian population as a whole with a margin of sampling error of plus or minus 2 percent at a 95 percent confidence level.

The Perceived Morality of Campaign Manipulation

As a first step, I ask whether African citizens regard vote buying and violence as right or wrong. One might expect that voters would ascribe a different moral status to each transgression: violence visits heavy costs upon unwilling victims, whereas the purchase of votes at least holds out the promise of a material benefit to those who voluntarily participate.

A clear majority of Nigerians say political violence is always wrong. Almost four out of five (79 percent) see political violence as "never justified," even "in support of a just cause." The same proportions think it better to find lawful solutions to social problems and that "politicians and political parties should not be allowed to form their own private security forces." Only 5 percent—notably younger and less educated Nigerians—strongly support the "necessity" of using violence in pursuit of political goals.

Most Nigerians also condemn efforts by politicians to purchase support at the polls. Almost six in ten (58 percent) say that it is "wrong and punishable" for "a candidate or party official to offer money in return for a vote." An additional 30 percent consider vote buying "wrong but understandable," adding the qualifying phrase perhaps because they think that political patrons are obliged to steer kickbacks to clients. Nicolas van de Walle suggests that voters in Nigeria take vote-buying offers as signals of a patron's wealth and capability of winning elections (cited in Kitschelt and Wilkinson 2007: 64; see also Chabal and Daloz 1999: 39–44). Less charitably, Richard Banégas reports that voters in Benin see the payment of money for votes as reparation for public funds that politicians are assumed to have stolen (1998: 78). Importantly, only 7 percent of Nigerians would characterize vote buying as "not wrong at all." Education is a powerful solvent to acquiescence: people with primary education are only half as likely as those without formal schooling to see candidate handouts as "not wrong at all."

When they look in the mirror, however, Nigerians are less critical of their *own* behavior. Barely half (49 percent) think that it is "wrong and punishable" for a *voter* to "accept money in return for a vote." The other half of the adult population is willing to excuse participation in a vote-buying transaction as "wrong but understandable" (35 percent) or "not wrong at all" (10 percent). The main extenuating circumstance is poverty; people on the lowest rung of a 5-point poverty scale are only half as likely as those on the top rung to say that the sale of votes is "wrong and punishable."

Between these two electoral violations, which is regarded as the greater evil? When asked about the most important issues in upcoming elections, many more Nigerians demand that "Nigerians should be secure from violence" than those who demand that "vote buying should be controlled" (14 versus 2 percent of all election issues mentioned). These findings suggest that while Nigerians are resistant on moral grounds to both vote buying and electoral violence, they worry more deeply about political intimidation, and many are inclined to forgive voters for succumbing to campaign inducements.

Frequency of Campaign Irregularities

To estimate the frequency and distribution of vote buying and violence in Nigerian election campaigns, I use survey questions about whether individuals encountered offers of "something" (money, food, or a gift) "in return for your vote." or threats of "negative consequences in order to get you to vote a certain way." The survey also asked respondents to report whether they thought "other people in your neighborhood or village" had experienced such encounters.

By midway through the 2007 general election campaign, some 12 percent of interviewed Nigerians acknowledged that a candidate or party agent had offered "something in return for your vote." This level of direct experience with vote buying was slightly lower than that recalled for the 2003 elections, at 16 percent. But the 2007 figure captured only half the campaign period, whereas the 2003 figure covered the entire campaign. We know from research in Taiwan that the pace of vote buying accelerates as the day of the election approaches (Wang and Kurzman 2007), so it is reasonable to project that vote buying in Nigerian elections was at least as frequent in 2007 as in 2003, and quite possibly more so.

Moreover, vote buying may have been more extensive in both campaigns than implied by the figures cited. Experience from Argentina suggests that some people are understandably reluctant to admit that they had been approached with a forbidden offer, especially if they had subsequently entered an agreement and complied with its terms (Brusco, Nazareno, and Stokes 2004). The existence of undercounting in self-assessments is reflected in the respondents' 2007 estimate that fully 28 percent of *other* voters were offered gifts during the 2003 campaign. I therefore consider that the "true" level of vote buying exists within a zone bracketed by a wide confidence interval. I contend that the real frequency of this activity probably lies somewhere between reported levels of personal experience (12 percent in

Nigeria in 2007, which may be an underestimate), and assumed levels of involvement by fellow citizens (28 percent, which may be an overestimate).

In vote-buying transactions in Nigeria, voters are usually offered money (68 percent of all reported attempts), commodities (such as food or clothing, 26 percent) or jobs (6 percent). In 2007 the most common inducement was 500 naira (about US$4). But the median price of a vote payment rose between 2003 and 2007, from 1,750 to 2,250 naira, largely because the proportion of large payments (10,000 naira or more per vote) increased over time.

Relatively few Nigerians report being directly affected by electoral violence. By February 2007, just 4 percent of survey respondents nationwide said they had received "threats of negative consequences." To be sure, political intimidation was geographically concentrated in certain electoral "hot spots," especially the Niger Delta region, where the Afrobarometer recorded personal (13 percent) and observed (18 percent) experiences with electoral violence at rates more than three times higher than the national norm.

The negative consequences of political intimidation include—in approximately equal proportions—perceived reductions in personal safety, in the safety of family members, and in the loss of property. Reports of violent encounters midway through the 2007 campaign were almost as frequent as for the whole 2003 election (5 percent). If the pace of violence also quickens as the vote approaches, one can infer that the actual level of electoral violence was higher in 2007 than 2003 (Human Rights Watch 2007). And because the gap between reported personal and estimated third-party abuses (a difference of 6 percentage points in 2007) was smaller for violence than for vote buying, we can invest greater confidence in the violence data.

Who Are the Victims?

In seeking to control voter behavior, politicians are likely to focus their efforts on vulnerable elements in society. The poor are likely to be victimized by vote buying because their limited means makes them susceptible to material inducements, including offers of basic commodities or modest amounts of money (Stokes 2007). Moreover, people with limited education may be unaware of individual political rights and therefore possess weak defenses against intimidation.

In Nigeria, however, the survey revealed few demographic correlates of exposure to electoral violence. Political intimidation was spread rather evenly across all social groups, whether rich or poor, urban or rural, even male or female. This smooth distribution constitutes further evidence that violence is a general "atmospheric" condition that tends to affect everyone touched by an election campaign. In the only observable statistical effect, education performed as expected: it tended to inoculate Nigerians against explicit threats of retaliation for making the "wrong" vote choice. Whereas 5 percent of people with no formal schooling experienced such threats, just 2 percent of those with postsecondary education did.

By contrast, there were clear demographic correlates of vote buying. Poor Nigerians were most likely to report an encounter with a politician (or a politician's agent) who offered to buy their vote. Those who suffered "many" shortages of basic needs were over four times more likely to be "often" approached with a vote-buying offer than those who could cover their needs. But the poor still drove a hard bargain; they did not quote a lower price than the going rate for selling a vote. Nor were they more likely than anyone else to accept payment in the form of goods-in-kind as opposed to cash. Educated people are not entirely immune from temptation, being almost twice as likely as those without formal schooling to think that a vote is worth 10,000 naira or more.

At face value, it is unclear whether vote buying would be more prevalent in urban or rural areas. On the one hand, poor and uneducated people are concentrated in rural villages, making these areas prime targets for the distribution of patronage. On the other hand, outlying areas are hard for politicians to reach and monitor, which suggests that rural dwellers can easily refuse or defect from reward-driven agreements. The Afrobarometer data show that vote buying in Nigeria is more common in rural than urban areas, a result that is consistent with research from East Asia and Latin America (Ramsayer and Rosenbluth 1993; Shugart and Nielsen 1999). Indeed, in 2003, residential location was the most important demographic consideration of all, trumping both poverty and education. By 2007, however, education and urban residence were equally important considerations in reducing the likelihood of vote buying.

Voting Behavior

I now turn to voting behavior. Intended *voter turnout* is measured by the 66 percent of survey respondents who reported in 2007 that "I am a registered voter and I will vote." Intended *vote choice* is measured by a question that asked, "If elections were held tomorrow, which party's candidate would you vote for as member of the national assembly?" This variable is coded on a 3-point scale running from incumbent-party partisan, through nonpartisan, to opposition-party partisan. As Table 7.1 shows, voters were split in February 2007 between supporters of the incumbent party, the PDP (one-third), and supporters of all opposition parties (a combined two-fifths). Alone, however, the largest opposition party, the All Nigeria People's Party (ANPP), attracted less than one-quarter of the intended votes. Together,

Table 7.1 Vote Choice in Nigeria, 2007 (percentages)

Election	Respondents Who Indicated Support for the Incumbent Party	Respondents Who Were Undecided	Respondents Who Indicated Support for an Opposition Party
National president	33.3	23.0	43.7
National assembly	34.1	27.8	38.1
State governor	36.0	23.0	41.0
State assembly	32.5	28.6	38.9
Mean	34.0	25.6	40.4

Source: Afrobarometer survey, 2007.
Note: Sample size of 2,410 respondents.

these data suggest that neither incumbents nor opposition held a decisive edge in most national races.

How Effective Is Campaign Manipulation?

How do citizens respond to the mix of irregular carrots and sticks employed by politicians in African election campaigns? Are vote buying and violence effective strategies of electoral manipulation?

Voter Turnout

The results of a logistic regression analysis are shown in Table 7.2. Poverty and education perform as expected—the former is negative for turnout and the latter is positive; because neither is statistically significant, both can be discounted. Second, rural residence remains important for turnout since country dwellers are more likely to vote than their urban counterparts (Yadav 2000; Bratton, Chu, and Lagos 2010; Krishna 2008). Third, other demographic considerations now enter the analysis: older people are significantly more likely to vote than younger people, and women are very much less likely to vote than men. Political partisanship, however, is unrelated to voter turnout.

Our main interest is in campaign irregularities. Table 7.2 shows that individuals who experience a vote-buying offer are less likely to vote than those who do not, though the relationship is not significant. As such the Nigeria data do not validate any claim to the effect that vote buying "works," at least in the limited sense of boosting voter turnout. One possible interpretation is that recipients of such offers feel ambivalent: they agonize about whether to comply with the wishes of the vote buyer or to act according to conscience. To resolve this dilemma, individuals sometimes

Table 7.2 Determinants of Voter Turnout in Nigeria, 2007

	B	S.E.	Sig.
Constant	0.773	0.327	0.016
Controls			
Poverty	–0.055	0.053	0.297
Education	0.017	0.023	0.449
Rural	0.427	0.098	0.000
Age	0.009	0.004	0.019
Female	–0.511	0.095	0.000
Incumbent partisan	–0.035	0.055	0.518
Campaign malpractices			
Experienced vote-buying offer	–0.121	0.086	0.163
Experienced threat of violence	–0.796	0.137	0.000

Source: Afrobarometer survey, 2007.
Notes: B = beta coefficient, S.E. = standardized error, Sig. = significance. Nagelkerke R^2 = 0.069. Sample size of 2,229 respondents.

avoid voting altogether. In other words, they engage in a form of defection. An alternative interpretation is that, in some cases, vote buyers succeed in their aim of preventing their opponents' supporters from casting a ballot. This possibility—which then must be interpreted as compliance—arises wherever voters report that they have sold their voter registration cards in return for a payment (Vicente 2008; see also Chauvet and Collier 2009; Collier and Vicente 2011).

Much more powerful is the effect of threatened campaign violence. The effect is again negative, but now it is strong and statistically significant. For an average Nigerian (say, a female rural dweller), and with other variables controlled at their mean level, a threat of violence reduces the odds of intending to vote by 52 percent. Moreover, intimidation's effect seems to be long-lasting, since the model works almost as well if exposure to violence is measured for 2003 rather than 2007. To all appearances, Nigerians who encounter a threat against voting freely often withdraw from the electoral process—that is, they abstain from voting, perhaps persistently. So political intimidation apparently makes citizens so fearful that they abandon their right to vote.

Vote Choice

Do illicit campaign methods affect not only *whether* people vote, but also *how* they vote? A further distinction is necessary for this inquiry: the valence of campaign malpractices. In other words, from where do illegal interventions originate: from incumbent or opposition parties? I assume that both sides are implicated. Take vote buying. Because there were more crimes than victims (485 cases of vote buying experienced by 296 respondents), it follows that many individuals (196, or about two-thirds of all victims) received more than one offer from more than one partisan group. The largest political parties were the most active in vote buying. According to the survey respondents, the ruling PDP made 40 percent of all reported attempts, followed by the leading opposition groups: the ANPP at 31 percent and the Action Congress at 10 percent.

Table 7.3 displays factors that affect whether an individual chooses the incumbent party at the ballot box. The object to be explained is a dummy variable scored as 1 if the individual preferred a PDP candidate in the April 2007 national assembly election and 0 otherwise. Importantly, the incumbent party was apparently much more successful than opposition parties in building support among eligible voters. It is unclear whether this advantage was due to an explicit effort by incumbents to concentrate voter registration drives in their own electoral strongholds. Alternatively, well-known candidates may have found it easier to generate popular enthusiasm than opposition candidates, some of whom were fresh faces newly arrived on the political scene. Whatever the reason, the supporters of Nigerian opposition parties were significantly less likely to plan to turn out on the day of the election.

Table 7.3 Determinants of Choosing the Incumbent Party in Nigeria, 2007

	B	S.E.	Sig.
Constant	−1.323	0.315	0.000
Controls			
Poverty	−0.005	0.053	0.925
Education	0.053	0.023	0.019
Rural	0.182	0.097	0.060
Age	−0.007	0.004	0.069
Female	−0.017	0.094	0.852
Intended voter	0.476	0.102	0.000
Campaign malpractices			
Experienced vote-buying offer from incumbent party	1.633	0.203	0.000
Experienced vote-buying offer from opposition party	−0.063	0.199	0.754
Experienced threat of violence	−0.559	0.155	0.000

Source: Afrobarometer survey, 2007.
Notes: B = beta coefficient, S.E. = standardized error, Sig. = significance. Nagelkerke R^2 = 0.077. Sample size of 2,265 respondents.

But the issue under review is the effectiveness of vote buying and violence. As Table 7.3 shows, violence was counterproductive for the ruling party. People who felt threatened by political intimidation were consistently *less* likely to vote for the incumbent PDP. We do not have the data to determine whether particular incidents of intimidation originated from incumbents or opposition. But I note that the PDP unleashed significant campaign repression as a means to control its own members. Since all political parties in Nigeria have short histories and shallow institutional roots, there is reason to believe that party leaders might easily resort to heavy-handed measures as a means of overcoming weak party discipline, even in their own electoral strongholds. But, contrary to leaders' presumed intentions, violence was associated with *lower* levels of electoral support.

Importantly, partisan choice is also strongly associated with vote buying, but this time positively. In Nigeria in 2007, citizens who received a vote-buying offer from the incumbent party were significantly more likely to express an intention to vote *for* the PDP in the April elections. For an average Nigerian (say, a female rural dweller), and with other variables controlled at their mean level, vote buying by an incumbent was linked to an increase in voting for the ruling party by 38 percent. In other words, efforts by rulers to reward loyalists and attract others to the ruling party told apparently paid off. In this regard, we can interpret vote buying as one aspect of the larger phenomenon of patronage politics in which leaders exchange material rewards in return for political allegiance. It is unclear, however, whether campaign inducements were essential to cementing the loyalty of citizens who already felt an affinity with the PDP, or whether these individuals would have voted for the PDP anyway.

Vote buying by incumbents was apparently more effective than vote buying by opposition parties. True, a vote-buying bid by an opposition party is connected to an opposition vote when the latter is used as the dependent variable (not shown). But in Table 7.3, the effect of opposition vote buying looks weak. One obvious interpretation is that office holders enjoy the advantage of political incumbency. Rulers are able to make offers to voters that are more credible and binding than those of the cash-starved opposition because they enjoy access to a larger pool of resources, including the public purse controlled by the state. The resource edge of incumbency is borne out by supporters of the ruling party, who are more likely than opposition partisans to estimate the price of a vote at 10,000 naira or more.

Popular Reactions: Comply, Defect, or Refuse?

Politicians manipulate campaigns in order to maximize votes. So far, I have shown that material inducements are a more effective means to this end than political intimidation. Because threats of violence suppress voter turnout, intimidation is not a useful campaign tactic except perhaps to counteract an impending electoral loss. By contrast, vote buying appears to boost partisan support, and therefore can be considered—morality and legality aside—as a campaign tactic that "works."

But these judgments make sense mainly from the pragmatic perspective of a politician who seeks to obtain or hang on to office. What courses of action are available to voters in the face of vote buying and violence? Do specific forms of campaign manipulation invite different responses? Under what circumstances do citizens comply, defect, or refuse?

I concentrate the analysis on vote buying because fuller survey data are available on this subject. The Afrobarometer asked, "What would you do if a candidate or party official offered you money for your vote?" Would you "refuse the money and vote for the candidate of your choice" (that is, refuse), "take the money and vote for him/her" (that is, comply), or "take the money and vote for the candidate of your choice" (that is, defect)? The survey also asked respondents to judge the reactions of "other people in your neighborhood or village."

The distribution of responses is shown in Table 7.4. Only a small minority said they would comply (8 percent) by voting for the purchaser's party, attributing exactly the same level of compliance to other people in their locality. Most people said they would defect (42 percent) by taking the money but voting according to conscience. A similar proportion said they would refuse from the outset to enter any vote-buying agreement (41 percent). One respondent elaborated that he would "drive that person away" and another said that she would "call the police."

As might be expected, popular reactions to vote buying depend in part on socioeconomic status. Poor people are slightly more likely to comply and educated people are slightly more likely to refuse. But residential location

Table 7.4 Popular Reactions to Vote Buying in Nigeria, 2007 (percentages)

Reaction to Vote-Buying Offer	"How do you think you would react?"	"How do you think other people would react?"
Comply	8	8
Defect	42	28
Refuse	41	24
Other (including "don't know")	9	40

Source: Afrobarometer survey, 2007.
Note: Sample size of 2,410 respondents.

again makes the largest difference, with rural dwellers being markedly more likely to comply than urban dwellers (10 percent versus 6 percent). Concomitantly, rates of refusal are significantly higher in towns than in the countryside (54 versus 43 percent). Thus, if there is a culture of vote buying in Africa—in which votes are exchanged for campaign rewards—it is predominantly (though not exclusively) a rural phenomenon.

The effectiveness of vote buying also depends in part on the source of the offer (not shown). By a small but significant margin (15 percent versus 11 percent), the PDP was more likely to get a Nigerian voter to say that he or she would comply. Again, the incumbents' ability to offer attractive rewards may be part of the explanation, though we should not discount mass loyalty to ruling parties, which have deeper social roots than insurgent oppositions. Moreover, citizens are also somewhat more likely to defect from the opposition by promising support but then voting freely. Especially where the opposition is unlikely to win, the voter has less reason to fear that defection will result in subsequent retribution from powerful office holders.

I hypothesize that defection is most likely when would-be voters receive vote-buying offers from more than one party. Under these conditions, voters are faced with cross-pressures. They find themselves in the uncomfortable position of being unable to simultaneously comply with the preferences of both sides. Usually, they comply with the wishes of only one party (probably the party they judge most likely to win), hoping that the other party will not be able to punish them. Or they refuse all offers, knowing that it is impossible to keep more than one party happy at the same time.

But there is a third option. As some respondents indicated, it is feasible for voters to take the money and not vote at all. The data reveal that this outcome is especially likely if voters accept inducements from more than one party. We already know that entering a vote-buying agreement has a slight suppressive effect on voter turnout. We now discover that this effect is large when voters face cross-pressures from competing vote buyers. Whereas, in January 2007, 66 percent of Nigerian survey respondents said they intended to vote in the April elections, just 58 percent did so if they had received a vote-buying offer from a political party. But the intention to vote falls even further—to less than half of all eligible voters (49 percent)—when individuals entertain vote-buying offers from more than one political party.

Correlates of Defection

In a democracy, a responsible citizen would refuse to enter a vote-buying agreement. Most Nigerians acknowledge this moral precept and many adopt it in practice. Citizen compliance with the wishes of vote buyers may be the path of least resistance, but it is fraught with ethical and legal dilemmas and undermines the development of democratic citizenship. Perhaps the most rational response—though hardly the most honest one—is defection, when citizens take any money that may be on offer but vote as they wish anyway. Some civic educators even encourage this course of action (Schaffer 2007: 161–179). But the implications for democratization are mixed: while citizens retain and exercise a right of free choice at the polls, they also implicate themselves in an electoral malpractice. One possible saving grace is that if enough citizens repeatedly defect, politicians will learn that vote buying does not work.

Because defection is the most ambiguous and interesting option—not to mention the most common one in Nigeria—I conclude the discussion of vote buying by delving into possible determinants. What drives defection? I propose three hypotheses.

First, the prospect of defection from a vote-buying agreement raises a collective action problem. In order to avoid revealing that they have acted alone—thus exposing themselves to punishment—citizens will seek strength in numbers. They will only violate the agreement if they think others will do so too. Hence, one would expect to find a positive relationship between an individual's own reaction to a vote-buying offer and his or her estimate of what other people would do under the same circumstances. Specifically, people will defect only if they think others will defect too.

Second, voters are more likely to defect if they think that the ballot is secret. If politicians cannot discover how individuals or small groups voted, then the possible costs of defection are greatly reduced. At the time, the Afrobarometer contained no direct measure of whether voters regard the ballot as secret. But a proxy measure can be constructed from a question about how often "people have to be careful of what they say about politics." Those who say "often" or "always" are deemed to express political fear (66 percent in Nigeria); this group probably also worries that the ballot may not be secret.

Third, citizens who are committed to democracy as their preferred political regime are unlikely to surrender the right to vote lightly. It is reasonable to expect that most will refuse offers to buy their votes. But even if such persons succumb to illicit campaign inducements, they are still likely to want to make a free choice. I therefore propose that committed democrats are more likely to defect than individuals who harbor nostalgia for authoritarian rule. Commitment to democracy is measured by a standard index that combines an expressed preference for democracy with rejection of several alternative authoritarian regimes (Bratton, Mattes, and Gyimah-Boadi 2005). By this criterion, about half (49 percent) of adult Nigerians could be characterized as "committed democrats" in 2007.

These correlates of defection from vote buying are entered, along with the usual controls, into the logistic regression model in Table 7.5. All three hypotheses are confirmed. First, a committed democrat is unlikely to sell his or her vote lightly. Even if some of these individuals accept payments from vote buyers, they still report that they vote according to conscience (i.e., they defect). This explanation does not preclude, of course, that such voters might choose the vote buyer's party, but they assert that the preferences underlying this partisan choice are their own.

Moreover, people who are fearful of expressing themselves have a reduced propensity to defect. Especially if voters suspect that the ballot is not secret—an impression that unscrupulous politicians are in no hurry to dispel—defection will be seen as too risky. The biggest danger is that vote buyers will discover that voters have not kept their part of the bargain, an outcome that invites retaliation and punishment. So it stands to reason that those who doubt that freedoms of expression and voting will be protected are unlikely to become defectors.

Finally, I report a definitive result: defection from vote buying depends on solving the collective action problem. Voters defect if they have some assurance that others in their locality will do so too. As revealed in Table 7.5, the strongest and most significant relationship with defection is voters' own expectations that they are partaking in the collective behavior of a larger group. For an average Nigerian (say, a female rural dweller), and with other variables controlled at mean levels, the expectation that others will defect is associated with an increase in one's own odds of defecting by 59 percent. I do not know for sure whether would-be defectors have reliable

Table 7.5 Determinants of Defection from Vote Buying in Nigeria, 2007

	B	S.E.	Sig.
Constant	−0.357	0.378	0.344
Controls			
Poverty	−0.146	0.061	0.017
Education	−0.028	0.026	0.291
Rural	0.272	0.110	0.014
Age	−0.014	0.004	0.001
Female	−0.219	0.108	0.042
Determinants			
Think that others will defect	2.811	0.130	0.000
Express political fear	−0.166	0.053	0.002
Committed to democracy	0.235	0.099	0.017

Source: Afrobarometer survey, 2007.
Notes: Nagelkerke $R^2 = 0.371$. Sample size of 2,166 respondents.

information about the planned voting behavior of their friends and neighbors. But such subjects are surely a topic of communal conversation. As
such, citizens can probably figure out whether they can subsume their own
behavior within that of a larger group, and thus avoid being singled out for
retribution. Under these circumstances, they are very much more likely to
take the money and run.

Complementary or Alternative Strategies?

I have treated vote buying and political intimidation as if political campaign-
ers see such interventions as alternatives. Accordingly, politicians who lack
sufficient resources to buy off voters will be prone to resort to heavy-handed
methods. Or if violence backfires, then they will try to tempt voters with rewards. A third possibility is that voters will experience promises of reward
from one side of the partisan divide and threats of violence from another.

Table 7.6 teases out the links between, on the one hand, a combination
of vote buying and violence and, on the other, voting behavior. It displays a
cross-tabulation of two ordinal scales: a scale of exposure (to none, one, or
both violations) and a scale of intended compliance (ranging from refusal,
through defection, to compliance). It shows that combining vote buying and
violence had little appreciable association with the likelihood that a voter
would refuse to enter an agreement (to vote a certain way) or comply with
such an agreement (if they did enter). In other words, a threat of violence or
an offer of a material inducement alone would be just as effective as a combination of these influences.

But a voter who experienced both vote buying and violence was more
likely to defect, either by not voting at all or by exercising a free vote choice.
The probability of this connection rises by 6 percentage points when he or

Table 7.6 Combined Effects of Vote Buying and Violence on Voter Behavior in Nigeria, 2007 (percentages)

Reaction to Vote-Buying Offer	Experienced *Neither* Vote Buying *Nor* Threat of Violence	Experienced *Either* Vote Buying *Or* Threat of Violence	Experienced *Both* Vote Buying *And* Threat of Violence
Refuse	51	30	29
Defect	42	57	63
Comply	8	13	9

Source: Afrobarometer survey, 2007.
Note: Respondents who answered "don't know/other" about how they would react to vote buying
are excluded. Sample size of 2,252 respondents.

she is subjected to both treatments. The most extreme scenario involves a voter who is induced to vote one way (say by an incumbent party) but threatened to vote another way (say by an opposition group). This harsh combination of cross-pressures is also much more likely to be linked to defection than compliance.

Conclusion

This chapter has shown that vote buying and political intimidation are important, if epiphenomenal, dimensions of Nigerian election campaigns. According to survey-based estimates, fewer than one out of five Nigerians are personally exposed to vote buying and fewer than one in ten experience threats of electoral violence. But when, as commonly happens, campaign irregularities are targeted at the rural poor, their effects are concentrated. I find that violence reduces turnout, and vote buying enhances partisan loyalty. But perhaps because most citizens condemn campaign manipulation as wrong, compliance with the wishes of politicians is not ensured. Defection from threats and agreements is more common than compliance, especially where voters are cross-pressured from both sides of the partisan divide.

That vote buying and violence affect relatively few people and rarely work well does not mean that these malpractices are inconsequential. As others have noted, the intrusion of money and violence into election campaigns damages the quality of democracy (Schedler 2006; Schaffer 2007). These transgressions undermine democratic norms of political liberty (by depriving voters of free choice) and political equality (by benefiting the rich at the expense of the poor). They diminish the legitimacy of electoral outcomes by giving "losers" reason to think that the vote was fraudulent. Even without other methods of manipulation—such as ballot stuffing, ballot stealing, and tampering with vote tallies—Nigeria's disastrous April 2007 elections suffered precisely this fate.

Negative consequences may be long-lasting, because defective election campaigns set the stage for governance by corruption. As a defeated gubernatorial candidate in Nigeria said: "Anyone who is willing to steal a ballot box will [also] steal public money" (author interview 2000). Vote buying and violence elevate unsuitable cronies, criminals, and strong-arm "godfathers" to public office. As a result, policy debates—for example on the balance between taxation and services—remain distorted: the preferences of the rich are amplified and the views of the poor are muffled (Stokes 2007; Acemoglu and Robinson 2006). All told, irregular elections reduce the institutionalization of political accountability.

Campaign irregularities may also infect the quality of democratic citizenship. It is encouraging that most Nigerians see vote buying and electoral violence as wrong. But morality, as well as behavior, may be communally defined. We know that people who enter vote-buying agreements are more likely to defect if they think others will do so too. The normative dimension of this solution to the collective action problem, however, is that participants in vote buying and violence are also likely to regard these infractions as "wrong but understandable" or "not wrong at all." If participation in electoral malpractices reduces critical citizenship, it can hardly be healthy for the development of democracy.

8

Museveni and the 2011 Ugandan Election: Did the Money Matter?

Jeffrey Conroy-Krutz and Carolyn Logan

On February 18, 2011, Ugandan president Yoweri Museveni won a resounding reelection victory, extending his tenure until 2016, some thirty years after he first seized power. The length of Museveni's reign is striking even by African standards, particularly in light of the promise he offered at his first inauguration, in 1986, that "we [his National Resistance Army] shall be here for only four years, after which we shall hand over power to a free and fairly elected civilian government." Museveni is in many ways a study in contradictions. He has been lauded at home and abroad for his pathbreaking policies on universal primary education, HIV/AIDS, and decentralization, yet criticized for his long record of antiparty sentiments, corruption, and most recently, harsh crackdowns on nascent public demonstrations. This mix of carrot and stick has made Museveni one of the most durable rulers in postindependence Africa.

In the run-up to the 2011 electoral campaign, however, many of Museveni's opponents sensed that his days might be numbered. Steadily growing support for opposition candidates over the course of the last several elections, well-publicized corruption scandals, deepening rifts within the ruling National Resistance Movement (NRM), and increasing disquiet among key ethnic groups seemed to augur poorly for the incumbent. However, when the Afrobarometer released results from a preelection survey in December 2010 revealing that nearly two-thirds of Ugandans intended to vote for Museveni, the news was met in some quarters with anger or even outright disbelief. Several subsequent surveys, however, produced similar findings, ultimately confirmed by the eventual outcome of the election: Museveni secured 68 percent of the vote, while his main challenger, Kizza Besigye, garnered 26 percent.

Rather than emerging from this victory with renewed confidence and a strengthened hand, Museveni seemed more challenged than ever. In the months after the election, Kampala and other urban centers were roiled by demonstrations. Opposition supporters took to the streets, joined by lawyers, women's groups, and—perhaps most worrisome for Museveni—the merchant class, primarily (though not exclusively) to protest skyrocketing prices for fuel and basic commodities.

Ironically, the roots of these troubles, as well as the constraints on the state's capacity to mitigate them, may lie in the president's successful—but very expensive—reelection campaign. By all accounts, the government and ruling party spent lavishly during the campaign. State resources purchased everything from extensive advertising to public goods, as well as reported attempts to buy the political support of powerful local brokers and individual voters through cash disbursements (Izama and Wilkerson 2011: 67–68). In the aftermath of the election, many observers attributed Museveni's comfortable win to this spending, which, they contended, had severely tilted the playing field.

While the monetization of Ugandan politics amounted to an undemocratic use of state resources, we find little evidence in public opinion data to substantiate claims that Museveni essentially "bought" reelection. Rather, we find that the outcome can best be attributed to widespread public satisfaction with sustained economic growth, and especially with the peace dividend enjoyed in the north, alongside discontent with a fractionalized and uninspiring slate of opposition candidates. Self-reported beneficiaries of vote buying and public goods were not significantly more likely to have supported Museveni than their counterparts who reported no such largesse. In other words, the unprecedented level of campaign spending may not have yielded significant electoral gains for the incumbent. But the massive economic infusion likely exacerbated the inflationary pressures that became the source of many of the president's woes while, at the same time, depleted state coffers constrained the government's capacity to respond. The paradox—and tragedy—is that in the wake of harsh crackdowns on dissent, Uganda appeared to be backsliding democratically just months after an election that was perhaps the most peaceful and representative in several decades.

The Run-Up: Opposition Optimism

Going into the 2011 elections, many opponents of Museveni and the NRM were convinced of an impending electoral turnover in Uganda. This optimism stemmed from three factors. First, Museveni's support had tracked downward over three previous elections, from 76 percent of the vote in 1996, to 69 percent in 2001, to 59 percent in 2006, the latter being the first elections after the restoration of multiparty competition (in a deal that also eliminated presidential term limits). Many believed that this downward trajectory indicated that the public were tiring of Museveni.

Second, opposition adherents also saw opportunity in an apparent rift between Museveni and the Baganda, the country's largest ethnic group. Museveni had first won the allegiance of many Baganda during the bush war of the 1980s, when his National Resistance Army fought against President Milton Obote, whose troops had been committing atrocities in the Luweero Triangle. His status was further cemented when he restored traditional kingdoms in 1993, invited the exiled Kabaka (Buganda king) to return to the country, and allowed for the restoration of the Lukiiko (Buganda parliament) and other traditional institutions. As a result, the Baganda, who live primarily in the central region of the country around Kampala, threw the bulk of their electoral support behind Museveni.

However, two more recent developments opened a growing schism. First, in September 2009, the government blocked the king from attending a ceremony in Kayunga, arguing that since parts of that district had recently announced, unilaterally, their secession from Buganda, the king's presence might spark violence. The perceived insult to the king was met with outrage, resulting in days of rioting in Kampala and other areas, and several dozen deaths.

Potentially even more damaging to the relationship was the burning of the Kasubi Tombs in March 2010. As the burial place of four Buganda kings and declared a World Heritage Site by the United Nations Educational, Scientific, and Cultural Organization, the tombs are revered by Baganda. When Museveni tried to visit the site the following day, angry protesters initially blocked him, and two people were killed in subsequent violence. An investigation attributed the burning to a deranged individual, and Museveni promised support for rebuilding, but the event was a serious blow to relations between the government and Buganda.

A parliamentary by-election in Mukono North, near Kampala, in May 2010, just weeks after the Kasubi incident, was seen as a bellwether for how Museveni might fare in Buganda in 2011. The Democratic Party, the most pro-Buganda opposition group, ran Betty Nambooze, a former radio host and fervent critic of Museveni, who referred to herself as the *Omukungu wa Kabaka*, or "king's loyal envoy." Her NRM opponent, Reverend Peter Bakaluba Mukasa, warned voters, "If you vote for Nambooze, it will be a vote of no confidence in President Museveni," and Museveni made several campaign visits in an attempt to save the seat (Kiggundu 2010). Nambooze claimed victory with nearly 53 percent of the vote, leaving many in the opposition increasingly bullish about 2011.

Third, opposition hopes were boosted further by the perceived high caliber of several candidates. First among them was Kizza Besigye, who was making his third attempt at the presidency. A former NRM stalwart and physician to Museveni, Besigye split with the NRM in the 1990s, and thereafter became Museveni's most prominent opponent. He had gained increasing support over the two previous elections, from 28 percent of the vote in 2001 to 37 percent in 2006.

Others were excited about the candidacies of Olara Otunnu, Uganda's former ambassador to the United Nations and a noted human rights advocate, who ran under the banner of the Uganda Peoples' Congress (UPC), and Norbert Mao, a smooth-talking lawyer, who tried—with some success (Nalugo 2010)—to present himself as Uganda's Obama. Mao, a northerner who won the nomination of the Buganda-centered Democratic Party, had the perceived advantage of being from mixed parentage, with an Acholi father and a Munyankole mother, a potentially significant asset in an environment where ethnicity is perceived to play an important role in vote choice.

There were abortive attempts to field a single opposition candidate under the banner of the Inter-Party Coalition (IPC), which had signed an alliance protocol in 2009. The IPC brought together several parties, including Besigye's Forum for Democratic Change (FDC), the UPC, the Justice Forum, and the Conservative Party. The effort collapsed, however, over the selection of a presidential flag bearer as well as questions about whether to participate in elections without first winning changes in the composition of the national electoral commission, which was filled with Museveni appointees. Otunnu, whose successful return from a twenty-three-year exile might not have been possible without the support of the IPC, eventually pulled out because of these issues (Mubangizi 2010), while the Democratic Party never signed on. Nonetheless, many in the opposition likely calculated that the two-round system reduced the need for a preelection pact.

The Result: A Resounding Opposition Defeat

The opposition's confidence waned during the campaign, in part due to the release of the December 2010 Afrobarometer survey. Besigye lagged with just 12 percent of intended votes, Mao and Otunnu languished in low single digits, and several other candidates barely registered any support (Afrobarometer 2010). Although the opposition and some media commentators dismissed the findings and questioned the methodologies and the loyalties of the Afrobarometer (Among 2010; Mulondo 2010; Kalyegira 2010, 2011; Mugerwa 2011), a second Afrobarometer survey, conducted in January 2011 (Afrobarometer 2011), as well as surveys commissioned by the state-run *New Vision* newspaper (Olupot 2011), and by the opposition itself (Olupot 2010), all put Museveni ahead with 65–70 percent of the prospective vote.

These results were borne out on election day with a remarkable degree of accuracy, when Museveni took 68 percent of valid votes cast, an increase of over 9 points from 2006. Besigye captured just 26 percent, a decline of 10 points, while Mao and Otunnu took 1.9 percent and 1.6 percent respectively. Even in Kampala, long an opposition stronghold, Museveni came within 4,000 votes of topping Besigye, a difference of less than 1 percentage point. In the meantime, Besigye claimed just four districts: Kampala and three in the Teso subregion. And Mao won only his home of Gulu and two neighboring districts. Besigye does appear to have won the votes of many of those who reported themselves to be "undecided" in the Afrobarometer and other surveys—he overperformed compared to the preelection surveys by an average of 11 points—but this was clearly not enough to put him within striking distance of Museveni. Even though turnout was not robust by Ugandan standards—59 percent of registered voters cast a ballot, as opposed to 69 percent in 2006—the results demonstrated a resounding victory for the NRM.

None of the opposition presidential candidates accepted the results. In a press conference, Besigye called the election a "sham" and accused the government of organizing "well planned electoral rigging that we have never seen before" (Bareebe 2011). Otunnu said the results were indicative of "subjugation and suppression" and quickly called for protests (Khisa 2011). Mao characterized Museveni as "an obstacle to democracy" under whom "elections have become a meaningless ritual," and called for "a campaign of defiance." Within a week, these three candidates were calling for peaceful protests to challenge the results. They sought to take advantage of the cracks that appeared in the armor of many longtime incumbents in the wake of the prolonged protests in Cairo's Tahrir Square, which had succeeded in ousting Egyptian president Hosni Mubarak only a week before the Ugandan election. But early protests were not sustained and did little more than create some hours of inconvenience in Kampala.

In contrast, the Ugandan public was relatively sanguine about the quality of the electoral process, at least prior to the election. In the January 2011 Afrobarometer survey, 61 percent said they expected the election to be completely free and fair, or free and fair with only minor problems. Similar majorities believed that the national electoral commission was unbiased in its work (57 percent), and that the security forces were performing their duties in an impartial and neutral manner (60 percent). More than two-thirds (70 percent) reported that, on the whole, media coverage of all candidates and parties had been either "somewhat fair" or "very fair." And the police got especially high marks for performing "fairly well" or "very well" in "maintaining a secure environment for the elections" (85 percent) and for acting "somewhat fairly" or "very fairly" in "regulating public demonstrations and campaign rallies" (81 percent). However, Ugandans were sharply divided on these issues along party lines: three-quarters (75 percent) of NRM supporters anticipated that the election would be mostly or completely free and fair, compared to just 33 percent of opposition supporters.

With regard to the quality of the elections, the findings of several international observer missions, as well as the domestic observer coalition DEMGroup, were decidedly mixed. All agreed that election day went considerably better than in 2006. But observers were also consistent in noting that the voting process in many locations was marred by significant administrative problems, and that the large deployment of security forces on voting day had the potential to intimidate voters. None suggested, however, that these problems were widespread enough to affect the final tally significantly. Several reports specifically cited the transparency of the vote-counting process (EAC-COMESA-IGAD 2011; African Union 2011), while DEMGroup (2011a) found that the final vote count reflected the ballots cast and concluded that the election was "mostly free and somewhat fair."

At the same time, most observers failed to endorse the election. The European Union and Commonwealth observers, in particular, strenuously objected to what they described as the "abuse of incumbency," and the "commercialization of politics" (COG 2011; EU-EOM 2011b). Describing the elections as Uganda's "most expensive ever" (EU-EOM 2011b: 19), observers saved their strongest critique for the rampant (mis)use of state resources on the part of Museveni and the NRM, and the fundamental failure, as a result, to establish a level playing field. Observers described a variety of problems, ranging from blatant vote buying and distribution of "vast amounts of money and gifts" to "other more subtle forms of buying allegiance" (EU-EOM 2011b: 19), including the use of government projects to secure support for the NRM, as well as the creation of new districts—sometimes announced by Museveni during his campaign rallies—as outlets for additional patronage (COG 2011: 25–26).

Critics note that the NRM increased spending in the 2010–2011 budget by a robust 16 percent. In addition, just halfway through the fiscal year, parliament approved a supplementary budget of 602 billion Ugandan shillings (approximately US$260 million), of which 85 billion (US$37 million) was assigned to the presidency (EU-EOM 2011b: 24). All told, about US$1.3 billion of the government's budget was spent in January 2011 alone (Izama and Wilkerson 2011: 68).

There were widespread suspicions that these funds had been allocated largely for campaign purposes. As part of the supplementary budget, each member of parliament (including opposition members) received a disbursement of 20 million Ugandan shillings (approximately US$8,700). According to the European Union's election observation mission, "most NRM candidates used government projects such as the National Agricultural Advisory Services (NAADS) and the Northern Uganda Social Action Fund (NUSAF) as tools to press voters to adhere to the NRM should they wish to benefit from such projects," this amid widespread accusations that the government was spending lavishly, building roads, schools, and clinics, providing agricultural implements and supplies, and undertaking other public-works projects as well (EU-EOM 2011b: 12). Some observers found the government's withdrawal of about US$740 million from Uganda's central bank during the campaign to be highly suspicious (Izama and Wilkerson 2011: 68). Reports cited NRM campaign spending figures as high as half a trillion Ugandan shillings (about US$200 million). The European Union's election observation mission cited the "persistent fusion of the state and the ruling party during the campaign," concluding that "the power of incumbency and state resources were used to such an extent as to compromise severely the level playing field between the competing candidates and political parties" (EU-EOM 2011b: 5, 20–25). DEMGroup likewise concluded that "the pervasive use of money to decide elections has become an entrenched norm in Uganda" (DEMGroup 2011b: 10).

Data and Analysis

What went so wrong for the opposition, and so right for Museveni? Did the outcome of the 2011 election depend as much on money as many commentators suggest? Or did other factors play an equal, or perhaps even greater, role? What of the opposition's confidence in its slate, the public's seeming weariness with Museveni, and the perception of a deep Baganda rift?

To explore these questions, we draw on data from two Afrobarometer preelection surveys, as well as two waves of a more geographically limited panel study that focused on Ugandans' attitudes regarding the campaign. The Afrobarometer surveys, conducted in November 2010 and January 2011, were based on random samples of 2,000 adults distributed across about half of Uganda's 112 districts. The panel study, independently designed by one of this chapter's authors, selected approximately 120 respondents from each of nine constituencies distributed around the country. All four of Uganda's regions were represented, with the constituencies chosen to ensure that all major ethnic groups were included. The first wave of the study, conducted in November 2010, comprised 1,072 interviews; the second wave, conducted in late March and early April 2011 following the February election, comprised 675 follow-up interviews. Unlike data from the Afrobarometer, data from the panel study are not nationally representative, but they nonetheless provide useful perspective on—and in some cases confirmation of—Afrobarometer findings.

For example, both methods yield little evidence that the reported beneficiaries of the government's massive distribution of resources were significantly more likely to report having voted for the incumbent. Rather, the surveys provide stronger evidence that Museveni's victory derived from voter unease with the crop of opposition candidates, the robustness of support for the NRM in Buganda, and a sense among many northerners that, with the conclusion of the war in the region against the Lord's Resistance Army, citizens were better off on election day 2011 than they were five years earlier.

Buying the Election?

As noted, opponents and observers charge the NRM with widely distributing largesse in the form of vote buying, an infusion of funds into community development projects, and the profligate designation of new districts. We examine each of these in turn.

Vote Buying

Vote buying is illegal in Uganda, but reportedly widespread. To begin, Ugandans believe that vote buying is rampant: in late 2010, 56 percent thought that candidates often or always buy votes during elections (Afrobarometer 2010). Asked whether they themselves had received a vote-buying offer in the 2011 campaign, 14 percent said they had received an offer by early December 2010, and 17 percent said they had received an offer by late January 2011 (Afrobarometer 2011). In the postelection wave of the panel study, approximately one month after the election, 25 percent of respondents reported that a candidate or party had offered them something during the campaign, while 43 percent said that they had witnessed such distributions to other people.

When the Afrobarometer (2011) asked Ugandans how they would respond to offers of money in exchange for their vote, 19 percent claimed they would refuse the offer. Fully three-quarters (76 percent) said they would defect, meaning that they would accept the offer but make their own choices about whether to vote and for whom. A mere 4 percent said they would comply. The figures shifted slightly when respondents were asked what other people in their neighborhood or village would do, but the overall pattern was similar: two-thirds (66 percent) believed that others would defect, compared to only 7 percent who believed that others would comply (18 percent were unsure). The low reported impact of vote buying could reflect some social desirability bias, but further analysis confirms the tactic's lack of significant effectiveness.

Consistent with the emerging storyline, the NRM was reported to be the source of most (67 percent) vote-buying offers. The FDC made 20 percent of the offers, while the UPC and the Democratic Party trailed at just 5 percent each. In line with Eric Kramon (see Chapter 6 in this volume; see also Vicente 2008), we find that recipients of offers from the NRM were more likely to report having turned out to vote (92 percent versus 84 percent). Importantly, however, those who reported receiving an offer from the NRM were actually slightly *less* likely to say that they intended to vote for the ruling party (see Figure 8.1). Similarly, in the postelection panel wave, self-reported voters were not significantly more likely to say they voted for Museveni if they received an offer from the NRM (81 percent) than if they did not (77 percent).

The evident lack of effectiveness of vote buying cannot be explained by how the offers were targeted. Early in the interviews, Afrobarometer respondents were asked, "Do you feel close to any particular political party?" and, if yes, "Which party is that?" In response, 62 percent reported feeling close to the NRM, 13 percent to the FDC, and 7 percent to other parties; 9 percent were not close to any party. Only 29 percent of the NRM's reported offers went to opposition partisans, of whom only 1 percent reported an intention to vote for Museveni; in the meantime, 5 percent of opposition partisans who did not receive an NRM offer reported an intention to vote for

Figure 8.1 Voting Intentions Relative to Vote-Buying Offers in Uganda, 2011

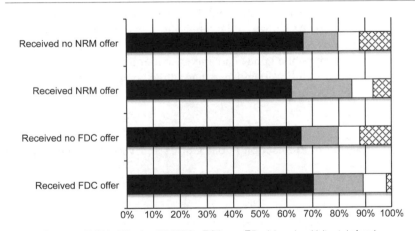

Source: Afrobarometer survey, 2011.
Notes: Afrobarometer question: "If a presidential election were held tomorrow, which party's candidate would you vote for as president?" Weighted sample: 1,712 respondents received no offer from the National Resistance Movement (NRM) and 288 respondents did; 1,916 respondents received no offer from the Forum for Democratic Change (FDC) and 84 did. Unweighted sample: 1,700 respondents received no offer from the NRM and 299 did; 1,909 respondents received no offer from the FDC and 90 did.

Museveni. Opposition offers seem similarly ineffective. Of the offers made by the opposition, 64 percent were directed at individuals affiliated with the NRM. But less than 3 percent of those NRM partisans who received an opposition offer said they would vote for an opposition candidate, compared to 2 percent of NRM partisans who did not receive an opposition offer. We thus find no evidence to suggest that any party's efforts to buy votes changed voter intentions or that vote buying gave the NRM any significant advantage over its competitors, at least in the presidential race.

Public Goods

The postelection wave of the panel study gathered data on the provision of public goods in the preelection environment. Respondents were asked whether their village or neighborhood had benefited from new or improved services in any of the following sectors during the previous six months: schools, health clinics, roads, water supply, and sanitation. As Table 8.1 shows, fully 47 percent of respondents reported at least one improved service, a remarkably high rate of investment. One-third (33 percent) reported new or improved roads in their area, 18 percent schools, 14 percent water supplies, 12 percent clinics, and 9 percent sanitary systems.

But the lack of effect on vote choice is notable. Those who benefited from improvements were actually slightly less likely to identify themselves as Museveni voters. As shown in the table, those who did not benefit from any improvements might have been slightly less likely to vote, so it is possible that receiving public goods had a modest mobilization effect. But this analysis offers no significant evidence that public goods outlays were an effective tool for boosting Museveni's support.

Table 8.1 Provision of Preelection Public Goods and Vote Choice in Uganda, 2011

Number of Improvements Reported	Number of Respondents	Percentage of Respondents	Percentage Who Voted	Vote Share for Museveni[a]
0	357	53	82	78
1	165	24	89	75
2	79	12	89	77
3–5	74	11	88	83
All respondents	675	100	88	78

Source: Panel study, postelection wave, March–April 2011.
Note: a. This is the vote share only among those in this group who said they did vote in the election.

Districtization

The NRM has also been accused of purchasing support through an innovative strategy: the proliferation of local district governments. When Museveni took office in 1986, there were just 33 districts in Uganda, but his government has more than tripled that number to 112 by the time of the 2011 elections. This rapid process of "districtization," as Ugandans have dubbed it (Green 2010), has made Uganda one of the most densely administered countries in the world, with more primary administrative units at the grassroots level than any other country. While the stated impetus for district proliferation has been a need to improve governance, Elliot Green (2010) finds little supportive evidence. Rather, he argues that districtization has served Museveni well, proving an effective means for expanding his patronage network, and helping him to win elections (see also Tripp 2010).

Of the 80 districts that existed at the time of the 2006 elections, 25 were subdivided (some more than once) into 57 districts; the other 55 districts were unaffected. This aggressive creation of new districts had only modest impacts on electoral outcomes. Table 8.2 shows the change in Museveni's vote share across new, parent, and old/unchanged districts between 2006 and 2011. While there was a large increase in Museveni's vote share across all three groups, his share increased by approximately 5 percentage points in new and parent districts relative to districts that saw no change. Since just over one-third (37 percent) of all registered voters live in new or parent districts, this translates at the national level into a roughly 2-point increase in Museveni's national vote share potentially due to districtization, out of a total increase of 9 points. In short, districtization appears to have helped Museveni, but the effects have been quite modest, and there is nothing to suggest that he would not have done quite well even in its absence. As with vote buying and public goods outlays, the evidence does not support the contention that these investments played a decisive role in

Table 8.2 Effects of Districtization on Vote Share in Uganda, 2011

Type of District (N)	Museveni's 2006 Vote Share	Museveni's 2011 Vote Share	Change in Museveni's Vote Share, 2006–2011
Old/unchanged (55)	58.9	66.0	+7.1
Parent (25)	49.5	62.4	+12.9
New (32)	56.1	68.3	+12.2

Source: Electoral Commission of Uganda.

Museveni's reelection. We thus conclude that the foundations of Museveni's 2011 success lie elsewhere, and turn to an exploration of several alternative explanations.

Opposition Weakness

Was the opposition fielding a strong slate of candidates? The first hurdle for any nonincumbent is name recognition. In Uganda, where independent media are relatively strong, the deck might not have been stacked as much against the opposition as in other places in Africa. The privately owned *Monitor* (daily) and *Observer* (weekly) newspapers compete with the state-owned *New Vision* (daily) newspaper. And dozens of private radio and television stations fill the airwaves, offering a wide array of alternatives to the state-run Uganda Broadcasting Corporation.

Even so, survey data suggest limitations in the public's recognition of candidates. Fully 91 percent of Afrobarometer respondents could name two candidates in December 2010, and 66 percent could name three (the maximum number allowed by that survey), suggesting that most Ugandans could name at least a couple of alternatives to Museveni. Results from the panel survey (in which there was no limit to the number of candidates respondents could list), however, suggest that, aside from Museveni and Besigye (96 percent and 74 percent recognition respectively), no other candidates were sufficiently widely known, at least at the campaign's outset in November 2010, to be considered serious contenders: only 36 percent named Otunnu, 33 percent Mao, and 29 percent Beti Kamya of the Uganda Federal Alliance, the only female candidate.

In order to be successful, a challenger needs not just name recognition, but a positive public image as well. Yet in general, opposition parties in Africa do not enjoy public confidence; they are often ranked among the least-trusted political institutions, falling well behind ruling parties (Logan 2008). Uganda is no exception: in the December 2010 Afrobarometer, 60 percent of respondents expressed trust in the ruling party, while just 39 percent trusted opposition parties.

Nor do opposition parties fare well individually. As shown in Figure 8.2, no more than one-quarter of respondents express a liking for any major opposition party, including the UPC and the Democratic Party. The relatively high numbers who say they are neutral (or "don't know") suggest that many Ugandans have still not formed opinions about specific opposition parties. These results are confirmed by the findings of the first panel wave. If respondents could name a candidate, they were then asked to rate how effective that candidate would be at reducing poverty and improving security, and his or her honesty. The opposition candidates consistently fared

Figure 8.2 Popular Assessments of Ruling and Opposition Parties in Uganda, 2011

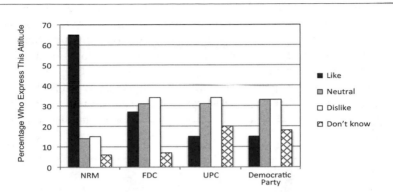

Source: Afrobarometer survey, 2010.

Note: Afrobarometer question: "What do you think about each of the political parties participating in the forthcoming elections? Please say whether you strongly dislike, dislike, feel neutral about, like, or strongly like that party."

far worse than Museveni. All of the opposition candidates except Mao started the campaign with net negatives—that is, more people rated them unfavorably than favorably on these grounds (see Figure 8.3). Moreover, even among those respondents who named the opposition candidates, large numbers could not express an opinion about their honesty or abilities (not shown).

Finally, panel respondents were also asked to name the most important issue facing the country, and then identify which candidate would be most capable of dealing with that issue. Again, Museveni was the overwhelming favorite: 61 percent identified him as most capable of addressing their priority issue, while all other candidates were identified by fewer than 10 percent of respondents. The panel also asked respondents to name the party they trusted most to deal with specific development tasks. On issue after issue—land reform, wealth distribution, fighting terrorism, creating jobs, public service provision, and controlling prices—the named party was the National Resistance Movement. On average, fully 64 percent named the NRM, compared to just 8 percent who named the FDC, and 3 percent each who named the Democratic Party and the UPC—well below the 7 percent who said "none of them" (14 percent said they didn't know).

In sum, opposition parties started the campaign at a severe disadvantage in terms of public perceptions. And over the course of the campaign, opposition candidates, rather than overcoming these deficits, appeared to lose ground. When asked in the November 2010 Afrobarometer whether "the opposition has presented a convincing vision and plan for Uganda," versus

**Figure 8.3 Net Favorable or Unfavorable Ratings of Candidates in
Uganda, 2011**

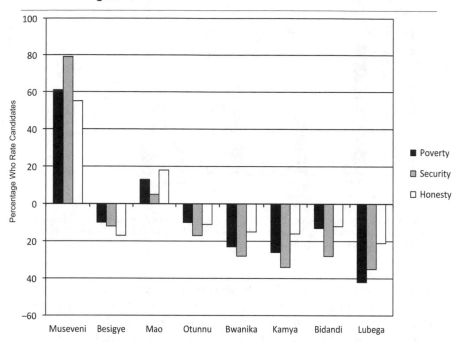

Source: Panel study, first wave, November 2010.
Notes: Panel study question: "In your opinion, how capable of reducing poverty, how capable of improving security, and how honest is [named candidate]?" Response options: "very,"
"somewhat," "not very," "not at all," and "don't know." The ratings portrayed here reflect only
the views of those who could name a given candidate.

whether "the opposition has not shown that it has the plans to solve the
country's problems," Ugandans were roughly evenly split in their assessment (45 percent versus 44 percent). When the same question was asked
again in January 2011, however, an 11-point gap had opened, and a majority
(53 percent) reported that the opposition was not presenting a convincing alternative vision, compared to just 42 percent who thought it was. It appears
that Besigye, Otunnu, Mao, and the others were having little success in convincing the Ugandan public that they were ready to take the helm.

 After the election, commentators made unfavorable contrasts between
the presidential candidates: "Where Besigye projected himself as a national
statesman, Museveni positioned himself as a local politician. Where Besigye articulated a grand, national vision, Museveni focused on mundane
local issues. Besigye came across as idealistic with a high sense of morality; Museveni was realistic, pragmatic and practical if not opportunistic"
(Mwenda 2011). A voter echoed this sentiment, suggesting that Besigye's

focus on possible electoral malfeasance was misguided: "Besigye forgot that he has to get the vote first before concentrating on protecting it" (Were 2011).

The opposition also overestimated the depth of the rift between Museveni and Buganda. Ultimately, the incumbent won twenty-two out of twenty-three districts in the region, and his vote share increased from 57 percent in 2006 to 61 percent in 2011. Concomitantly, Besigye's vote share dropped by 5 points, from 36 percent in 2006 to 31 percent in 2011.

The Democratic Party, long a favorite of Baganda monarchists (Carbone 2008: 12–13), also underperformed. The party's controversial nomination of Mao, a non-Muganda, might have backfired, since it exacerbated existing schisms within the party. Instead, Baganda voters continued to register high levels of satisfaction with Museveni's administration. In the end, Mao won only 2.2 percent of the vote in Buganda—down from the 2.7 percent that Democratic Party candidate John Ssebaana Kizito won in 2006.

Economic Gains, War Weariness

Finally, we recall the opposition's hope that the downward trend in Museveni's vote share over three previous elections suggested that the Ugandan public was growing weary of his rule. Afrobarometer data suggest that this hope, too, was misplaced.

It is true that overall ratings of government performance dropped between 2005 and 2011, often substantially. At the same time, Uganda experienced relatively strong economic growth despite the global economic downturn. This is reflected, albeit relatively modestly, in respondents' improved ratings of the country's general economic condition, as well as of their own economic status. Some 43 percent rated their own living conditions as "fairly good" or "very good" in January 2011, up from 35 percent in 2005, while the number who rated their situation as "fairly bad" or "very bad" dropped to 41 percent. Perhaps more significant, when asked at the start of the survey about the overall direction of the country, nearly two-thirds (64 percent) averred that it was "going in the right direction" (and among these, 76 percent said they would vote for Museveni). In short, despite weak performance in some sectors, the country's general economic successes appear to have favored Museveni, perhaps strongly. But there also appears to be more to the story that government performance alone cannot explain. Further analysis reveals that the additional factor is probably Museveni's success in finally bringing the war in the north to an end.

The opposition had largely taken the north for granted, assuming that it would remain an electoral stronghold. The question—they thought—was whether the IPC or the Democratic Party would dominate there, not whether Museveni and the NRM would. The Democratic Party apparently hoped that

Mao would bring a substantial block of northern votes into its orbit. However, Mao won only 5.9 percent of the northern vote, taking just three districts and even underperforming in his ethnic home of Acholiland (29 percent). Besigye also underperformed. A Munyankole from the west, he swept the north, save Karamoja, in 2006, when he took 59 percent of the vote compared to Museveni's 36 percent. But in 2011, Besigye's share plummeted to 25 percent, and he captured just three districts.

Instead, the northern vote swung heavily to Museveni, who took a majority (56 percent) in the region for the first time. Museveni's gains in the north (24 points versus 2006), which built upon what had previously been a very low base, were many times higher than his gains in the western and central regions (2.5 and 3.3 points respectively). Table 8.3 compares the breakdown within the north in terms of new, parent, and old/unchanged districts. It is clear that although districtization does have positive effects, as seen earlier, the effects of northern location (an increase of 21 points relative to the western or central regions) are significantly greater.

This large "northern effect" suggests that much of the explanation for Museveni's electoral success in 2011 lies in the waning of hostilities against the Lord's Resistance Army since 2006. Evidence from successive Afrobarometer surveys suggests that levels of hardship in the region have dropped markedly. In 2005, fully 46 percent of northerners reported having gone without enough food "many times" or "always" in the preceding year, a figure that plummeted to just 7 percent in January 2011. Similarly sharp

Table 8.3 Gains in Museveni's Vote Share, 2006–2011, in Uganda by Region

	Museveni's 2006 Vote Share	Museveni's 2011 Vote Share	Change in Museveni's Vote Share, 2006–2011
Region of Uganda			
Central	57.4	60.7	+3.3
East	52.9	65.5	+12.6
North	28.9	53.0	+24.2
West	75.4	77.9	+2.5
Type of district (north only)			
Old/unchanged	32.7	53.3	+20.6
Parent	24.4	49.9	+25.5
New	27.1	57.1	+29.9

Source: Electoral Commission of Uganda.
Note: Differences in numbers are due to rounding.

declines were evident in reported lack of access to clean water for household use (37 percent in 2005, down to 9 percent in 2011) and medical treatment (49 percent in 2005, down to 25 percent in 2011). While life is still considerably more difficult in the north than in the rest of the country, these improvements were nonetheless reflected in significantly stronger progovernment sentiments in the region in 2011 compared to 2005. As a consequence, popular trust in Museveni among northerners increased from 64 percent in 2005 to 71 percent in 2011, while approval ratings for his performance as president climbed from 63 percent to 79 percent. Simply put, most northerners reflected on their lives over the preceding five years, saw an improvement, and apparently rewarded Museveni accordingly.

Conclusion

The narrative of Uganda's 2011 presidential election, from the perspective of the press and election observers, was the money. The unprecedented amounts of funds dumped into election spending produced descriptions focused on monetization, commercialization, and vote buying: in short, the purchase of the election. The clear implication was that—absent abuse of the material advantages of incumbency—Museveni might have lost.

Survey data, however, tell a different story. The National Resistance Movement's distribution of largesse was not a deciding factor in rallying voters to Museveni, but rather icing on the cake for a strong contingent of supporters who were already committed to extending his tenure for other reasons. Museveni's success in finally settling the war in the north, and in keeping the economy largely on track, had not just preserved his status among Ugandans, but also enhanced it considerably, especially in the north. At the same time, the Ugandan opposition failed to convince the public that it was a preferable alternative. The press, Ugandan elites, and much of the international community might have grown weary of Museveni, but the average Ugandan had not.

Northerners in particular were weary after decades of war. However culpable Museveni might have been for the fighting's long duration, he nonetheless appears to get credit for its resolution, and the return of peace and relative prosperity to the north. Put simply, northerners' lives have improved over the preceding five years; as a result, their support swung dramatically in favor of Museveni. This appears to be the largest single factor that allowed Museveni not just to hang on in the 2011 presidential election, but also to gain support relative to 2006. At the same time, faced with an unconvincing slate of alternatives, a majority of Ugandans elsewhere in the country likewise opted to preserve the status quo rather than take a risk on an alternative. Despite whatever failures they attributed to Museveni, and whatever drawbacks they might see to extending his reign, overall, in the public's eyes, the balance still came out very much in his favor.

In the end, the large quantity of resources dumped into the election played a bit part rather than a starring role. While vote buying may have been fairly common, the evidence suggests it had limited impact. Ugandans apparently have enough confidence in the secrecy of the ballot box to accept "gifts" from politicians and then vote as they please. And the disbursement of public goods prior to the election likewise had little obvious effect on voters. Substantial investment in new districts appears to have paid off in a marginal increase in Museveni's share, especially in the north—perhaps enough to have mattered had the election been close, but hardly a decisive factor given his wide margin of victory. Ironically, his profligate—and evidently unnecessary—campaign spending may subsequently have undermined Museveni's more important strength: his ability to manage the economy over the long term. The cash infusion likely contributed to local inflation. And if there is any truth to the claims that the government was nearly broke soon after the election, Museveni's ability to buffer the threatening impacts of the rising global food and fuel prices was consequently constrained.

Indeed, despite his large victory, Museveni was deeply disconcerted by the public dissatisfaction over these issues. By April 2011, protests over rising food and fuel prices, dubbed the "Walk to Work" campaign, were gaining momentum. All three of the leading opposition candidates were arrested and detained at least briefly. Besigye was detained several times, shot in the hand during one event, and beaten at another. The heavy-handed response bespoke a surprising lack of confidence for a government that had just secured a resounding reelection victory. Walk to Work never attracted a mass following, but it was followed by further urban protests, particularly in Kampala, over the lack of democratic freedoms. Still, the collapse of Museveni's regime hardly seems imminent and the prospects for change in the near future seem limited at best.

But there are also reasons for democrats to be somewhat sanguine. Although Museveni's reelection raises many questions, the vast majority of Ugandans—including most of those who planned to vote for the opposition—reported that they were indeed free to vote as they please. It appears that, by and large, on February 18, 2011, Ugandans were voting their own hearts and minds, and not because they had sold their votes.

Part 3

Implications for Citizenship

9

Uncritical Citizenship: Mozambicans in Comparative Perspective

Robert Mattes and Carlos Shenga

Mozambique is one of the poorest and most underdeveloped societies in the world. While poverty and the lack of infrastructure have many
social and political consequences, perhaps the most important from the
standpoint of the country's democratic development are the limitations
these obstacles place on the ability of its people to act as full citizens. Even
compared to people in other poor societies, Mozambicans suffer extremely
low levels of formal education: the adult literacy rate is 46 percent, compared to an average of 61 percent across all low-income countries. The public also lacks access to information: per 1,000 people, the country has just 3
newspapers (compared to 44 for low-income countries), 14 television sets
(compared to 84), and 44 radios (compared to 198). Along with high levels
of illiteracy, these shortcomings strike at the core of the cognitive skills and
political information that enable citizens to assess social, economic, and political developments, learn about elections and other institutional rules,
form opinions about political performance, and care about the survival of
democracy.

Data from Round 3 of the Afrobarometer (2005) demonstrate that relatively high proportions of Mozambicans are consistently unable to answer
many key questions about the performance of government or the democratic regime, or to offer preferences about what kind of regime Mozambique ought to have. Those Mozambicans who are able to offer opinions
grant their political leaders and institutions high levels of trust and approval, and perceive low levels of official corruption. They offer these
glowing views even as many respondents tell interviewers they are critical
of what their government has done in several different policy areas, have
great difficulty working with government agencies, are dissatisfied with

their personal circumstances, and live in desperate poverty. Most important, those Mozambicans who are able to offer opinions exhibit some of the lowest levels of commitment to democracy measured by the Afrobarometer across eighteen African multiparty systems. At the same time, Mozambicans are some of the most likely people to say their country is democratic. Thus, there are many reasons to suspect that Mozambicans uncritically overrate the performance of their new democratic regime.

In a comprehensive overview of public opinion in older democracies, Pippa Norris traced a growing tension between the promise of democracy and the reality of the performance of democratic institutions to "the emergence of more 'critical citizens,' or 'dissatisfied democrats,' who adhere strongly to democratic values but who find the existing structures of representative government, invented in the eighteenth and nineteenth centuries, to be wanting" (1999: 3). Critical citizenship requires individuals who offer their leaders neither blind trust nor cynical distrust, but rather display a healthy skepticism (Almond and Verba 1963; Mishler and Rose 1997). However, the combination of Mozambicans' very high levels of trust in leaders and institutions with their very low levels of commitment to democracy means that they present precisely the opposite archetype: uncritical citizenship.

In this chapter, we explore the extent to which uncritical citizenship in Mozambique is a function of living in a low-information society, the primary features of which are a lack of schooling and limited access to news about public affairs. While modernization theory has cited education and cognitive skills as part of a broad bundle of social requisites of democracy (alongside urbanization, industrialization, affluence, and the expansion of the middle class) (Lipset 1959; Almond and Verba 1963; Inkeles and Smith 1974), Geoffrey Evans and Pauline Rose demonstrate that the actual evidence of the impact of education in developing societies is "surprisingly thin" (2007b: 2). And while a great deal of evidence links education to democratic attitudes in older democracies, some political scientists now argue that the role of knowledge and cognitive skills is overstated. They claim that poorly informed people tend to reach the same political opinions and decisions as the well informed, largely because they utilize "low-information reasoning," based on personal experience of commonly accessible information (like consumer goods prices, joblessness, and housing construction), as a heuristic cue to evaluate government performance (Popkin 1994; Lupia and McCubbins 2000). And latter-day modernization scholars see education as a "marker" of material security, which itself is the main driver of prodemocratic values (Inglehart and Welzel 2005).

But we also consider alternative explanations of the limited extent to which Mozambicans embrace the values of electoral competition and democracy. In their country, uncritical public attitudes may reflect not so much a lack of education and information as fear created by sixteen years of civil war, electoral dominance, and hegemonic control of political information by Frelimo (the Front for the Liberation of Mozambique, the governing party). We also investigate whether an uncritical mind-set reflects a socially embedded and culturally transmitted set of orientations shaped by indigenous tradition and centuries of Portuguese colonial occupation. Finally, we probe the extent to which Mozambique's proportional electoral system contributes to this syndrome of attitudes by removing critical cognitive linkages between citizens and the political system.

Popular Political Awareness and Evaluations

Our main purpose is to explore linkages between the characteristics of a low-information society—as embodied in schools and mass news media—and elements of democratic citizenship. In particular, we wish to assess Mozambicans' *political information,* or their ability to provide a range of basic political facts. Second we assess the degree of what we call *opinion ation,* or the extent to which people are able, or willing, to offer evaluations of regime and state. Third, we assess what we call *criticalness,* or the extent to which these evaluations are negative or disparaging. Finally, we assess two distinct dimensions of popular attitudes to democracy, namely the *perceived supply of democracy* provided by political elites, and the extent to which ordinary citizens exhibit a *demand for democracy.*

Political Information

Measuring citizens' information is a tricky affair. Results often differ sharply depending on whether researchers ask respondents to recall facts from memory, or to recognize them from a list of several possible answers. Because the Afrobarometer uses the recall method, results may understate the actual level of popular awareness.

Most Mozambicans know the identity of the largest political party in the country. In 2005, 68 percent were able to offer the name of Frelimo, which put the country near the median point among eighteen Afrobarometer countries. Yet while 73 percent of Frelimo identifiers could provide this information, just 56 percent of independent voters and an even lower 46 percent of opposition identifiers were able to do so.

However, Mozambicans are relatively unaware of other key political facts. Just one in five (20 percent)—the lowest percentage among Afrobarometer countries—knew how many terms the president is allowed to serve (two), with this proportion dropping to 16 percent in rural areas. By way of contrast, nine in ten Namibians and Batswana were able to supply the correct answer for their country. And just 8 percent of Mozambicans (4 percent in the countryside) knew that it is the responsibility of the courts to ensure that legislation is constitutional. While this very low proportion is similar in size to the tiny minorities measured in over half the Afrobarometer countries, it is far lower than the 45 percent of Nigerians who in 2005 demonstrated awareness of judicial review.

Mozambicans also have difficulty identifying the occupants of elected office. In 2005, less than one-third (30 percent) were able to offer the correct name of their local councilor, and only one in ten (13 percent) were able to give the correct name of their elected national representative (in Mozambique's system of proportional representation, legislators are elected on provincial lists). Information about local councilors is relatively similar across party identification, and across rural and urban areas. But awareness of a representative's identity is not: 18 percent of people living in urban areas knew their representative's name, compared to 10 percent in the countryside. The impact of partisan identification also reverses: 21 percent of opposition supporters could provide the correct name of their representative, compared to 14 percent of Frelimo identifiers and 8 percent of independents. Even so, as Figure 9.1 shows, Mozambique places close to the bottom among Afrobarometer countries in terms of citizen knowledge of elected representatives.

Opinionation

Beyond factual information, to what extent are Mozambicans able to express preferences and opinions about politics? Much depends on the immediacy

Figure 9.1 Knowledge of Elected Representatives in Sub-Saharan Africa, 2005

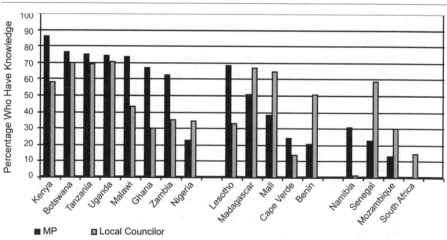

■ MP   ▣ Local Councilor

Source: Afrobarometer survey, 2005.

with which the issue at stake affects their personal lives. For example, respondents experience little difficulty in offering judgments about their material standards of living. Moreover, respondents are quite willing and able to state value preferences when provided with both sides of an argument over political or social values. For instance, when asked to indicate whether they agreed with either the statement that "people should look after themselves and be responsible for their own success in life" or the statement that "the government should bear the main responsibility for the well being of people," just 3 percent said they did not know and another 3 percent said they agreed with neither option. The combined percentage of these responses on a range of similar items in the 2005 Afrobarometer survey in Mozambique rarely exceeded 10 percent and never topped 15 percent.

However, people are far less able to state preferences when the question does not provide a balanced set of alternatives, or deals with an abstract concept like democracy. Thus, when asked to approve or disapprove of a range of nondemocratic alternatives to multiparty elections, 16 percent of Mozambicans had no view about the prospect of military rule, and 19 percent were unable to offer an opinion about the abolition of elections and parliament to allow for presidential dictatorship. And fully one-quarter (24 percent) had no opinion on whether democracy is preferable to all other forms of government. In fact, the term "democracy" is unfamiliar to significant proportions of the populace. While only 8 percent gave no response when asked, "What, if anything, does 'democracy' mean to you?" an additional 20 percent admitted that they could not understand the word "democracy," either in Portuguese or when translated into a local language.

Indeed, the proportions of Mozambicans who are unable to offer opinions on political issues increases consistently as the object of the question grows more distant from the daily purview of the respondent. In 2005, one in five (19 percent) could not offer an opinion on the performance of the elected parliament, and one in three (29 percent) cannot judge the performance of elected local councils. And one in five were unable to say whether members of parliament (18 percent) or local councilors (21 percent) "try their best to listen to what people like you have to say."

Once we move to more remote institutions or more sensitive issues, the proportions rise even higher. One-quarter were unable to say how well the country's electoral system performed in allowing people to replace bad leaders (28 percent) or in ensuring that elected representatives reflect public opinion (24 percent). At least one in four were unable, or unwilling, to offer an assessment of how many officials in the presidency (26 percent), parliament (26 percent), or local council (30 percent) were involved in corruption. And while only 10 percent were unable to offer a view on whether the 2004 elections had been free and fair, 16 percent could not rate their level of current satisfaction with the way democracy works, and 21 percent could not rate the level of democracy in the country.

In order to efficiently compare the level of opinionation among Mozambicans and other Africans, we created a valid and reliable summary index. It sums the number of substantive opinions (positive or negative) that respondents were able to offer across twenty question items on the quality of democracy (the freeness and fairness of elections, satisfaction with democracy, and the extent of democracy), and good governance (the extent of official corruption, the responsiveness of elected representatives, the degree to which the electoral system produces accountability, and the overall job performance of key incumbent leaders). On this scale, Mozambicans fall well below the Afrobarometer average (fourth lowest) in terms of being able to offer opinions on the quality of governance and democracy (a score of 16 out of a possible total of 24, as shown in Figure 9.2).

Criticalness

Among Mozambicans, those who do offer opinions are especially unlikely to be critical of the performance of the country's multiparty regime, institutions, or leaders. In 2005, eight in ten respondents said they trusted the

Figure 9.2 Opinion on Democratic and Government Performance in Sub-Saharan Africa, 2005

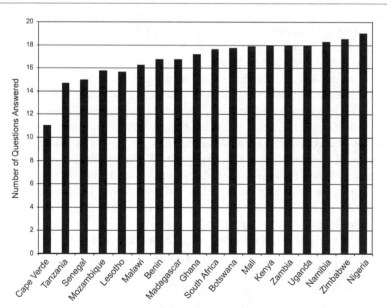

Source: Afrobarometer survey, 2005.
Note: Average number of questions (out of twenty) that respondents could answer on the supply of democracy and good governance.

president (81 percent) and approved of his performance in the previous twelve months (81 percent). And three-quarters said they trusted the parliament (75 percent) and approved of its overall job performance (73 percent).

Not only are Mozambicans far more likely to express trust than distrust, but they are also very likely to place *total* trust in their political leaders, choosing the most extreme response category available. Two-thirds of all respondents (67 percent) said they trusted the president a "very great deal." This pattern also applied to the public's view of parliament (56 percent trusted it a "great deal"). In fact, for every single institution that the 2005 Afrobarometer asked about, the modal response was one of total rather than qualified trust.

Levels of approval of government performance in specific policy areas were relatively lower, but still high in absolute terms, ranging from 70 percent approval of government handling of health and educational policy to a low of 42 percent approval of its job in narrowing income gaps. And even though both Transparency International (2006) and the World Bank (2004) rate Mozambique as one of the most corrupt countries in the world, a relatively modest 19 percent of Mozambicans felt that "all" or "most" national government officials were involved in corruption.

Yet popular responses reveal a pattern of internal contradiction in which Mozambicans express trust in institutions even in the face of poor performance. Three-quarters of Mozambicans (71 percent) said they trusted the police, even though four in ten (40 percent) said it was "difficult" or "very difficult" to get help from the police, and another 17 percent reported being victimized in the previous twelve months by a police demand for a bribe or a favor. And 65 percent said they trusted their local government council, though only 40 percent said their council was handling local road maintenance "fairly" or "very badly," and 34 percent said it was doing a bad job keeping their communities clean.

To compare Mozambicans with other Africans, we created an index that measures the balance of positive versus negative views among those who offer an opinion. From this perspective, Mozambicans rank as second to last among the eighteen African countries in terms of their propensity to distrust institutions or criticize incumbent or policy performance (see Figure 9.3).

Democracy: Supply and Demand

Following earlier work (Bratton, Mattes, and Gyimah-Boadi 2005; Mattes and Bratton 2007), we assess whether Mozambicans feel that they are living in a democracy and whether they wish to do so. On the supply side, Mozambicans apparently perceive a relatively high degree of democracy in

Figure 9.3 Critical Opinions on Political Performance in Sub-Saharan Africa, 2005

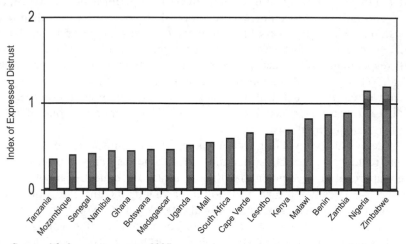

Source: Afrobarometer survey, 2005.
Note: Index of expressing distrust in institutions or offering critical assessments of policy and incumbent performance: 0 = trust/approve, 1 = distrust/disapprove, 2 = strongly distrust/ disapprove.

their country. In 2005, over three-quarters said that the country's 2004 election was either "completely free and fair" (57 percent) or "free and fair, with minor problems" (20 percent). And almost two-thirds believed that the country was "a full democracy" (35 percent) or "a democracy with minor problems" (29 percent). Three in five were either "very satisfied" (31 percent) or "fairly satisfied" (28 percent) with the way democracy works in Mozambique.

On the demand side, however, large minorities—even pluralities—of Mozambicans remain uncommitted to democratic government. While 80 percent agreed that "we should choose our leaders in this country through regular, open, and honest elections," they were not yet completely sold on the necessity of multiparty choice. Fully one-third (33 percent) agreed that "political parties create division and confusion; it is therefore unnecessary to have many political parties in Mozambique." Similarly, one-third (33 percent) approved of an alternative form of government whereby "only one political party is allowed to stand for election and hold office."

Many Mozambicans are also quite comfortable with the idea of strong, even dictatorial leadership. One-third (34 percent) agreed that "since the president was elected to lead the country, he should not be bound by laws or court decisions that he thinks are wrong"; four in ten (42 percent) said they would approve of an alternative system of governing the country whereby "elections and the parliament are abolished so that the president can decide everything"; and one in five (19 percent) said they would approve of the alternative whereby "the army comes in to govern the country."

We developed valid and reliable indices of supply and demand out of subsets of these items (see Figure 9.4). On the supply side, we calculated the proportion of people who think they are living in a democracy *and* are satisfied with the way democracy works. Barely one-half of all Mozambicans can be classified as feeling "fully supplied" (48 percent). Mozambique lags behind only Ghana (64 percent), Namibia (61 percent), Botswana (54 percent), and South Africa (53 percent). On the demand side, we calculated the proportion of people who reject presidential dictatorship, military rule, and one-party rule *and* prefer democracy to nondemocratic forms of government. By this measure, just one in five Mozambicans (18 percent) can be classified as "committed democrats." In sharp contrast to perceptions of supply, of which Mozambicans have some of the highest levels in Africa, this figure is tied for the lowest level among the eighteen Afrobarometer countries, statistically indistinguishable from the 19 percent of Namibians who are committed. Obviously, there are many Mozambicans who think they live in a democracy, but do so from a perspective of not being terribly concerned about whether they want to or not.

As argued at the start of this chapter, Western democracies are characterized by the rise of critical citizens—that is, people who support democracy but increasingly find the existing structure of government wanting. In

Figure 9.4 Consolidation of Regimes in Sub-Saharan Africa, Circa 2005

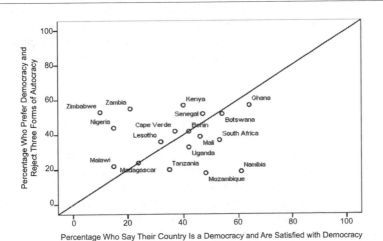

Source: Afrobarometer survey, 2005.
Note: Respondents who answered "don't know" are excluded.

Mozambique, by contrast, the combination of high trust in leaders and institutions with low levels of commitment to democracy presents precisely the opposite archetype: that of uncritical citizens.

In order to operationalize the concept of critical citizens, we created an individual-level measure of whether or not respondents received the level of democracy they desired, by taking each person's average scores for both supply and demand (which was scaled to range from 0 to 4) and subtracting the supply score from the demand score. This yielded a new score, ranging from +4 (indicating a sharply critical democrat who deeply wants democracy but perceives absolutely no democracy) to −4 (indicating a completely uncritical, acquiescent citizen who has no desire for democracy but feels his or her country is completely democratic). Across eighteen countries and 21,500 respondents, the average (mean) score is +0.61 (with a standard deviation of 1.5), indicating that the average African wants slightly more democracy than she or he thinks they are receiving. Yet it also indicates that a large proportion of African responses generate scores below the 0 point, meaning that these respondents' perceived supply of democracy outstrips their desire. The average (mean) Mozambican, however, has a score of −0.55, the lowest in all eighteen countries (though Namibians are in a statistical dead heat at −0.50).

Awareness of Politics

We now turn to the distinctive low-information profile of Mozambican society. We begin by describing various constituent elements of the broad concept of "cognitive awareness," which includes the information that people possess about politics and democracy, but also their exposure to information from a range of community and mass media sources. It also includes the cognitive skills acquired through formal education or interpersonal discussion.

Formal Education

As a legacy of Portuguese colonialism and civil war, Mozambican adults have the lowest level of schooling in southern Africa, and among the lowest on the continent. In 2005, 28 percent of all adult Mozambicans said they had no formal education (though 8 percent claimed some informal schooling). One in three (33 percent) had some primary education, 14 percent had completed primary school, and just one in ten adults had completed high school. A total of 3 percent had proceeded beyond high school, but just 0.03 percent had completed a university education.

Yet there is also some good news in these statistics. Once disaggregated by age, the Afrobarometer data reveal a positive impact of postcolonial education policies. In 2005, although 48 percent of those aged fifty-six to sixty-five had no formal schooling, just 15 percent of those aged eighteen to twenty-four fell into this category. Moreover, Mozambique's levels of educational attainment are higher than those of Benin, Mali, and Senegal (though about one in five Senegalese and Malians say they have had informal—usually Islamic—schooling).

News Media Use

Mozambicans also display low rates of access to, and use of, formal news media. In 2005, just 13 percent regularly read newspapers (8 percent every day and 5 percent a few times a week), a figure higher only than in Lesotho, Mali, and Benin. The Portuguese colonial state bequeathed Mozambique with a weak mass media network: just one radio station (*Rádio Moçambique*), two daily newspapers (*Diário de Moçambique* and *Notícias*), and one weekly newspaper (*Domingo*). Though the country now has greater media pluralism than before, few people have access to newspapers, since few are distributed outside of provincial capital cities. While one in five city dwellers (23 percent) read newspapers on a regular basis, just 5 percent of rural citizens do so.

Just one quarter said they regularly watched news programs on television (16 percent every day and 8 percent a few times a week). This proportion is lower than in all countries surveyed except Tanzania, Malawi, Lesotho, and Uganda. Television was only introduced in Mozambique in 1982, with a single public station that was accessible only in the Maputo area. Access was broadened to reach the country's second biggest city (Beira) in 1994 and has now spread to provincial capitals. Accordingly, 44 percent of those in urban areas said they got their news from television on a regular basis, compared to just 9 percent in the countryside. Viewership is also limited by the availability of affordable television sets: just 19 percent of Mozambicans said they owned a television in 2005, and most of those people were located in the cities (32 percent lived in urban areas, compared to 9 percent in rural areas).

Mozambique's public and private radio stations are by far the most accessible and widely used form of news media in the country. Yet while two-thirds of all adult Mozambicans said they got their news from the radio either every day (49 percent) or a few times a week (21 percent), this figure ranks higher only than in Madagascar, Zimbabwe, and Lesotho. Radio listenership is limited by the supply of radio stations. The only radio station that comes close to covering the entire country (*Rádio Moçambique*) is publicly owned. Community-based stations are owned both by the state and civil society agencies. Many rural areas still remain without any radio coverage. But access is also limited by the supply of affordable radio sets. Only two-thirds (66 percent) of Mozambicans said they owned a radio in 2005, far lower than the 81 percent of South Africans and the 80 percent of Senegalese and Malagasy who owned radios.

Cognitive Engagement

It is possible, however, that some citizens can make up deficits in formal education and news media exposure. They can become mentally engaged with public affairs by taking an active interest in and regularly talking about politics with their spouses, families, neighbors, or coworkers, adding their experiences to those of others (Richardson and Beck 2006).

The Afrobarometer data suggest that people who live in a low-information society like Mozambique remain relatively engaged with the political process. In 2005, two-thirds of respondents said they were either "very" (38 percent) or "somewhat" interested (29 percent) in politics and public affairs. A similar proportion said they talked about politics with friends and family "frequently" (25 percent) or "occasionally" (43 percent). Both figures put Mozambique near the Afrobarometer country mean.

Access to Alternative Sources of Information

Citizens in Mozambique may also access alternative sources of information about the larger political world they inhabit. These include the secondary associations they join, or the government or community leaders with whom they come in contact. Yet all of these alternative sources of information are not necessarily equal, especially in the degree to which they contribute to democratic citizenship. Richard Gunther, José Montero, and Mariano Torcal (2006) distinguish informational intermediaries that are explicitly partisan from those that are ostensibly apolitical. A finer distinction discriminates between informational sources that are aligned with the state and ruling party versus those that remain relatively independent (Shenga 2007).

The latter distinction is especially relevant in Mozambique, where ruling-party and government officials have been moving the political regime away from democracy. The country has regressed from an "electoral democracy" to a more "ambiguous" hybrid regime (Diamond 2002). Frelimo's three decades of political power (first through a one-party system, then through dominance under multipartyism) has limited the free flow of information. First, large sections of the electronic broadcast and print news media are under the control of the state: not only *Rádio Moçambique,* but the major television station and the largest-circulation newspapers are state-controlled. Independent weeklies like *Savana, Demos,* and *Embondeiero* face increasing government regulation (Mosse 2007). Second, significant sections of civil society are aligned with the state. For example, the predominant trade unions—

such as the Organização dos Trabalhadores Moçambicanos–Central Sindi-
cal—are explicitly pro-government, having been created or favored by Frelimo. The business community is also captured by a party elite whose
"main capital is precisely their link with Frelimo and its state" (Pereira and
Shenga 2005: 56). Thus Mozambicans are also probably more likely than
other Africans to get the little information that they do have from state-
aligned sources.

Associational Membership

Moreover, many people in Mozambique belong to civic associations, some
of which are aligned with party or state. For example, in 2005, one in four
(23 percent) Mozambicans were affiliated with either a trade union or
farmer association, and a surprising 16 percent mentioned affiliation with a
business or professional group. But an even larger proportion (81 percent)
claimed affiliation with some form of religious association. While about a
third (31 percent) characterized themselves as "inactive members," 44 percent said they were active in these groups, and another 6 percent said they
were official leaders in these groups. All these figures place Mozambique
around the middle of the eighteen Afrobarometer countries in terms of associational membership.

By contrast, just one in five (19 percent) Mozambicans said they were
affiliated in some way with a community development group, and just one in
ten of these were active (9 percent active, with 1 percent active as official
leaders). In this case, Mozambique places in the bottom half of our eighteen
countries, a position below Tanzania, Senegal, and Nigeria, and well below
Kenya and Malawi. Nevertheless, three-quarters of Mozambicans (76 percent) said they attended a community meeting in the previous year (37 percent "often"), and 69 percent reported "getting together with others to raise
an important issue" (28 percent "often"). Thus, while the party or state may
have sponsored many of these events, Mozambicans do not appear to possess an ingrained predisposition against involvement in community affairs.

Contacting Leaders

Mozambicans have extremely low rates of contact with elected leaders, including the lowest previous-year contact rate with local councilors recorded
by the Afrobarometer—(just 9 percent in 2005). And just 7 percent of
Mozambicans said they had contacted a parliamentary representative, representing a statistical tie for the lowest rank with Benin (6 percent), South
Africa (5 percent), and Madagascar (5 percent), as shown in Figure 9.5.

By contrast, Mozambicans have higher rates of contact with nonelected
leaders. Some 21 percent and 15 percent respectively said they had met a

Figure 9.5 Public Contact with Elected Officials in Sub-Saharan Africa, 2005

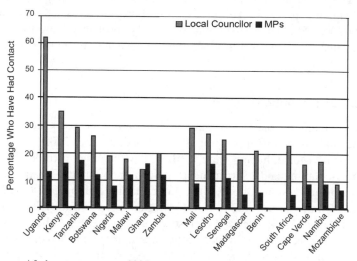

Source: Afrobarometer survey, 2005.

party official or a government official at least once during the previous year. While there is no difference in the rate of contact with party officials between opposition (23 percent) and Frelimo (22 percent) supporters, the latter are more likely to contact government officials or elected leaders.

But like other Africans, Mozambicans make most of their contact with religious leaders (53 percent, with 19 percent doing so "often" within the previous year, which matches Afrobarometer norms). Moreover, one in three (31 percent) contacted a traditional leader and 17 percent contacted some other community leader. As expected, but unlike for other leaders, rural dwellers are more likely than their urban counterparts to contact traditional leaders.

Cognitive Awareness and Democratic Citizenship in Mozambique

We now turn to multiple regression models to ask whether Mozambique's pattern of uncritical public attitudes are a function of citizens' lack of formal education, access to the news media, and political information. We also probe whether poorly informed citizens are able to use experiential means like interpersonal discussion, attending group meetings, or contacting officials to make up cognitive deficits. And we examine whether it matters if citizens use news media, belong to associations, or contact officials that are aligned with the state or governing party.

Our results, as shown in Table 9.1, indicate that political information is not a meaningless ability to answer "quiz-show" questions about political trivia. Political information in Mozambique is driven first and foremost by formal education. In addition, news programs seen on television and heard on radio (but not read in newspapers) also make an independent and positive contribution. Even so, people without formal education or access to news broadcasts can make up some of their informational deficit through interpersonal discussion, joining collective action groups, and perhaps surprisingly, contacting officials from government ministries.

We can see from the table that political information is, in turn, a potent predictor of several other important variables. Even after controlling for Mozambique's large rural-urban divide, and the privileged position of Portuguese-speakers, well-informed citizens enjoy greater ability to offer opinions about the performance of government and preferences about political regimes.

As noted earlier, formal education plays a crucial role in helping Mozambicans learn about the political system. Even after considering the role of political information from other sources, formal education continues to play an important role in preference formation. Yet the news media apparently have few effects on users' critical faculties or attitudes to democracy. Newspaper readership does contribute to demand for democracy, but those who obtain news from television (which is state-dominated) are actually less committed to democracy.

Cognitive awareness therefore has important but selective effects on the nature of citizenship. An individual's interest in politics is consistently more important than interpersonal discussion, but its contribution to democratic citizenship is not always positive. Political interest enables people to offer more opinions and preferences, yet among these respondents, interest in politics reduces the likelihood that they will offer critical opinions. And while it increases demand for democracy, interest also increases Mozambicans' tendency to uncritically overrate the supply of democracy in their country.

As for other sources of opinion formation, our analysis finds few consistent contributions from associational affiliation or contact with leaders. Membership in a community development group (or merely attending community meetings) does enable people to form political opinions. But it also induces them to become less critical, especially when judging the supply of governance. The only positive impact with any real consistency comes from citizen contact with religious leaders. Citizens who seek out priests, pastors, or imams are more likely than citizens who do not seek out contact with religious leaders to form preferences about democracy, to demand democracy, and to be critical citizens.

Table 9.1 Consequences of Cognitive Awareness and Alternative Information Sources in Mozambique, 2005

	Political Information	Opinionation		Criticalness			
		Supply of Governance and Democracy	Demand for Democracy	Supply of Governance	Supply of Democracy	Demand for Democracy	Supply of Democracy
Cognitive awareness							
Political information	—	0.211***	0.190***		−0.083*	0.096**	0.139***
Formal education	0.297***	0.110***	0.107**			0.177***	
Radio news	0.077**						
Television news	0.131***		0.072*			−0.080*	
Newspapers						0.096***	
Interest in politics	0.127***	0.107***	0.170***	−0.093*	−0.095**	0.106***	0.143***
Political discussion		0.103***					
Other sources							
Member, religious group						0.061***	
Member, development group		0.058*		−0.117*			0.141***
Member, trade union		0.087**					
Member, professional group			0.108***				
Attend community meetings		0.103***	0.085**	−0.125**	−0.132***		
Joined with others	0.058*						
Contact, religious leader			0.068**				
Contact, government official	0.088**					0.090***	
Contact, traditional leader					0.072**		
Control variables							
Rural	−0.070*	−0.183***	−0.031 ns	−0.068 ns	−0.092*	−0.089**	0.070*
Portuguese	−0.003 ns	0.002 ns	−0.060*	−0.060 ns	0.066*	−0.056 ns	−0.038 ns
Adjusted R²	0.243	0.183	0.168	0.045	0.045	0.116	0.070
N	1,199	1,197	1,198	480	883	1,199	1,199

Source: Afrobarometer survey, 2005.
Notes: Table reports standardized (beta) regression coefficients.
***$p < 0.001$, **$p < 0.01$, *$p < 0.05$; ns = not statistically significant.

Overall, cognitive factors explain almost a quarter of the variation in political information and more modest shares of opinionation about government performance, political regimes, and demand for democracy. However, cognitive awareness alone explains little about whether Mozambican opinions will be more or less critical.

Alternative Explanations

We also wonder whether alternative (noncognitive) approaches might better explain uncritical citizenship. Our analysis suggests the following:

- *Political values matter.* The narrow majority of Mozambicans who value freedom of expression are significantly more likely than those who support government suppression of dissent to have opinions and to demand democracy and less likely to say they are living in a democracy.
- *Fear is a minor factor.* Fear does not suppress political opinion and may even engender an expressive counterreaction. Compared to less fearful respondents, those who thought the interviewer was from a government agency or felt that it was unsafe to speak their minds about politics were actually more likely to provide an opinion about democracy and its alternatives.
- *Economic performance yields political dividends.* Mozambicans who think the national economy is improving and that they, personally, are not economically deprived are less likely to criticize the supply of governance and democracy.
- *Political partisanship works as expected.* Compared to nonpartisans, individuals who identify with Frelimo are more likely to offer opinions but are less likely to be critical. Predictably, opposition supporters too are likely to form regime preferences but are also likely to criticize the performance of the government of the day.

Importantly, none of these alternative explanations eliminates the strong and significant relationship between cognitive awareness and democratic citizenship. Political information remains the single strongest predictor of opinion formation and, along with formal education, continues to have a large impact on demand for democracy.

Electoral System

We also wonder whether Mozambicans' cognitive deficits in politics have been exacerbated by the country's choice of electoral system. Mozambique employs a proportional representation system based on party lists, which places inordinate power in the hands of party leaders. Candidates for office and elected legislators have far more incentive to please party bosses who control the lists than any identifiable group of voters. Thus, parliamentary representatives and ordinary citizens have little motivation to seek each other out or exchange information, by either expressing policy preferences or sharing experiences of problems.

Assessing the impact of a variable that affects an entire country (like a national electoral system) requires that we expand the scope of our regression analysis to compare respondents across countries. Thus we applied the full explanatory model (including all cognitive, cultural, economic, and partisan factors previously discussed) to all Round 3 Afrobarometer respondents (21,508) in all eighteen African countries. Party-list proportional representation (entered as a dummy variable, with single-member district systems as the excluded category) had a strong negative impact on political information (not shown). As might be expected, Africans who live in countries that use proportional representation are systematically less able to identify their member of parliament by name. Less predictably, they are also less able to give the correct name of their local councilor or the largest party in the legislature or know the correct limit on presidential terms or understand the role of the courts. And perhaps most important, over and above the effect of political knowledge, proportional representation also decreases people's ability to offer opinions or form preferences on issues of governance and democracy, decreases the frequency with which those with opinions will offer critical evaluations, and decreases the demand for democracy.

Although more research is necessary to probe this consequential finding (see Chapter 10 in this volume), it appears that proportional representation in Mozambique (and other similarly designed political systems) has the effect of "dumbing down" the body politic. List-based elections eliminate an important "cognitive hook" with which citizens might otherwise obtain a firmer grasp of the political process. Especially in deeply rural areas of agrarian societies, citizens in proportional representation systems lack key personal and institutional linkages to elected political representatives (Barkan 1995). This representation gap must be counted among the key factors that incline them to become uncritical citizens.

Conclusion

Mozambicans exhibit a problematic structure of public attitudes toward democracy and governance. Uncritical citizenship is characterized by low levels of political information and extremely positive (and possibly unreflective) political evaluations among those who hold opinions. This syndrome is accompanied by high levels of satisfaction with the supply of democracy juxtaposed with low levels of demand for it. Mozambicans say they are satisfied with the progress of Mozambique's democratic experiment. Yet paradoxically, this optimism stops short of creating a widespread demand for democracy.

Cognitive factors (political information, formal education, and interest in politics) have important impacts here, even after taking into account alternative explanations. Our findings suggest that the fate of Mozambique's fledgling democracy will rest in important part on the speed and degree to which the government and donors are able to expand educational opportunities and access to news media, particularly independent media, in order to build critical skills across the body politic. Finally, we have found strong evidence that Mozambique has chosen an electoral system that does nothing to reverse, and probably exacerbates, the deleterious effects of a low-information society. By removing institutional and personal links between voters and elected representatives, party-list proportional representation appears to reduce citizens' ability (or incentive) to learn about, and demand, democracy. Consequently, electoral reform also ought to occupy a central place on the reform agenda of Mozambican democrats.

10

Accountability or Representation? How Electoral Systems Promote Public Trust

Wonbin Cho

Citizens' political support for important government institutions such as legislatures is critical for achieving stability in emerging democracies (Easton 1965; Norris 1999). Citizens put their trust in political institutions based on their evaluations of the performance of those institutions (March 1988; Mishler and Rose 2001). More specifically, citizens judge a legislature according to whether it provides what people want and whether it provides a reasonably fair chance for them to influence decisionmaking processes through periodic multiparty elections. Different electoral systems have distinct mechanics for allowing citizens to express their interests. Without knowing how ordinary citizens understand the mechanics of a given electoral system, we are hardly able to understand how they build their trust in the legislature.

In a democracy, elections establish the connection between citizens and policymakers. Voting is the means through which citizens encourage policymakers to pay attention to their interests. However, institutional designs differ in the vision of representation that elections promote. Some electoral systems emphasize accountability whereas others emphasize representativeness. While the former arrangement establishes elections as an instrument for citizens' direct control over policymakers, the latter enables elections to increase broad participation in government and cultivate widespread agreement on policies.

Electoral systems are conventionally classified into two types: majoritarian systems and proportional representation (PR) systems (Lijphart 1999). Majoritarian systems most often use single-member districts. In this system, voters cast a vote for an individual candidate, and the candidate receiving the most votes is the winner (winner-take-all). On the other hand, proportional representation is an electoral system in which voters cast votes for political parties, and the percentage of the vote that each party receives translates into a share of seats in the legislature.

Majoritarian electoral systems help promote accountability. They usually offer voters a clear-cut choice between two major parties at the national level, and the national vote clearly translates into winning and losing parties. Majoritarian electoral systems in turn produce legislative bodies that are especially reflective of the wishes of the majority but may neglect the goal of representativeness by excluding smaller groups from meaningful participation. Systems that distribute legislative seats proportionally, meanwhile, ensure broader representativeness in the legislature but may fracture power to such an extent that leaders fail to achieve compromise policy solutions and the majority cannot hold the leadership sufficiently accountable (Lijphart 1994; Cox 1997; Katz 1997; Reynolds 1999; Norris 2003).

These differences in institutional priorities pose an interesting dilemma for public trust in legislative institutions. The electoral system may shape people's evaluation of institutions themselves. A majoritarian system likely will generate trust when it succeeds at providing accountability. Under such a system, citizens who perceive an ability to control their members of parliament (MPs) directly through voting would in turn show higher levels of trust in the legislature. A proportional representation system, on the other hand, might generate trust according to its success at being representative. It brings into the policymaking arena representative agents from all factions of society, who then bargain with each other in a flexible and accommodative fashion. In other words, electoral institutions mediate how citizens translate their judgments of legislative performance into overall trust in the legislative branch itself.

This chapter tests that proposition using Afrobarometer survey data collected from sixteen sub-Saharan African countries. I first examine the impact of citizens' perceptions of accountability and representation on their confidence in the legislature at individual and country levels. I then allow the relationship between those perceptions and overall confidence to depend upon the type of electoral system present in each country. I find that African citizens typically value the representation function of elections more than their accountability roles when they judge the legislature. Moreover, proportional representation systems are much better at boosting public trust in the legislature than are majoritarian electoral systems when citizens believe that elections actually improve their political representation. These findings have important implications for democratic development in Africa. They help us to understand how ordinary citizens build trust in the institutions that are intended to represent them, and thus in the legitimacy and effectiveness of democratic government.

Public Trust in the Legislature

Several studies show evidence of a direct relationship between institutional trust and democratic legitimacy for emerging democracies (Rose, Mishler, and Haerpfer 1998; Bratton, Mattes, and Gyimah-Boadi 2005). Three theoretical traditions—cultural theories, theories of government performance, and institutional theories—attempt to explain the origins of institutional trust, and they provide very different perspectives on how ordinary citizens develop high levels of trust in political institutions.

First, cultural theories emphasize the role of deep-rooted norms and socialization experiences (Almond and Verba 1963; Putnam 1993; Inglehart 1997). Individuals learn to trust or distrust other people by interacting with family members, friends, and formal social networks from their early youth. This socialization process results in a collective sense of interpersonal trust in a given society, and high levels of interpersonal trust are strongly associated with high levels of institutional trust. However, William Mishler and Richard Rose (2001), based on survey data from postcommunist countries, find few empirical results supporting the cultural explanations.

A second type of theory focuses on the effects of government performance—whether subjectively or objectively measured—on institutional trust (Weatherford 1992; Anderson and Guillory 1997; Hetherington 1998). The high quality of policy outcomes and improvement in economic evaluations lead ordinary citizens to perceive government to be working effectively. These positive perceptions result in increased institutional trust. In addition to economic outcomes, political outcomes—such as removing restrictions on individual liberty, providing increased freedoms, and reducing corruption—contribute to high levels of institutional trust, particularly in emerging democracies. These studies, however, show inconsistent results. For example, Mishler and Rose (2001) find strong evidence supporting the perspective of institutional performance, but Ian McAllister (1999) and Arthur Miller and Ola Listhaug (1999) report nonsignificant results.

Finally, a third group of scholars emphasizes the influence of political institutions on public trust in other institutions (Norris 1999; Anderson et al. 2005; Cho and Bratton 2006; Criado and Herreros 2007). Variations in public trust in institutions across countries seem to result from characteristics of electoral systems, executive types, and party systems. The direct effects on popular attitudes toward political institutions vary in different studies. Pippa Norris (1999), for example, finds that countries with majoritarian electoral systems have higher general levels of institutional confidence than ones with proportional electoral systems. However, Christopher Anderson and colleagues (2005) and Wonbin Cho and Michael Bratton (2006) show that electoral systems that are more proportional increase citizens' confidence in the political system. These discrepancies in empirical results suggest that the effects of institutions on institutional confidence remain understudied.

Instead of direct effects, I contend that the design of electoral systems has indirect effects on institutional trust. To understand how ordinary citizens develop trust, this study combines two existing bodies of knowledge: theories of government performance and theories of institutional design. I argue that the effects of citizens' perception of government performance on their levels of institutional trust are mediated by electoral institutions.

Unlike previous studies focusing on citizens' trust in institutions generally, my research emphasizes a specific institution: the legislature. Weakness of legislatures is a common phenomenon in Africa (van de Walle 2003; Barkan 2009). The legislature, however, is intended to be the embodiment of the sovereignty of the people. In addition to its legislative role, the legislature is expected to serve both as an agency of restraint on the executive branch of government and as a public arena for the mobilization of popular participation in governmental decisionmaking. Legislatures, in turn, are supposed to have a significant role in establishing and consolidating democracy in the region. Because the legislature effectively shapes political debates, and democratic politics revolve around these representative bodies, my study attempts to understand the legitimacy of African legislatures from the perspective of ordinary citizens. The legitimacy of the legislature depends heavily on whether citizens approve of the work their lawmakers are doing. In this way, public trust in institutions is necessary for the success of democratic governments.

Parliamentary Elections: Accountability and Representation

What determines the levels of popular trust in African legislatures? At first glance, one might expect that popular perceptions of the quality of multiparty elections affect confidence in the legislative bodies. Between 1990 and 2006, forty-four of the forty-eight sub-Saharan African countries introduced multiparty electoral competition (Bratton and van de Walle 1997; Lindberg 2006). In some cases, elections are improperly conducted and results are disputed, often leading to violence, as observed in Kenya after the 2007 elections and in Zimbabwe after the first round of presidential voting in 2008. Indeed, many African elites and some scholars argue that multiparty elections exacerbate ethnic conflicts and polarize societies in the region (Sisk and Reynolds 1998; LeBas 2006). However, in other cases, such as South Africa, Mozambique, and Liberia, among others, elections have proved a useful device for conflict resolution, especially where voting is perceived by citizens to have been freely and fairly conducted. In these instances, multiparty elections are a means for connecting ordinary voters with political elites and provide a peaceful way for citizens to demand representation or accountability at the national level.

But political outcomes may depend on electoral systems. There is no consensus on what kind of electoral system is better for political accommodation and stability in emerging democracies. One group of scholars strongly recommends majoritarian electoral systems, which should motivate parties to approach moderate positions (Horowitz 1991, 2003; Sartori 1997; Reilly 1997; Barkan 1998). Others recommend a system of proportional representation to allow minority parties to gain representation in the legislature (Lijphart 1999, 2004; Reynolds 1999; Powell 2000; Shugart and Wattenberg 2000).

G. Bingham Powell (2000) distinguishes two visions of elections as "instruments of democracy": accountability and representation. Accountability models design elections to enable direct voter influence over policymakers. Under this model, citizens are reluctant to allow autonomy to elected representatives and are more likely to trust elected officials who are accountable to voters. Furthermore, voters are likely to see elections as a periodic opportunity to replace unsatisfactory policymakers. Additionally, the accountability model argues that anticipation of possible rejection shapes the policies of the incumbents. Competitive elections create pressure on all incumbents to worry about the next elections and make policy with voter review in mind. During election campaigns, MPs clamor for personal votes and are inclined to seek out regular contact with individual voters. Citizens, meanwhile, like to pinpoint responsibility for policymaking and exercise direct control over who will become a policymaker. When voters feel they have the ability to reward or punish elected officials in elections, their resulting confidence seems to shape their positive attitudes toward the legislature as a group of individual MPs who are accountable to their constituents' interests.

On the other hand, the representation model emphasizes that citizens should be treated evenhandedly at the decisive stage of public policymaking. According to this model, legislation should represent a full range of citizen opinion, not just the opinion of an electoral majority. In the representation model, citizens are suspicious of majorities (especially those created by elections), less worried about the autonomy of policymakers (so long as citizens have had a role in selecting them), and unconcerned about negotiated inaction. Elections are instruments of citizen influence, not direct control. They work as an instrument to choose representatives who reflect all points of view and can bargain for voters' interests in postelection policymaking. While the accountability model conceives of elections as a one-stage device to locate the true majority position, the representation model emphasizes the bargain process of representatives to find the most preferred policy after the elections. This latter model therefore suggests that citizens who feel elections enhance representation in the legislature are more likely to express high levels of trust in parliament.

The Mediating Effects of Electoral Systems

The choice of electoral systems has important implications for citizen expectations of representation and accountability. Different kinds of electoral systems tend to perform better in achieving different goals.

As discussed earlier, proportional representation systems employ multiseat districts, usually with party lists, and typically produce a high degree of proportionality between a party's vote share and its seat share in parliament. Because PR systems make it easier for smaller parties to win seats in parliament, they offer voters more opportunities for representation. If electoral thresholds are low and district magnitudes are reasonably large, almost all votes cast in PR systems can be translated into seats in the legislature. In PR systems, however, voters choose between parties, not candidates, and have little ability to mandate and monitor the elected officials. Elected officials' election and reelection chances depend mainly on where the candidate selectors, not voters, place them within the party list. Because PR systems are more complex than majoritarian systems, they are also more likely to confuse voters. The voters may not be entirely certain of how their votes are counted into seats in parliament, and they may end up with a government that is very different from the one imagined. Nevertheless, I expect that the effect on trust of popular evaluations of the representation mechanism should be higher in PR systems than in majoritarian electoral systems.

By contrast, majoritarian systems usually employ single-seat districts with a plurality rule that tends to give rise to one or two large parties. As a result, majoritarian rules produce governments that have a clear political mandate and locus of responsibility, thus enabling citizens to easily target demands for accountability. Under plurality—or first-past-the-post voting rules—voters have the ability to reelect or reject their particular representative, whose identity is well known to them. An elected official's belief that chances of reelection depend significantly on voter evaluations of individual performance builds individual accountability among members of parliament. Under first-past-the-post, on the other hand, legislatures will be less representative, since the composition of MPs will reflect voter preferences less accurately. A significant number of votes cast for losing candidates will be "wasted" in the sense that supporters of those candidates will lack a voice in the legislature. But because majoritarian electoral systems are designed to promote citizens' direct control over policymakers, I expect that citizens in countries with majoritarian electoral systems should be more likely than those in PR systems to base their confidence in the legislature on perceptions of their ability to replace elected officials.

Majoritarian electoral systems are more common in sub-Saharan Africa than proportional representation systems. Only about one-third of the countries of the region—Angola, Benin, Burkina Faso, Burundi, Cape Verde, Equatorial Guinea, Guinea-Bissau, Liberia, Mozambique, Namibia, Niger, Rwanda, São Tomé and Príncipe, Sierra Leone, and South Africa—have adopted various forms of proportional representation. All the rest feature majoritarian systems with plurality rules or some form of mixed system.

Data and Methods

This study draws mainly upon individual-level survey data collected by the Afrobarometer in sixteen sub-Saharan Africa countries between March 2005 and March 2006. The data are derived from national probability samples that range in size from 1,161 in Lesotho to 2,400 in South Africa, Nigeria, and Uganda. By the time of the surveys, all countries had held a founding (re-democratizing) election and undertaken some degree of political liberalization. The results thus cannot be seen as representative of sub-Saharan Africa as a whole: they epitomize the continent's most liberalized regimes.

Dependent Variable

The object of explanation is the level of confidence that people place in the legislature. Respondents were asked: "How much do you trust the parliament?" The response options were: "not at all" (coded 0), "just a little" (1), "somewhat" (2), and "a lot" (3). Figure 10.1 shows the distribution of mean values in public trust in the legislature across countries. On the average, countries score 1.71 on this scale of 0 to 3. The graph shows considerable cross-national variation in popular trust in the legislature, ranging from 0.82 in Nigeria to 2.39 in Mozambique.

Independent Variables

Two types of explanatory factors are used in regression models: at the individual level and at the country level. At the individual level there are two main independent variables: *accountability* and *representation*. Accountability measures whether the respondent believes that elections "enable voters to remove from office leaders who do not do what the people want." On average, 54 percent of respondents think that elections "well" or "very well" offer them a periodic opportunity to replace elected officials. Representation

Figure 10.1 Public Trust in the Legislature in Sub-Saharan Africa, 2005–2006

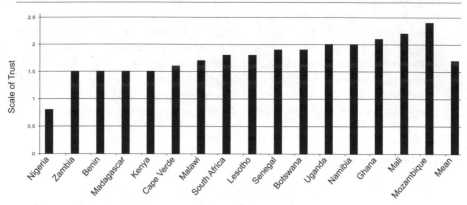

Source: Afrobarometer survey, 2005–2006.
Note: Trust is measured on a 0–3 scale from "not at all" through "just a little" and "somewhat" to "a lot."

measures whether the respondent perceives that elections "ensure that the members of parliament reflect the views of voters." On average, 53 percent of respondents believe that elections "well" or "very well" bring to bear all points of view into the government decisionmaking process. I expect that these two individual-level independent variables should have a positive effect on public trust in the legislature.

While accountability and representation are related concepts, they are also conceptually distinct. The correlation coefficient between the two indicators is 0.55. Among respondents who believe that elections provide a chance to replace leaders, only 62 percent think that elections also facilitate political representation in the legislature. For this reason, and because these dimensions of public opinion are expected to diverge under different electoral systems, the explanatory models that follow treat perceptions of accountability and representation as separate explanatory factors.

At the country level, I capture electoral systems by reference to *mean district magnitude*. This variable is a measure of the proportionality of the electoral system, which allows us both to distinguish majoritarian from proportional systems and to introduce wide variation within the proportional representation group in the country sample. Table 10.1 displays country-level characteristics.

I am specifically interested in whether electoral systems condition the relationship between public perceptions of accountability and representation on the one hand, and citizens' confidence in the parliament on the other. To test the accountability hypothesis, I add a cross-level interaction

Table 10.1 Descriptive Statistics for Country-Level Characteristics in Sub-Saharan Africa, 2005–2006

	2005 Freedom House Index (political rights, civil liberties)	Mean District Magnitude (lower house)	Electoral System	Effective Number of Political Parties
Benin	2, 2	6.9	Party-list PR	6.16
Botswana	2, 2	0.9	First past the post	1.42
Cape Verde	1, 1	4.5	Party-list PR	2.07
Ghana	1, 2	1.0	First past the post	2.16
Kenya	3, 3	0.9	First past the post	3.22
Lesotho	2, 3	1.5	Mixed-member proportional	1.02
Madagascar	3, 3	1.3	First past the post & Party-list PR	4.89
Malawi	4, 4	1.0	First past the post	2.68
Mali	2, 2	1.0	Two-round	1.31
Mozambique	3, 4	22.7	Party-list PR	1.99
Namibia	2, 2	72.0	Party-list PR	1.66
Nigeria	4, 4	1.0	First past the post	2.22
Senegal	1, 2	36.2	Parallel party block	2.40
South Africa	2, 3	44.4	Party-list PR	2.15
Uganda	5, 4	1.0	First past the post	1.15[a]
Zambia	4, 4	1.0	First past the post	2.88
Mean		11.7		2.46

Sources: World Bank 2007; International IDEA 2005.
Notes: "Mean district magnitude" is the mean score of the number of candidates to be elected in the district. A greater mean district magnitude means more proportional electoral system.
   a. Based on 2006 parliamentary elections. In Uganda, political parties were not allowed to participate in general elections between 1986 and 2005.

term—*accountability × mean district magnitude*—into the models. I expect that the interaction term should have a negative coefficient. In other words, proportional electoral systems are expected to mitigate the positive effects of popular perceptions of accountability on popular confidence in parliament. The models also include an additional cross-level interaction term—*representation × mean district magnitude*—to test if a more proportional electoral system is likely to reinforce the positive relationship between mass perceptions of representation and popular trust in the legislature. In this case, I expect the interaction term to have a positive coefficient.

Control Variables

The models also include a series of control variables that may have an impact on popular trust in the legislature. At the country level, I control for the effective number of parliamentary parties, and levels of democratization (a reversed average score of political rights and civil liberties as calculated by Freedom House in 2005). Variations in both party systems and regime type should shape citizens' confidence in legislature. A larger effective number of parliamentary parties implies that voters have greater choice in elections and, especially if parties are linked with voters' ethnic groups, increased popular trust in the parliament. The development of the legislature may in turn be dependent on a country's degree of democratization, with higher levels of democracy encouraging greater public trust in the legislature.

A number of individual-level variables are also used to control for attitudinal and demographic factors. In African politics, the discretionary decisions of strong presidents and neopatrimonial elites often marginalize the roles of the legislature. If survey respondents feel positively about a president's dominant power in policymaking, they should have lower levels of trust in the legislature. The quality of elections should also matter for citizens' ability to express confidence in the legislature; people who highly rate the freeness and fairness of the elections that brought their national representatives to power are more likely to express high levels of trust.

Multiparty elections in Africa have often led to the formation of ethnic parties rather than ideological or programmatic ones (Sisk and Reynolds 1998). Thus members of minority ethnic groups should grant legitimacy to the legislature to the extent that they can find a party to represent their interests. Because numerous studies also find that perceptions of the economy influence attitudes about the performance of political institutions (Weatherford 1992; Anderson and Guillory 1997), I include two evaluations of economic conditions, one personal (egocentric) and the other national (sociotropic).

Finally, to control for party affiliations, this study includes an individual's identification with ruling political parties. Existing studies find that such "winners" are likely to express higher levels of trust in institutions (Norris 1999; Anderson et al. 2005; Cho and Bratton 2006; Chapter 12 in this volume). I also control for age, education, gender, and urban or rural habitation. Descriptive statistics for all individual-level variables are shown in Table 10.2.

Multilevel Analysis

Due to the multilevel structure of the Afrobarometer dataset—survey respondents are nested within countries—I estimate a model of institutional trust using multilevel analysis (Raudenbush and Bryk 2002). A multilevel model is a type of regression analysis that is particularly suitable for such a dataset. Unlike the ordinary least squares regression, the equation has two

Table 10.2 Descriptive Statistics for Individual-Level Variables in Sub-Saharan Africa, 2005–2006

	Number of Persons Surveyed	Mean	Standard Deviation	Minimum	Maximum
Trust in the legislature	21,231	1.71	1.09	0	3
Perceptions of accountability	20,131	1.57	0.97	0	3
Perceptions of representation	20,157	1.55	0.90	0	3
Quality of elections	20,953	3.02	1.07	1	4
Dominant executive	21,641	2.00	0.91	1	4
Minority ethnic group	20,092	0.81	0.99	0	3
Personal economic condition	22,963	2.65	1.19	1	5
National economic condition	22,541	2.62	1.26	1	5
Winner	23,045	0.39	0.49	0	1
Age	22,789	36.58	14.93	18	130
Education	22,954	3.11	2.03	0	9
Gender (male = 0, female = 1)	23,045	0.50	0.50	0	1
Urban (rural = 0, urban = 1)	23,045	0.39	0.49	0	1

Source: Afrobarometer survey, 2005–2006.
Note: Minimum and maximum indicate the range of survey responses; mean indicates the average response for all individuals surveyed.

error terms: one for the individual level and one for the country level. In addition, a multilevel model helps to overcome a number of statistical problems associated with ordinary least squares, including underestimating the standard errors for country-level predictors, which constitute key independent variables in this study. Ordinary least squares regression also assumes that there is constant variance and no clustering across countries. Multilevel modeling, in contrast, allows us to estimate a model with varying intercepts and slopes among countries in this study, and provides for direct estimation of variance components at both levels of the model (Steenbergen and Jones 2002).

Results

To test for significant variation in public trust in the legislature at the individual and country levels, I first estimate an analysis of variance, which decomposes the variance in the dependent variable between the two different levels of analysis. If both variance components are statistically significant, then both levels of analysis are important. Indeed, I find significant variance in public confidence in the parliament at both levels. The results of the analysis of variance are not shown. But the maximum-likelihood estimate of individual-level variance was 1.028 and its standard error was 0.009; the maximum-likelihood estimate of country-level variance was 0.136 and its standard error was 0.050. These results clearly suggest that both individual- and country-level variance be taken into account in order to fully understand the levels of public trust in the legislature.

I therefore construct a multilevel model of institutional trust in two forms (see Table 10.3). Model 1 examines the independent effects of two public perceptions about how elections work in practice (accountability and representation) on citizen trust in the legislature. Model 2 adds two cross-level interaction terms (*accountability × mean district magnitude* and *representation × mean district magnitude*) to take into account the relative and contingent effects of electoral systems. In model 1, I consider the two key explanatory variables at the individual level: one measures popular perceptions of the voters' ability to replace elected officials (accountability) and the other measures popular perceptions of the social composition of members of parliament (representation).

The results show that attitudes toward accountability do not have any significant effects on popular trust in the legislature. Whether or not citizens believe that they can use elections to reward or punish elected officials is not a significant factor when they express trust in the legislature. The results suggest that periodic multiparty elections are not seen as offering any practical control for ordinary people to select a better-performing candidate for the seat in the national assembly. In this respect, elections in Africa do not seem to activate an important aspect of democracy: the accountability mechanism. Even after the introduction of multiparty elections, one-party dominance and infrequent instances of executive power turnover are still the order of the day in many countries. The prevalence of ethnically based parties also limits electoral choice, since there are strong incentives for voters to merely endorse coethnic candidates and reject the rest. In short, the analysis in Table 10.3 offers no support for the hypothesis that voters feel they have the ability to reward or punish elected officials in elections by holding them accountable to constituents' interests.

On the other hand, popular perceptions of representation have a large, positive, and statistically significant effect on the levels of trust in the legislature. This result is consistent with the hypothesis that citizens who feel that elections enhance representation in the legislature are more likely to express trust. It suggests that multiparty elections do work as an instrument of democracy, in this case via the representation mechanism. In some countries, a transition to multiparty elections significantly increased the number of political parties and enabled some of them, including small ethnic parties, to gain seats in the national legislature. As of 2012, Benin has twelve parties in the national assembly, Kenya ten, and South Africa twelve. If voters have a preferred party in the legislature, they are more likely to feel that their

Table 10.3 Individual- and National-Level Predictors of Popular Trust in the Legislature in Sub-Saharan Africa, 2005–2006

	Model 1	Model 2
Fixed effects		
Individual-level predictors		
Accountability	0.001	−0.011
	(0.010)	(0.011)
Accountability × mean district magnitude		0.001
		(0.001)
Representation	0.171**	0.152**
	(0.011)	(0.012)
Representation × mean district magnitude		0.002**
		(0.001)
Dominant executive	−0.016*	−0.015
	(0.008)	(0.009)
Quality of election	0.122**	0.122**
	(0.008)	(0.008)
Minority ethnic group	−0.088**	−0.088**
	(0.008)	(0.009)
National economic condition	0.071**	0.071**
	(0.008)	(0.008)
Personal economic condition	0.026**	0.026**
	(0.008)	(0.008)
Winner	0.230**	0.231**
	(0.017)	(0.017)
Age	0.001	0.001
	(0.001)	(0.001)
Education	−0.044**	−0.044***
	(0.005)	(0.005)
Female	−0.007	−0.007
	(0.016)	(0.016)
Urban	−0.108**	−0.107**
	(0.017)	(0.017)
Country-level predictors		
Mean district magnitude (electoral system)	0.001	−0.004
	(0.003)	(0.004)
Democratization	0.012	0.006
	(0.071)	(0.071)
Effective number of political parties	0.157	0.154
	(0.088)	(0.089)
Constant	0.642	0.711
	(0.328)	(0.333)
Variance components		
Country-level	0.260**	0.263**
	(0.054)	(0.055)

(continues)

Table 10.3 Continued

	Model 1	Model 2
Individual-level	0.946**	0.945**
	(0.005)	(0.005)
–2 × log-likelihood	41,725.892	41,722.954
N	15,243	15,243

Source: Afrobarometer survey, 2005–2006.
Notes: Estimates are maximum-likelihood estimates (generalized least squares). Standard errors appear in parentheses.
***$p < 0.001$, **$p < 0.01$, *$p < 0.05$.

voices will be heard and that their particular interests will be represented in the governmental decisionmaking process.

Most of the individual-level control variables are statistically significant, and in some cases their effects are quite substantial. In particular, people who accept the dominance of chief political executives (by agreeing that "since the president represents all of us, he should pass laws without worrying what the parliament thinks") are less likely to express confidence in parliament. Compared with the president, ordinary people apparently still believe that the legislature possesses relatively weak power in the policymaking process and in the operations of the state. By contrast, the quality of elections has a positive and significant effect on public trust in the legislature. People who think that the last national elections were largely or completely "free and fair" are much more likely to feel that the elected parliament is trustworthy. In short, high-quality elections provide a boost the popular legitimacy of the legislature.

I also find that people who feel that their own ethnic group is treated unfairly by the government are more likely to show lower levels of trust in the legislature. One of the main roles of the legislature is to represent the various and conflicting interests of the society as a whole; those ethnic groups who are marginalized from the governmental decisionmaking process are very likely to express their distrust in the legislature. Public perceptions of economic performance also matter: higher ratings of national and personal economic conditions are associated with more optimistic assessments about the parliament's performance. Consistent with existing studies, ordinary Africans tend to build their own levels of trust in political institutions based on their evaluations of economic performance. Moreover, citizens who identify with parties in power ("winners") reveal higher trust in the legislature than those who support opposition parties.

Meanwhile, urbanized and educated respondents exhibit lower levels of trust in the legislature. Both urban dwellers and highly educated citizens are likely to have more information on the governmental decisionmaking process. Perhaps as a result, these Africans are more critical of how the political system generally, and the legislature in particular, work in the region. Age and gender have no significant effect on public trust in the legislature.

In model 1 in Table 10.3, none of the three country-level predictors is statistically significant at the 0.05 level. This result may be due to the small amount of variance in political regime across the sixteen countries included in this study, which are among the most politically open on the continent. At this stage of the analysis, the results show that, on their own, electoral systems do not have any direct impact on public trust in the legislature, a conclusion inconsistent with existing studies (Norris 1999; Cho and Bratton 2006). Instead, country-level variance in the model must be due to other factors unrelated to the design of the electoral system, the effective number of political parties, or the level of democracy. I tested for the possible impact of ethnic fractionalization and the average annual growth rate in gross domestic product in the decade prior to 2005, but neither was statistically significant (not shown).

To deepen the analysis, model 2 in Table 10.3 includes two cross-level interaction terms to explore whether and how electoral systems matter for public trust in the legislature. Recall that I hypothesized that the impact of popular perceptions of either accountability or representation on public trust may be contingent upon electoral systems.

Does a majoritarian electoral system boost public trust in the legislature by means of the accountability mechanism? Under majoritarian systems, which feature one candidate per geographically defined constituency, voters are assumed to have more opportunities for direct contact with elected representatives. They can place the locus of responsibility for providing public goods to the locality squarely on the shoulders of their "own" individual member of parliament. Voters are thus well placed to reward or punish particular leaders at election time—that is, to hold them accountable, if necessary by electing someone else. The results of model 2, however, show that the cross-level interaction term between public perceptions of accountability and mean district magnitude is not statistically significant at a conventional level. I found no evidence suggesting that citizens in countries with majoritarian electoral systems are much more likely than those in proportional representation systems to base their confidence in the legislature on perceptions of their ability to replace policymakers. Electoral systems designed to directly connect voters and political elites apparently fail to establish an accountability mechanism for establishing popular trust in the national legislature.

This result raises a second possibility. Does a proportional electoral system boost public trust in the legislature by means of a mechanism of representation? At face value, one might expect that the positive relationship previously observed between representation and trust is due to the representational qualities of PR electoral systems. In this case, the results of model 2 reveal a positive (if small) and significant (at conventional levels) coefficient for the cross-level interaction term between popular perceptions of MPs' representation and mean district magnitude. This finding suggests that that PR electoral systems have an advantage over majoritarian systems when it comes to boosting trust in representative institutions. Under PR systems, as we expect, citizens perceive that even small parties can easily win seats in the legislature and that minority views and opinions are included in the process of governmental decisionmaking. This inclusive feature of PR systems encourages minority groups and small parties to work within the political system, which in turn contributes to increase public trust in the legislature.

Conclusion

Elections—especially free and fair, competitive, multiparty elections—are a critical component of regime survival in emerging democracies. While sometimes intensifying the polarization of a society along ethnic lines, competitive elections force political elites to legitimate their rule through the ballot box. However, scholars still wonder whether and how multiparty elections work as instruments of democracy in Africa's hybrid regimes. Moreover, we are still debating about the electoral mechanisms that link voters and elected officials. While one group of scholars emphasize the directness and clarity of the connection between voters and policymakers, others point to representation of all segments in society. This chapter has explored how, in practice, ordinary Africans perceive two different mechanisms (accountability and representation) linking them to the legislature and whether these mechanisms shape levels of public trust in the legislative institutions.

I have found that when ordinary Africans build confidence in the national legislature, they focus more on whether elections facilitate the scope of representation of all the factions of society than on whether they can directly reward or punish their representative at the polls. Citizens who positively perceive that elections ensure that members of parliament broadly reflect the views of voters are likely to express higher levels of trust in the legislature. Much also depends on the type of electoral system. Proportional representation systems work better for boosting the positive effects of perceived political representation on public trust in the legislature than do majoritarian systems. On the other hand, I have found no evidence indicating that citizens' popular perceptions about their ability to replace elected officials have a greater effect on their confidence in the legislature in countries with majoritarian electoral systems than in countries with proportional representation systems.

The results show that elections are not fully developed as instruments of democracy in Africa. True, elections are instruments of citizen influence, not direct control, over their representatives. To at least some extent, elections in selected African countries have apparently enabled voters to send leaders who represent their interests to the national parliament. However, voters tell Afrobarometer researchers that they do not at the same time believe that they have a controlling ability to reward or punish elected officials in periodic elections based on performance in office. While the continent has undergone a series of multiparty elections and while some countries have even experienced power alternations as a result of their founding election or subsequent elections, legislator turnover has in fact been a relatively infrequent occurrence. As such, citizens have yet to take full advantage of new opportunities for political representation by turning them into meaningful measures to ensure political accountability (see Chapter 11, this volume).

11

Voters But Not Yet Citizens: The Weak Demand for Vertical Accountability

Michael Bratton and Carolyn Logan

Transitions to competitive, multiparty politics in African countries during the 1990s were jubilantly welcomed, both on the continent and internationally. Today, Africans enjoy unprecedented opportunities to vote, and many still revel in greater individual and political freedoms. But the full potential of democracy—including the promise of accountable governance—has yet to be fulfilled. Economic growth is fragile, corruption remains widespread, and aid dependency continues to frustrate recipients and donors alike. Questions therefore have been raised about indigenous capacity to absorb an influx of new funds without exacerbating old problems. A program of effective aid would seem to require that African political leaders are held accountable—not only to donor agencies but, more importantly, to their own people—for sound policy choices and the effective use of resources.

But why has democratization so far failed to secure better governance? If elected leaders are supposed to be rewarded for good choices and sanctioned for bad ones, why is policy performance still so poor? Why haven't competitively elected governments in Africa demonstrated a significantly greater degree of accountability to their publics than the authoritarian systems that they replaced? How is it, for example, that the multiparty regimes in Kenya, Uganda, Zambia, and Nigeria receive lower scores on corruption-perception indices than much less open societies like Burkina Faso, Gabon, Rwanda, Equatorial Guinea, and Côte d'Ivoire (Transparency International 2005)? After nearly two decades of promoting democracy, citizens and donors have joined the chorus asking why democratization has, so far, fallen short of expectations.

One answer concerns how Africans themselves understand the contours of new political regimes and, in particular, their own roles in a democracy. Analysts and practitioners often assume that voting in elections automatically endows individuals with a sense of ownership of their political system and a will to control leaders. But this may not necessarily be so. Our intention in this chapter is to explore African understandings of political accountability and their own responsibility for securing it. To what extent do they demand answers from elected leaders? To what extent do they feel they receive satisfactory responses? And what are the implications for public policy?

Our findings suggest that the road to accountable governance may be a long one. On the one hand, Africans enthusiastically support electoral politics, which in principle constitutes the most direct means for influencing leaders. They do not, however, believe that elections have been particularly effective at securing political accountability. And when it comes to monitoring leadership performance in the intervals between elections, a substantial number of Africans do not see any role for themselves. Instead, a majority apparently opts for a broadly *delegative* form of democracy, granting authority to oversee elected representatives either to the president, or to other political actors. Only about a third of the Africans we interviewed apparently feel confident in asserting that elected leaders must answer directly to them. Nor do many Africans feel that they receive accountability from leaders; the reported supply of vertical accountability is even lower than the demand for it.

Guillermo O'Donnell has proposed that democracy is ultimately based not on voters, but on *citizens* (2007). To an important extent, Africans may have begun to transform themselves from the "subjects" of past authoritarian systems into active "voters" under the present dispensation. But at the same time, they do not appear to fully grasp their political rights as "citizens," notably the right to regularly claim accountability from leaders. As such, most African political regimes have yet to meet the minimum requirements of representative democracy. Some indicators point toward these regimes as "delegative democracies," albeit in a somewhat broader form than originally described by O'Donnell (1994). But this description does not necessarily capture the crux of the deficiencies that we observe. In fact, the problem for many new democracies in Africa is not so much that citizens knowingly *delegate* authority to strong presidents but that democracy remains *unclaimed* by mere "voters."

This chapter reveals that the public's understanding of its role in governmental accountability appears, in part, to be a historical legacy. Unclaimed democracy is partly a product of previous, top-down authoritarian precedents, which implies that a popular sense of ownership of government will most readily develop at the local level—that is, from the bottom up.

Elections continue to play a powerful role in engaging the public in the political arena. They serve as a starting point for publicizing the broader rights and responsibilities of citizenship; civic education and election monitoring serve as seeds for organizations focused on demanding postelection performance. Public access to information, including about government budgets and expenditures, is a fundamental condition for effective oversight of officials. Finally, public-attitude surveys play a critical role in exposing leaders' self-serving claims that they alone comprehend popular preferences. Taken together, a package of policy programs aimed at administrative decentralization, budget transparency, civic education, and public opinion surveys will likely go a good way toward assisting African citizens to demand accountability for themselves.

Accountability in Perspective

The obligation of political leaders to answer to the public for their actions and decisions—the obligation of *accountability*—is a cornerstone of a well-functioning democracy. In principle, accountability serves multiple purposes. It checks the power of the political class, diminishes arbitrary or abusive rule, and helps to ensure that governments operate effectively and efficiently. Moreover, accountability is intimately linked to citizen participation, leadership responsiveness, and the rule of law, three other pillars that define the practice of democracy. Particularly in representative systems, the level of accountability of elected leaders to their constituents is a key indicator of the quality of democracy (Diamond and Morlino 2005: xiii).

O'Donnell (1994) has coined a useful distinction between two primary types of political accountability: horizontal and vertical. Horizontal accountability refers to restraints imposed by the state on itself, or, more specifically, by one state institution upon another. It rests on the separation of powers between branches of government and refers to the checks on the executive branch exercised by legislative, judicial, regulatory, and monetary institutions. Initially, vertical accountability was defined in terms of elections, or making elected officials answerable to the ballot box. By definition, this type of vertical accountability exists in every democracy, as long as the political system provides voting opportunities and real choice.

But the inherent limitations of individual votes in enforcing accountability upon elected leaders are well known. Most obvious, voters enjoy infrequent opportunities to cast a ballot; for president or parliament this opportunity arises only once every four or five years. Moreover, elections force voters to compress myriad preferences—of political identity, competing policies, retrospective evaluation, and future expectation (see Chapter 5)—into a single choice. In Africa, elections rarely offer real programmatic alternatives, thus limiting choice itself. Moreover, incumbent leaders can easily break promises and resort to evasion (Maravall 1996). And voting does almost nothing to hold bureaucrats, the judiciary, or security forces to account for their actions. Elections thus constitute a blunt instrument for enforcing accountability.

Analysts increasingly recognize that popular demands for accountability are far more varied and important than those captured by elections alone. In the long intervals *between* elections, there is considerable scope for popular initiative—both individual and collective—through mass mobilization and public protest, advocacy and lobbying campaigns, lawsuits, and other "new accountability initiatives" such as participatory budgeting and expenditure monitoring (Anderson 2006; Goetz and Jenkins 2005; Malena, Forster, and Singh 2004). Many of these initiatives presuppose an active and effective civil society that can aggregate interests and engage in political advocacy. But Anne Marie Goetz argues that "the new accountability agenda is characterized by an *expansion* of accountability . . . [to] include more ordinary people seeking to engage directly—rather than relying upon intermediaries—in efforts to make power-holders answer for their actions" (2003: 4–5).

If accountability mechanisms do not include formal means of *enforcement,* then they may be ineffective. Andreas Schedler suggests that "exercises of accountability that expose misdeeds but do not impose material consequences will usually appear as weak, toothless, 'diminished' forms of accountability. They will be regarded as acts of window dressing, rather than real restraints on power" (1999: 15–16). But accountability can still be advanced even when the punishment component is missing. Schedler himself cites the value of institutions like South Africa's Truth and Reconciliation Commission, which focused on publicizing abuses of power and was effective even when sanctions were limited to public exposure and disapproval (1999: 17). Catalina Smulovitz and Enrique Peruzzotti (2000) argue that even symbolic measures can serve to control public servants, potentially destroying their reputations and political capital, as well as activating horizontal mechanisms of accountability. In fact, political leaders who face genuine elections may have considerable incentive to establish or enforce institutional checks and balances. As such, "the linkage between voters and elected representatives sets the tone for all other accountability relationships" (Mainwaring and Welna 2003: 21), because "the effective operation of vertical accountability, through the electoral process, the news media and concerted civic action, causes governments to take seriously the perils of failing to sustain horizontal accountability" (Schacter 2001: 3).

But the literature on vertical accountability fails to address whether individuals are *willing and able* to seek accountability from elected leaders. How do ordinary people understand their own relationships to political representatives and thus their own political roles in a democracy? It is easy to assume that competitive elections automatically unleash public desires and expectations for answerability. But it is not at all clear that popular understandings of political rights and obligations can be taken for granted. Ayesha Jalal argues that, due to embedded culture and the colonial experience, "the extension in India of universal adult franchise did not energize the polity with the spirit of citizens' rights as distinct from the formal periodic exercise of voters' rights." Relations between voters and leaders were largely limited to elections, and considerations of "caste and communal modes of mobilizing voters" inhibited "the rise of an ethic of representatives' accountability to citizens that would be the hallmark of any substantive democracy" (1995: 19–20).

Frederic Schaffer highlights the importance of understanding local intentions, interpretations, and explanations of politics—that is, "how local populations understand their own actions" (1998: 7). He finds that, in Senegal, people vote for reasons of community solidarity or for personal gain rather than to influence public policy or ensure accountability. He argues that the very notion of public accountability must be questioned in Senegalese society, where many people have a weak sense of a "national good" that politicians should be expected to pursue, or a weak sense of themselves as individuals with democratic rights in the national arena. Yet Gabriela Ippolito-O'Donnell proposes that "democracy entails a particular conception of the human being *cum* citizen as an *agent* . . . an autonomous, reasonable and responsible individual" (2006: 10–11; see also O'Donnell, Cullel, and Iazetta 2004: 24–31). Similarly, Smulovitz and Peruzzotti note that societal mechanisms of civic action tend to be activated by actors "that recognize themselves as legitimate claimants of rights" (2003: 310). Yet immense metamorphoses may be required for individuals to transit from "subjects" under authoritarian rule, to "voters" in electoral democracies, and thereafter to rights- and accountability-demanding "citizens." The assertion by individuals of *superior authority* over public officials is no small step. History matters: democratic citizenship is not built in a day, and a legacy of authoritarianism cannot be wiped out overnight (see North 1990).

In new electoral regimes that lack deep democratic traditions, it is more common for the members of general public to *delegate* rather than claim their legitimate political rights. In Latin America, for example, voters may demand vertical accountability at election time, but they all too readily grant presidents a mandate to rule essentially unilaterally once elected. In O'Donnell's words: "Delegative democracies rest on the premise that whoever wins election to the presidency is thereby entitled to govern as he or she sees fit. . . . After the election, voters/delegators are expected to become a passive but cheering audience of what the president does" (1994: 59–60). O'Donnell characterizes the key distinction between delegative and representative democracies as an institutional rather than an individual infirmity (1994: 61–62). But by emphasizing the institutional weaknesses that impair horizontal accountability, his formulation may overlook the crux of the problem: the failure of the public to *claim* a representative democracy. While he implicitly conceives of the public in transitional societies as having an underdeveloped desire for accountability, he treats such demand-side failures as secondary to the supply-side shortcomings of governmental institutions and to the president's successful efforts to undermine them.

We thus offer an alternative characterization that focuses on whether individuals *demand* vertical accountability, especially between elections. We contend that political accountability remains incomplete in Africa because individuals have a limited appreciation of political rights, of reasonable expectations, and of their own public roles and responsibilities. In other words, the general public's adoption of an ethic of citizenship may lag well behind their enjoyment of the freedom to vote in competitive elections. In effect, the inherent potential of democracy in these societies remains *unclaimed* by the people. Many Africans may be evolving from subjects into voters, but too few of these voters can be regarded as fully formed citizens.

Afrobarometer data—here pooled from eighteen countries in 2005–2006—present novel opportunities to explore individual attitudes toward vertical accountability between elections. Only if people routinely demand accountability from elected leaders can we conclude that average Africans are evolving into democratic citizens. As an indication of the quality of emerging African democracies, and in a quest to find points of leverage for policy reform, we will also be interested to know whether people think that leaders are supplying accountability.

Vertical Accountability: Who Wants It?

Delving into the demand side of the political process, we first explore forms of vertical accountability other than elections. We ask whether Africans see roles for themselves—beyond voting—as citizens in a representative democracy. We limit our inquiry to the public's interaction with elected representatives (the president, members of parliament or deputies in the national assembly, and local government councilors), rather than all government officials. We want to know whether ordinary people feel responsible for holding these elected leaders accountable between elections, or whether they would rather delegate the monitoring function to other agents or institutions.

Africans appear divided on whether they prefer a representative or delegative form of democracy. When asked, "Who should be responsible for making sure that, once elected, members of parliament do their jobs," they split into two main camps. Across eighteen African countries based on

2005–2006 survey data, one-third of the survey respondents say that "the voters" should take the lead in holding legislators accountable (34 percent). Countering this view, however, a proportion of equal size believe that "the president" (or "the executive branch of government") should supervise the work of legislators (33 percent). The remainder of the survey respondents either say they "don't know" who is responsible for ensuring accountability (10 percent) or that the political parties represented in the parliament should police their own members (23 percent).

One can make a case from these results that Africans *prefer* a broadly *delegative* form of democracy. Adding together all valid responses that do not cite "the voters," we can see that, between elections, more than half of all adults (56 percent) apparently stand ready to abdicate their democratic right to discipline their representatives. In lieu of vertical accountability, they seem willing to accept some form of horizontal accountability exercised by either the legislative or executive branches of government. Let us be clear: these are weak substitutes for popular oversight. Accountability of elected representatives to a legislature or party requires leaders to monitor themselves without any form of popular check or balance. And accountability to a president constitutes an extreme form of horizontal accountability in which the arrow of sovereignty—which, in a democracy, grants precedence to an elected legislature—is reversed. It proposes that the legislature should be held accountable to an executive branch whose members, save usually the president, are unelected.

Do Africans everywhere spurn vertical accountability between elections? Not necessarily. Figure 11.1 shows the percentage of survey respondents in each country who say that "the voters" are responsible for making sure parliamentary representatives do their work. The Afrobarometer mean score (34 percent) conceals a remarkably wide range of cross-national variation. To be sure, only 6 percent of Namibians say they want members of parliament (MPs) to be answerable to voters in a context where almost half the adult population (48 percent) would gladly delegate this task to the executive president. A further 17 percent regard the ruling party, the South West Africa People's Organization, as a reliable agent of restraint. By contrast, a clear majority of almost three-quarters of Malawians prefer that MPs report directly to voters, in a country where only 12 percent countenance entrusting such authority to the president.

Similar patterns prevail when people consider local government councilors. Once again, Malawians (76 percent) are more insistent than other Africans on the right of popular review. They are followed by Malagasy (74 percent), in whose vast country local government is often more visible than central authority, and Ugandans (61 percent), who enjoy a strong recent tradition of participatory local administration. As before, Namibians readily surrender their political rights (just 12 percent demand vertical accountability),

Figure 11.1 Popular Demand for Vertical Accountability in Sub-Saharan Africa, 2005–2006

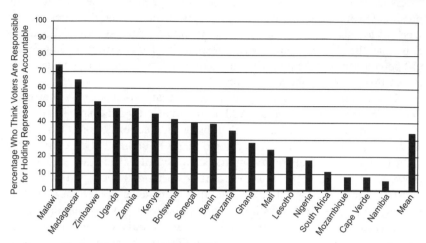

Source: Afrobarometer surveys, 2005–2006.

but now less so than Cape Verdians (5 percent), whose local government is seen as highly dependent on, and therefore largely indistinguishable from, national government.

Importantly, the Africans we interviewed demand more popular accountability from local government than from central government. Overall, some 40 percent think that local government councilors should be subject to oversight from voters, compared to 34 percent for legislators. Moreover, only 19 percent think that the national president should have any role in supervising councilors, some 15 points lower than for MPs. These differences reflect the relative physical proximity of voters to local councilors and, by contrast, the remoteness of the office of the president, other agencies of central government, and even members of parliament, from the areas where citizens live. The data also suggest that a popular constituency for *representative* democracy (rather than delegative democracy) is likely to emerge first at the local government level, and only later with regard to the national parliament.

Nonetheless, popular attitudes about the accountability of elected representatives at all levels are forged from the same mold. Public opinion about the locus of responsibility for responsive governance is correlated across central and local government levels (Pearson's $r = 0.711$, $p < 0.001$). At both levels, there are strong delegative and weaker representative tendencies. Because these attitudes are linked, for purposes of further analysis it is possible to combine them into a valid and reliable item that refers generally to elected representatives, both local and central. This produces a single variable on a 3-point scale that we call "popular demand for vertical accountability." It constitutes the object of explanation in the analysis that follows.

A Multivariate Test

To understand what factors determine an individual's inclination to demand vertical accountability, we use regression analysis. Model 1 in Table 11.1 tests three sets of explanatory factors: social characteristics, political attitudes, and national-level political and institutional legacies.

We already know that mass demand for vertical accountability varies substantially across countries. So it is reasonable to expect that the aggregate-level features of nation-states—whether historical, economic, or institutional—will play a significant role in explaining differences in whether Africans grant voters the leading role in seeking accountability. Before leaping to this conclusion, however, we wish to probe alternative explanations embedded in the social characteristics and political attitudes of individuals. For example, it is reasonable to expect that urban residents would be more politically sophisticated than rural dwellers and thus more likely to think that voters should be responsible for monitoring leaders. We might also expect that those with more education would have a better understanding of the rights and responsibilities of citizens in a democracy. Additionally, it is also plausible to propose that people who possess relevant political knowledge—such as the names of elected representatives or the requirements of presidential term limits—would be more insistent about vertical accountability.

Other things equal, however, the effects of standard social indicators are very limited. Rural residence and gender are not significant determinants of the demand for vertical accountability. Age, education, and wealth all have positive and significant—but quite small—effects. It is hardly surprising that people who are better educated and have amassed personal assets will be more active in seeking direct accountability, as they have both an economic stake in political outcomes and the social status to make effective demands on their representatives. But the effects of these factors are nonetheless marginal, so the moving force behind accountability must lie elsewhere, perhaps in the attitudinal realm.

We considered a wide array of potential attitudinal predictors. For the record, we find that an individual's level of political engagement and sense of personal political efficacy (not shown in Table 11.1) play no role in shaping demand for accountability, nor does a belief that elected leaders should listen to their constituents rather than follow their own ideas. Even persons who say they are inclined to "question leaders" rather than to automatically "respect authority" are no more likely than anyone else to want leaders to

Table 11.1 Popular Demand for Vertical Accountability in Sub-Saharan Africa, 2005–2006

	Model 1			Model 2		
	B	Beta Coefficient	Adjusted Block R^2	B	Beta Coefficient	Adjusted Block R^2
Constant	1.851***			1.340***		
Social characteristics			0.007			0.007
Rural	−0.011	−0.008		0.018	0.013	
Female	−0.003	−0.002		−0.007	−0.005	
Age	0.002***	0.046		0.001***	0.028	
Employment status	−0.026	−0.018		0.000	0.000	
Education	0.015***	0.041		−0.005	−0.013	
Wealth	0.019***	0.036		0.026***	0.048	
Political attitudes			0.060			0.060
Know political leaders	0.041***	0.048		0.088***	0.103	
Know term limits	0.046***	0.033		0.026	0.018	
Reject one-person rule	0.023***	0.035		0.028***	0.043	
Perceive corruption	0.028***	0.032		0.016	0.018	
Question leaders	0.007	0.015		0.012***	0.025	
Leaders should listen	0.008	0.011		0.027***	0.036	
Country contexts			0.160			
South Africa	−0.429***	−0.190				
Nigeria	−0.349***	−0.163				
Namibia	−0.471***	−0.154				
Mozambique	−0.528***	−0.150				
Lesotho	−0.474***	−0.128				
Cape Verde	−0.592***	−0.120				
Ghana	−0.185***	−0.056				
Botswana	−0.135***	−0.043				
Mali	−0.134***	−0.043				
Benin	0.152***	0.045				
Madagascar	0.361***	0.116				
Malawi	0.450***	0.128				
Institutional legacies						0.085
Years of independence				0.009***	0.156	
Past presidential rule				−0.109***	−0.117	
Liberation movement				−0.002***	−0.070	
Plurality electoral system				0.063***	0.043	
Adjusted R^2	0.183			0.103		

Source: Afrobarometer survey, 2005–2006.

Notes: For country dummies in model 1, Tanzania is the excluded category. Only countries for which the unstandardized ordinary least squares regression coefficient (B) is significant at $p < 0.001$ (***) are shown.

answer directly to voters. Instead, what matters most is an individual's level of political knowledge. Not surprisingly, people who know the names of their legislative representatives and local government councilors are most likely to demand accountability from them. People who know the constitutional rule about how many terms in office a national president may serve (usually just two) are also more likely to call their representatives to account. People who reject a "strong-man" presidential regime in which "elections and parliament are abolished so that the president can decide everything" (i.e., "one-man rule") also want an assertive citizenry. Finally, the more that people perceive that elected representatives are corrupt, the more likely they are to want to hold them to account.

But we again concede that the overall explanatory power of the effects of political attitudes is quite small. In the realm of public opinion, demand for the accountability of elected leaders to voters is nascent at best. And the limited demand that does exist is widely dispersed among all classes and categories of people. We can only conclude that, even in new African democracies, most people are only just beginning to form the preferences that would enable a personal transition to active citizenship.

From where, then, does the low demand for accountability originate? Our findings confirm that, rather than being an attribute of particular individuals or groups, this prevalent mind-set is better understood at the country level through the shared experiences of whole populations. In particular, people who live in South Africa, Nigeria, Namibia, and Mozambique, among other countries, are less likely than the average African to demand popular accountability (see Chapter 9, this volume). By contrast, living in Malawi or Madagascar significantly increases such demand.

But attributing demand for vertical accountability simply to "country effects," indicating that characteristics specific to each country are the determining factors, is unhelpful for building theory or prescribing policies. The challenge is to replace country names with *common* historical and institutional features. In model 2 of Table 11.1, we test several alternatives that offer insight into the factors that underlie fixed country effects. Nonetheless, the total explanatory power of these alternatives is just over half that of the "country effects" alone, so we conclude that other omitted influences, as yet unidentified and unmeasured, are also at work.

First, African citizens are more likely to demand vertical accountability if their countries have been independent for a long time. This implies that demand for public accountability is an attribute that people learn gradually, and that learning occurs largely through accumulated experience—good or bad—with self-governance. In other words, citizens usually seek to hold leaders to account only after they discover that the latter are not governing in the public interest. This insight helps us to interpret the relatively high levels of demand for vertical accountability in countries like Benin, Madagascar, and Malawi, all of which gained independence in the early 1960s and which subsequently suffered indigenous dictatorships. In newly free countries, such as South Africa (1994) and Namibia (1990), insufficient time has elapsed for citizens to learn this lesson. Like other Africans before them, South Africans and Namibians are allowing leaders considerable latitude in the early years of the founding democratic regime.

But the way that leaders governed after independence is also important, especially the extent to which they concentrated power in the presidency. As a way of differentiating countries on this dimension, we calculated the number of years between independence and 1989 that each country spent under personal dictatorship, military rule, or plebiscitary one-party rule as a share of the total years since independence ("past presidential rule"). We think that the relatively low demand for accountability in Nigeria, for example, can be traced in part to eighteen years of highly centralized military dictatorship during this period (Sklar, Onwudiwe, and Kew 2006: 102), which counteracts the positive effects of the country's early independence. At a general level, a legacy of past presidential rule is negatively and significantly correlated with demand for accountability. To state the result differently, Africans who were socialized under the rule of strong presidents in the past and who thus have limited experience with representative democracy are likely to default to a delegative form of democracy today. A long period of independence therefore helps the development of democratic citizenship in all countries, but it helps those who lived under a repressive system much less than those who lived under more open regimes.

Third, the mode of decolonization also matters. National liberation movements led armed struggles in the latecomer countries mentioned earlier, plus Cape Verde, Mozambique, and Zimbabwe. This mode of decolonization featured dominant political parties based on revolutionary discipline and democratic centralism. These organizational features were carried over into the postcolonial phase, with leaders like Samora Machel, Sam Nujoma, and Robert Mugabe being resistant to, even intolerant of, political pluralism and competition. Instead, they sought to indoctrinate their compatriots to follow an official party line. In this way, the legacy of national liberation has discouraged a political culture of bottom-up accountability.

Finally, as an alternative to historical path dependencies, we consider contemporary political institutions, notably the electoral system (see also Chapters 9 and 10). Among the countries studied here, eleven possess plurality systems (first-past-the-post elections in single-member districts) and five employ proportional systems (like party-list proportional representation, with various district magnitudes). We find that plurality systems have a more positive effect than proportional and mixed systems on popular demands for political accountability. This stands to reason, since under plurality systems citizens can identify and locate a single representative, whom they can potentially hold accountable. Under the party-list proportional representation system—as in South Africa, where the whole country forms one electoral district for parliamentary elections—citizens do not know who to approach as "their" representative. But the accountability benefits of plurality systems must be weighed against benefits (of representativeness and inclusivity) of proportional systems before taking a strong position on this matter.

Vertical Accountability: Are Africans Getting It?

To measure the supply of vertical accountability, we focus on the perceived credibility of politicians. The Afrobarometer survey asks, "In your opinion, how often do politicians keep their campaign promises after elections?" Like people elsewhere in the world, Africans have skeptical views on this subject. Across eighteen African countries based on 2005–2006 survey data, an average of just 15 percent think that elected leaders keep their word "often" or "always." Some 38 percent say that elected leaders do so "rarely," and a plurality (44 percent) say "never." With only 3 percent who "don't know," almost everyone has an opinion on this hot topic.

Figure 11.2 depicts the extent to which people think campaign promises are credible across African countries. Whereas more than one-third of Namibians put faith in the pledges of politicians, just 3 percent do so in Benin. A visual comparison of Figures 11.1 and 11.2 reveals two insights. First, fewer people perceive a supply of vertical accountability than the (already low) proportion who demand it (15 versus 34 percent). And second, there is a systematic inverse relationship between demand and supply of vertical accountability at the aggregate, country level (Pearson's $r = 0.690$,

Figure 11.2 Perceived Supply of Vertical Accountability in Sub-Saharan Africa, 2005–2006

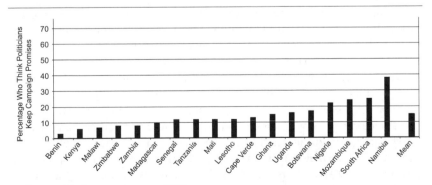

Source: Afrobarometer survey, 2005.

$p < 0.001$). However, this relationship does not hold at the individual level. For example, Namibians and Mozambicans are very unlikely to say they *want* accountability, and also much more likely to report that they are *getting* it. In these places, low popular expectations are easily satisfied. By contrast, Malawians and Zimbabweans insist that they *want* leaders to be beholden to citizens, but they do not report *getting* much responsive service. In these settings, widespread popular demands are routinely frustrated.

Africans also doubt that politicians "do their best to deliver development after elections." Instead, people commonly complain that candidates for office make grandiose guarantees of social and economic investments that are never subsequently fulfilled. The distribution of this attitude closely mirrors opinion about campaign promises (Pearson's $r = 0.634$, $p < 0.001$). Accordingly, we calculate an average construct of "the perceived supply of vertical accountability" to serve as the object of explanation.

What accounts for the generally low levels of this indicator in sub-Saharan Africa? In particular, why are most Africans getting less accountability than they say they want? Table 11.2 reports results. Performance evaluations now loom large. Even when controlled for country contexts or institutional legacies, these assessments lie at the heart of how people evaluate whether or not their leaders are accountable.

First, from a popular perspective, an accountable leader is seen primarily as one who listens carefully to constituents. The most important determinant of supply of accountability is the evaluation of political responsiveness, or the extent to which citizens think elected representatives actually "listen" (see Chapter 14). The interviewers asked, "How much of the time do you think MPs try their best to listen to what people like you have to say?" Again, local leaders fare slightly better than national leaders: 62 percent of survey respondents think local councilors listen at least "sometimes," compared to 54 percent for national legislators. But importantly, only about one-quarter of all adults think that either set of leaders listen "often" or "always."

Confidence in the effectiveness of elections also matters. As reported earlier, less than half of all Afrobarometer respondents think that elections work well at replacing unresponsive leaders and ensuring that popular preferences are aired in parliament. Those who "think elections work" are significantly more likely to believe that they are being supplied with accountable governance. This result helps to confirm the centrality of elections to any popular conception of vertical accountability, including in Africa.

The next most important consideration is whether people think leaders get special treatment under the law. The survey asks, "How likely do you think it would be that the authorities could enforce the law if a top official: (a) committed a serious crime; or (b) did not pay tax on some of the income they earned?" The same questions were then asked about the likelihood of law enforcement if "a person like you" committed these offenses. The "en-

Table 11.2 Perceived Supply of Vertical Accountability in Sub-Saharan Africa, 2005–2006

	Model 1			Model 2		
	B	Beta Coefficient	Adjusted Block R^2	B	Beta Coefficient	Adjusted Block R^2
Constant	0.394			(0.920)		
Social characteristics			0.006			0.006
Rural	−0.005	−0.003		−0.008	−0.005	
Female	0.018	0.012		0.024	0.015	
Age	0.000	0.006		0.000	−0.009	
Employment status	0.016	0.010		0.042***	0.027	
Education	0.007	0.017		0.020***	0.052	
Wealth	0.016***	0.028		0.014	0.024	
Performance evaluations			0.106			0.106
Political leaders do listen	0.114***	0.135		0.115***	0.137	
Think elections work	0.075***	0.118		0.070***	0.110	
Enforcement gap: rule of law	−0.043***	−0.093		−0.058***	−0.125	
Trust representative institutions	0.043***	0.076		0.032***	0.057	
Performance gap: MP service	−0.042***	−0.072		−0.057***	−0.097	
Perceive corruption	−0.050***	−0.054		−0.038***	−0.041	
Country contexts			0.068			
Nigeria	0.379***	0.149				
Namibia	0.455***	0.137				
South Africa	0.257***	0.094				
Mozambique	0.336***	0.083				
Uganda	0.130***	0.056				
Zambia	0.166***	0.047				
Madagascar	0.108***	0.034				
Botswana	−0.119***	−0.035				
Malawi	−0.203***	−0.057				
Institutional legacies						0.016
Years of independence				−0.008***	−0.114	
Past presidential rule				0.001***	0.045	
Liberation movement				0.006	0.280	
Plurality electoral system				0.008	0.005	
Adjusted R^2	0.158			0.123		

Source: Afrobarometer survey, 2005–2006.
Notes: For country dummies in model 1, Kenya is the excluded category. Only countries for which the unstandardized ordinary least squares regression coefficient (B) is significant at $p < 0.001$ (***) are shown.

forcement gap" is wide. For example, whereas 90 percent think that ordinary citizens would be punished for committing a serious crime, only 53 percent think that a top official would receive the same treatment. The uneven application of the rule of law is another leading factor that explains the perceived supply of accountability: if citizens think that leaders benefit from a culture of impunity, then they doubt that vertical accountability is being supplied.

Leadership performance between elections is also important. In this case, we probe whether legislative representatives actually perform constituency service with the intensity expected by citizens. The survey asks two related questions: "How much time *should* your MP spend in this constituency?" and "How much time *does* your MP spend?" The "performance gap" between these two estimates is again wide. Whereas 33 percent of interviewed Africans want their legislative representative to visit the community at least weekly, only 8 percent report that he or she actually does so. The performance gap on MP service is a solid, negative predictor: the larger the gap between expectation and delivery, the less the general public thinks that service is being supplied with vertical accountability. The clear implication is that leaders must be present and visible in the locality for citizens to think that they are being served.

Finally, two other important considerations pull in opposite directions. On the positive side, citizens who trust representative institutions (the national assembly and local government council) are more likely to perceive accountable governance. But on the negative side, citizens who see corruption among assembly and council representatives are less likely to think they are being supplied with accountability. As expected, institutional trust and perceptions of official corruption are inversely related (Pearson's $r = -0.377, p < 0.001$).

Before we conclude that political attitudes and performance evaluations are the primary factors explaining the supply of vertical accountability, it is necessary to confirm that these evaluations are not trumped by institutional legacies. Model 1 in Table 11.2 shows that "country contexts" are again significant. A familiar pattern emerges: Nigerians, along with Namibians, South Africans, and Mozambicans, think they are getting more accountability than does the average African, whereas Malawians think they are getting less.

But are these "country effects" again interpretable as institutional legacies? In model 2, longer duration of independence actually has a negative effect on the perceived supply of vertical accountability. This could mean that even as demand for accountability goes up over time, the perceived supply goes down. Alternatively, citizens may more readily give elected representatives the benefit of the doubt in newly liberated countries: because popular expectations are lower (relative to other countries), so evaluations of supply are higher. Consistent with our earlier argument, citizens have not yet learned—either because insufficient time has passed, or because representatives are so far doing a good enough job—that, in the long run, leaders are rarely effective at holding themselves to account. Likewise, duration of "past presidential rule" once again partially counteracts the effects of duration of independence. The effects of this factor on perceived supply of accountability are positive, suggesting that individuals who spent many years living under systems of centralized, repressive rule are likely to be less critical than those who have lived in more open and competitive societies.

Importantly, however, neither country context nor institutional legacies displace an explanation based mainly on political attitudes and performance evaluations. On the supply side, we get considerably more explanatory mileage from a set of performance evaluations—especially whether citizens think that leaders listen to constituents, think that elections are effective, and think that leaders subject themselves to equal treatment under a rule of law—than from shared institutional histories. This is just as well for purposes of devising policies to improve vertical accountability. After all, institutional histories can hardly be changed. But elite behaviors (like failing to listen to constituents or attempting to evade the law) are prospectively subject to at least a measure of reengineering.

Conclusion

This chapter has explored the stance of ordinary Africans in relation to delegative and representative forms of democracy. At first glance, the concept of delegative democracy would seem to travel well: there is an apparent affinity between O'Donnell's image of unrestrained presidential government in Latin America and the continued dominance, even after democratic transitions, of Africa's political big men. We find evidence—for example that one-third of the electorate wants the *president* to hold legislators accountable—suggesting that a substantial proportion of Africans prefer a delegative model of governance to a representative one.

Yet the evidence also requires that the delegative model be adjusted to African circumstances. First, an equal proportion of the electorate thinks that *voters*—not the president—should be responsible for holding leaders accountable. Second, large majorities in every country firmly oppose the notion of one-man rule in which the president decides everything. And perhaps most telling, two out of three interviewed Africans say that, at least in principle, the legislature and the courts should limit the decisionmaking power of the political chief executive. In this regard, ordinary Africans reject a key tenet of delegative democracy, namely that the president should be unrestrained by horizontal checks.

In reality, however, the legislative and judicial branches of government remain weak in Africa and usually prove ineffective in the face of presidential power. We therefore paid greater attention to vertical accountability, both as a mode of direct popular control of elected leaders, and as an essential complement to horizontal agencies of restraint. We expanded the definition of vertical accountability beyond the common references in the literature to periodic elections, or even to the watchdog functions of organized civil society. Putting a spotlight on individual Africans in the periods between elections, we asked instead whether ordinary people demand vertical accountability from elected representatives, and whether they think such accountability is actually supplied.

Across virtually all social and attitudinal groups, we find low effective demand for representatives to do their jobs between elections. In short, we discern a vacuum in African politics in the arena where pressures for representative democracy are expected to originate—that is, at the mass level, where individual citizens *claim their right* to monitor leaders. In newly minted democracies, especially in countries without previous experience of indigenous dictatorship, people tend to absolve representatives of the responsibility of reporting back to the grassroots communities, and instead defer to the authority of rulers. Moreover, since people broadly agree that the promises of politicians lack credibility, we find even lower perceived levels of a supply of accountability. Which few leaders are deemed accountable? Only those who have developed a reputation for listening to the needs of constituents and of subjecting themselves to equal treatment under a rule of law.

What implications does limited vertical accountability hold for democratization? Africans clearly value open and competitive elections and vote in large numbers. In this role, they undoubtedly help to underpin fragile new electoral democracies in Africa. But elections are hardly inconsistent with delegative democracy; indeed, elections are the very device by which delegation of authority occurs from people to president. A more rigorous test is whether Africans demand—and think they receive—vertical accountability in the long intervals between elections. To do so, Africans would have to assert citizenship rights more regularly and vigorously than the survey evidence so far reveals. In the absence of a popular groundswell in this direction, we cannot describe African political regimes as representative democracies.

Are African regimes therefore best regarded as being delegative democracies? Not completely. The term "delegative" suggests a degree of agency on the part of individual members of society that may be misleading. Emerging from authoritarian pasts, Africans may not so much be intentionally delegating power to their governments as *failing to claim it* from them. Whether unwilling, unable, or simply unaware, many Africans have hesitated to take advantage of the rights and opportunities—along with accompanying responsibilities—that are meant to be theirs in a liberalized political world. They have adopted the attitudes of "voters," who show strong support for the electoral process but have yet to transform themselves into "citizens," who take on the added responsibility of monitoring and, where appropriate, sanctioning leaders in the long intervals between elections. Too many ordinary people instead assume that the head of state (or, to a lesser extent, other arms of the government and the political system) will somehow perform the role of holding elected representatives to account. Thus, to the extent that democracy is supposed to mean "power to the people" and not just "a vote to the people," democracy in Africa remains largely unclaimed.

Part 4

Implications for Democracy

12

Critical Citizens and Submissive Subjects: Election Losers and Winners in Africa

Devra Moehler

Elections have the potential to confer legitimacy, moderate dissent, engender compliance, and heighten citizen efficacy. But do elections fulfill these functions in Africa, where electoral competition is often unfamiliar and imperfect? Specifically, do citizens who feel close to ruling parties (winners) believe that their government institutions are significantly more legitimate than do citizens aligned with opposition parties (losers)? If losers are more disgruntled than winners, is it because they doubt the procedural fairness of the recent elections?

Analyses of Afrobarometer survey data from more than 20,000 respondents in twelve African countries demonstrate that winners are more inclined than losers to trust their political institutions, consent to government authority, and feel politically efficacious. Contrary to initial expectations, however, winners are less willing than losers to defend political institutions—such as judicial courts, independent media, and elected legislatures—against manipulation by elected officials. While losers doubt the trustworthiness, rightful authority, and responsiveness of their political institutions, winners are willing to support their current governments even as they undermine the pillars of liberal democracy. It seems that elections in Africa may generate too little support for the current government among losers and too much support among winners. Critical losers may withhold their consent from current institutions, but they nonetheless are willing to protect imperfect institutions against elite sabotage. Satisfied winners easily comply with the current establishment, but they are also more willing to acquiesce as their chosen leaders erode the independence of political institutions.

This chapter also investigates the hypothesis that winners and losers express different levels of political support because they view elections

219

differently. The analysis indicates that partisan affiliation is strongly associated with perceptions of electoral integrity: winners tend to excuse imperfections and judge recent elections as free and fair, whereas losers are more inclined to report that the elections were fraudulent. Importantly, however, divergent attitudes about the fairness of elections may only be responsible for a small portion of the gap in political support between winners and losers. It seems that the legitimacy gap results more from loser dissatisfaction with what happens between elections than with what happens during them. All else being equal, losers have a hard time accepting their government as legitimate even if they think the election was free and fair. By contrast, winners are overly supportive of their government even if they think the election was fraudulent. These findings suggest that efforts to ensure free and fair elections—and to help citizens perceive them as such—will have only a limited effect in creating constructive and shared levels of political legitimacy in new democracies.

Perceived Institutional Legitimacy in Unconsolidated Electoral Regimes

For democracies to survive and govern effectively, losers as well as winners must accept electoral outcomes and comply with the laws set by elected leaders. Stephen Craig argues that "a crucial aspect of legitimacy has to do with losers' acceptance of the election outcome as valid and with their willingness to consent to the winners' rightful authority to implement policies advocated during the campaign—policies to which losers may be strongly opposed" (2004: 2). Equally important, democratic survival requires that winners do not use their current position of power to undermine structures of political accountability and that citizens aligned with the ruling party do not condone or participate in such antidemocratic behavior (Anderson et al. 2005; Anderson and Lotempio 2002; Anderson and Tverdova 2001, 2003; Banducci and Karp 2003; Clarke and Acock 1989; Fuchs, Guidorossi, and Svensson 1995; Listhaug and Wiberg 1995; Nadeau and Blais 1993; Nadeau 2000; Norris 1999). Mass perceptions of political legitimacy are especially crucial in transitional polities where political systems are unstable and democracy is not yet "the only game in town." If a sizable portion of the population desires, or is apathetic about, institutional change, then there is little to protect the system from elite tampering or more severe challenges. Citizens who deem the system illegitimate may not take up arms against the state, but they will also fail to act as a buffer to those who do seek to alter the political system from within or from without. Understanding how citizens across the political spectrum evaluate the legitimacy of their institutions is important for anticipating the trajectories of hybrid and nascent democratic regimes.

In theory, elections are legitimating institutions because they provide citizens with fair procedures for selecting leaders. Research shows that when individuals believe that decisionmaking procedures are fair, they tend to be more satisfied with the leaders who oversee the process and more accepting of the outcomes of the process—even when the outcomes are deemed undesirable (Anderson et al. 2005; Tyler, Casper, and Fisher 1989; Tyler 1989). In practice, however, most electoral contests in hybrid systems and new democracies are plagued by irregularities, either by design or due to lack of resources, infrastructure, and experience. Furthermore, it is difficult for citizens to assess the causes and consequences of irregularities because election observers and investigative journalists have limited reach and public opinion surveys and exit polls are rare. In the face of uncertainty and poor information, one would expect winners to give their leaders the benefit of the doubt; citizens who emerged from an election victorious will tend to believe that alleged irregularities were unintentional, that the proper candidate won, and that the system is legitimate. In contrast, one would expect losers to assume the worst and conclude that electoral fraud was deliberate and consequential. Additionally, losers might actually witness or be subject to more abuse during campaigns and elections than are winners, especially if the winning party was an incumbent party. As a result, losers may withhold their support not only from elected leaders but also from political institutions.

Individual-level research on electoral outcomes in new democracies or hybrid systems is quite limited (exceptions include Anderson et al. 2005; Bratton, Mattes, and Gyimah-Boadi 2005; Cho and Bratton 2006; Norris 2002). Instead of evaluating citizen attitudes, most studies of transitional elections rely on expert assessments of electoral quality. Expert assessments are well suited for determining whether electoral outcomes accurately reflect the wishes of the voters and are also very revealing of elite behavior. However, expert assessments are less well suited for informing us about whether elections have a legitimizing effect on the mass public. Elections may be deemed free and fair by experts, but not by citizens, and vice versa. Furthermore, even if elections are perceived as free and fair, they may not confer legitimacy on government institutions. Therefore this chapter departs from expert assessments by means of an individual-level approach that examines ordinary citizens' assessments of electoral integrity as expressed in public opinion surveys.

Individual-level survey data are employed to evaluate two hypotheses based on the preceding discussion. The first hypothesis is that Africans who feel close to parties in power tend to award their government institutions greater legitimacy than do nonpartisan independents and those who identify with losing parties. The second hypothesis is that (to the extent that there is a legitimacy gap in political support between winners, independents, and losers in Africa) the relationship between identification with the winning party and perceived legitimacy is mediated by evaluations of electoral fairness. This second hypothesis generates the following predictions: (1) winner status is positively associated with perceived legitimacy of government institutions; (2) winner status is positively associated with opinions of the freeness and fairness of elections; (3) evaluations of electoral honesty are positively related to perceived political legitimacy; and (4) the initial relationship between winner status and perceived legitimacy is attenuated or eliminated in the presence of electoral evaluations. Figure 12.1 depicts these four predictions.

Before proceeding, several weaknesses in the analysis must be addressed. First, the Baron-Kenny procedure (see Baron and Kenny 1986), used to identify mediation, relies on a number of untestable assumptions (Imai et al. 2011). Second, cross-sectional data are used to test for associations that are consistent with the hypothesized causal links shown in Figure 12.1. Given the available data, however, it is impossible to establish the direction of causation between the associated variables. It may be that alternative causal explanations are consistent with the same evidence. For example, it is possible that individuals who feel the government is illegitimate would be subsequently motivated to support opposition parties and also believe the election was forged (Mondak 1993). Or, citizens who witnessed election fraud and corruption may think the resulting government is illegitimate and switch their allegiance to the opposition (McCann and Domínguez 1998). More conclusive tests of the causal influences will have to await panel data, field experiments, or qualitative interviews. Nonetheless, the analysis here provides suggestive evidence regarding the hypotheses represented in Figure 12.1. Furthermore, given what is known about the continuity of party identification (Lindberg and Morrison 2005), the proposed causal theory is the most plausible one.

Figure 12.1 Effect of Winner Status on Political Legitimacy with Evaluation of Electoral Integrity as a Mediating Variable

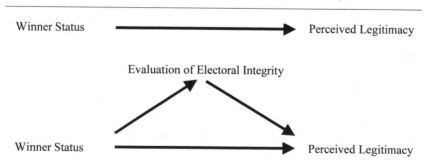

Data and Measurement

This study employs data from Afrobarometer surveys administered between 1999 and 2001 in twelve sub-Saharan African countries undergoing political and economic reform. The dozen countries surveyed were not representative of the continent as a whole, since they tended to be more democratic than the African average. However, they did include a range of regime and election types: two "liberal democracies" (South Africa and Botswana); four "electoral democracies" (Ghana, Mali, Namibia, and Malawi); three "ambiguous regimes" (Tanzania, Nigeria, and Zambia); and three "liberalized autocracies" (Lesotho, Zimbabwe, and Uganda) (Bratton, Mattes, and Gyimah-Boadi 2005; Diamond 2002; Freedom House 2005). Observers judged the most recent elections prior to the first-round Afrobarometer surveys as (1) fully free and fair only in Botswana; (2) exhibiting deficiencies that did not affect the outcome of the elections in Ghana, Lesotho, Malawi, Namibia, South Africa, Tanzania, and Uganda, and (3) containing numerous irregularities that affected the election results in Mali, Nigeria, Zambia, and Zimbabwe. Zimbabwe's election was wracked by widespread and coordinated violence, while Lesotho, Malawi, Mali, Nigeria, South Africa, Tanzania, and Zambia experienced violence primarily in the form of isolated incidents. At the time of the surveys, Botswana had just had its seventh consecutive democratic election; Mali its third; Ghana, Malawi, South Africa, Tanzania, and Zimbabwe their second; and Lesotho, Namibia, Nigeria, and Uganda their first. Namibia and South Africa had proportional representative electoral systems, Mali had a majoritarian system, and the remaining countries had plurality systems (Lindberg 2006).

Institutional legitimacy, or diffuse support, is a multidimensional concept that is defined and measured in slightly different ways by different authors. Vanessa Baird discusses the concept of legitimacy as follows: "Diffuse support is the belief that although at times specific policies can be disagreeable, the institution itself ought to be maintained—it ought to be trusted and granted its full set of powers" (2001: 334). James Gibson writes: "Legitimate institutions are those one recognizes as appropriate decision making bodies even when one disagrees with the outputs of the institution" (2004: 294). Gibson and Gregory Caldeira add: "We define diffuse support as institutional commitment—that is, willingness to defend the institution against structural and functional alterations that would fundamentally alter the role of the institution in society. At the extreme, this means willingness to defend the institution against attempts to abolish it" (1995: 471). Finally, Stephen Weatherford notes: "Political legitimacy is too unwieldy and complex a concept to be grappled in a frontal assault, and virtually all the empirical literature follows the tactic of breaking it into component parts. Thus various lines of research (on alienation, political trust, modes of participation, political efficacy) all partake of a common interest in how citizens evaluate governmental authority" (1992: 149).

Rather than selecting a single dimension of this complex concept, this analysis includes a range of indicators that reflect the descriptions of institutional legitimacy quoted in the previous paragraph. The Afrobarometer instrument necessarily limits what indicators are available, but it nonetheless yields four measures associated with different aspects of institutional legitimacy: institutional trust, consent to authority, external efficacy, and defending democracy.

The first variable measuring legitimacy, *institutional trust,* is a valid and reliable index that sums trust in four government institutions: the electoral commission, courts of law, the army, and the police. The second variable, *consent to authority,* is derived from a question that asks respondents how much they agree or disagree with the statement: "Our government has the right to make decisions that all people have to abide by whether or not they agree with them." The third variable, *external efficacy,* gauges whether citizens feel the system is responsive. Finally, citizens should be more willing to act in defense of institutions they deem legitimate than ones they think are illegitimate. Accordingly, the fourth variable, *defending democracy,* is a valid and reliable index constructed from questions that asked what citizens would do if the government "shut down newspapers that criticized the government," "dismissed judges who ruled against the government," and "suspended the parliament and cancelled the next elections."

For purposes of comparison, these four dependent variables were recoded so that they range from −1 (no legitimacy) to +1 (full legitimacy), with intermediate responses arrayed evenly between the two poles. Negative numbers indicate that citizens think their political institutions are illegitimate, and positive numbers indicate that individuals think their institutions are legitimate. Neutral answers were coded 0. As mentioned earlier, and as confirmed by factor and reliability analyses, these four indicators measure independent dimensions of legitimacy rather than a single unified concept and are thus analyzed separately rather than in combination.

The intervening variable, *free and fair election,* records citizens' evaluations of electoral integrity. It is based on a question that asks respondents to rate the freeness and fairness (or honesty) of the most recent presidential, parliamentary, or general election. The variable has five possible values and is also recoded to range from −1 to +1 for ease of comparison.

Winner status is the key independent variable of interest in this chapter and it takes on three different values, corresponding to winners, nonpartisans, and losers. Citizens who say they feel close to the parties that make up the government (winners) are coded as 2. Citizens who claim they are not close to any party (nonpartisans) are coded as 1. Citizens who report feeling close to opposition parties in the legislature or parties that did not win seats at all (losers) are coded as 0. Michael Bratton, Robert Mattes, and E. Gyimah-Boadi acknowledge that citizens may not truthfully or accurately report their partisan attachments, but argue that the measure is still valid: "Of course, some respondents may rewrite their personal histories by reporting voting records deemed politically correct. Despite the possibility that we were sometimes intentionally misled, we still expect that being a self-proclaimed 'winner' increases one's loyalty to incumbent leaders and reduces one's willingness to criticize their performance" (2005: 259). Roughly 17 percent of respondents would be considered losers, 45 percent are nonpartisans, and 38 percent are coded as winners, although there is considerable variation in the distributions across countries.

Winner Status and Perceived Legitimacy

Is there a winner-loser legitimacy gap? If so, how deep and widespread are the expected doubts about political legitimacy among losers in Africa? Figures 12.2 through 12.5 allow us to compare the mean perceived legitimacy scores for losers, nonpartisans, and winners in the twelve countries surveyed. Where a question was not asked, the country is eliminated from the analysis for that indicator only. The signs indicate differences between winners and losers at the 0.05 level of significance. A positive sign (+) indicates that, on average, winners are significantly more supportive than losers; a negative sign (−) indicates that, on average, winners are significantly less supportive than losers; and a zero (0) indicates that, on average, winners are not significantly different from losers in their attitudes. The bars for the figures depict (1) whether losers and winners, on average, see their

Figure 12.2 Institutional Trust Among Losers, Nonpartisans, and Winners in Sub-Saharan Africa, 1999–2001

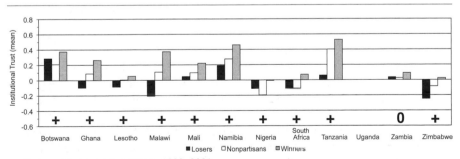

Source: Afrobarometer survey, 1999–2001.
Notes: Afrobarometer question: "How much do you trust the following institutions [to do what is right]: the police, courts of law, the army, the electoral commission?" Sign indicates winner-loser gap at 0.05 level of significance.

Figure 12.3 Consent to Authority Among Losers, Nonpartisans, and Winners in Sub-Saharan Africa, 1999–2001

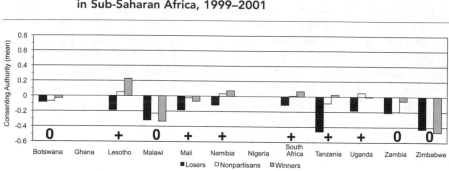

Source: Afrobarometer survey, 1999–2001.

Note: Afrobarometer question: "Please say whether you agree or disagree with the following: 'Our government has the right to make decisions that all people have to abide by, whether or not they agree with them.'" Sign indicates winner-loser gap at 0.05 level of significance.

Figure 12.4 External Efficacy Among Losers, Nonpartisans, and Winners in Sub-Saharan Africa, 1999–2001

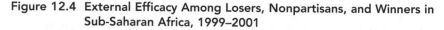
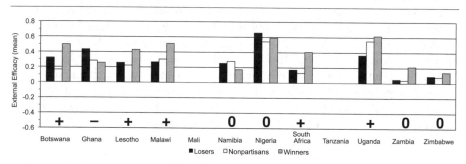

Source: Afrobarometer survey, 1999–2001.

Note: Afrobarometer question: Respondents were asked which of two statements they agreed with, either "No matter who we vote for, things will not get any better in the future" or "We can use our power as voters to choose leaders who will help us improve our lives." Sign indicates winner-loser gap at 0.05 level of significance.

government institutions as legitimate (above zero) or illegitimate (below zero); (2) whether there are cross-national differences in the level of legitimacy; and (3) whether there are cross-national differences in the legitimacy gap—the difference between the first bar and the last for each country.

Figure 12.2 reveals a positive gap in institutional trust between winners and losers in ten countries where the relevant questions were asked. With the exception of Zambia, the winner-loser gaps are statistically significant at the 0.05 level. Winners express significantly greater trust in the electoral commission, courts of law, the army, and the police than do losers in nearly every country. On average, winners say that they can trust their government

Figure 12.5 Willingness to Defend Democracy Among Losers, Nonpartisans, and Winners in Sub-Saharan Africa, 1999–2001

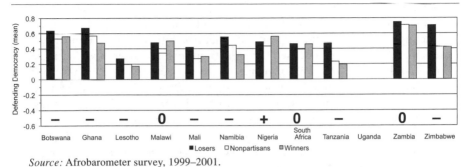

Source: Afrobarometer survey, 1999–2001.

Note: Afrobarometer question: "What would you do if the government took any of the following actions: shut down newspapers that criticized the government, dismissed judges who ruled against the government, suspended the parliament, and canceled the next elections?" Sign indicates winner-loser gap at 0.05 level of significance.

institutions in ten of the eleven countries (Nigeria being the exception), although the means are significantly above zero in only seven of those countries. Taking all countries together, winners express significant trust in their political institutions (winner mean = 0.270), while losers are significantly distrustful (loser mean = –0.023).

The picture is bleaker with regard to popular consent to authority, as depicted in Figure 12.3. Regardless of political affiliations, most citizens are unwilling to grant their governments authority to make binding decisions. However, once again, there is a legitimacy gap whereby winners are significantly more willing than losers to consent to government decisions (winner mean = –0.049, loser mean = –0.231). The winner-loser gap is significantly positive in six of the ten countries. And for losers, the mean value of granting authority is significantly negative in every country.

Figure 12.4 reveals that external efficacy ratings are generally quite high. In the ten countries where the question was asked, Africans agree that they can improve their circumstances by electing responsive leaders. The average winner is significantly positive in all countries, as are most losers. A winner-loser gap is evident for external efficacy, but it is smaller than for other perceived legitimacy measures (winner mean = 0.370, loser mean = 0.313). There is a statistically significant positive gap in half the countries, but the gap is not significant in four others. In Ghana there is a significant reverse gap—losers feel they have more power through the ballot box than do the winners. Indeed, following the survey, the opposition managed to win the 2000 election and change Ghana's leaders.

Finally, Figure 12.5 presents the mean values for whether citizens say they will act to defend their democratic institutions from threatening government actions. Most surveyed Africans report that they would act against hypothetical government attacks on media freedom, judicial independence, and democratic elections. This is important because if legitimacy is to be meaningful for political outcomes, it must induce supportive behavior as well as attitudes. Surprisingly and importantly, the winner-loser gap in defending democracy is the opposite of what was hypothesized. Winners are less inclined to act in defense of their system than are losers (winner mean = 0.404, loser mean = 0.535). Winners in seven countries are significantly less inclined to act in defense of their system. Only in Nigeria is the mean value for winners significantly higher than it is for losers. There is no significant winner-loser gap in the remaining three countries.

Why is it that the losers seem to place a higher value on protecting core democratic institutions than do the winners? Why is the legitimacy gap the reverse of what it is for all other indicators of democratic governances? It is impossible to give a conclusive answer post hoc, although informed analysis suggests a possible explanation. The original assumption was that willingness to defend democratic institutions is a good measure of citizens' perceptions of institutional legitimacy. However, a careful review of the question's wording indicates that the instrument pits support of the current government against the legitimacy of democratic institutions. In other words, it asks: "If the government took an action against current democratic institutions, what would you do?" Both winners and losers, on average, would act to support democratic institutions. However, when forced to choose between the in-power government and their nascent democratic institutions, winners are more willing to support a government that violates democracy than are the losers. This interpretation is consistent with the finding of Bratton and colleagues that "winning is negatively related to citizen rejection of authoritarian rule" (Bratton, Mattes, and Gyimah-Boadi 2005: 260). In this sense, there is such a thing as too much government legitimacy and citizen compliance. Some Africans are willing to support the government even as it violates fundamental democratic precepts—and winners are more susceptible to "overcompliance" with their governments than are the losers. This result also suggests that although government legitimacy and citizen compliance may be good for government effectiveness, such attitudes are not necessarily beneficial for democratic survival, especially in unconsolidated democracies.

In sum, Figures 12.2 through 12.5 depict a common and consistent legitimacy gap between citizens who feel close to winning parties and those who are aligned with losing parties. Winners exhibit greater support for their institutions than do losers. The gap is evident across the different attitude dimensions and most countries. Even so, the figures do not depict a severe legitimacy crisis for losers in most states. Losers are less sanguine about their political institutions, but they do not indicate that they are inclined to withdraw from the political sphere or reject democratic governance as a result. Instead losers say their vote matters nearly as much as winners and, additionally, losers express a greater willingness to act to defend democratic institutions than do those citizens whose favored party is in power. Furthermore, the size of the gap varies considerably by country.

An additional test is warranted to see if the bivariate relationships between winner status and perceived legitimacy remain significant after possibly confounding factors are taken into account. Table 12.1 displays the results of the multivariate regression analyses. In Model A, the indicators of perceived legitimacy are regressed on winner status and a series of control variables. Previous research in old and new democracies found that these traits are often related to partisan affiliation and to perceived legitimacy (Anderson et al. 2005; Anderson and Tverdova 2001, 2003; Clarke and Acock 1989; Listhaug and Wiberg 1995; Nadeau and Blais 1993; Nadeau 2000).

The controls include indices that gauge citizen satisfaction with the political and economic outcomes (government performance and economic performance). The logic is that citizens who think their government is performing well are also more likely to view it as legitimate. The controls also include measures of civic participation and engagement (electoral participation, political interest, and exposure to mass media) because citizens who are actively involved in public affairs tend to view their governments as legitimate.

Finally, the model controls for standard demographic items (education, gender, and age) in order to ensure that personal characteristics do not confound the relationship between winner status and perceived legitimacy (Mattes and Bratton 2007). The model also incorporates dummy variables for each country in the Afrobarometer (as required when an exhaustive set of dummies is employed, one country is excluded, in this case Botswana). There are likely to be cross-national differences in how citizens feel as a result of historical legacies, type of political system, ethnic makeup, margins of victory, electoral quality, length of democracy, level of democracy, and economic development. Including country dummy variables ensures that differences in perceived legitimacy among the twelve countries are not confounded with the differences in perceived legitimacy between winners and losers.

Table 12.1 shows that the coefficients on winner status are substantively and statistically significant for all four aspects of political legitimacy. For the first three dimensions of legitimacy (trust, consent, efficacy), winners are more supportive than losers, even when controlling for confounding factors. For defending democracy, the relationship is negative such that losers are more willing to defend democracy than are winners, all else being equal. Importantly, a comparison of the standardized regression coefficients shows that government performance, economic performance, and education have larger substantive effects than winner status in nearly all of the equations. However, partisan status (winner or loser) is typically more

Table 12.1 The Effects of Electoral Influences on Perceived Institutional Legitimacy in Sub-Saharan Africa, 1999–2001

	Institutional Trust		Consent to Authority		External Efficacy		Defending Democracy	
	Model A	Model B	Model A	Model B	Model A	Model B	Model A	Model B
Electoral influences								
Winner status	0.109***	0.071***	0.039***	0.024	0.034***	0.026**	-0.023**	-0.019*
Free and fair election	n/a	0.169***	n/a	0.060	n/a	0.050***	n/a	-0.020*
Performance evaluations								
Government performance	0.199***	0.171***	0.113***	0.102***	0.073***	0.065***	-0.059***	-0.056***
Economic performance	0.140***	0.116***	0.068***	0.061***	0.124***	0.116***	0.015	0.018
Participation and engagement								
Electoral participation	0.038***	0.024**	-0.004	-0.009	0.043***	0.038***	0.051***	0.053***
Political interest	0.042***	0.038***	0.004	0.002	0.039***	0.038***	0.067***	0.067***
Exposure to mass media	-0.066***	-0.060***	-0.016	-0.015	0.018	0.019	0.132***	0.131***
Social structure								
Education	-0.121***	-0.111***	-0.062***	-0.060***	0.069***	0.071***	0.119***	0.118***
Gender (female)	-0.023**	-0.020**	0.019*	0.020*	-0.010	-0.009	-0.044***	-0.045***
Age	-0.026***	-0.028***	-0.005	-0.006	0.012	0.011	-0.017*	-0.017*
Countries								
Ghana	n/a	n/a	n/a	n/a	n/a	n/a	n/a	n/a
Lesotho	-0.121***	-0.098***	0.064***	0.072***	0.012	0.019	-0.142***	-0.144***
Malawi	-0.072***	-0.051***	-0.078***	-0.071***	0.027*	0.034**	-0.049***	-0.051***
Mali	-0.152***	-0.112***	-0.026	-0.012	n/a	n/a	-0.094***	-0.099***
Namibia	0.005	0.015***	0.021	0.025*	-0.070***	-0.067***	-0.097***	-0.098***

(continues)

Table 12.1 Continued

	Institutional Trust		Consent to Authority		External Efficacy		Defending Democracy	
	Model A	Model B	Model A	Model B	Model A	Model B	Model A	Model B
Nigeria	-0.383***	-0.353***	n/a	n/a	0.064***	0.073***	-0.107***	-0.111***
South Africa	-0.113***	-0.108***	0.103***	0.105***	-0.047***	-0.045***	-0.175***	-0.175***
Tanzania	0.037**	0.055***	-0.011	-0.004	n/a	n/a	-0.220***	-0.222***
Uganda	n/a	n/a	0.015	0.020	0.042**	0.046***	n/a	n/a
Zambia	-0.069***	-0.062***	-0.007	-0.005	-0.073***	-0.071***	0.048***	0.047***
Zimbabwe	-0.070***	-0.070***	-0.078***	-0.066***	-0.041***	-0.031*	-0.079***	-0.082***
Adjusted R^2	0.231	0.253	0.065	0.067	0.084	0.086	0.118	0.118
N	15,715	15,715	14,141	14,141	13,656	13,656	15,524	15,524

Source: Afrobarometer survey, 1999–2001.

Notes: Entries are standardized regression coefficients (beta). To facilitate interpretation, the results of ordinary least squares regressions are presented here. Ordered logit analyses were also conducted because the dependent variables are categorical ranks. The statistical significance of the key independent variable (winner status) and intervening variable (free and fair election) remains virtually identical in every model.

***$p < 0.001$, **$p < 0.01$, *$p < 0.05$.

n/a = data not available.

influential than other variables (electoral participation, political interest, exposure to mass media, gender, and age). The substantive effect of winner status is largest in the equation predicting institutional trust, and lowest for the measure of defending democracy.

In sum, electoral winners are significantly more pleased with political outcomes than are electoral losers. However, feeling close to the winning party is not the most important factor affecting legitimacy beliefs. The results in Table 12.1 indicate that performance evaluations matter more than partisan attachments. Poor performance of the economy or the government can overwhelm the loyalty of winners, and good performance can gain the allegiance of even opposition supporters. Ultimately, state institutions have to work well or both winners and losers will withhold their support (see Chapter 5 in this volume).

Free and Fair, or Fraudulent and Forged?

Given the evidence of winner-loser gaps in legitimacy beliefs, the question remains as to why the gaps exist. Earlier I hypothesized that the causal pathway between partisan status and institutional legitimacy runs through procedural evaluations of elections. In this section three observable implications of this theory are tested: I hypothesize that winner status is positively associated with evaluations of the freeness and fairness of recent elections; electoral evaluations are associated with perceived institutional legitimacy; and the influence of winner status on perceived legitimacy is attenuated or eliminated when electoral evaluations are added to the analysis.

Partisan Attachments and Electoral Evaluations

Do winning voters in African elections have more positive views of electoral fairness than do losers? Figure 12.6 shows the mean values of the perceived quality of the last election for losers, nonpartisans, and winners in each of the twelve countries surveyed. For each country, the winners' average ratings of electoral freedom and fairness are significantly higher than the losers' average ratings. The difference between winners and losers is highly significant at the 0.005 level, except for Zambia, which is significant at the standard 0.05 level. Furthermore, the winners' average rating is significantly greater than zero in eleven of the twelve countries surveyed, but the losers' average rating is significantly greater than zero in only six countries. In sum, there seems to be a vast gulf separating winners and losers in how they rate the quality of national elections.

Table 12.2 shows that winner status in Africa is positively related to the perception of a free and fair election, even when controlling for other pos-

Figure 12.6 Free and Fair Election Ratings Among Losers, Nonpartisans, and Winners in Sub-Saharan Africa, 1999–2001

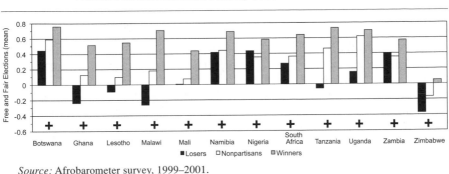

Source: Afrobarometer survey, 1999–2001.

Note: Afrobarometer question: "On the whole, how would you rate the freeness and fairness [honesty] of the last national election?" Sign indicates winner-loser gap at 0.05 level of significance.

sible influences. Notably, when the same model is run on each country separately, the coefficients on winner status are all significant with 99 percent confidence. The substantive effects are largest in Malawi and Tanzania. Compared with all other variables in the model, winner status has the largest influence on evaluations of electoral integrity in substantive as well as statistical terms. In the face of elections of uncertain quality, winners tend to think they won fair and square, whereas losers are far more inclined to cry foul.

Fair Elections and Perceived Legitimacy

Are evaluations of electoral fairness related to the perceived legitimacy of government institutions? Model B in Table 12.1 provides evidence of an association between opinions of procedural fairness and citizen satisfaction with the outcomes of the process. The coefficients on free and fair election are positive and significant in both substantive and statistical terms ($p < 0.001$) for three of four aspects of legitimacy. All else being equal, citizens who believe that the most recent election was free and fair also tend to exhibit these three traits: they trust their government institutions, grant government the authority to make binding decisions, and believe that their vote matters. In regard to predicting citizens' willingness to defend democracy, the effect is negative and somewhat less significant ($p < 0.018$). In other words, citizens who think that the last election was free and fair are less willing to act to defend democratic institutions against government incursion—perhaps because they are inexorably devoted to their current government.

Table 12.2 Effects of Winner Status on Free and Fair Election Ratings in Sub-Saharan Africa, 1999–2001

	B	S.E.	Beta
Electoral influences			
Winner status	0.204	0.007	0.214***
Performance evaluations			
Government performance	0.024	0.001	0.166***
Performance of economy	0.025	0.002	0.142***
Participation and engagement			
Electoral participation	0.080	0.006	0.098***
Political interest	0.015	0.004	0.027***
Exposure to mass media	−0.004	0.001	−0.031***
Social structure			
Education	−0.043	0.006	−0.062***
Gender (female)	−0.015	0.009	−0.011
Age	0.001	0.000	0.012*
Countries			
Ghana	n/a	n/a	n/a
Lesotho	−0.348	0.026	−0.129***
Malawi	−0.320	0.026	−0.119***
Mali	−0.476	0.024	−0.227***
Namibia	−0.160	0.027	−0.056***
Nigeria	−0.278	0.022	−0.171***
South Africa	−0.063	0.023	−0.032**
Tanzania	−0.200	0.023	−0.100***
Uganda	−0.155	0.024	−0.074***
Zambia	−0.105	0.027	−0.037***
Zimbabwe	−0.514	0.027	−0.184***
Constant	−0.012	0.030	
Adjusted R^2	0.212		

Source: Afrobarometer survey, 1999–2001.
Notes: B = unstandardized ordinary least squares regression coefficient, S.E. = standard error, Beta = standardized coefficient. Botswana is the excluded category.
***$p < 0.001$, **$p < 0.01$, *$p < 0.05$.
n/a = data not available.

The Mediating Effect of Electoral Evaluations

The final step is to determine whether the relationship between winning an election and perceived legitimacy is reduced or eliminated when electoral evaluations are taken into account. A rough estimate of the amount of mediation can be gauged from Table 12.1 by comparing the coefficients for winner status in the absence (Model A) and in the presence (Model B) of the *free and fair election* variable.

For all four dependent variables, there is evidence of partial mediation. The inclusion of the indicator of electoral fairness reduces slightly (but does not eliminate) the estimated effect of winning the election. For each of the four legitimacy measures, the coefficient on winner status in Model B is closer to zero than it is in Model A, but remains substantively and statistically significant. The estimated effect of winning never decreases by more than half of its original value. Winners and losers have different opinions about the fairness of the electoral process and those opinions matter for institutional legitimacy, but there must be alternative aspects of winning that also boost political support. The evidence suggests that perceived electoral integrity may be a causal pathway linking partisan attitudes and legitimacy, but it is not the only (or even the most important) causal connection. This analysis suggests that even if losers could be convinced that they lost fair and square, they would still doubt the legitimacy of their government institutions—at least in comparison to nonpartisans and winners.

Conclusion

Whereas some incumbent rulers may be satisfied with substandard elections, most foreign and domestic policy actors in Africa are concerned with improving electoral quality. Donors, advisers, and activists direct significant resources toward making electoral procedures more free, fair, and transparent. One of the primary goals of electoral reform is to increase the legitimacy of nascent democratic institutions, especially among citizens who are aligned with opposition parties. This chapter has evaluated the extent to which African elections build institutional legitimacy among losers as well as winners, and whether or not winner-loser legitimacy gaps are the result of perceptions of electoral integrity. The analysis yields a number of insights.

First, the evidence indicates significant gaps in perceived legitimacy between winners and losers. While not ubiquitous, these gaps are relatively common across three indicators and twelve countries. In general, citizens who feel close to winning parties think that their governments are more trustworthy, acceptable, and responsive than do citizens who are unaligned or aligned with the losing side. In sum, African elections reveal a distinction in political attitudes between insiders and outsiders who have quite different perceptions of the probity of political institutions.

Second, the analysis shows reverse gaps with respect to prospective political behaviors, such as acting in defense of democracy. Compared to losers, winners are more attached to sitting governments than they are to a regime of democratic institutions; winners are less willing to defend press freedoms, judicial independence, and parliamentary elections if it means going against the government. Some level of government legitimacy and citizen compliance is necessary for democracy to function effectively, but unconditional allegiance can be dangerous for democratic development, especially in hybrid systems. It seems that winners in Africa grant too much support to their current government while losers may offer too little.

Third, the analysis reveals a possible causal explanation (although only a partial one) for the winner-loser gaps in perceived legitimacy. In all twelve African countries where the surveys were conducted, winners and losers express significantly different opinions about whether their country's last national election was free and fair. Many Africans who watch their favored party lose an election doubt the integrity of the contest (and often they have many tangible reasons to be suspicious). In contrast, winners tend to overlook or excuse irregularities. Once again it seems that winners are more willing to acquiesce to undemocratic behavior by their chosen leaders.

In Africa, the divergent views of procedural fairness are also associated with different levels of acceptance of political outcomes. In theory, elections generate legitimacy and ensure the compliance of losers because they provide fair mechanisms for choosing leaders and resolving disputes. However, in practice, Africans who feel attached to losing parties are less inclined to think the process is fair, and are also less likely to view the outcomes as legitimate. This evidence is consistent with the second hypothesis; different perceptions of procedural fairness among winners and losers help explain gaps in legitimacy beliefs. But additional panel, experimental, or qualitative data would be required to firmly establish that the causal pathways are as hypothesized.

While there is some evidence that electoral evaluations play a mediating role between partisan affiliations and perceived legitimacy, the causal explanation evaluated in this chapter does not tell the full story. Even after accounting for respondent attitudes about elections, there are significant gaps in perceived legitimacy between winners and losers. Africans who emerge from an electoral contest victorious not only have a more favorable view of their elections, but apparently they also have other reasons to view political life more auspiciously.

A fruitful avenue for future research would be to specify alternative causal pathways. Evaluations of government and economic performance are plausible links; previous research indicates that winners have higher opinions of government performance than do losers (Bratton, Mattes, and Gyimah-Boadi 2005: 260) and performance evaluations exert a large influence on perceived legitimacy (see Table 12.1 and Chapter 5 in this volume).

Additionally, there is considerable variation across countries in the level of perceived legitimacy and the size of the winner-loser gaps. Thus national traits such as the level of democracy and rule of law, the type of political system, opposition-party behavior, and institutional performance would also seem to influence the link between partisanship and perceived legitimacy. This preliminary analysis reveals an insignificant relationship between the beta coefficients on winner status for all four measures of legitimacy and (1) whether an election was judged free and fair by outside observers; (2) whether the parliamentary electoral system was proportional representation instead of majoritarian or plurality; and (3) the level of civil and political rights at the time of the election (not shown) (see also Moehler and Lindberg 2009). Unfortunately, with less than twelve country cases per dependent variable in this analysis, it is difficult to statistically evaluate the influence of such national-level characteristics.

Regardless of the reason for partisan differences, it is important to recognize that performance evaluations have a strong estimated effect on institutional legitimacy even after electoral influences are accounted for. Partisan affiliations and the fairness of elections matter for institutional legitimacy, but government performance and economic conditions matter more. This evidence suggests that institutional legitimacy in Africa is based more on a learning theory of cognitive rationality than on citizens' affective party loyalties (Bratton, Mattes, and Gyimah-Boadi 2005: 347–349). Regardless of what happens during intermittent election periods, the institutions of the state have to perform in the intervening years if they are to gain the full allegiance, support, and protection of the citizenry.

Finally, this chapter offers a mix of positive and negative news for democracy activists and policymakers who have devoted their energies to improving electoral quality in Africa. The good news is that, to the extent that electoral reforms and assistance help Africans to feel better about the integrity of their elections, individuals will become more supportive of government institutions and more willing to consent to official policies. However, the bad news is that individuals often diverge in their views of electoral processes—improvements in the quality of elections may not always be perceived as such by African citizens, especially by those described here as electoral losers. Furthermore, even if losers can be convinced that the electoral procedures are fair, they will still hold some residual negative attitudes. Cleaning up elections alone will not be enough to win the full support of Africans aligned with the losing side.

13

Does the Quality of Elections Affect the Consolidation of Democracy?

Ari Greenberg and Robert Mattes

Virtually every political scientist sees elections as a necessary feature of modern representative democracy. Accordingly, international donors and domestic democracy advocates have devoted a great deal of effort and resources over recent decades to supporting regular, free, and fair elections in countries that have initiated transitions away from authoritarian rule. Indeed, some democratic theorists have even averred that elections are a sufficient condition for popular self-government.

Joseph Schumpeter (1942), for example, asserted that competition among multiple candidates and political parties for the free votes of the electorate is sufficient to generate a range of democratic externalities beyond the electoral arena, such as increased freedom of speech, association, and news media, as well as greater accountability and responsiveness. Similarly, Carl Friedrich (1963), in his "law of anticipated reactions," argued that any government whose policies and actions will be subsequently reviewed by an electorate with the power to punish bad actions or reward good ones is likely to consider the opinions and preferences of voters in the policymaking process. Finally, Dankwart Rustow argued that democracy "is by definition a competitive process, and this competition gives an edge to those who can rationalize their commitment to it, and an even greater edge to those sincerely believe in it. . . . In short, the very process of democracy institutes a double process of Darwinian selectivity in favor of convinced democrats: one among parties in general elections, and the other among politicians vying for leadership within these parties" (1970: 358).

Yet an important line of research on emerging democracies has warned against an overemphasis on competitive elections, or what Terry Karl (1986) called the "fallacy of electoralism." In a wide-ranging attack on the "transition paradigm," Thomas Carothers (2002) argued that many countries that had moved away from authoritarianism, and toward holding regular elections, were no longer transiting toward democracy, but were forming new types of hybrid regimes. For Marina Ottaway (2003), elections often serve as a way for "semiauthoritarian" or "competitive authoritarian" regimes—which have no intention of moving to genuine democracy—to placate domestic opponents and the international community (see also Schedler 2006; Levitsky and Way 2010). These authors have highlighted a wide range of democratic shortcomings and abuses that seem to endure even as countries hold successive elections that are reasonably free and fair, and that sometimes even result in defeat of the ruling party. The bottom line, for this school of analysts, is that recurring elections—in and of themselves—generate few if any positive externalities for the larger democratic process. In Carothers' words, "greatly reduced expectations are in order as to what elections will accomplish as generators of deep-reaching democratic change" (2002: 16).

Staffan Lindberg (2006, 2007, 2009), however, has assembled systematic evidence from sub-Saharan Africa corroborating Schumpeter's thesis that repeated elections may produce other democratic goods. By examining 287 elections between 1989 and 2005, Lindberg showed not only that African elections were gradually becoming freer and fairer, but also that, as the number of unbroken consecutive elections in a given country accumulated, opposition parties were more likely to participate, "old guard" bureaucrats were more likely to retire, presidential (but not legislative) elections became more competitive, electoral losers were more likely to accept the results, campaigns became more peaceful, and multiparty regimes became increasingly stable. More provocatively, he demonstrated that most of these effects existed even where elections were flawed (though the effects were generally smaller than when elections were free and fair).

Most important, by examining changes in Freedom House data before and after these 287 elections, Lindberg found that repeated elections did, in fact, produce subsequent incremental advances in the quality of civil liberties. And again, he showed that flawed elections also tended to produce increases in civil liberties, though with smaller effects than with free elections (the only deviation occurred among countries holding flawed fourth or subsequent elections, which was largely driven by Zimbabwe) (Lindberg 2006). In sum, he concluded that "elections are a powerful force for political change. They are sometimes the ignition that sparks other processes that tend to cause direct improvements in a country's level of political freedom and rights" (2009: 45).

The causal mechanisms, according to Lindberg (2006), are multifaceted. By turning individuals into voters, elections engage people in the exercise of their rights and increase the likelihood that they will exercise and defend other democratic rights and expect elected leaders to defend those rights. Organizations that conduct key services during elections, such as monitoring or voter education, come to apply their skills to other areas of democracy between elections. The authorities, civil servants, security officials, and judges who maintain elections will be less likely to then engage in antidemocratic behaviors as soon as the campaign is done. Elections also create new spaces for news media to push back boundaries on what is permissible, and those boundaries are less likely to retract in the postelection period. Finally, elections bring countries under increased international scrutiny, and criticisms may be addressed in the subsequent interelection periods.

In fact, increasing levels of international scrutiny suggest that authoritarian entrepreneurs cannot take elections lightly; instead they face what Susan Hyde (2011) calls the "pseudo-democrat's dilemma." Hyde has found evidence of an increasingly powerful international norm according to which countries should invite international observers to observe elections, and according to which nonobserved elections are by definition undemocratic. She reports data from a cross-national survey in seventeen developed and developing countries that found almost two-thirds popular support (64 percent, rising to over 80 percent in Kenya) for international observation "when there are concerns about freeness and fairness of elections" (2011: 87). She also found majority popular agreement with the statement that the respondent's nation would "benefit from having international observers monitor elections here" (rising as high as 85 percent in Kenya and 74 percent in Nigeria). By 2006, over 80 percent of all elections across the world were internationally monitored, including virtually all elections where there were preelection concerns of fraud—a very sharp increase since 1989.

However, the dilemma is that while pseudo-democrats may invite international monitors in a bid to maintain foreign aid, attract direct investment, tourism, and trade, or gain access to membership in international organizations, they increase the risks of getting caught in electoral malpractice. A negative international verdict on an election, in contrast, might bring cutoffs in aid, international sanctions, ejection from international organizations, and even domestic uprisings.

But as argued elsewhere, what ultimately matters for the survival of democracy are neither international observer reports of elections, nor expert ratings of civil liberties or political rights, but rather whether putative advances in elections, rights, and liberties are registered by ordinary citizens and translated into increased support for democracy (Bratton, Mattes, and Gyimah-Boadi 2005; Mattes and Bratton 2007). Previous analyses of Afrobarometer data found that people who rated their most recent elections as free and fair were far more likely to be satisfied with democracy and feel that they lived in a democracy, compared to those who thought their election had been a charade. But these analyses found no link between people's ratings of elections and whether or not they supported democracy or rejected nondemocratic regime alternatives. However, these studies did not explore the accuracy of popular election evaluations. Nor did they examine whether these micro-level associations accumulated to produce tangible macro-level shifts in public opinion. Thus, we argue that the real test of Lindberg's thesis is whether or not Africans accurately distinguish between free and flawed elections. Do elections of varying quality produce different aggregate levels of popular satisfaction with and commitment to the larger democratic regime?

Methodology

In this chapter we explore these questions using public opinion data regarding thirty-three elections in eighteen countries collected over three separate rounds of the Afrobarometer, as well as using data on electoral quality from Lindberg's elections dataset. We seek to determine, first, whether there is a link between the "objective" quality of African elections and popular evaluations of those elections, and second, whether the quality of an election results in aggregate increases or decreases in the popular demand for democracy and popular evaluation of democratic supply.

Following Lindberg, we hypothesize that elections in Africa's multiparty systems matter, and that they generate externalities for the larger democratic regime. National elections constitute the largest mobilization of the citizenry outside of war (Mozaffar 2002) and, in the multiparty systems of sub-Saharan Africa, constitute the most salient democratic activity of which citizens may be aware. Thus, electoral quality should have a major impact on people's overall sense of how democracy works in practice. We anticipate that public evaluations of electoral quality will indeed be related to the actual quality of that election, at least as measured by independent expert ratings. More important, we expect that these evaluations will help shape public attitudes toward the democratic regime.

But in contrast to Lindberg's thesis, we expect to find important differences in the nature of this impact, depending on the quality and integrity of elections. In young, emerging multiparty regimes in societies with relatively low levels of formal education and poorly developed communications infrastructure, a flawed election should lead people to reevaluate and downgrade the perceived supply of democracy. However, since demand for democracy is an aspiration, and given that previous research has demonstrated that individual-level differences in demand are based largely on differences in cognitive skills and cognitive awareness of politics, we do not expect to find that demand for democracy is reduced substantially by flawed elections. But neither should flawed elections increase public attachments to democracy.

In order to measure the quality of African elections, we use Lindberg's dataset of 284 elections held between 1989 and 2005. He collected information from domestic monitoring organizations, news media, and academic sources to determine the freeness and fairness of those elections. Based on this information, he coded elections using a 4-point scale, with 0 indicating that an election was wholly unfair and an obvious charade orchestrated by the incumbent rulers, 1 indicating that an election had a legal and practical potential to be free and fair but that numerous flaws or serious frauds affected the result, 2 indicating that an election had deficiencies, whether unintended or organized, but that these deficiencies did not affect the election outcome, and 3 indicating that an election was considered free and fair, even though there might have been human errors or logistical restrictions in the process. Overall, Lindberg judged that 60 percent of the elections covered during this time period were "somewhat" or "entirely" free and fair, and that 30 percent led to government turnover.

To measure public evaluations of electoral quality, we use responses to the Afrobarometer survey question: "How would you rate the freeness and fairness of the most recent [presidential or parliamentary] election in your country held on [specific date]." Again responses were coded using a four-point scale, with 0 indicating "Not free and fair," 1 indicating "Free and fair but with major problems," 2 indicating "Free and fair but with minor problems," and 3 indicating "Completely free and fair."

Following Michael Bratton, Robert Mattes, and E. Gyimah-Boadi (2005), we define the perceived supply of democracy in each country as a combination of public evaluations of the current level of democracy in that country, and current popular satisfaction with the way democracy works in that country. The first concept is measured with an Afrobarometer survey item that asks citizens whether they consider their country, "on the whole," as "a full democracy," "a democracy with minor problems," "a democracy with major problems," or "not a democracy." The second concept is measured by the standard survey item that asks people how "satisfied" they are with "the way democracy works" in their country. A citizen feels fully supplied with democracy if she or he believes that the country is democratic and also is satisfied with the way democracy works.

We define demand for democracy as a combination of explicit support for a democratic regime combined with rejection of authoritarian alternatives to democracy. Support for democracy is measured by the widely used item that asks people to choose between the statements "democracy is preferable to any other kind of government," "in some circumstances, a nondemocratic government can be preferable," and "it doesn't matter what kind of government we have." Rejection of authoritarianism is measured by three items that ask people to approve or disapprove systems whereby "only one political party is allowed to stand for election and hold office," "the army comes in to govern the country," and "elections and parliament are abolished so that the president can decide everything."

For each indicator, we created two separate measures. The first gives each country the mean response on the original survey scale of 0 to 4. The second indicator uses the simple absolute percentage of people who express a particular combination of attitudes. For electoral quality, the second indicator sums the percentage who say the election was "completely free and fair" or "free with minor exception." For the supply of democracy, the second construct captures those individuals who *both* are satisfied with democracy *and* believe that the country is democratic. For demand for democracy, we counted only those respondents who *both* prefer democracy *and* reject all three forms of nondemocratic regime.

Citizen and Expert Evaluations of Electoral Quality

We begin by assessing the relationship between expert observer ratings of election quality and public evaluations of those same elections. Do citizen and expert assessments of electoral quality converge or diverge? For the twenty-nine elections for which we had data on both scores, Table 13.1 shows a very strong, positive correlation. Fewer than one-third (an average of 32 percent) of all respondents gave their election a passing mark for the single election where media and observer reports suggested that the election was "not free" (Zimbabwe 2005) and for the five elections where "irregularities affected the outcome" (Zambia 1996, Zimbabwe 1996, Nigeria 2003, Malawi 2004, and Zimbabwe 2005). In contrast, 61 percent of all respondents in those countries saw mostly or completely free elections in the twenty contests that experts rated as "somewhat fair." And finally, the three elections that qualified as "completely free" were rated as mostly or wholly free or fair by an average of 71 percent of citizens. The correlation persists whether we measure public opinion as the aggregate percentage of people who felt their election was free and fair ($r = 0.705$, $p < 0.001$) or the mean micro-level response on a scale of 0 to 4 ($r = 0.748$, $p < 0.001$). If the expert score is the standard-bearer for objective quality of elections, these findings strongly suggest that African electorates pay attention not only to who wins and who loses, but also to the means by which they do so.

The single biggest deviation between mass and expert opinion occurs with regard to Zambia's 1996 election. While international observers sharply criticized the integrity of the outcome because of the Zambian electoral commission's exclusion of former president Kenneth Kaunda, 65 percent of

Table 13.1 Electoral Quality: Expert and Citizen Ratings in Sub-Saharan Africa Compared, 1989–2005

		Citizen Rating	
Expert Rating		Mean	Absolute Percentage
No, not at all	Mean	2.20	14%
	N	1	1
	Standard error	—	—
Irregularities affect outcome	Mean	2.30	35%
	N	5	5
	Standard error	0.19	7.5
Somewhat fair	Mean	3.08	61%
	N	20	20
	Standard error	0.05	12.6
Completely free	Mean	3.27	71%
	N	3	3
	Standard error	0.06	10.4
	Eta	0.808***	0.730***
	Pearson's *r*	0.748***	0.705***

Sources: Lindberg 2007; Afrobarometer surveys, 1999–2006.
Notes: Eta is a measure of association for ordinal data.
***$p < 0.001$.

Zambians rated the election as mostly or wholly free, probably because they concluded that Kaunda was so discredited that his presence in the race would not have affected the outcome. Indeed, observer organizations noted that the actual election poll was mostly transparent and peaceful. In contrast, Zambia's 2001 election was also rated by observers as unfree, but in this instance just 29 percent of citizens saw it as free.

Mass Evaluations of Electoral Quality and the Perceived Supply of Democracy

We now turn to assessing whether African publics condition their attitudes to democracy on their evaluations of the quality of elections. We take data from twenty-eight Afrobarometer surveys that contain both measures of the perceived freeness and fairness of the previous election and subsequent measures of satisfaction with the perceived extent of democracy (which together measure the supply of democracy). As we can see in Figure 13.1, there is a strong correlation between the two measures ($r = 0.820$, $p < 0.000$ when the absolute percentage is used, and $r = 0.774$, $p < 0.000$ when using

Figure 13.1 Electoral Quality and Perceived Supply of Democracy in Sub-Saharan Africa, 1989–2005

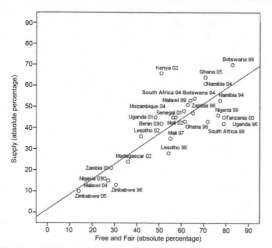

Sources: Lindberg 2007; Afrobarometer surveys, 1999–2006.
Note: R² linear = 0.673.

the mean response). Where mass publics sense significant degrees of electoral irregularity, fraud, corruption, or intimidation—like in Zimbabwe (1996 and 2005), Nigeria (2003), Malawi (2004), and Zambia (2001)—they are significantly more likely to offer a critical assessment of the supply of democracy in their country.

Thus we can see that, in the aggregate, popular perceptions of democratic supply covary in relation to public perceptions of electoral quality. To be more precise, if absolutely no one felt the election was free and fair, the predicted value (intercept) for the supply of democracy would be 1 percent, but this popular assessment would increase to 72 percent if all citizens saw the election as free and fair. Stated differently, where elections are judged by experts as flawed (a combination of Lindberg's lower two ordinal categories), an average of just 21 percent of respondents in those countries both felt their country was democratic and were satisfied with the way democracy works. In contrast, the average level of perceived supply following free elections (a combination of Lindberg's upper two categories) was more than twice as large, at 47 percent.

Does this relationship hold up once we take into consideration other potentially important influences on the way people evaluate democracy? We know from previous micro-level research that people base their estimates of the supply of democracy not only on their assessment of the electoral process, but also on the delivery of other "political goods" such as the performance of the president, levels of official corruption, and the availability of civil liberties as well as the delivery of "economic goods" such as recent economic trends (Bratton, Mattes, and Gyimah-Boadi 2005; Mattes and Bratton 2007; Bratton and Chang 2006; Sall, Smith, and Dansokho 2004; and Wolf, Logan, and Owiti 2004).

As we can see in Table 13.2, aggregate Afrobarometer measures of presidential job approval and economic satisfaction are significantly and strongly correlated with the perceived supply of democracy, though at a slightly lower strength than are evaluations of electoral quality (Pearson's $r = \sim 0.650$), while perceptions of corruption are not. However, once we regress aggregate levels of democratic supply on all these indicators simultaneously, we see that evaluations of both electoral quality and economic performance retain an independent and relatively equal effect.

Electoral Quality and Demand

Having found a strong relationship between perceived electoral quality and the perceived supply of democracy, we apply the same methods to determine whether electoral quality is related to the overall level of popular demand for democracy. As shown in Figure 13.2 and as hypothesized, we find

Table 13.2 Correlations with Supply of Democracy in Sub-Saharan Africa, 1989–2005

	Zero-Order Correlation	Regression Coefficient	Standardized Beta Coefficient
Constant		0.266 (0.475)	
Elections free and fair	0.820***	0.515* (0.239)	0.469
Presidential performance	0.608***	0.089 (0.116)	0.116
Official corruption	0.257	–0.180 (0.201)	–0.169
Economic performance	0.681***	0.355* (0.145)	0.474
N		18	
Adjusted R^2		0.659	

Sources: Lindberg 2007; Afrobarometer surveys, 1999–2006.
Notes: Standard errors appear in parentheses.
*** $p < 0.01$, ** $p < 0.05$, * $p < 0.10$.

Figure 13.2 Electoral Quality and Demand for Democracy in Sub-Saharan Africa, 1989–2005

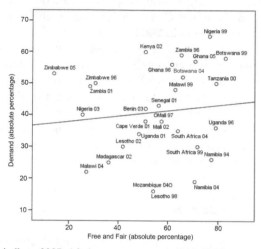

Sources: Lindberg 2007; Afrobarometer surveys, 1999–2006.

no significant bivariate relationship between the popular evaluations of electoral quality and expressed levels of demand for democracy ($r = -0.114$, not significant using the absolute percentage, and $r = -0.102$, not significant using the overall mean response). Neither is there any significant difference between expressed levels of demand among countries that have experienced either free or flawed elections. Moreover, introducing the three control variables discussed previously fails to reveal any new relationship between electoral evaluations and demand for democracy.

Changes in Supply and Demand: A Natural Experiment

While the preceding analysis suggests that African electorates revise their assessments of the supply of democracy upward after a successful election or downward after a flawed one, the static cross-sectional analysis does not speak to actual opinion change. Thus, to generate stronger evidence about the causal impact of electoral quality on public attitudes to democracy, we identified fifteen overtime pairs, or dyads, of Afrobarometer country surveys that contain an intervening election, some of which were free and some of which were flawed. As a control group, we also identified thirteen other pairs of country surveys in which there was no intervening election.

In Table 13.3, we display the overtime change in perceived democratic supply for each set of dyads: that is, those that contain an intervening free election, an intervening flawed election, and no election. Across the ten dyads that contain a free election, we find an average *increase* in the perceived supply of democracy of 10 percentage points. In contrast, we find average *decreases* in the perceived supply of democracy both in the five dyads of country surveys that contain a flawed election (–10.2 percentage points) as well as in the thirteen pairs of country surveys that contain no intervening election (–8.5 percentage points). The size of the average decrease subsequent to a flawed election would be even stronger (–16 percentage points) were we to remove the effect of the arguably unique circumstances surrounding the 2002 Zimbabwean election. As shown by Annie Chikwana, Tulani Sithole, and Michael Bratton (2004), that election and the subsequent 2003 survey coincided with the rise of Jonathan Moyo and his control of the propaganda arm of the Zimbabwean government, which had produced a short-term increase in overall level of democratic supply—an increase that was confined largely to those who read and listened exclusively to government media.

While the cross-sectional data fail to identify any impact of electoral quality on popular demand for democracy, the natural experiment suggests more promising trends, though ultimately nonsignificant results. Table 13.4 shows that popular demand for democracy *decreases* after a flawed election (–9.8 percentage points) but basically holds steady after a high-quality election (+1.7 percentage points) or where there is no intervening election (–1.4 percentage points). However, because the standard errors are as large as the observed changes, the results are not statistically significant. Again, the size of the decrease would be even larger (–18.5 percentage points) were we to remove the unique resurgence in demand for democracy that occurred be-

Table 13.3 Change in Perceived Supply of Democracy in Sub-Saharan Africa, 1989–2005

Expert Rating	N	Supply of Democracy (absolute percentage)	Standard Error	Eta
Flawed election	5	–10.2	6.5	
No election	13	–8.5	3.4	
Free and fair election	10	+8.9	3.5	0.592**
Total	28	–2.6	2.8	

Sources: Lindberg 2007; Afrobarometer surveys, 1999–2006.
Notes: Eta is a measure of association for ordinal data.
** $p < 0.05$.

Table 13.4 Change in Demand for Democracy in Sub-Saharan Africa, 1989–2005

Expert Rating	N	Demand of Democracy (absolute percentage)	Standard Error	Eta
Flawed election	5	−9.8	9.1	
No election	13	−1.4	2.9	
Free and fair election	10	+1.7	3.5	0.314 ns
Total	28	−1.8	2.4	

Sources: Lindberg 2007; Afrobarometer surveys, 1999–2006.
Notes: Eta is a measure of association for ordinal data.
** $p < 0.05$; ns = not statistically significant.

tween the Round 2 and Round 3 Zimbabwe surveys (e.g., related to its equally flawed 2005 election).

Comparing Countries

We end by examining within-country longitudinal trends that span several elections but also enable us to hold country-specific factors constant. Here we separate Afrobarometer countries into those that had convened at least one flawed election (see Figure 13.3) and those whose elections were consistently free and fair (at least within the time span covered by the Afrobarometer project) (see Figure 13.4). This distinction produces a clear difference in terms of the supply of democracy. By the end of the third round of surveys, all of the countries that had at least one flawed election during this period (1999–2005) registered levels of perceived supply below 25 percent. All of these countries also displayed net overall declines over this time span. In contrast, the countries that had held consistently free and fair elections all had levels of supply above 30 percent, with most falling above 45 percent. Furthermore, there were no clear trends within this group, with some showing increases over time, but others showing declines. Finally, there are no such clear differences or patterns across these two clusters of countries in terms of the demand for democracy.

Conclusion

In this study we have found clear evidence that African electorates pay attention to the quality of their national elections, and are quite good judges

Figure 13.3 Change in Perceived Supply of Democracy in Sub-Saharan African Countries with at Least One Flawed Election, 1989–2005

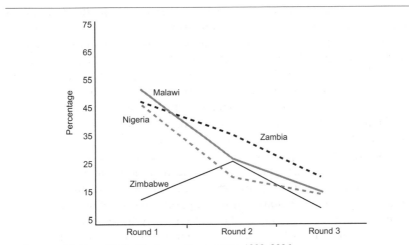

Sources: Lindberg 2007; Afrobarometer surveys, 1999–2006.

Figure 13.4 Change in Perceived Supply of Democracy in Sub-Saharan African Countries with Consistently Free and Fair Elections, 1989–2005

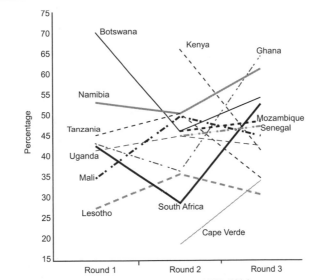

Sources: Lindberg 2007; Afrobarometer surveys, 1999–2006.

of their freeness and fairness. In turn, publics then base their assessments of the overall state of democracy, in large part, on the quality of the most recent election. Thus, with Staffan Lindberg, and against the electoral fallacy argument, we find that elections matter to at least one important attitudinal dimension of the process of democratization in sub-Saharan Africa. But contrary to Lindberg, we find that not all elections make a positive contribution: the quality of elections matters greatly (see also Chapter 2 in this volume). Moreover, the effect is asymmetrical: bad elections do far more damage than quality elections do good. Above and beyond dissatisfaction with economic trends, the performance of the president, or perceptions of corruption, flawed elections decrease satisfaction with democracy and lead people to downgrade the extent of perceived democracy in their country. Finally, we also have suggestive, but not statistically significant, evidence that flawed elections also lead people to question the value of democracy.

Thus, to the extent that public opinion is important, simply convening regular competitive elections will not support the consolidation of young democracies. In fact, holding regular, but regularly flawed, elections might be a successful strategy for authoritarian entrepreneurs who wish to simultaneously hold the international community at bay, yet reduce popular demand for further democratization. These findings hold out clear implications for donor strategy: to the degree that donors wish to expand their democracy assistance portfolio to other areas such as legislative strengthening, or civil society development, they should not do so if it means abandoning or sharply reducing election support.

14

Do Free Elections Foster Capable Governments?

Michael Bratton

Over the past two decades, Africa's political environment has opened up. To varying degrees in different countries, military and de jure one-party regimes have made way for multiparty competition. To be sure, the quality of democracy in Africa is often strained. In many countries, fragile multiparty regimes coexist with persistent social conflict, imperfect elections, weak political institutions, and presidents who seek to govern outside the rule of law.

But there is no gainsaying the fact that, over the period from 1988 to 2011, sub-Saharan Africa became a more democratic region. According to Freedom House, the number of countries designated "not free" dropped by half (from thirty-two to sixteen), alongside an almost doubling of those that moved from "not free" to "partly free" (from twelve to twenty). Most important, the number of countries that became "free" increased from two to nine (Freedom House 2012). From a very low starting point, and despite setbacks in recent years (Puddington 2010; Petrovic 2012), the rate of political liberalization in the post–Cold War period was actually greater in sub-Saharan Africa than in any other world region apart from the former Soviet bloc (Finkel et al. 2006; Markoff 2009).

But does democratization lead to improved governance? Do freely elected regimes automatically perform better at public management than regimes installed by authoritarian means? Even if multiparty rule offers certain advantages, do these apply equally to all dimensions of governance? And what is the causal direction of any democracy-governance connection? After all, if democratization occurs more commonly in countries that are already relatively well governed, then it would be a mistake to attribute any improvements in governance to political liberalization and free elections.

This chapter seeks preliminary answers to these questions with reference to a cross-section of sub-Saharan African countries in 2005. I examine the democracy-governance connection at both the macro level, using aggregate data, and the micro level, drawing on a comparative survey of the attitudes of African citizens. The analysis also employs intertemporal analysis in a bid to advance the debate on causality. I compare perceived governance performance before and after electoral alternations, both across countries and in one particular country (Ghana).

A Democracy-Governance Connection?

A valid inquiry into linkages between democracy and governance requires strict independence of key concepts. It is necessary to set aside at the outset the conflated, hybrid notion of "democratic governance," which merges concepts by definition. A more fruitful approach begins by breaking apart the two components and describing each separately. For the purposes of this chapter, I define *democracy* in minimal, procedural terms as a political regime installed by a free and fair multiparty election in which all contenders accept the results (Collier and Levitsky 1997). I define *governance* broadly as the act or process of imparting authoritative direction and coordination to organizations in an environment (Hyden and Bratton 1992; Pierre 2000). But I apply the concept narrowly to central governments, excluding global, corporate, civic, and local forms of governance (Hirst 2000). Thus, when the democracy-governance connection is boiled down to operational essentials, we are left with the following research question: Do free elections foster capable governments?

It seems sensible to suppose that the advent of a freely elected political regime would have beneficial consequences for governmental performance. One possible reason is that elections confer political legitimacy: having voted for rulers, citizens are more willing to comply with their directives, thus reducing the costs of enforcing public policies, especially unpopular ones. Second, democratic regimes are installed by means of a mechanism of political equality: one person, one vote. Especially where poverty is widespread, political democratization implies an enhanced prospect of social and economic redistribution, including by making public services more accessible, efficient, and fair. A final and more explicit route from democracy to good governance concerns political responsiveness. Because political leaders—from local government councilors all the way up to the national president—are subject to re-election after a fixed term of office, they face incentives to attend to the expressed needs of constituents in the intervals between elections.

Of course, democratization may undermine good governance, for example by encouraging populist policy responses that exceed the limits of prudent management (Huntington 1968; Kitschelt and Wilkinson 2007). A transition to democracy may also allow an increase in corruption; since the prospect of open elections raises political insecurity for incumbent elites, they may choose to discount the future by accelerating the rate at which they grab rents (Bates 2008; Gandhi and Lust-Okar 2009). Or by diffusing power and multiplying the number of potential veto points, the introduction of democratic procedures may make decisionmaking more difficult, less transparent, and more confusing to ordinary citizens (Tsebelis 2002).

In theorizing mechanisms through which democratic elections might plausibly affect governance, it becomes apparent that governance has multiple aspects. Analysts have long recognized the multidimensionality of the concept. The World Bank Institute, for example, proposes six dimensions ranging from "voice and accountability" to "control of corruption" (Kauffmann, Kraay, and Mastruzzi 2008). I find this classification useful and employ it in an initial analysis here. But for theoretical and methodological reasons, I prefer to decompose governance along different lines, both to identify additional governance dimensions and to enable operational research using indicators available in Afrobarometer surveys.

My alternate scheme proposes three main types of governance: administrative, economic, and political. Each can be broken down in three ways, making a total of nine dimensions in all.

The *administrative* dimensions of good governance concern:
> *Legality*—whether the government observes a rule of law.
> *Transparency*—whether government procedures are open for all to see.
> *Honesty*—whether government officials are free of corruption.

The *economic* dimensions of good governance cover:
> *Effectiveness*—whether government is able to attain its stated policy goals.
> *Efficiency*—whether public goods are delivered on a cost-effective basis.
> *Equity*—whether citizens enjoy equality of access to available public goods.

Finally, the *political* dimensions of governance consist of:
> *Responsiveness*—whether elected officials act according to popular priorities.
> *Accountability*—whether unresponsive public officials can be disciplined.
> *Legitimacy*—whether citizens willingly obey government commands.

A fine-grained framework of this sort allows us to unpack the encompass-
ing notion of governance as a prelude to exploring the possibility that democratization has differential effects. For example, I hypothesize that free
elections will boost the political legitimacy of an incumbent government,
especially if elections precipitate an alternation of ruling parties. On the
other hand, I expect that elections and alternations offer no guarantees that
political representatives will readily respond to popular preferences in the
periods between elections. Having presented evidence in support of these
hypotheses, I conclude the chapter by arguing that new African democracies manifest a worrisome "representation gap" between the electorate and
representative institutions.

Macro Connections

If the recent wave of free elections in sub-Saharan Africa has fostered gains
in the quality of public management, then a general democracy-governance
connection should be evident across countries. The availability of aggregate
indicators of democracy (e.g., from Freedom House) and governance (e.g.,
from the World Bank Institute) facilitates such an analysis.

But words of caution are due about the limitations of these common
data sources (Bollen 1993; Arndt and Oman 2006; Kurtz and Schrank 2007;
Coppedge, Alverez, and Maldonado 2008). Take the measurement of democracy. The Freedom in the World survey, published annually since 1972
by Freedom House, evaluates the political rights and civil liberties available
to citizens, now across 193 states. It measures the range of voter choices
and the enjoyment (or not) of supportive constitutional guarantees. As such,
the survey tends to capture the openness of political regimes as experienced
within society—that is, popular freedoms—rather than the democratic qualities of political institutions per se. Hence, freedom indicators are best sup-
plemented and validated by institutional indicators. The Polity IV Project
(2008), for example, distinguishes democratic and autocratic forms of authority (on a scale of +10 to -10) with reference to institutional characteristics like the mode of executive recruitment, the extent of constraints on executive authority, and the degree of political competition.

Due to complex dimensionality of the concept of governance, its measurement is not straightforward. The World Governance Indicators currently
set the methodological standard by providing systematic estimates of relative
public sector performance for 212 countries and territories from 1996 onward. Reflecting inherent imprecision, the World Bank Institute provides explicit margins of error for each country estimate. For the purposes of this
study, I find utility in just five of the six World Governance Indicator dimensions of governance: political stability, government effectiveness, regulatory

quality, rule of law, and control of corruption. The sixth dimension—voice and accountability—is based partly on Freedom House scores for civil liberties and political rights (among ten other representative sources). Thus, to reduce possible circularity in estimates of the effects of democratization on good governance, I drop the "voice and accountability" dimension of governance.

Table 14.1 presents a summary of the macro-level connections between metrics of democracy—as measured by Freedom House and Polity IV—and the World Governance Indicators. All aggregate data are drawn from the forty-eight sovereign states in sub-Saharan Africa. Cell entries are bivariate correlation coefficients.

The first result worth noting is that, regardless of the method of measurement, democracy has substantively strong and statistically significant links to governance. Democracy is positively associated with every governance dimension (as these are conceived by the World Bank Institute) and with a mean World Governance Indicator score calculated as an average of five dimensions (excluding "voice and accountability"). Without at this stage imputing directionality to the relationship, a simple macroanalysis of this sort suggests an apparent structural affinity within African countries between democracy and good governance: the more democratic the regime, the better its record at governance.

Second, the strength of this democracy-governance connection depends on the method of measurement. When democracy is measured using Freedom House scores, correlations are systematically stronger than when democracy is measured using Polity IV indicators. Indeed, the Freedom House–World Governance Indicator coefficients are so large ($r = 0.774$, $p < 0.001$ for a mean index, rising to $r = 0.830$, $p < 0.001$ when the dimension of "voice and accountability" is included in the index) as to call into question the independence of indicators. Could it be that *all* World Bank Institute indicators overlap with Freedom House scores? Stated differently, are the World Bank Institute indicators a methodological analog of the hybrid concept of "democratic governance"? One possibility is that the compilers of the World Bank Institute source materials inadvertently incorporate knowledge about a country's status of freedom into their judgments about the quality of its governance. The Polity indicators were developed for a separate purpose and are not employed as a World Governance Indicator source. Perhaps for this reason, the Polity–World Governance Indicator coefficients—although positive, strong, and significant (mean $r = 0.545$, $p < 0.001$)—are more plausible because they provide a greater degree of assurance that democracy and governance were conceived and measured separately.

Third, and notwithstanding the method of measurement, there is rough equivalence in the relative importance of democracy to different dimensions of governance. For both Freedom House and Polity, democracy is more

Table 14.1 Democracy and Governance in Sub-Saharan Africa: Macro Connections, 2005

World Governance Indicators	Indicators of Democracy	
	Freedom House	Polity IV
Political stability	0.706***	0.455***
Government effectiveness	0.730***	0.525***
Regulatory quality	0.684***	0.488***
Rule of law	0.751***	0.526***
Control of corruption	0.693***	0.488***
Mean World Governance Indicator score	0.774***	0.545***

Sources: Freedom House 2008 (forty-eight countries); Polity IV Project 2008 (forty-one countries); Kauffmann, Kraay, and Mastruzzi 2008.
  Notes: Cell entries are bivariate correlation coefficients.
  ***$p < 0.001$.

closely associated with the rule of law and government effectiveness than with regulatory quality and control of corruption. I take this as prima facie evidence that, if democratization has formative effects on the subsequent quality of governance (a proposition yet to be confirmed), then it does so more through some governance channels than via others. I would expect, for example, that democracy—a form of constitutional rule requiring regular elections and term limits on office holders—helps to reinforce a rule of law. But precisely because free elections may compel politicians to seek an expanded pool of patronage resources, democratization is less strongly associated with policies to deregulate economic markets or to control corruption. A key purpose of the rest of this chapter is to further explore such differential effects.

Micro-Level Connections

So far, macro-level analysis suggests a crude association between democracy and governance, with the strength of the connection dependent on the dimension of governance. Here I seek to refute, corroborate, or refine these results at the micro level using survey data on the popular perceptions of ordinary Africans. Do Africans themselves think they are obtaining good governance? By way of answer, I compare public opinions across democratic and nondemocratic regimes.

Data are drawn from 25,397 face-to-face interviews conducted in 2005 during Round 3 of the Afrobarometer. The data are pooled from eighteen country surveys, all of which used a standard survey instrument. To measure the extent of democracy, the Afrobarometer asks: "In your opinion, how much of a democracy is [this country] today?" The response options are coded using a 4-point scale: "not a democracy" (1), "a democracy with major problems" (2), "a democracy with minor problems" (3), and "a full democracy" (4). For the purposes of this analysis, those whose answers are coded 3 or 4 are held to live in a "democracy"; those whose answers are coded 1 or 2 are said to reside in a "nondemocracy." The distinction between democracies and nondemocracies, shown in Table 14.2, is employed as a device to distinguish among popular attitudes toward governance.

To confirm the face validity of Afrobarometer's democracy indicator, I note that, in 2005, fully 71 percent of Ghanaians thought that their country (a model of clean elections) was a democracy, compared to just 14 percent of Zimbabweans (whose leader has become increasingly dictatorial) for their country. Moreover, in an external validity test for the same year, Afrobarometer assessments of the extent of democracy (aggregated to country level) correlate extremely highly with the Freedom House index ($r = 0.802$), which suggests that citizens and experts come to remarkably similar judgments about each country's democratic attainments. And to address the conceptual validity of a minimal, electoral definition of democracy, it is reassuring to discover that public opinion about the quality of the last election (how free and fair was it?) is the best single predictor of whether Africans think that they live in a democracy (Bratton 2007a).

The nine dimensions of governance, as defined earlier, appear as row headings in Table 14.2. For example, to assess if the government operates within a framework of *legality,* the survey asks whether citizens think that "the president usually observes (or often ignores) the constitution." A strong and significant difference in public opinion is detectable between regime types: in democracies, almost two-thirds of citizens (65 percent) perceive respect for a constitutional rule of law in the president's office as compared to less than half (46 percent) in nondemocracies. Take another example. To evaluate whether the civil service is *honest,* the survey asks citizens how many public officers they perceive to be corrupt. Whereas in democracies just over one-quarter of citizens (28 percent) perceive corruption among "most or all" government officials, more than half (51 percent) do so in nondemocracies. In this initial test, therefore, we find no evidence that democratization is associated with higher levels of perceived corruption. Indeed, on this dimension of governance, the positive democracy connection is especially strong.

It is also worth noting that, in democracies, most interviewed Africans (69 percent) consider that their government is *effective* at solving the most important problems in society. When quizzed in open-ended fashion about the nature of these problems, respondents most often mention unemployment,

Table 14.2 Democracy and Governance in Sub-Saharan Africa: Micro Connections, 2005

Dimension of Governance	Indicator	Democracy[a]	Nondemocracy[b]	R	
				Democracy[c]	Free Elections[d]
Administrative					
Legality	The president usually observes the constitution	65	46	0.268***	0.216***
	The president often ignores the constitution	16	36		
Transparency	Government procedures are easy to understand	21	17	0.102***	0.069***
	Government procedures are too complicated	64	71		
Honesty	Few or no government officials are corrupt	72	49	0.280***	0.286***
	Most or all government officials are corrupt	28	51		
Economic					
Effectiveness	Government can solve most important problems	69	45	0.265***	0.253***
	Government cannot solve important problems	31	55		
Efficiency	Public services are easily accessible	64	51	0.160***	0.152***
	Public services are difficult to obtain	36	49		
Equity	Government usually treats people equally	56	37	0.207***	0.173***
	Government often treats people unequally	44	63		

(continues)

Table 14.2 Continued

Dimension of Governance	Indicator	Democracy[a]	Nondemocracy[b]	R Democracy[c]	R Free Elections[d]
Political Responsiveness	Elected representatives usually try to listen	30	18	0.172***	0.139***
	Elected representatives often fail to listen	70	82		
Accountability	Elections allow people to remove poor leaders	51	31	0.262***	0.240***
	Elections do not ensure the will of the people	28	48		
Legitimacy	The government can rightfully demand compliance	90	84	0.088***	0.108***
	If you did not vote for a government, you need not obey	9	13		

Source: Afrobarometer survey, 2005.

Notes: Cell entries are percentages of adults surveyed. Calculated using binary or 3-point scales. Totals may not sum to 100 where "don't knows" are not reported.

a. Respondents regard the political regime as a full democracy or a democracy with minor problems.
b. Respondents regard the political regime as having major problems or as not being a democracy at all.
c. Pearson's product moment correlation coefficient (range 0–1), calculated using full variable ranges (i.e., 4- and 5-point scales).
d. Freedom House 2006.
***$p < 0.001$.

food security, and the paucity of healthcare. One is struck that affirmative views of administrative capability are at odds with academic portrayals of African governance as an arena of state fragility (Rotberg 2004; Bates 2008). To be sure, the survey data reveal variations across regimes—only 45 percent of citizens in nondemocracies see the state as effective—but even this result hardly amounts to the journalistic stereotype of African state collapse. For serious analysis, we require a nuanced portrayal of state failure as a variable quality, whose manifestations are hardly universal across the continent.

Admittedly, democracy's association is weaker on other dimensions of governance. According to the 2005 Afrobarometer data, the public sees more tenuous linkages to government *efficiency,* procedural *transparency,* and regime *legitimacy.* To be sure, all these relationships are positive and statistically significant, suggesting an underlying democracy advantage, but they are feebler than democracy's association with a rule of law and official probity. For example, in both democracies and nondemocracies, majorities within the national adult population think that public services are easily accessible (64 and 51 percent) and that the government should always be obeyed, despite whether an individual voted for it (90 and 84 percent). As such, perceptions of government efficiency and regime legitimacy are widespread across a range of regime types in Africa, including electoral autocracies.

Citizens in democratic regimes also see a slight advantage with regard to the *transparency* of governmental operations, thus undermining the hypothesis about the complicating and obscuring effects of veto points. Perhaps press freedoms help to offset shortages of information. But it is worth noting that majorities everywhere, regardless of the type of political regime, regard government procedures as too complex to fully understand (64 and 71 percent). Reportedly, the process of political decisionmaking is relatively more transparent in Africa's emergent democratic regimes, but even there this dimension of governance remains opaque to almost two-thirds of the citizens.

Because these results are based on pooled data, it is necessary to ask whether the democracy-governance connection holds true for all the eighteen countries studied. There is strong evidence that the general model fits well. When run separately for each country, the same variables almost always generate coefficients with the same signs as in Table 14.2. To be sure, the democracy-governance connection fits more tightly in some countries than in others. In Senegal, Uganda, and Zimbabwe, citizens perceive an especially strong linkage between the extent of democracy and legal, effective, and accountable governance. In Senegal, which has a long history of multiple parties and a relatively strong legal tradition, the connection is at the high end of both scales. In Zimbabwe, which faces twin crises of illegitimate government and state fragility, both democracy and governance are seen to be well below average. There are very few country exceptions. Only in Tanzania do citizens perceive a link between democratization and unequal treatment, and only in Uganda do they worry that free elections are tied to a lack of responsiveness among public officials.

I end this stage of analysis by considering the centrality of free elections to the associations with governance just described. The last column of Table 14.2 depicts coefficients when the nine governance dimensions are correlated with popular African perceptions of the freeness and fairness of the last national election in their country. Without exception, the perceived quality of elections generates predictions about governance with the same sign and statistical significance as for a broader democracy standard. Since democracy is more than mere elections, the observed relationships may not always be quite as strong. But importantly, citizens seem to see a *direct* line of connection between free and fair elections and two leading elements of governance: control of corruption and the legitimacy of government. Stated differently, high-quality elections seem to give citizens confidence that abuse of public office will be reined in and that official policy directives ought to be obeyed.

The Arrow of Causality

So far, this chapter has established a democracy-governance connection in sub-Saharan Africa at both macro and micro levels. But correlation is not causation. To establish the direction of any arrow of attribution, it is necessary to ask: Is democracy in Africa built on the foundation of strong states that have already established a semblance of capable governance? Or—in the key question—does the installation of multiparty electoral democracy in Africa *create* conditions for improvements in public governance?

The preponderance of relevant theory in political science suggests that statebuilding, including the governance function of effective policy implementation, is a prerequisite for democratization. Juan Linz and Alfred Stepan stake out a definitive position: "No modern polity can become democratically consolidated unless it is first a state" (1996: 7). Richard Rose and Doh Shin (2001) add that new democracies tend to be unstable because they democratize "backwards"—that is, by introducing mass elections without prior benefit of modern state institutions, including a rule of law and a working bureaucracy. With reference to Yugoslavia among other places, Edward Mansfield and Jack Snyder (2005) contend that, lacking foundational political order, new democracies are more susceptible to conflict compared to stable autocracies, a proposition pertinent to sub-Sahara's conflict-prone settings.

I am persuaded by the powerful argument that democracy can hardly be established in the absence of political order. Simply stated, the existential dilemma for an African citizen is this: Why should they turn out to vote in a founding election if, in so doing, they risk being intimidated, assaulted, or killed? The establishment of political order requires a capable state that can, without abuse, assert authority throughout a territory. One irreducible requirement of such authority is that citizens voluntarily comply with state commands, thus granting legitimacy to rulers. But what better way has been found to establish political legitimacy in the modern world than through the installation of rulers in open and competitive elections? In other words, democratization may itself be a prerequisite for well-governed and consolidated states.

The question of which comes first—democracy or governance—has found expression in the so-called sequencing debate among democracy scholars and practitioners. Thomas Carothers argues that, because "persuading people to defer their ambition to vote in a free election is most often not an option," democracy promoters should *not* "put . . . off for decades or indefinitely the core element of democratization—fair and open processes of political competition and choice" (2007: 23, 25). Rather than "sequentialism" (rule of law first, elections second), Carothers favors what he calls "gradualism," which involves slowly creating conditions for free and fair elections wherever possible. Indeed, "prescribing more rule of law . . . as the basis for eventual democratization gets it backwards: more democratization is vital to strengthening the rule of law" (2007: 17). Those democratic theorists who see the rule of law as a pillar of democracy support this view (O'Donnell 2005; Diamond and Morlino 2005; Hadenius and Back 2008).

Testing the sequencing debate against African materials, Eric Chang and I (Bratton and Chang 2006) find some support for both sides. On the one hand, we report that democratic regimes (measured as Freedom House's "free" countries) have only ever arisen in stronger African states (that is, those with an above-average World Governance Indicator mean score). In other words, the continent's emergent democracies—from Benin to South Africa—are all erected on a foundation of states that enjoy relatively solid capacity to create political order, govern through legal means, and control corruption. On the other hand, we employ a simultaneous equations model to show that the relationship between statebuilding and democratization is thoroughly recursive. Not only do strong states breed democratic regimes but also, in turn, democratic regimes foster the law enforcement capacity and political legitimacy necessary for good governance. By demonstrating that the establishment of a rule of law is an implicit product of democratization, we make a case that democratization can come first.

Electoral Alternation

I build on this groundwork by devising an additional test of causality in the democracy-governance relationship. On the common assumption that prior events are candidate causes for subsequent outcomes—what Robert Franzese calls "poor man's exogeneity" (2007: 65)—this "with-and-without" test rests on the concept of electoral alternation. An electoral alternation is the peaceful transfer of power from one ruling party to another by means of a free and fair election. Sometimes called a "turnover" of government, alternation is a relatively infrequent outcome in African elections, having occurred some 64 times across 344 elections between 1990 and 2011 (Lindberg 2006, updated to 2011 by author; see Table 2.2).

I start by observing that electoral alternation boosts mass commitments to democracy, both on the demand side and (especially) in terms of popular estimates of the supply of democracy (Bratton 2004). By demonstrating that incumbency is not forever, alternation deepens democracy by giving both electoral winners and (especially) electoral losers an incentive to support the rules of the democratic game (Anderson et al. 2005). It seems reasonable to wonder whether, as a core attribute of democratization, a turnover of political elites also contributes to improved governance. I therefore propose that an electoral alternation will be followed in time by positive upward increments in indicators of good governance.

Table 14.3 presents largely supportive evidence. It distinguishes African countries that underwent an electoral alternation at any time *after* the country's founding multiparty election but *before* the Afrobarometer measured perceptions of governance in 2005. An alternation is scored as 1, its absence as 0. On eight out of the nine governance dimensions, significant differences in popular perceptions of performance are evident for citizens in countries that experienced alternations. In six out of these nine cases, differences run in the expected direction. For example, citizens who experienced a democratic turnover were significantly more likely to regard the government as *effective* at problem solving and to regard few or no public officials as *corrupt*.

But there are anomalies. The coefficients for three dimensions of governance have unexpected signs. One is not statistically significant: the occurrence of an electoral alternation seemingly makes no difference to popular perceptions of equity in treatment by government. And two dimensions of governance—transparency and responsiveness—stand in significant negative relationships to democratization. Even after democracy begins to take root through peaceful electoral alternation, citizens are apparently less likely to find government procedures easy to understand or to consider that elected representatives listen to them. Perhaps citizens remain uncertain about the exact roles that elected representatives are supposed to play. Or they soon discover that the new occupants of these offices are even less responsive than the leaders they replaced. These inverted democracy-governance relationships, although hardly strong, nonetheless raise red flags about possible areas of governance in which the affinity with democratization begins to break down.

Table 14.3 Electoral Alternation and Governance in Sub-Saharan Africa: Popular Perceptions, 2005

Dimension of Governance	Indicator	Country Has Had an Electoral Alternation[a]	Sign[b]
Administrative			
Legality	The president usually observes the constitution	0.056***	E
Transparency	Government procedures are easy to understand	−0.074***	U
Honesty	Few or no government officials are corrupt	0.068***	E
Economic			
Effectiveness	Government can solve most important problems	0.109***	E
Efficiency	Public services are easily accessible	0.040***	E
Equity	Government usually treats people equally now (versus before)	−0.011 ns	U
Political			
Responsiveness	Elected representatives usually try to listen	−0.065***	U
Accountability	Elections are efficacious	0.071***	E
Legitimacy	The government must always be obeyed	0.123***	E

Source: Afrobarometer survey, 2005.

Notes: Cell entries are Pearson's product moment correlation coefficients (R, range 0–1), calculated using full variable ranges (i.e., 4- and 5-point scales).

a. Scored 1 for electoral alternation if any presidential election after 1989 led to a turnover of the ruling party, 0 if not. Legislative elections are used in parliamentary systems.

b. E = expected sign, U = unexpected sign.

***$p < 0.001$; ns = not statistically significant.

The Case of Ghana

The previous section unearthed trace evidence that an electoral alternation—an event that signals the deepening of democracy—has positive causal impact on citizen perceptions of the quality of governance. This result was based on a cross-sectional research design, which compared average citizen attitudes to governance in groups of countries "with-and-without" alternation. We still do not know whether these average results apply evenly in all African countries or whether specific changes in governance are discernible in particular countries over time.

One solution is to devise a "before-and-after" test of governance conditions in a given country, with a democratic alternation as the pivotal event. But which country? At the time of writing in mid-2012, nine countries in the Afrobarometer had undergone an electoral alternation. But, by then, we had gathered survey data on a full array of before-and-after governance indicators for only a few of these countries: Benin, Cape Verde, Ghana, and Mali. In an earlier version of this chapter drafted in 2009, I found largely positive results in the case of Mali: citizens were more likely to see the government as legitimate, legal, capable, efficient, and honest after alternation than before. A military coup in Mali in March 2012, however, rendered moot most of those governance gains.

I therefore offer Ghana as an alternative test case. Ghana experienced an alternation of leaders and ruling parties (the second such occurrence since the restoration of democracy in 1993) as a result of closely fought presidential and parliamentary elections in December 2008 (Gyimah-Boadi 2009; Jockers, Kohnert, and Nugent 2009; Whitfield 2009). In January 2009, President John Kufuor of the New Patriotic Party handed over peacefully to John Atta Mills of the National Democratic Congress. Applicable data are found in Afrobarometer surveys for Ghana conducted in March 2005 (the "before" survey) and May 2012 (the "after" survey).

Ghana—a continental leader in democratization and good governance (APRM Secretariat 2005; Rotberg and Gisselquist 2008)—is an interesting case in its own right. A managed transition from military rule to civilian democracy culminated when Jerry Rawlings conceded the country's first electoral alternation in 2001. Thereafter, the center-right New Patriotic Party government of John Kufuor pursued the rule of law and a liberal economy by respecting institutional checks and balances, encouraging media freedom, and maintaining fiscal discipline. Political institutions established in the democratic constitution of 1992—such as presidential term limits—began to take root. By 2012, the country's respected electoral commission had held five free and fair elections and enjoyed an international reputation for independence and competence. The central bank of Ghana expanded its autonomy. And the parliament, the courts of law, and a commission on human rights and administrative justice "gained popular and elite acceptance as the legitimate avenues for settling differences between contending political factions" (Gyimah-Boadi and Prempeh 2012: 95).

This is not to say that all has gone smoothly in Ghana on the governance front. The president continues to enjoy inordinate powers, notably to name political allies to public office (Kopecky 2011). And because he appoints all mayors and one-third of local assembly members, decentralization remains seriously incomplete. As in earlier periods, the parliament's hands are tied in terms of initiating legislation or investigating official corruption and mismanagement. The integrity of the voter register remains questionable, and electioneering within Ghana's two-party system is becoming increasingly personalized and polarized. Finally, the discovery of offshore oil wealth in 2007 presents new challenges that "could potentially worsen the country's patronage-fueled politics and foster stagnation in governance and public management" (Gyimah-Boadi and Prempeh 2012: 107).

The survey data from Ghana reflect these political tensions. Table 14.4 shows changes in public opinion along eight of the nine dimensions of governance from surveys before and after the 2008 electoral turnover. Because the margin of sampling error is at least plus or minus 2 percentage points for each survey, I infer changes in opinion only if there is a difference of 4 percentage points across surveys. By this criterion, Ghanaians perceived no discernible change in the efficiency or equity of governance procedures (up 3 points and down 1 point respectively) that could be attributed to democratic alternation. Nor was there meaningful change from before to after alternation in the popular legitimacy of the government of Ghana (already extremely high) or the perceived transparency of government procedures (which remained stubbornly low).

Table 14.4 The Effects of Electoral Alternation on Good Governance in Ghana: Popular Perceptions, 2005–2012

Dimension of Governance	Indicator	2005[a]	2012[b]	Change
Administrative				
Legality	The president usually observes the constitution	67	82	+15
Transparency	Government procedures are easy to understand	20	22	+2
Honesty	Few or no government officials are corrupt	52	62	+10
Economic				
Effectiveness	Government can solve most important problems	68	77	+9
Efficiency	Public services are easily accessible	49	52	+3
Equity	Government usually treats people equally	56	55	−1
Political				
Responsiveness	Elected representatives usually try to listen	26	10	−16
Accountability	Elections allow people to remove poor leaders	79	not asked	n/a
Legitimacy	The government can rightfully demand compliance	95	93	−2

Source: Afrobarometer survey, 2012.
Notes: Cell entries are percentages of adults surveyed.
a. An alternation of leader and ruling party occurred in Ghana's presidential and parliamentary elections of December 2008. Afrobarometer Round 3 in Ghana (the "before" survey) was conducted prior to the March 2005 alternation. Survey size of 1,200 respondents.
b. Afrobarometer Round 5 in Ghana (the "after" survey) was conducted more than three years following the May 2012 alternation. Survey size of 2,400 respondents.

Other alternation dividends are more plausible. Between 2005 and 2012, many more Ghanaians regarded the government as legally constituted (up 15 percentage points), its officials as honest (up 10 points), and its capacity to solve problems as effective (up 9 points). These perceived improvements constitute meaningful evidence of a possible causal impact of electoral alternation on public opinion about the quality of governance.

Notably, however, a before-and-after comparison in Ghana reveals that electoral alternation had negative implications regarding the perceived responsiveness of elected officials. This incongruous result repeats a pattern seen earlier in cross-sectional analysis. In the case of Ghana, the proportion of adults who—in response to an identical question in each survey—thought that members of parliament listened to their needs in March 2005 (26 percent) was more than halved by May 2012 (10 percent). A 16-point negative gap between pre- and post-alternation observations is very likely to reflect a real diminution in the receptiveness of elected leaders to constituent needs in the aftermath of a landmark election. In sum, declining popular satisfaction among Ghanaians with the political responsiveness of the government to popular needs stands in stark contrast to their growing satisfaction with government performance in other areas.

A Representation Gap

This finding draws attention to an enduring representation gap in new African democracies. Notwithstanding gains in political competition and electoral alternation, a chasm persists in the link between voters and elected leaders. This deficit of political responsiveness is a hallmark of new African democracies.

Consider the evidence. African citizens have high expectations about the amount of time that legislative representatives should spend on constituency service: on average, some 12 percent unrealistically think that members of parliament (MPs) should reside in their electoral districts "all the time," more so in places like Mali (19 percent) and Malawi (26 percent). Yet citizens estimate that, in practice, only 3 percent of MPs or legislative deputies actually establish a permanent presence. The rest are judged to stay away for longer periods of time and, on average, 35 percent are held to "never" visit the district (Mali represents the Afrobarometer norm in this respect). The representation gap can be measured by subtracting citizen estimates of the amount of time legislators actually spend with constituents from the amount of time citizens think they should spend. Whereas three-quarters (76 percent) think it reasonable that representatives ought to visit constituents at least once per month, only one-quarter (26 percent) say that they actually do so.

A huge, 50-point representation gap (with Mali again exactly representing the Afrobarometer mean) bespeaks of African electorates estranged from their leaders. This sort of public alienation is common in representative democracies in other parts of the world and hardly unique to Africa.

But is the African version a real governance problem or a manifestation of unrealistic expectations on the part of citizens? One way to address this question is to test whether popular perceptions of a representation gap are reinforced by an absence of actual contact between constituents and elected agents. With reference to the year prior to the surveys, the Afrobarometer asks, "How often have you contacted any of the following persons: a member of parliament or legislative deputy?" Across eighteen countries, an average of only 11 percent of respondents had experienced any interaction with a parliamentary representative. Citizens report infrequent political contacts in countries at all levels of democratic development, whether in South Africa's liberal democracy (just 6 percent) or in Nigeria's ambiguous regime (a mere 8 percent). But such contacts tend to be more commonplace in countries that have undergone an electoral alternation, as in Ghana (17 percent) or Kenya (16 percent). Moreover, counter perhaps to intuition, the rate of citizen-legislator contact is slightly—but significantly—higher in Africa's rural rather than urban areas. If nothing else, this result suggests that legislators face greater demands for personal, face-to-face service from villagers rather than from townsfolk.

The available data also suggest that the representation gap is an empirical reality rather than simply a function of excessively high expectations among the electorate. Table 14.5 shows that the higher the frequency of actual citizen-legislator contact, the lower the perceived representation gap. At minimum, therefore, popular attitudes to legislator performance seem to be based on citizens' concrete experiences. This conjecture is strengthened

Table 14.5 Behavioral Correlates of the Representation Gap in Sub-Saharan Africa, 2005

	Representation Gap	Time MP Should Spend on Constituency Service	Time MP Actually Spends on Constituency Service
Citizen-legislator contact	−0.096***	0.009 ns	0.126***

Source: Afrobarometer survey, 2005.
Notes: Cell entries are Pearson's product moment correlation coefficients.
***$p < 0.001$; ns = not statistically significant.

when I separate expectations—how much time the MP should spend in the constituency—and actual performance—how much time the MP actually spends. There is no statistical relationship between expectations and contact, but there is a strong and significant link between the physical presence of the legislator in the district and the reported frequency of citizen contacts. As such, I conclude that the representation gap is an existential reality and not simply a figment in the imaginations of African citizens who long for more responsive forms of governance.

Explanations for shortfalls in the responsiveness of governance in Africa are plentiful. The representation gap could be a function of formal institutions. Electoral systems based on proportional representation, for example, especially where representatives on national party lists are not tied to any defined electoral district, provide little inducement to legislators to attend to popular preferences (Mattes 2008; see also Chapters 9 and 10 in this volume). Alternatively, informal institutions may matter more. The representation gap may be a manifestation of a deep-seated cultural preference for a direct (rather than representative) form of democracy, in which Africans insist on personal, face-to-face contacts with elected officials. Or it could result from patronage demands that representatives encounter every time they set foot in their home districts, a deluge whose size provides strong incentives to shirk constituency service (Davies 2008). Or perhaps citizens themselves bear responsibility. The gap could reflect a lack of effective popular demand for vertical accountability; other research shows that one-third of African citizens are willing to delegate to national presidents the authority for "making sure MPs do their jobs" (see Chapter 11). Whatever the reason, the accumulated evidence suggests that responsiveness by elected officials is the weakest link in the chain that connects democracy to good governance.

Conclusion

In this chapter I have tried to disentangle democratization from the quest for good governance in sub-Saharan Africa. Beyond having a vague sense that these processes are somehow related, development practitioners rarely know which to tackle first or which dimensions of governance are more susceptible to reform in multiparty settings. Internally, political elites tend to be preoccupied with the acquisition and maintenance of political power; as such, they neglect needed administrative reforms and development priorities once they have won an election. Externally, donors face the conundrum of reform sequencing, as evidenced by meta-policy debates on whether a rule of law is a necessary prerequisite to the survival and sustenance of a democratically elected regime.

Having defined and measured democracy and governance separately, I have shown consistent patterns of association. Various sorts of evidence—macro, micro, and temporal—indicate a structural affinity between free elections and improved governance. This observation may seem glaringly obvious, but only if democracy and governance are conflated by definition. We know from recent experience in Africa that nominal democratization via less-than-perfect elections provides little guarantee of improvement in the performance of state institutions. And current cases of "tiger" development in Asia—notably in China, Malaysia, and Singapore—indicate that aspects of good governance can sometimes be attained by authoritarian regimes. Given, therefore, that democracy and governance can vary with a considerable degree of independence, it is therefore encouraging—if not entirely unexpected—to discover that, in sub-Saharan Africa, the two types of reform tend to go together empirically.

Nonetheless, the democracy connection is more consistent in relation to some dimensions of good governance than to others, namely administrative, economic, and political dimensions. Regarding administrative dimensions, democratic elections are linked more strongly and consistently to the establishment of a rule of law and the control of corruption than to the attainment of transparency in decisionmaking procedures. A lingering concern for institutional development is that mass populations still lack a broad and deep understanding of essential procedures of democratic governance such as the separation of governmental powers and the rights of citizens with regard to decisionmaking.

Regarding economic dimensions, whatever the nature of the test, democracy and elections have surprisingly strong and consistent associations with perceived governmental *effectiveness*. But the links to *efficiency* and (especially) *equity* in public goods provision are less reliable. In sum, while hardly absent in Africa, state failure does not occur always and everywhere. Yet even where state institutions are well established, they too often operate below capacity, at excessive cost, or with uneven coverage.

Regarding political dimensions, unsurprisingly, democratic elections are closely associated with legitimate and accountable governance, especially so where elections enable the peaceful alternation of rulers. Unexpectedly, however, democratic elections do not reliably guarantee that elected leaders will subsequently be more responsive to their constituents. A principal challenge in deepening democratic governance in Africa is to strengthen procedures for ensuring that representatives listen to the populace and respond to their needs between elections.

Over the past two decades, elites and masses in sub-Saharan Africa have evinced a measure of political learning. Some (but not all) citizens have begun to realize that democratic elections offer an opportunity to eject underperforming leaders. And some (but not all) elected officials have adapted their strategies for maintaining power and extracting resources to the uncertainties of electoral competition and a gradually tightening rule of law (Posner and Young 2007). In the tension between formal constitutional rules and informal ethnic ties, the latter still win the day across much of Africa, and elites and masses alike are complicit in supporting prevailing institutions of patronage and clientelism. But the advent of free elections has made it more feasible for internal and external actors to enforce norms of better governance, if only because, under democracy, there is a political price to be paid for nonperformance.

The chapter also offers evidence to support the claim that democratization and good governance are mutually constitutive. On the one hand, democracies emerge more readily on the foundations of a steady and orderly state—meaning one that is already well governed. But by introducing a rule of law and providing electoral legitimacy, democratization itself contributes to the consolidation of trustworthy state institutions and, in turn, to good governance. As a rule of thumb for policy sequencing, therefore, democracy promotion need not await the prior establishment of a rule of law.

Part 5

Conclusion

15

Voting and Democratic Citizenship in Africa: Where Next?

Michael Bratton

On March 25, 2012, voters in Senegal triggered an electoral alternation. In a second round of voting for a president they resoundingly ejected the octogenarian incumbent, Abdoulaye Wade, in favor of Macky Sall, a fifty-year-old former prime minister turned opposition leader. The election symbolized popular resistance to arbitrary rule by an African "big man" who had overstayed his welcome by running for a third term and by grooming his son as a prospective presidential successor (Kelly 2012). The challenger attracted a public following, including young people who had taken to the streets in violent protest, by opposing the incumbent's efforts to sidestep the law and create a family dynasty. Instead, Sall's campaign pledged to serve the "sovereign people" of Senegal by shortening presidential terms from seven to five years, enforcing the constitution's two-term limit, and "bring[ing] in measures to reduce the price of basic foodstuffs" (Look 2012; Fessey 2012). In making these promises, he explicitly acknowledged the central role that ordinary people played in defending one of Africa's longest-lived and most promising democracies.

Lessons Learned

In this volume we have drawn attention to the involvement of voters and citizens in building democratic institutions. Political developments in postcolonial Africa have demonstrated that institution building involves much more than constitutional engineering from above. Departing colonial powers and indigenous would-be dictators alike have discovered that political institutions that fail to acknowledge the values and serve the interests of popular constituencies are destined to have a limited shelf life. Instead, because durable institutions can only flourish in a supportive political culture, ordinary people have important functions to perform in the process of "getting the institutions right." In a democracy, a "sovereign people" (to use President Mack's language) holds the trump card of political legitimacy, which can be granted or withheld—not only to particular political institutions, but also to individual leaders or whole political regimes—depending on mass acceptance and approval. It therefore behooves political leaders to design and implement institutional rules in close consultation with expressed popular preferences.

Elections are the essential democratic institution; without elections a regime of democracy is impossible. In this book we have further insisted that the quality of elections matters. Electoral contests must be free and fair—and acknowledged as such by both voters and international observers—in order to make reliable contributions to the consolidation of democracy. Recognizing that elections alone are not a sufficient condition for democracy, however, we have noted in addition that voting alone—even in free and fair elections—is insufficient for the full blossoming of democratic citizenship. Ordinary people also require a full appreciation of the rights and responsibilities of citizenship as expressed through action—individual and collective—to hold leaders accountable between elections. In order to do so, there is need for additional democratic institutions that, so far in Africa, are less well developed than elections.

A decade-long series of Afrobarometer surveys across a variety of African countries reveals both good and bad news. On the positive side, survey respondents confirm that competitive elections, regularly held in an open environment, are overwhelmingly the most popular institution for selecting political leaders. Furthermore, the Africans we interviewed are proficient judges of the quality of elections, being able to distinguish contests that accurately reflect a popular will from those that are marred by elite malpractice. Moreover, Africans in the surveyed countries see a direct connection between the construction of high-quality elections and the subsequent consolidation of democracy. In countries with free and fair voting, they judge democracy to be taking root and express satisfaction with the way the political regime actually works. Remarkably, there is even evidence that individuals who vote for parties that lose elections are more deeply committed to defending the rules of competitive elections than those who emerge as winners.

Other results, while mixed, are ultimately encouraging. Over time, the Africans we interviewed evince a growing acceptance of multiple political parties, even though the emergence of these institutions sometimes spawns violent conflict. These citizens apparently see overt competition as a risk worth taking in order to guarantee real political choice and the prospect of leadership accountability. Offsetting the institutionalization of political competition, however, is a lingering reservoir of popular distrust for opposition parties, which are often seen as weak and feckless (Logan 2008).

As political competition intensifies, however, so do electoral malpractices, perpetrated mainly, though not exclusively, by political elites. The weight of evidence from Afrobarometer surveys suggests that, while violence may depress voter turnout, vote buying is not always effective at securing voters' political loyalty. Indeed, our research suggests that many Africans use an instrumental logic in arriving at voting decisions; even as they hew to social (especially ethnic) identities, their choices at the polls are driven principally by rational considerations of policy performance. A principal determinant of vote choice is whether incumbents have "delivered the goods" in terms of employment, inflation, and income distribution. Finally, elections that are conducted according to standards of high quality serve to increase confidence among citizens that political leaders will be made honest and state institutions will become more effective. If not, then voters—like those in Senegal—are seemingly gaining confidence that they can change governments at the next election.

On the negative side, ethnic bloc voting remains a notable feature of African elections. While survey respondents find it politically incorrect to admit to voting on identity grounds, actual voting behavior sometimes belies widespread popular claims of toleration of ethnic differences (Bratton and Kimenyi 2008). The political salience of ethnicity depends importantly on the closeness (both in time and outcome) of electoral contests and on whether individuals think their political rivals will vote on ethnic grounds.

There is also evidence that electoral malpractices are more effective among some voters than others: vote buying and threats of violence have greatest impact among the poor (who are most needy) and the ill educated (who are most easily intimidated). The phenomenon of "uncritical" citizenship—manifest in low levels of political knowledge, unreflective evaluations of policy performance, and unconditional support of incumbents—is most common among these social groups. Along with electoral "winners," uncritical citizens fail to demand accountability from leaders or fully claim their rights under democracy. And while electoral "losers" are willing to fight hardest to defend democracy, they also express low levels of trust in public institutions and are guarded about granting legitimacy to state authority.

Thus there are sound reasons why observers ought to remain cautious about recent democratic gains on the African continent. Apart from elections, the most important political and economic decisions remain beyond popular reach. Self-serving leaders continue to capitalize on their tenure in public office—made all the more uncertain by the threat of ejection at the next election—in order to make the most of opportunities to extract rents from the country's wealth. Nor have some ruthless elites given up on efforts to tilt the playing field in their own direction, including by resorting to violence, the better to emerge victorious whenever exposed to elections.

The countries of sub-Saharan Africa, and even the more open societies so far covered by the Afrobarometer, therefore continue to move in divergent political directions. For every Senegal, which enjoys a strengthening democracy, there is a Zimbabwe, where an entrenched authoritarian regime is determined to bend the rules of political competition in its own favor. Strikingly, the opposition upset in the 2012 Senegalese election came only days after a military coup in neighboring Mali, just one month before that country was scheduled to hold its own presidential vote. Some Malians reportedly celebrated the return of soldiers to political life while others vigorously condemned it (Nossiter 2012). The actual distribution of these opinions remains to be studied by a future Afrobarometer survey. But the easy interruption of a once promising democratic regime in Mali and the apparent diversity of public reactions testify to the long-term challenges involved in building democratic political institutions. Democratization in sub-Saharan Africa remains a work in progress.

A Research Agenda

Although considerable advancement has been made over the past decade in understanding the dynamics of voting behavior and political participation in Africa, much more can be done. In this concluding section, I float some ideas for future investigation.

Who Votes?

Research across a range of African countries confirms certain articles of received wisdom in political science. For example, as in the rest of the world, voter turnout in African elections is positively related to age, with young people in their late teens and early twenties voting at far lower rates than their elders. But the same studies disconfirm other established comparative generalizations about the social demographics of voting. Unexpectedly, voters in African elections are drawn disproportionately from marginalized populations, including rural dwellers, the poor, and those with low levels of education (Bratton 2008; Isaksson 2010; Kuenzi and Lambright 2007). This profile of voter turnout stands in stark contrast to patterns of higher turnout by middle-class and well-educated strata in the economically developed parts of the world. And features of Africa's demographic transition—a youth bulge accompanied by rapid urbanization—would appear to augur badly for voter turnout rates in future African elections.

These results pose a number of interesting research questions. Why do the rural poor in Africa turn out to vote? Why, by contrast, are some people with wealth and education apparently spurning opportunities to do so? Could it be because they regard with disdain electoral processes that feature patronage and violence rather than reasoned debate about programmatic policy alternatives? Certainly, middle-class persons display a pervasive suspicion that their fellow citizens are incapable of casting a responsible vote. Afrobarometer surveys repeatedly show that, as education rises, individuals are more likely to agree that "only those who are sufficiently well educated should be allowed to choose our leaders" and to disagree that "all people should be permitted to vote, even if they do not fully understand all the issues in an election." In this respect, recent economic growth and the rise of an African middle class (Handley 2012; Radelet 2010; Severino and Ray 2012) may not automatically herald the spread of democratic values.

Election Campaigns

With the exception of Part 2 on vote buying, this book says little about the roles of voters and citizens in election campaigns. More work is needed on the various channels of communication—canvassing, posters, radio, rallies—used by politicians and their agents to reach and persuade voters. How do ordinary voters respond? Which campaign messages and media are most effective? Do campaign rallies have observable consequences, for example by encouraging citizens to register as voters, join political discussions, or work on behalf of candidates? We should be especially interested in the cross-pressures faced by prospective voters, for example between the positive incentives of patronage and the negative sanctions of violence.

As for patronage, it is becoming clear that the token gifts distributed by African politicians (for example, small amounts of food, cash, or clothing) are too modest to shape political allegiances substantially or permanently. A more promising line of research suggests that vote buying of this sort serves as a signal that, if elected, the politician will deliver more generous rewards after the election (Conroy-Krutz 2012). So far, however, ordinary people have yet to be convinced that such commitments are credible, since, in every Afrobarometer country, a large (often very large) majority of survey respondents believe that politicians never or rarely "keep their campaign promises after elections." We therefore need deeper study of the subject of political clientelism in African elections. For example, we want to know which sorts of patronage rewards motivate voters, the mechanisms by which material rewards create political loyalty, and the durability (or evanescence) of patron-client ties.

Regarding electoral violence, we also have a lot to learn. A critical factor is the crisis of unemployment among urban youth. Lacking the material means to earn a living, settle down, and start families, young people, especially males, provide a reservoir of recruits for the private armies of unscrupulous politicians (Mueller 2008; Reno 2011). The mobilization of violent youth wings usually centers on election periods, with the best predictor of postelection outbreaks of violence being armed clashes during the preelection campaign.

But what causes some young people to join political gangs or party militias whereas others do not? Is there a connection between electoral disenfranchisement and propensity to resort to aggression? To what extent is electoral violence an expression of ethnic—as opposed to partisan or economic—identity? A study in urban Kenya of the 2008 postelection violence found substantial variation in the salience of ethnicity across neighborhoods (LeBas 2010). In neighborhoods unaffected by fighting, citizens tended to hold back from public criticism of coethnic politicians who resorted to violence. But in neighborhoods substantially victimized by conflict, individual citizens are as likely to criticize their coethnics for vicious electoral tactics as to sanction a politician from a different ethnic group for similar behavior. But we need more evidence of this kind before we can confirm the tantalizing possibility that electoral violence may backfire rather than prime ethnic identity or reinforce ethnic polarization.

Vote Choice

It must be admitted that survey data on partisan preferences, expressed voting intentions, and reported vote choice may be somewhat unreliable. There is a tendency for survey respondents to censor their answers to questions about party identification or ballot behavior. For example, those who think that Afrobarometer interviewers are sent by a government agency (an incorrect assumption) or those who say that people "must be careful what they say about politics" (the Afrobarometer's standard indicator of political fear) are somewhat more likely to report identification with the ruling party and to say that they would vote for the incumbent. Masipula Sithole has memorably described this tendency as "a margin of terror" (personal communication 2002; Bratton and Masunungure 2012). One or other of these variables should therefore be included as controls in any multivariate analysis of vote choice. It would also be advisable (where possible) to supplement opinion surveys conducted during preelection periods with official voting returns, with exit polls, or with surveys conducted at other times, especially if these allow fine-grained analysis at the constituency level or below.

For analytic purposes, however, descriptive point estimates are less important than the social, economic, and political correlates of partisanship. We can be confident in the results of inferential analysis—who votes how and why—because broad patterns remain consistent across countries and over time. For example, a systematic geographical pattern is evident in the choices at polling booths—whether for incumbent or opposition—made by African voters. Rural dwellers are strongly inclined to support incumbent governments. By contrast, urban residents regularly cast their votes for opposition parties, an effect amplified by the rural turnout advantage noted earlier. Robin Harding (2010) explains this underanalyzed feature of voting behavior in terms of the demography of democratic majorities: he contends that ruling parties adopt policies that reward rural dwellers, thus incurring what he calls "urban incumbent hostility." Kate Baldwin (2011) adds detail to this story: African politicians devolve power to traditional leaders, in part by giving them greater responsibility over the allocation of land, as a means of mobilizing electoral support from noncoethnics. In addition, I would draw attention to the calculus of unpopular national leaders. The longer they are in office, the more likely they will seek political refuge in a rural electorate who are relatively satisfied with small patronage rewards, less exposed to critiques of government performance, and more accustomed to taking political cues on the basis of social pressure.

This raises the important issue of the quality of voting. Are voters making autonomous political decisions, or are they participating as part of a mobilized bloc (Bratton, Mattes, and Gyimah-Boadi 2005; Bratton 2008)? If the latter, then by what institutional mechanism is rural support mobilized? In recent years, incumbent politicians in Africa have routinely employed political parties, traditional leaders, and community organizations as instruments to get out the rural vote. The time therefore has come to renew studies of local organizations in African politics. We need to understand whether in fact rural voters are more likely than urban voters to act on community-wide consensus about who to vote for. If bloc voting is a demonstrable feature of African elections, then how is it enforced? Through the economic inducements of patronage? Through the application of violence or threats of retribution after elections? Or through appeals to social solidarity and the avoidance of conflict in the locality? Or all of the above? Of special interest is the effect on the popular legitimacy of chiefs and headmen who have been co-opted by authoritarian leaders to deliver a guaranteed quota of rural votes.

In a related inquiry, we need to ask whether voters make sincere or strategic choices. Do they choose a political candidate as a genuine first preference? Or do they line up behind the likely winner? Alternatively, is strategic voting driven by efforts to avoid unpalatable alternatives, such as parties associated with ethnic rivals? In the context of limited competition, dominant ruling parties, and weak opposition challengers, strategic voting is a risk-averse approach. But it hardly bespeaks of an electorate taking full advantage of the opportunities of democratic citizenship.

Collective Action

Indeed, when it comes to citizenship, as we have argued in this book, voting is merely a first step. Citizenship in a democracy also involves civic engagement, both horizontally through collective action alongside fellow citizens and vertically through linkages with political institutions. Such engagement may occur through either formal or informal channels.

The puzzle of collective action is central to the concerns of political science (Olson 1965; Hardin 1982; Ostrom 1990, 1998). It asks whether individuals and groups can devise institutional rules that limit everyone's short-term interests in order for all to benefit in the longer run. Consistent with this approach, recent work on African development emphasizes the role of political coalitions in building locally appropriate institutions (Kelsall 2011; Leftwich 2012).

But many research questions remain unanswered. Who gets involved in electoral and developmental coalitions, especially at the grassroots level? The survey data suggest that—as with voter turnout and vote choice—rural dwellers are more active in cooperative political projects than are their urban counterparts. Recent analysis has even begun to question whether young Africans who live in cities are any more likely than anyone else to join advocacy groups and engage in political protest (Resnick and Casale 2011). It is likely that the experience of urbanization is socially atomizing, undermining precisely the sorts of social ties that might provide a foundation for locally appropriate institutions. In order to support a case for rural collective action, however, one would have to disprove the conventional wisdom that scattered peasant societies are difficult to organize. One would also have to show that popular involvement in community meetings in rural areas actually challenges, rather than reinforces, local power structures. Viable local initiatives—say by groups of women farmers—often face difficulty in organizational "scaling up" and resistance or co-optation by entrenched political interests. Thus, despite the appealing idea of social embededness, there are clear limits to the degree to which a patrimonial political culture can provide a firm foundation for building developmental or democratic institutions.

On the positive side, however, there is scattered evidence of emerging democratic citizenship. As shown in this book, a context of high-quality elections seems to stimulate ordinary Africans to increase their involvement in public debate and organized community action. The likely mechanism—yet to be confirmed—runs through political legitimacy, both procedural and substantive. Procedurally, free and fair elections signal that citizen preferences will be accurately recorded, thus making it worthwhile for individuals to invest in civic engagement. And substantively, high-quality contests build political support for policy implementation, even if policies are initially unpopular among citizens.

What other conditions prompt collective political action? Modernization theory points to the formative influence of education on democratic citizenship, probably directly through value change rather than indirectly through material advantage (Evans and Rose 2007a, 2007b). Even though, as shown earlier, educated people vote less and doubt that their under-educated compatriots make good citizens, they are otherwise likely to be politically active. Analysis of four pooled rounds of Afrobarometer data confirms that an individual's level of education is positively related to his or her discussion of public affairs, collaboration with others to raise issues, and attendance at a demonstration or protest march. But people with education apparently still hold back from participation in community meetings. This result points either to persistent social differences that block coalition formation or to the resistance of educated, rights-bearing citizens to authoritarian controls on political activity at the local level. So, while education is spur to citizenship, it does not dissolve all barriers.

As a supplement or alternative to formal education, one might expect that new information and communications technologies would encourage collective action among democratic citizens. The rapid spread of mobile phone technology is connecting people to one another, initially in terms of social and economic interactions (as in East Africa) but potentially also politically (as during the Arab Spring in North Africa). The Internet, which is only beginning to penetrate the continent at a popular level, also holds the prospect of growing cosmopolitanism—meaning awareness and tolerance of a range of world values (Appiah 2006; Brown and Held 2012; Hannerz 1990). The Afrobarometer has already detected tantalizing hints that the use of cellular telephones is linked to support for, and satisfaction with, market-oriented policy reforms (Bratton and Lolojih 2013), with engagement in political discussion (Bratton 2013), and with acceptance of a critical role for opposition parties (Ismail and Graham 2009). The challenge going forward is to establish whether (and if so, how) new modes of interpersonal communication facilitate the construction of democratic institutions from below.

Toward Accountability

Finally, much work remains to be done in conceptualizing, measuring, and explaining the vertical linkages between African citizens and political institutions. The range of relevant institutions is wide—political parties, legislatures, executive ministries, courts, independent agencies of restraint, civic associations—and citizens may relate differently to each type. And rival models of linkage—whether patronage or policy, interest or identity—are surely too crude in contexts where relations between citizens and institutions are fluid, situational, and hybrid.

Yet analysts can probably agree that, in a democracy, institutional rules aim at ensuring the accountability of political leaders. To arrive at a usable theory of political accountability, however, we must first finish basic tasks of conceptual definition. I detect a good deal of overlap and imprecision in

the use of three central concepts in the literature: responsiveness, representation, and accountability. As I see it, *responsiveness* refers to the willingness of leaders to register the preferences of constituents—that is, by paying attention to their requests and complaints. It can be differentiated from
representation, which refers to the role of elected officials in conveying
popular demands onward to deliberative and decisionmaking bodies. These
two concepts are further distinguished from political *accountability,* which
refers to the periodic ability of citizens to evaluate leadership performance,
most commonly but not exclusively through elections. While all three concepts are closely related, even cumulatively nested, they should be explored
separately.

Empirically, this book has established that African citizens regard the
responsiveness of elected leaders between elections as the greatest shortfall
in the practice of democratic governance in Africa. In short, most people
hold that leaders do not listen. We have also uncovered a representation gap
between citizens and legislators that can be summarized in the common
complaint that they only visit the locality at election time. Finally, the
Africans interviewed in the latest complete round of Afrobarometer surveys
are undecided about how well elections enable voters to remove unresponsive and unrepresentative leaders: 45 percent say "well," 43 percent say
"not well," and 12 percent "don't know." In this way, they signal that they
find elections to be less than fully adequate to the task of securing political
accountability.

The onus for guaranteeing accountable governance in the longer run
therefore falls on citizen links with other institutions. Here the news is
mixed. Take political parties. Although multiparty competition is becoming
more widely accepted among Africans, a sizable minority still worry that
this competition leads to violent political conflict. Accordingly, while one-
third of interviewees report feeling "very close" to a preferred political
party, just as many prefer to remain politically unaffiliated. And, even after
two decades of democracy on the continent, people consistently lend far
less trust to opposition parties than to ruling parties. As for parliament, here
understood as the lower house of the legislature, citizens are gradually displaying more institutional trust over time. But by the same token, almost
half of the electorate continue to doubt that members of parliament reliably
reflect the views of voters. And they do not trust members of parliament or
assembly deputies to make decisions on citizens' behalf. Thus, for too many
African citizens, the formal institutions of state and the official realm of
politics remain remote and alien. Majorities in every Afrobarometer country except Botswana and Cape Verde continue to report that they experience
difficulty in making their voice heard between elections.

We have argued in these pages that liability for this outcome lies as
much with masses as with elites. Our research has revealed conflicting pop-

ular conceptions of democratic citizenship. These differences contrast notions of "delegative" democracy with alternative forms of representative or participatory democracy. On one hand, uncritical citizens tend to blindly trust the institutions of the status quo and to defer authority to the occupants of state office for most political decisions except voting. On the other hand, critical citizens express greater demand for regular, direct, face-to-face contacts with elected representatives than the latter can reasonably be expected to deliver. Some individual Africans even hold delegative, representative, and participatory preferences in their minds at the same time, an indication that the development of democratic citizenship—including its full array of both rights and responsibilities—is still embryonic in many places.

In the end, however, lasting democracy cannot be built without democrats. It may be possible to temporarily install a nominally democratic regime in the absence of full elite commitment, for example when incumbent leaders reluctantly accept the liberalization of political rules in order to avoid losing power. But the consolidation of a democratic regime can only be consummated when a set of culturally embedded institutions holds political elites accountable for their actions in office. Since political executives are not self-restraining, others must take the initiative to restrain them. This task falls (horizontally) to legislative, judicial, and watchdog bodies, and (vertically) to an active and organized citizenry. In this book, we have argued that high-quality elections can set in motion a process of vertical accountability, most vividly illustrated when incumbent rulers are voted out of power. But because institutions are only as durable as their cultural underpinnings, much depends on the subsequent development and sustainability of democratic citizenship among African populations at large.

Acronyms

ANC	African National Congress
ANPP	All Nigeria Peoples' Party
AU	African Union
DRC	Democratic Republic of the Congo
ECOWAS	Economic Community of West African States
EU	European Union
FDC	Forum for Democratic Change (Uganda)
FPTP	First Past the Post
Frelimo	Front for the Liberation of Mozambique
GDP	gross domestic product
IPC	Inter-Party Coalition (Uganda)
KANU	Kenyan African National Union
LDP	Liberal Democratic Party (Kenya)
MDM	mean district magnitude
MP	member of parliament
NARC	National Rainbow Coalition (Kenya)
NRM	National Resistance Movement (Uganda)
PDP	Peoples' Democratic Party (Nigeria)
PR	proportional representation
SADC	Southern African Development Community
UNDP	United Nations Development Programme
UPC	Uganda Peoples' Congress
USAID	US Agency for International Development

References

Accmoglu, Darren, and James Robinson. 2006. *The Economic Origins of Dictator-ship and Democracy.* New York: Cambridge University Press.

African Union. 2011. *AU Observer Mission to Elections in Uganda.* Addis Ababa.

Afrobarometer. 2009. "Neither Consolidating Nor Fully Democratic: The Evolution of African Political Regimes, 1999–2008." *Afrobarometer Briefing Paper* no. 67. http://www.afrobarometer.org/files/documents/briefing_papers/AfrobriefNo 67.pdf.

———. 2010. "Summary of Results: Round 4.5.1 Afrobarometer Pre-Election Sur-vey in Uganda 2010." http://www.afrobarometer.org/files/documents/summary _results/uga_r4-5_SOR.pdf.

———. 2011. "Summary of Results: Round 4.5.2 Afrobarometer Pre-Election Sur-vey in Uganda 2011." http://www.afrobarometer.org/files/documents/summary _results/uga_r4-5-2_sor.pdf.

Ake, Claude. 1996. *Democracy and Development in Africa.* Washington, DC: Brook-ings Institution.

Aldrich, John. 1993. "Rational Choice and Turnout." *American Journal of Political Science* 87 (2): 246–278.

Alesina, Alberto, et al. 2002. "Fractionalization." *Journal of Economic Growth* 8 (2): 155–194.

Alesina, Alberto, Reza Baqir, and William Easterly. 1999. "Public Goods and Eth-nic Divisions." *Quarterly Journal of Economics* 114 (4): 1243–1284.

Alford, Robert. 1967. "Class Voting in the Anglo-American Political Systems." In Seymour Martin Lipset and Stein Rokkan (eds.), *Party Systems and Voter Alignments: Cross National Perspectives.* New York: Free Press, 67–93.

Almond, Gabriel, and Sidney Verba. 1963. *The Civic Culture: Political Attitudes and Democracy in Five Nations.* Boston: Little, Brown.

Among, B. 2010. "Parties Rubbish Poll Survey." *Saturday Vision* (Kampala), De-cember 18.

Anderson, Benedict. 1996. *Imagined Communities: Reflections on the Origin and Spread of Nationalism.* London: Verso.

Anderson, Christopher. 2000. "Economic Voting in Political Context: A Compara-tive Perspective." *Electoral Studies* 19 (2–3): 151–170.

291

————. 2007. "The End of Economic Voting? Contingency Dilemmas and the Limits of Democratic Accountability." *Annual Review of Political Science* 10 (1): 271–296.

Anderson, Christopher, Andre Blais, Shaun Bowler, Todd Donovan, and Ola Listhaug. 2005. *Losers' Consent.* New York: Oxford University Press.

Anderson, Christopher, and Christine Guillory. 1997. "Political Institutions and Satisfaction with Democracy: A Cross-National Analysis of Consensus and Majoritarian Systems." *American Political Science Review* 91 (1): 66–81.

Anderson, Christopher, and Andrew Lotempio. 2002. "Winning, Losing, and Political Trust in America." *British Journal of Political Science* 32 (3): 335–351.

Anderson, Christopher, and Yuliya Tverdova. 2001. "Winners, Losers, and Attitudes About Government in Contemporary Democracies." *International Political Science Review* 22 (2): 321–338.

————. 2003. "Corruption, Political Allegiances, and Attitudes Toward Government in Contemporary Democracies." *American Journal of Political Science* 47 (1): 91–109.

Anderson, D. 2002. "Vigilantes, Violence, and the Politics of Public Order in Kenya." *African Affairs* 101 (405): 531–555.

Anderson, G., and Robert Tollison. 1990. "Democracy in the Marketplace." In M. Crain and Tollison (eds.), *Predicting Politics: Essays in Empirical Public Choice.* Ann Arbor: University of Michigan Press, 285–303.

Anderson, Leslie. 2006. "The Authoritarian Executive? Horizontal and Vertical Accountability in Nicaragua." *Latin American Politics and Society* 48 (2): 141–169.

Appiah, Kwame Anthony. 2006. *Cosmopolitanism: Ethics in a World of Strangers.* London: Allen Lane.

APRM (African Peer Review Mechanism) Secretariat. 2005. *African Peer Review Mechanism: Republic of Ghana.* Midrand, June.

Arndt, Christiane, and Charles Oman. 2006. *Uses and Abuses of Governance Indicators.* Paris: Organization for Economic Cooperation and Development.

Ayee, Joseph, ed. 1997. *The 1996 General Elections and Democratic Consolidation in Ghana.* Accra: University of Ghana Press.

Baek, Mijeong. 2009. "A Comparative Analysis of Political Communication Systems and Voter Turnout." *American Journal of Political Science* 53 (2): 376–393.

Baird, Vanessa. 2001. "Building Institutional Legitimacy: The Role of Procedural Justice." *Political Research Quarterly* 54 (3): 333–354.

Baldwin, Kate. 2011. "When Politicians Concede Control of Resources: Land, Chiefs, and Coalition-Building in Africa." *Afrobarometer Working Paper* no. 130. http://www.afrobarometer.org/files/documents/working_papers/Afropaper No130.pdf.

Banducci, Susan, and Jeffrey Karp. 2003. "How Elections Change the Way Citizens View the Political System: Campaigns, Media Effects, and Electoral Outcomes in Comparative Perspective." *British Journal of Political Science* 33 (3): 443–467.

Banégas, Richard. 1998. "Marchandisation du vote, cioyenneté et consolidation démocratique au Bénin." *Politique Africaine* 69 (1): 75–88.

Bareebe, G. 2011. "Besigye Rejects 'Sham' Elections." *Daily Monitor* (Kampala), February 19.

Barkan, Joel. 1979. "Bringing Home the Pork: Legislative Behavior, Rural Development, and Political Change in East Africa." In Joel Smith and Lloyd Musolf (eds.), *Legislatures in Development*. Durham, NC: Duke University Press, 265–288.

———. 1995. "Elections in Agrarian Societies." *Journal of Democracy* 6 (4): 106–116.

———. 1998. "Rethinking the Applicability of Proportional Representation for Africa." In Timothy Sisk and Andrew Reynolds (eds.), *Elections and Conflict Management in Africa*. Washington, DC: US Institute of Peace Press, 57–70.

———. 2008. "The Causes and Consequences of Flawed Democracy in Kenya." Testimony before the Foreign Relations Committee, Subcommittee on African Affairs, US Senate, February 7.

———, ed. 2009. *Legislative Power in Emerging African Democracies*. Boulder: Lynne Rienner.

Baron, Reuben, and David Kenny. 1986. "The Moderator-Mediator Variable Distinction in Social Psychological Research: Conceptual Strategic and Statistical Considerations." *Journal of Personality and Social Psychology* 51: 1173–1182.

Bates, Robert. 1983. "Modernization, Ethnic Competition, and the Rationality of Politics in Contemporary Africa." In Donald Rothchild and Victor Olorunsola (eds.), *State Versus Ethnic Claims: African Policy Dilemmas*. Boulder: Westview, 152–171.

———. 2000. "Ethnicity and Development in Africa: A Reappraisal." *AEA Papers and Proceedings* 90 (May): 131–134.

———. 2008. *When Things Fell Apart: State Failure in Late Century Africa*. New York: Cambridge University Press.

Bawumia, Mahamadu. 1998. "Understanding Rural-Urban Voting Patterns in the 1992 Ghanaian Election." *Journal of Modern African Studies* 36 (1): 47–70.

Bekker, Simon, Martine Dodds, and Meshak Khosa, eds. 2001. *Shifting African Identities*. Pretoria: Human Sciences Research Council.

Berman, Bruce, Dickson Eyoh, and Will Kymlicka, eds. 2004. *Ethnicity and Democracy in Africa*. Oxford: Currey.

Bhavnani, Ravinder, and Daniel Miodownik. 2009. "Ethnic Polarization, Ethnic Salience, and Civil War." *Journal of Conflict Resolution* 53 (1): 30–49.

Billig, Michael. 1995. *Banal Nationalism*. London: Sage.

Birch, Sarah. 2011. *Electoral Malpractice*. Oxford: Oxford University Press.

Bjornlund, Eric. 2004. *Beyond Free and Fair: Monitoring Elections and Building Democracy*. Baltimore: Johns Hopkins University Press.

Blais, Andre, and R. K. Carty. 1990. "Does Proportional Representation Foster Voter Turnout?" *European Journal of Political Research* 18 (2): 167–181.

Blaydes, Lisa. 2006. "Who Votes in Authoritarian Elections and Why? Determinants of Voter Turnout in Contemporary Egypt." Paper presented at the annual meeting of the American Political Science Association, Philadelphia, August 31–September 3.

Bollen, Kenneth. 1993. "Liberal Democracy: Validity and Method Factors in Cross-National Measures." *American Political Science Review* 37 (4): 1207–1230.

Bossuroy, Thomas. 2011. "Individual Determinants of Ethnic Identification." Working Paper no. 2011-06. Paris: UMR-DIAL.

Bovcon, Maja. 2012. "Why Repeated Elections Don't Always Lead to Better Democracy: The Case of Côte d'Ivoire." Draft paper. Oxford: Oxford University.

Bratton, Michael. 1999. "Political Participation in a New Democracy: Institutional Considerations from Zambia." *Comparative Political Studies* 32 (5): 549–589.

———. 2004. "The 'Alternation Effect' in Africa." *Journal of Democracy* 15 (4): 147–158.

————. 2007a. "Formal Versus Informal Institutions in Africa." *Journal of Democracy* 18 (3): 96–110.

————. 2007b. "How Africans View Elections." In Richard Soudriette and Juliana Geran Pilon (eds.), *Every Vote Counts: The Role of Elections in Building Democracy.* Washington, DC: International Foundation for Electoral Systems, 63–79.

————. 2008. "Poor People and Democratic Citizenship in Africa." In Anirudh Krishna (ed.), *Poverty, Participation, and Democracy.* New York: Cambridge University Press, 28–64.

————. 2013. "Citizens and Cell Phones in Africa." *African Affairs* 112 (447).

Bratton, Michael, and Eric Chang. 2006. "State Building and Democratization in Sub-Saharan Africa: Forwards, Backwards, or Together?" *Comparative Political Studies* 39 (9): 1059–1083.

Bratton, Michael, Yun-Han Chu, and Marta Lagos. 2010. "Who Votes? Implications for New Democracies." *Taiwan Journal of Democracy* 6 (1): 107–136.

Bratton, Michael, and Mwangi Kimenyi. 2008. "Voting in Kenya: Putting Ethnicity in Perspective." *Journal of East African Studies* 2 (2): 273–290.

Bratton, Michael, and Peter Lewis. 2007. "The Durability of Political Goods? Evidence from Nigeria's New Democracy." *Commonwealth and Comparative Politics* 45 (1): 1–33.

Bratton, Michael, and Peter Lolojih. 2013. "Rationality, Cosmopolitanism, and Adjustment Fatigue: Public Attitudes to Economic Reform in Zambia." In Paul Collier, Christopher Adam, and Caleb Fundanga (eds.), *Zambia: Policies for Prosperity.* Oxford: Oxford University Press.

Bratton, Michael, and Eldred Masunungure. 2012. "Voting Intentions in Zimbabwe: A Margin of Terror?" *Afrobarometer Briefing Paper* no. 103. http://www.afro barometer.org/files/documents/briefing_papers/afrobriefno103-2.pdf.

Bratton, Michael, Robert Mattes, and E. Gyimah-Boadi. 2005. *Public Opinion, Democracy, and Market Reform in Africa.* New York: Cambridge University Press.

Bratton, Michael, and Nicolas van de Walle. 1997. *Democratic Experiments in Africa: Regime Transitions in Comparative Perspective.* New York: Cambridge University Press.

Brown, Garrett, and David Held. 2012. *The Cosmopolitanism Reader.* Cambridge: Polity.

Brown, Michael, Owen Cote, Sean M. Lynn-Jones, and Steven E. Miller. 1997. *Nationalism and Ethnic Conflict.* Cambridge: Massachusetts Institute of Technology Press.

Brusco, Valeria, Marcelo Nazareno, and Susan Stokes. 2004. "Vote Buying in Argentina." *Latin American Research Review* 39 (2): 65–88.

Brynin, M., and David Sanders. 1997. "Party Identification, Political Preferences, and Material Conditions." *Party Politics* 3 (1): 53–77.

Burnell, Peter. 2002. "Zambia's 2001 Elections: The Tyranny of Small Decisions, 'Non-Decisions,' and 'Not Decisions.'" *Third World Quarterly* 23 (6): 1103–1120.

Butler, David, and Donald Stokes. 1974. *Political Change in Britain.* London: Macmillan.

Campbell, Angus, Phillip Converse, Warren Miller, and David Stokes. 1960. *The American Voter.* Ann Arbor: University of Michigan Press.

CAPF (Coalition for Accountable Political Finance) Election Monitoring Initiative. 2007. "Election 2007: Interim Report on National Voter Bribery Survey." Nairobi.

Carbone, G. 2008. *No-Party Democracy? Ugandan Politics in Comparative Perspective.* Boulder: Lynne Rienner.

Carothers, Thomas. 2002. "The End of the Transition Paradigm." *Journal of Democracy* 2 (1): 5–21.

———, ed. 2006. *Promoting the Rule of Law Abroad: In Search of Knowledge.* Washington, DC: Carnegie Endowment for International Peace.

———. 2007. "The 'Sequencing' Fallacy." *Journal of Democracy* 18 (1): 12–27.

Carter Center. 2003. "Observing the 2002 Kenya Elections." Atlanta.

Chabal, Patrick, and Jean-Pascal Daloz. 1999. *Africa Works: Disorder as Political Instrument.* Oxford: James Currey.

Chandra, Kanchan. 2004. *Why Do Ethnic Parties Succeed? Patronage and Ethnic Head Counts in India.* New York: Cambridge University Press.

Chauvet, Lisa, and Paul Collier. 2009. "Elections and Economic Policy in Developing Countries." *Economic Policy* 24 (59): 509–550.

Chen, Jie, and Yang Zhong. 2002. "Why Do People Vote in Semi-Competitive Elections in China?" *Journal of Politics* 64 (1): 178–197.

Chikwana, Annie, Tulani Sithole, and Michael Bratton. 2004. "The Power of Propaganda: Public Opinion in Zimbabwe, 2004." *Afrobarometer Working Paper* No. 42. http://www.afrobarometer.org/files/documents/working_papers/Afro paperNo42.pdf.

Cho, Wonbin, and Michael Bratton. 2006. "Electoral Institutions, Partisan Status, and Political Support in Lesotho." *Electoral Studies* 25: 731–750.

Christopher, A. J. 1996. "Regional Patterns in South Africa's Post-Apartheid Election in 1994." *Environment and Planning Government and Policy* 14 (1): 55–69.

Clapham, Christopher, ed. 1982. *Private Patronage and Public Power: Political Clientelism in the Modern State.* London: Pinter.

Clark, Terry, and Seymour Martin Lipset, eds. 2001. *The Breakdown of Class Politics.* Baltimore: Johns Hopkins University Press.

Clarke, Harold, and Alan Acock. 1989. "National Elections and Political Attitudes: The Case of Political Efficacy." *British Journal of Political Science* 11: 551–562.

COG (Commonwealth Observer Group). 2011. *Uganda Presidential and Parliamentary Elections, 18 February 2011.* London: Commonwealth Secretariat.

Collier, David, and Steven Levitsky. 1997. "Democracy with Adjectives: Conceptual Innovation in Comparative Research." *World Politics* 49 (3): 430–451.

Collier, Paul. 2001. "Implications of Ethnic Diversity." *Economic Policy* 16 (2): 129–166.

———. 2009. *Wars, Guns, and Votes: Democracy in Dangerous Places.* New York: Harper Collins.

Collier, Paul, and Pedro Vicente. 2011. "Violence, Bribery, and Fraud: The Political Economy of Elections." *Public Choice.* www.springerlink.com.proxy1.cl.msu .edu/content/55537kw65446t581/fulltext.pdf.

Conroy-Krutz, Jeffrey. 2012. "Mixed Signals? Petty Patronage as a Signaling Strategy in African Campaigns." Unpublished paper. East Lansing: Michigan State University.

Coppedge, Michael, Angel Alverez, and Claudia Maldonado. 2008. "Two Persistent Dimensions of Democracy: Contestation and Inclusiveness." *Journal of Politics* 70 (3): 632–647.

Cox, Gary. 1997. *Making Votes Count: Strategic Coordination in the World's Electoral Systems.* New York: Cambridge University Press.

Cox, Gary, and Mathew McCubbins. 1986. "Electoral Politics as a Redistributive Game." *Journal of Politics* 48 (2): 370–389.

Craig, Stephen. 2004. "Winners, Losers, and Perceived Mandates: Voter Explanations of the 1998 Gubernatorial and 2000 Presidential Elections in Florida." Paper presented at the annual meeting of the American Political Science Association, Chicago, September 2–5.

Crewe, Ivor, Jim Alt, and Bo Sarlvik. 1977. "Partisan Dealignment in Britain, 1964–1974." *British Journal of Political Science* 7: 129–190.

Crewe, Ivor, and David Denver, eds. 1985. *Electoral Change in Western Democracies: Patterns and Sources of Electoral Volatility.* New York: St. Martin's.

Criado, Henar, and Francisco Herreros. 2007. "Political Support: Taking Into Account the Institutional Context." *Comparative Political Studies* 40 (12): 1511–1532.

Daalder, Hans, and Peter Mair, eds. 1985. *Western European Party Systems.* London: Sage.

Daddieh, Cyril, and Jo Ellen Fair, eds. 2002. *Ethnicity and Recent Democratic Experiments in Africa.* New Brunswick, NJ: African Studies Association.

Dalton, Russell, Scott Flanagan, and Paul Allen Beck, eds. 1984. *Electoral Change in Advanced Industrial Democracies: Realignment or Dealignment?* Princeton: Princeton University Press.

Davies, Joanne. 2008. "Parliamentarians and Corruption in Africa: The Challenge of Leadership." Report by Oxford University for the African Parliamentarians' Network Against Corruption (APNAC) and the Parliamentary Center of Canada.

DEMGroup. 2011a. "Despite Challenges, DEMGroup Finds That the Final Vote Count Reflects Ballots Cast." www.demgroup.org/sites/default/files/election_day_statement.pdf.

———. 2011b. "Report on Money in Politics: Pervasive Vote Buying in Uganda Elections." www.demgroup.org/downloads/pervasive-vote-buying-uganda-elections.

Diamond, Larry. 2002. "Thinking About Hybrid Regimes." *Journal of Democracy* 13 (2): 21–35.

———. 2008a. "The Democratic Rollback: The Resurgence of the Predatory State." *Foreign Affairs* 87 (2): 36–48.

———. 2008b. "The Rule of Law Versus the Big Man." *Journal of Democracy* 19 (2): 138–149.

Diamond, Larry, and Leonardo Morlino, eds. 2005. *Assessing the Quality of Democracy.* Baltimore: Johns Hopkins University Press.

Diamond, Larry, and Marc Plattner, eds. 2010. *Democratization in Africa: Progress and Retreat.* 2nd ed. Baltimore: Johns Hopkins University Press.

Diaz-Cayeros, Alberto, Federico Estevez, and Beatriz Magaloni. 2007. "Strategies of Vote Buying: Social Transfers, Democracy, and Welfare in Mexico." Unpublished manuscript.

Downs, Anthony. 1957. *An Economic Theory of Democracy.* New York: Harper.

Dulani, Boniface. 2011. "Personal Rule and Presidential Term Limits in Africa." PhD diss. East Lansing: Michigan State University.

EAC-COMESA-IGAD Observer Mission. 2011. "Interim Statement on 2011 General Elections in Republic of Uganda." Press release.

Easton, David. 1965. *A Systems Analysis of Political Life.* New York: Wiley.

Economist Intelligence Unit. 2010. *Democracy Index, 2010: Democracy in Retreat.* London.

EISA (Electoral Institute for the Sustainability of Democracy in Africa). 2012. *Comprehensive African Election Calendar.* http://www.eisa.org.za/WEP/calaf.htm.

Eldridge, Matt, and Jeremy Seekings. 1996. "Mandela's Lost Province: The African National Congress and the Western Cape Electorate in the 1994 South African Elections." *Journal of South African Studies* 22 (4): 517–540.

Englebert, Pierre. 2002. *State Legitimacy and Development in Africa.* Boulder: Lynne Rienner.

Erdmann, Gero. 2007. "Ethnicity, Voter Alignment, and Political Party Affiliation—An African Case: Zambia." Working Paper no. 45. Hamburg: German Institute for Global and Area Studies.

Erdmann, Gero, and Ulf Engel. 2007. "Neopatrimonialism Revisited: Critical Review and Elaboration of an Elusive Concept." *Journal of Commonwealth and Comparative Politics* 45 (1): 95–119.

Erikson, Robert, Michael MacKuen, and James Stimson. 2000. "Peasants and Bankers Revisited: Economic Expectations and Presidential Approval." *Electoral Studies* 19 (2–3): 295–312.

Esteban, Joan, and Debraj Ray. 2008. "Polarization, Fractionalization, and Conflict." *Journal of Peace Research* 45 (2): 163–182.

EU-EOM (European Union Election Observation Mission). 2011a. "Preliminary Statement: Uganda 2011 Elections—Improvements Marred by Avoidable Failures." Kampala, February 20.

———. 2011b. "Uganda: Final Report—General Elections, 18 February 2011." http://www.eeas.europa.eu/eueom/pdf/missions/eueom_uganda2011_final _report_en.pdf.

Evans, Geoffrey. 1999. *The Decline of Class Politics?* Oxford: Oxford University Press.

Evans, Geoffrey, and Robert Andersen. 2006. "The Political Conditioning of Economic Perceptions." *Journal of Politics* 68 (1): 194–207.

Evans, Geoffrey, and Pauline Rose. 2007a. "Support for Democracy in Malawi: Does Schooling Matter?" *World Development* 35 (5): 904–919.

———. 2007b. "Testing Mechanisms of Influence: Education and Support for Democracy in Sub-Saharan Africa." *Afrobarometer Working Paper* no. 75. http://www.afrobarometer.org/files/documents/working_papers/Afropaper No75.pdf.

Evrensel, Astrid, ed. 2010. *Voter Registration in Africa: A Comparative Analysis.* Johannesburg: Electoral Institute for the Sustainability of Democracy in Africa (EISA).

Fearon, James, Kimuli Kasara, and David Laitin. 2007. "Ethnic Minority Rule and Civil War Onset." *American Political Science Review* 101 (1): 187–193.

Ferree, Karen. 2006. "Explaining South Africa's Racial Census." *Journal of Politics* 68 (4): 803–815.

Fessey, Thomas. 2012. "Senegal's President-Elect Macky Sall Hails 'New Era.'" *BBC News,* March 26.

Finkel, Steven, Anibal Perez-Linan, Mitchell Seligson, and Dinorah Azpuru. 2006. *Effects of U.S. Foreign Assistance on Democracy Building: Results of a Cross-National Quantitative Study.* Washington, DC: US Agency for International Development.

Fox, Jonathan. 1994. "The Difficult Transition from Clientelism to Citizenship: Lessons from Mexico." *World Politics* 46 (2): 151–184.

Franklin, Mark. 2004. *Voter Turnout and the Dynamics of Electoral Competition in Established Democracies Since 1945.* New York: Cambridge University Press.

Franklin, Mark, Tom Mackie, and Henry Valen. 1992. *Electoral Change: Responses to Evolving Social and Attitudinal Structures in Western Countries.* Cambridge: Cambridge University Press.

Franzese, Robert. 2007. "Multi-Causality, Context-Conditionality, and Endogeneity." In Carles Boix and Susan Stokes (eds.), *The Oxford Handbook of Comparative Politics.* Oxford: Oxford University Press, 27–72.

Freedom House. 1973–2012, annual. *Freedom in the World.* Online database. www.freedomhouse.org.

Fridy, K. 2007. "The Elephant, Umbrella, and Quarrelling Cocks: Disaggregating Partisanship in Ghana's Fourth Republic." *African Affairs* 106: 281–305.

Friedrich, Carl. 1963. *Man and His Government.* New York: McGraw-Hill.

Fuchs, Dieter, Giovanna Guidorossi, and Palle Svensson. 1995. "Support for the Democratic System." In Hans-Dieter Klingemann and Dieter Fuchs (eds.), *Citizens and the State.* Oxford: Oxford University Press, 323–354.

Gandhi, Jennifer, and Ellen Lust-Okar. 2009. "Elections Under Authoritarianism." *Annual Review of Political Science* 12: 403–422.

Gellner, Ernest. 1983. *Nations and Nationalism.* Oxford: Blackwell.

Gerber, A., D. Green, and C. Larimer. 2008. "Social Pressure and Voter Turnout: Evidence from a Large-Scale Field Experiment." *American Political Science Review* 102 (1): 33–48.

Gibson, Clark. 2002. "Of Waves and Ripples: Democracy and Political Change in Africa in the 1990s." *Annual Review of Political Science* 5: 201–221.

Gibson, Clark, and James Long. 2008. "What Explains the African Vote? Using Exit Poll Data from Kenya to Explore Ethnicity and Government Performance in Vote Choice." Unpublished paper. La Jolla: University of California, San Diego.

Gibson, James. 2004. *Overcoming Apartheid: Can Truth Reconcile a Divided Nation?* New York: Russell Sage.

Gibson, James, and Gregory Caldeira. 1995. "The Legitimacy of Transnational Legal Institutions: Compliance, Support, and the European Court of Justice." *American Journal of Political Science* 39 (3): 459–489.

Giliomee, Hermann. 1998. "South Africa's Emerging Dominant Party Regime." *Journal of Democracy* 9 (4): 124–142.

Githongo, John. 2007. "Kenya's Fight Against Corruption: An Uneven Path to Political Accountability." Development Briefing Paper no. 2. Washington, DC: Cato Institute.

Goetz, Anne Marie. 2003. "Reinventing Accountability: Making Democracy Work for the Poor." Presentation to the Community of Practice on Social Accountability Launch, World Bank, Washington, DC, November 12.

Goetz, Anne Marie, and Rob Jenkins. 2005. *Reinventing Accountability: Making Democracy Work for Human Development.* New York: Palgrave Macmillan.

Green, Elliot. 2010. "Patronage, District Creation, and Reform in Uganda." *Studies in Comparative International Development* 45 (1): 83–103.

Grossman, G., and E. Helpman. 1996. "Electoral Competition and Special Interest Politics." *Review of Economic Studies* 63 (2): 265–286.

Gunther, Richard, José Ramón Montero, and Mariano Torcal. 2006. "Democracy and Intermediation: Some Attitudinal and Behavioral Dimensions." In Richard Gunther, José Ramón Montero, and H. J. Puhle (eds.), *Democracy, Intermediation, and Voting on Four Continents.* Oxford: Oxford University Press, 31–52.

Gurr, Ted. 1993. "Why Minorities Rebel: A Global Analysis of Communal Mobilization and Conflict Since 1945." *International Political Science Review* 14 (2): 161–201.

———. 2000. *Peoples Versus States.* Washington, DC: US Institute of Peace.

Gyimah-Boadi, E. 2009. "Another Step Forward for Ghana." *Journal of Democracy* 20 (2): 138–152.

Gyimah-Boadi, E., and Daniel Attoh. 2009. "Are Democratic Citizens Emerging in Africa?" *Afrobarometer Briefing Paper* no. 70. http://www.afrobarometer.org/files/documents/briefing_papers/AfrobriefNo70.pdf.

Gyimah-Boadi, E., and H. Kwasi Prempeh. 2012. "Oil, Politics, and Ghana's Democracy." *Journal of Democracy* 23 (3): 94–108.

Hadenius, Axel, and Hanna Back. 2008. "Democracy and State Capacity: Exploring a J-Shaped Relationship." *Governance* 21 (1): 1–24.

Handley, Antoinette. 2012. "Economic Growth and Democracy in Africa: What the Past Twenty Years Tells Us." Paper presented at the symposium "Elections, Accountability, and Democratic Governance in Africa," Institute for African Development, Cornell University, Ithaca, April 20–21.

Hannerz, U. 1990. "Cosmopolitans and Locals in World Culture." *Theory, Culture, and Society* 7 (2): 237–251.

Hardin, Russell. 1982. *Collective Action.* Baltimore: Johns Hopkins University Press.

Harding, Robin. 2010. "Urban-Rural Differences in Support for Incumbents Across Africa." *Afrobarometer Working Paper* no. 120. http://www.afrobarometer.org/files/documents/working_papers/AfropaperNo120.pdf.

Hesli, Vicki, and Elena Bashkirova. 2001. "The Impact of Time and Economic Circumstances on Popular Evaluations of Russia's President." *International Political Science Review* 22 (4): 379–398.

Hetherington, Marc. 1998. "The Political Relevance of Political Trust." *American Political Science Review* 92 (4): 791–808.

Hirschmann, Albert. 1970. *Exit, Voice, and Loyalty: Responses to Decline in Firms, Organizations, and States.* Cambridge: Harvard University Press.

Hirst, Paul. 2000. "Democracy and Governance." In Jon Pierre (ed.), *Debating Governance.* Oxford: Oxford University Press, 13–35.

Ho, Danial, Kosuke Imai, Gary King, and Elizabeth Stuart. 2006. "Matching as Nonparametric Preprocessing for Reducing Model Dependence in Parametric Causal Inference." *Political Analysis* 15: 199–236.

Holmberg, Soren. 1994. "Party Identification Across the Atlantic." In M. Kent Jennings and Thomas Mann (eds.), *Elections at Home and Abroad.* Ann Arbor: University of Michigan Press, 93–122.

Horowitz, Donald L. 1985. *Ethnic Groups in Conflict.* Berkeley: University of California Press.

———. 1991. *A Democratic South Africa? Constitutional Engineering in a Divided Society.* Berkeley: University of California Press.

———. 1993. "Democracy in Divided Societies." *Journal of Democracy* 4: 18–38.

———. 2003. "Electoral Systems: A Primer for Decision Maker." *Journal of Democracy* 14: 115–127.

Human Rights Watch. 2007. "Criminal Politics: Violence, 'Godfathers,' and Corruption in Nigeria." Report no. A1916. New York, October.

Huntington, Samuel. 1968. *Political Order in Changing Societies.* New Haven: Yale University Press.

———. 1991. *The Third Wave: Democratization in the Late Twentieth Century.* Norman: University of Oklahoma Press.

Hyde, Susan. 2011. *The Pseudo-Democrat's Dilemma: Why Election Observation Became an International Norm.* Ithaca: Cornell University Press.

Hyde, Susan, and Nikolai Marinov. 2011. *National Elections Across Democracy and Autocracy (NELDA).* Data codebook. New Haven: Yale University Press. http://hyde.research.yale.edu/nelda.

Hyden, Goran. 2012. "Challenges to Studying Governance in Africa: What to Look For and How." Keynote address to the symposium "Elections, Accountability, and Democratic Governance," Institute for African Development, Cornell University, Ithaca, April 20–21.

Hyden, Goran, and Michael Bratton, eds. 1992. *Governance and Politics in Africa.* Boulder: Lynne Rienner.

Ibrahim, Jibrin. 2007. "Nigeria's 2007 Elections: The Fitful Path to Democratic Citizenship." Special Report no. 182. Washington, DC: US Institute of Peace, January.

Imai, Kosuke, Luke Keele, Dustin Tingley, and Teppei Yamamoto. 2011. "Unpacking the Black Box of Causality: Learning About Causal Mechanisms from Experimental and Observational Studies." *American Political Science Review* 105 (4): 765–789.

Imai, Kosuke, Gary King, and Oliva Lau. 2007. *Zelig: Everyone's Statistical Software.* http://gking.harvard.edu/zelig.

Inglehart, Ronald. 1997. *Modernization and Postmodernization: Cultural, Economic, and Political Change in 41 Societies.* Princeton: Princeton University Press.

Inglehart, Ronald, and Christian Welzel. 2005. *Modernization, Cultural Change, and Democracy: The Human Development Sequence.* Cambridge: Cambridge University Press.

Inkeles, Alex, and David Smith. 1974. *Becoming Modern: Individual Changes in Six Developing Societies.* Cambridge: Cambridge University Press.

International Crisis Group. 2008. "Kenya in Crisis." Africa Report no. 137. Nairobi/Brussels, February 21.

International Foundation for Electoral Systems. 2012. *Election Guide: Country Profile—Kenya.* http://electionguide.org/election.php?ID=498.

International IDEA (International Institute for Democracy and Electoral Assistance). 2002. *Voter Turnout Since 1945: A Global Report.* Stockholm.

Ippolito-O'Donnell, Gabriela. 2006. "Political Clientelism and the Quality of Democracy." Paper presented at the twentieth annual World Congress of the International Political Science Association, Fukuoka, July 9–13.

Isaksson, Ann-Sofie. 2010. "Political Participation in Africa: Participatory Inequalities and the Role of Resources." *Afrobarometer Working Paper* no. 121. http://www.afrobarometer.org/files/documents/working_papers/AfropaperNo120.pdf.

Ismail, Zenobia, and Paul Graham. 2009. "Citizens of the World? Africans, Media, and Telecommunications." *Afrobarometer Briefing Paper* no. 69. http://www.afrobarometer.org/files/documents/working_papers/AfropaperNo69.pdf.

Izama, Angelo, and Michael Wilkerson. 2011. "Uganda: Museveni's Triumph and Weakness." *Journal of Democracy* 22 (3): 64–78.

Jackman, Robert. 1987. "Political Institutions and Voter Turnout in the Industrial Democracies." *American Political Science Review* 81 (2): 405–423.

Jalal, Ayesha. 1995. *Democracy and Authoritarianism in South Asia: A Comparative and Historical Perspective.* Cambridge: Cambridge University Press.

Jeffries, Richard. 1998. "The Ghanaian Elections of 1996: Toward the Consolidation of Democracy?" *African Affairs* 97: 189–208.

Jockers, Heinz, Dirk Kohnert, and Paul Nugent. 2009. "The Successful Ghana Election of 2008: A Convenient Myth?" *Journal of Modern African Studies* 48 (1): 95–115.

Kalyegira, T. 2010. "Holes in 2010 Afrobarometer Election Poll." *Daily Monitor* (Kampala), December 20.

———. 2011. "How the 2011 Opinion Polls Took On Their Own Life." *Daily Monitor* (Kampala), January 17.

Karl, Terry. 1986. "Imposing Consent: Electoralism and Democratization in El Salvador." In Paul Drake and Eduardo Silva (eds.), *Elections and Democratization in Latin America, 1980–1985.* La Jolla: University of California, San Diego, Center for International Studies, 9–36.

Katz, Richard. 1997. *Democracy and Elections.* New York: Oxford University Press.

Kauffmann, Daniel, Aart Kraay, and Massimo Mastruzzi. 2008. *Governance Matters VII: Aggregate and Individual Governance Indicators, 1996–2007.* Washington, DC: World Bank.

Keefer, Philip. 2004. "Clientelism, Credibility, and Democracy." Washington, DC: World Bank, Development Research Group, March.

Keefer, Philip, and Razvan Vlaicu. 2008. "Democracy, Credibility, and Clientelism." *Journal of Law, Economics, and Organization* 24 (2): 371.

Kelley, Judith. 2010. *Quality of Elections Data (QED).* Data codebook. Durham, NC: Duke University. www.duke.edu/web/diem/docs/CodebookQEDlinked.pdf.

———. 2012. *Monitoring Democracy: When International Election Observation Works, and Why It Often Fails.* Princeton: Princeton University Press.

Kelly, Catherine. 2012. "Senegal: What Will Turnover Bring?" *Journal of Democracy* 23 (3): 121–131.

Kelsall, Tim. 2011. "Developmental Patrimonialism: Rethinking Business and Politics in Africa." Africa Power and Politics Project, Policy Brief no. 2. London: Overseas Development Institute.

Key, V. O. 1964. *Politics, Parties, and Pressure Groups.* New York: Crowell.

Khaila, Stanley, and Catherine Chikwana. 2005. "Ten Years of Democracy in Malawi: Are Malawians Getting What They Voted For?" *Afrobarometer Working Paper* no. 46. http://www.afrobarometer.org/files/documents/working_papers/AfropaperNo46.pdf.

Khisa, I. 2011. "Otunnu Calls for Protests." *Daily Monitor* (Kampala), February 21.

Kiggundu, E. 2010. "Nambooze Has Edge in Mukono Election." *The Observer* (Kampala), May 23.

Kinder, Donald, and D. Roderick Kiewiet. 1981. "Sociotropic Politics: The American Case." *British Journal of Political Science* 11: 129–141.

Kitschelt, Herbert, and Steven Wilkinson, eds. 2007. *Patrons, Clients, and Policies: Patterns of Political Competition and Democratic Accountability.* New York: Cambridge University Press.

Koehn, Peter. 1989. "Competitive Transition to Civilian Rule: Nigeria's 1st and 2nd Experiments." *Journal of Modern African Studies* 27 (3): 401–430.

Kopecky, Petr. 2011. "Political Competition and Party Patronage: Public Appointments in Ghana and South Africa." *Political Studies* 59: 713–732.

Kostadinova, Tatiana, and Timothy Power. 2007. "Does Democratization Depress Participation? Voter Turnout in the Latin American and Eastern European Transitional Democracies." *Political Research Quarterly* 60 (3): 363–377.

Krishna, Anirudh, ed. 2008. *Poverty, Participation, and Democracy.* New York: Cambridge University Press.

Kuenzi, Michelle, and Gina Lambright. 2001. "Party System Institutionalization in 30 African Countries." *Party Politics* 7 (4): 437–468.

———. 2007. "Voter Turnout in Africa's Multiparty Regimes." *Comparative Political Studies* 40 (6): 665–690.

Kurtz, Marcus, and Andrew Schrank. 2007. "Growth and Governance: Models, Measures, and Mechanisms." *Journal of Politics* 69 (2): 538–554.

Laakso, Lisa. 2002. "The Politics of International Election Observation: The Case of Zimbabwe in 2000." *Journal of Modern African Studies* 40 (3): 437–464.

———. 2007. "Insights into Electoral Violence in Africa." In Matthias Basedau, Gero Erdmann, and Andreas Mehler (eds.), *Votes, Money, and Violence: Political Parties and Elections in Sub-Saharan Africa*. Uppsala: Nordic Africa Institute, 224–252.

Laakso, Marku, and Rein Taagepera. 1979. "'Effective' Number of Parties: A Measure with Application to Western Europe." *Comparative Political Studies* 12 (1): 3–27.

Lacey, M. 2002. "Panel Tries Hard to Keep Kenya Vote Aboveboard." *New York Times*, December 23.

Landman, Todd. 2000. *Issues and Methods in Comparative Politics*. London: Routledge.

Lanegran, K. 2001. "South Africa's 1999 Election: Consolidating a Dominant Party System." *Africa Today* 48 (2): 81–102.

LeBas, Adrienne. 2006. "Polarization as Craft: Explaining Party Formation and State Violence in Zimbabwe." *Comparative Politics* 38 (4): 419–438.

———. 2010. "Ethnicity and the Willingness to Sanction Violent Politicians: Evidence from Kenya." *Afrobarometer Working Paper* no. 125. http://www.afrobarometer.org/files/documents/working_papers/AfropaperNo125.pdf.

Leftwich, Adrian. 2012. "Riker in the Tropics: *The Theory of Coalitions* and the Politics of Change in Developing Countries." Development Leadership Program, Concept Paper no. 2. http://www.dlprog.org/ftp/info/Public%20Folder/Concept%20Papers/Riker%20in%20the%20Tropics.pdf.html.

Lehoucq, F. 2007. "When Does a Market for Votes Emerge?" In Frederic Schaffer (ed.), *Elections for Sale: The Causes and Consequences of Vote Buying*. Boulder: Lynne Rienner, 33–46.

Lever, Henry. 1979. "Ethnicity and Voting Patterns in South Africa." *Political Studies* 27 (3): 458–468.

Levitsky, Steven, and Lucan Way. 2010. *Competitive Authoritarianism: Hybrid Regimes After the Cold War*. New York: Cambridge University Press.

Lewis-Beck, Michael. 1988. *Economics and Elections: The Major Western Democracies*. Ann Arbor: University of Michigan Press.

Lewis-Beck, Michael, William Jacoby, Helmut Norpoth, and Herbert Weisberg. 2008. *The American Voter Revisited*. Ann Arbor: University of Michigan Press.

Lewis-Beck, Michael, Richard Nadeau, and Angelo Elias. 2008. "Economics, Party, and the Vote: Causality Issues and Panel Data." *American Journal of Political Science* 52 (1): 84–95.

Lewis-Beck, Michael, and Andrew Skalaban. 1992. "France." In Mark Franklin, Tom Mackie, and Henry Valen (eds.), *Electoral Change: Responses to Evolving Social and Attitudinal Structures in Western Countries*. New York: Cambridge University Press, 167–178.

Lewis-Beck, Michael, and Mary Stegmaier. 2000. "Economic Determinants of Electoral Outcomes." *Annual Review of Political Science* 3: 183–219.

———. 2008. "The Economic Vote in Transitional Democracies." *Journal of Elections, Public Opinion, and Parties* 18 (3): 303–323.

Lijphart, Arend. 1978. *Democracy in Plural Societies*. New Haven: Yale University Press.

———. 1994. *Electoral Systems and Party Systems: A Study of Twenty-seven Democracies, 1945–1990*. New York: Oxford University Press.

———. 1999. *Patterns of Democracy*. New Haven: Yale University Press.

————. 2004. "Constitutional Design for Divided Societies." *Journal of Democracy* 15: 96–109.

Lindberg, Staffan. 2003. "'It's Our Time to Chop': Do Elections in Africa Feed Neopatrimonialism Rather Than Counteract It?" *Democratization* 10 (2): 121–140.

————. 2006. *Democracy and Elections in Africa*. Baltimore: Johns Hopkins University Press.

————. 2007. *African Elections Database, 1990–2006*. Unpublished. Gainesville: University of Florida.

————, ed. 2009. *Democratization by Elections: A New Mode of Transition*. Baltimore: Johns Hopkins University Press.

Lindberg, Staffan, and Minion Morrison. 2005. "Exploring Voter Alignments in Africa: Core and Swing Voters in Ghana." *Journal of Modern African Studies* 43 (4): 565–568.

————. 2008. "Are African Voters Really Ethnic or Clientelistic? Survey Evidence from Ghana." *Political Science Quarterly* 123 (1): 95–122.

Linz, Juan, and Alfred Stepan. 1996. *Problems of Democratic Transition and Consolidation*. Baltimore: Johns Hopkins University Press.

Lipset, Seymour Martin. 1959. "Some Social Requisites of Democracy: Economic Development and Political Legitimacy." *American Political Science Review* 53: 69–105.

Lipset, Seymour Martin, and Stein Rokkan. 1967. *Party Systems and Voter Alignments*. New York: Free Press.

Listhaug, Ola, and Matti Wiberg. 1995. "Confidence in Political and Private Institutions." In Hans-Dieter Klingemann and Dieter Fuchs (eds.), *Citizens and the State*. Oxford: Oxford University Press, 298–323.

Logan, Carolyn. 2008. "Rejecting the Disloyal Opposition? The Trust Gap in Mass Attitudes Toward Ruling and Opposition Parties in Africa." *Afrobarometer Working Paper* no. 94. http://www.afrobarometer.org/files/documents/working_papers/AfropaperNo94.pdf.

Look, Anne. 2012. "Senegal Votes in Tight Presidential Run-Off." *Voice of America News,* March 25. http://www.voanews.com/content/polls-open-in-senegal-presidential-run-off-144101006/179462.html.

Lupia, Arthur, and Mathew McCubbins. 2000. "The Institutional Foundations of Political Competence: How Citizens Learn What They Need to Know." In Arthur Lupia, Matthew McCubbins, and Samuel Popkin (eds.), *Elements of Reason: Cognition, Choice, and the Bounds of Rationality*. New York: Cambridge University Press, 47–66.

MacKuen, Michael, Robert Erikson, and James Stimson. 1992. "Peasants or Bankers? The American Electorate and the U.S. Economy." *American Political Science Review* 86 (3): 597–611.

Mainwaring, Scott, and Christopher Welna, eds. 2003. *Democratic Accountability in Latin America*. Oxford: Oxford University Press.

Malena, Carmen, Reiner Forster, and Janmejay Singh. 2004. "Social Accountability: An Introduction to the Concept and Emerging Practice." Social Development Papers, Participation and Engagement Paper no. 76. Washington, DC: World Bank, December.

Mamdani, Mahmood. 1996. *Citizen and Subject: Contemporary Africa and the Legacy of Late Colonialism*. Princeton: Princeton University Press.

Mansfield, Edward, and Jack Snyder. 2005. *Electing to Fight: Why Emerging Democracies Go to War*. Cambridge: Massachusetts Institute of Technology Press.

Manson, Katrina. 2007. "Tribal Voting Key to Sierra Leone Run-Off." *Reuters AlertNet,* August 26.

Manza, Jeff, and Clem Brooks. 1999. *Social Cleavages and Political Change: Voter Alignments and U.S. Party Coalitions.* New York: Oxford University Press.

Maravall, José María. 1996. "Accountability and Manipulation." Working Paper no. 92. Madrid: Instituto Juan March de Estudios e Investigaciones.

March, James. 1988. *Decisions and Organizations.* Oxford: Blackwell.

Markoff, John. 2009. "The Global Wave of Democratization." In Christian Haerpfer, Ronald Inglehart, Christian Welzel, and Patrick Bernhagen (eds.), *Democratization in a Globalized World.* Oxford: Oxford University Press, 55–73.

Mattes, Robert. 2008. "The Impact of Electoral Systems on Citizenship in Africa." Unpublished paper. Cape Town: University of Cape Town, Democracy in Africa Research Unit, Centre for Social Science Research.

Mattes, Robert, and Michael Bratton. 2007. "Learning About Democracy in Africa: Awareness, Performance, and Experience." *American Journal of Political Science* 51 (1): 192–217.

Mattes, Robert, and Amanda Gouws. 1999. "Race, Ethnicity, and Voting Behavior: Lessons from South Africa." In Timothy Sisk and Andrew Reynolds (eds.), *Elections and Conflict Resolution in Africa.* Washington, DC: US Institute of Peace Press, 119–142.

Mattes, Robert, and Jessica Piombo. 2001. "Opposition Parties and the Voters in South Africa's General Election of 1999." *Democratization* 8 (3): 101–128.

Mattes, Robert, Helen Taylor, and Cherrel Africa. 1999. "Judgment and Choice in the 1999 South African Election." *Politikon* 16 (2): 235–247.

McAllister, Ian. 1999. "The Economic Performance of Government." In Pippa Norris (ed.), *Critical Citizens.* New York: Oxford University Press, 188–203.

McCann, James, and Jorge Domínguez. 1998. "Mexicans React to Electoral Fraud and Political Corruption: An Assessment of Public Opinion and Voting Behavior." *Electoral Studies* 17 (4): 483–503.

McLaughlin, Eric. 2008. "Beyond the Racial Census: The Political Salience of Ethnolinguistic Cleavages in South Africa." *Comparative Political Studies* 40 (4): 435–456.

Melson, Robert. 1971. "Ideology and Inconsistency: The 'Cross-Pressured' Nigerian Worker." *American Political Science Review* 65 (1): 167–171.

Melson, Robert, and Howard Wolpe. 1970. "Modernization and the Politics of Communalism: A Theoretical Perspective." *American Political Science Review* 64 (4): 1112–1130.

Miguel, Edward. 2004. "Tribe or Nation? Nation-Building and Public Goods in Kenya Versus Tanzania." *World Politics* 56 (2): 327–362.

Miller, Arthur, and Ola Listhaug. 1999. "Political Performance and Institutional Trust." In Pippa Norris (ed.), *Critical Citizens.* New York: Oxford University Press, 204–216.

Mishler, William, and Richard Rose. 1997. "Trust, Distrust, and Skepticism: Popular Evaluations of Civil and Political Institutions in Post-Communist Societies." *Journal of Politics* 59 (2): 418–451.

———. 2001. "What Are the Origins of Political Trust?" *Comparative Political Studies* 34 (1): 30–62.

Moehler, Devra, and Staffan Lindberg. 2009. "Narrowing the Legitimacy Gap: Turnovers as a Cause of Democratic Consolidation." *Journal of Politics* 71 (4): 1448–1466.

Mondak, Jeffrey. 1993. "Institutional Legitimacy and Procedural Justice: Reexamining the Question of Causality." *Law and Society Review* 27: 599–608.

Montalvo, José G., and Marta Reynal-Querol. 2005. "Ethnic Polarization, Potential Conflict, and Civil Wars." *American Economic Review* 95 (3): 796–816.

Morgan, Stephen, and Christopher Winship. 2007. *Counterfactuals and Causal Inference: Methods and Principles for Social Research.* New York: Cambridge University Press.

Mosse, Marcelo. 2007. "Tendências contra o pluralismo dos media em Moçambique." Altera no. 1. Maputo: Centro de Integreidade Pública.

Mozaffar, Shaheen. 1997. "Electoral Systems and Their Political Effects in Africa: A Preliminary Analysis." *Representation* 34 (3–4): 148–156.

———. 2002. "Patterns of Electoral Governance in Africa's Emerging Democracies." *International Political Science Review* 23 (1): 85–101.

Mubangizi, M. 2010. "IPC Bashes Olara Otunnu for 'Betrayal.'" *The Observer* (Kampala), October 3.

Mueller, Suzanne. 2008. "The Political Economy of Kenya's Crisis." *Journal of Eastern African Studies* 2 (2): 185–210.

Mugerwa, Y. 2011. "Rivals Reject New Poll Giving Museveni 65 Percent." *Daily Monitor* (Kampala), February 9.

Mughan, Anthony. 1983. "Accommodation or Diffusion in the Management of Ethnic Conflict in Belgium." *Political Studies* 31: 431–451.

Mulondo, E. 2010. "Opposition Dismiss Election Survey." *Saturday Monitor* (Kampala), December 18.

Mustapha, Raufu. 2006. "Nigeria Since 1999: Revolving Door Syndrome or the Consolidation of Democracy?" Paper presented at the conference "Africa Since Democratization," Oxford University, Oxford, December.

Mwenda, Andrew. 2011. "Why Museveni Won and Besigye Lost and What Can Be Done for the Future." February 24. http://andrewmwendasblog.blogspot.com/2011/04.

Nadeau, Richard. 2000. "Elections and Satisfaction with Democracy." Paper presented at the annual meeting of the American Political Science Association, Washington, DC, September 2–5.

Nadeau, Richard, and Andre Blais. 1993. "Accepting the Election Outcome: The Effect of Participation on Losers' Consent." *British Journal of Political Science* 23: 553–563.

Nalugo, M. 2010. "DP Has Resurrected, Says Mao." *Daily Monitor* (Kampala), October 26.

Ndegwa, Stephen. 2001. "A Decade of Democracy in Africa." *Journal of Asian and African Studies* 36 (1): 1–16.

———. 2003. "Kenya: Third Time Lucky?" *Journal of Democracy* 14 (3): 145–158.

Neto, Octavia, and Gary Cox. 1997. "Electoral Institutions, Cleavage Structures, and the Number of Parties." *American Journal of Political Science* 41 (1): 149–174.

Nichter, Simeon. 2008. "Vote Buying or Turnout Buying? Machine Politics and the Secret Ballot." *American Political Science Review* 102 (1): 19–31.

Nie, Norman, Sidney Verba, and John Petrocik. 1976. *The Changing American Voter.* Cambridge: Harvard University Press.

Nohlen, Dieter, Michael Krennerich, and Bernhard Thibaut. 1999. *Elections in Africa: A Data Handbook.* Oxford: Oxford University Press.

Norris, Pippa. 1999. *Critical Citizens: Global Support for Democratic Governance.* Oxford: Oxford University Press.

———. 2002. *Democratic Phoenix: Reinventing Political Activism*. New York: Cambridge University Press.

———. 2003. *Electoral Engineering: Voting Rules and Political Behavior*. New York: Cambridge University Press.

North, Douglass. 1990. *Institutions, Institutional Change, and Economic Performance*. New York: Cambridge University Press.

Nossiter, Adam. 2012. "Pressed on All Sides, Coup Leader in Mali Is Digging In." *New York Times*, March 31.

Nugent, Paul. 1995. *Big Men, Small Boys, and Politics in Ghana*. London: Pinter.

O'Donnell, Guillermo. 1994. "Delegative Democracy." *Journal of Democracy* 5 (1): 55–69.

———. 2005. "Why the Rule of Law Matters." In Larry Diamond and Leonardo Morlino (eds.), *Assessing the Quality of Democracy*. Baltimore: Johns Hopkins University Press, 3–17.

———. 2007. "The Perpetual Crises of Democracy." *Journal of Democracy* 18 (1): 5–11.

O'Donnell, Guillermo, Jorge Vargas Cullel, and Osvaldo Iazetta, eds. 2004. *The Quality of Democracy: Theory and Applications*. South Bend, IN: University of Notre Dame Press.

O'Leary, Cornelius. 1962. *The Elimination of Corrupt Practices in British Elections, 1868–1911*. Oxford: Clarendon.

Ojo, O. J. B. 1981. "The Impact of Personality and Ethnicity on the Nigerian Elections of 1979." *Africa Today* 28 (1): 47–58.

Olorunsola, Victor. 1972. *The Politics of Cultural Sub-Nationalism in Africa*. Garden City, NY: Doubleday.

Olson, Mancur. 1965. *The Logic of Collective Action*. Cambridge: Harvard University Press.

Olupot, M. 2010. "Opposition Poll Gives Museveni 67 Percent." *New Vision* (Kampala), December 31.

———. 2011. "New Poll Gives Museveni 65 Percent Rating." *New Vision* (Kampala), January 2.

Ordeshook, Peter, and Olga Shvetsova. 1994. "Ethnic Heterogeneity, District Magnitude, and the Number of Parties." *American Journal of Political Science* 38 (1): 100–123.

Ostrom, Elinor. 1990. *Governing the Commons: The Evolution of Institutions for Collective Action*. New York: Cambridge University Press.

———. 1998. "A Behavioral Approach to the Rational Choice Theory of Collective Action." *American Political Science Review* 92 (1): 1–22.

Ottaway, Marina. 2003. *Democracy Challenged: The Rise of Semi-Authoritarianism*. Washington, DC: Carnegie Endowment for International Peace.

Pacek, Alexander, and Benjamin Radcliff. 1995. "The Political Economy of Competitive Elections in the Developing World." *American Journal of Political Science* 39 (3): 745–759.

Palmberg, Mai, ed. 1999. *National Identity and Democracy in Africa*. Pretoria: Human Sciences Research Council.

Pederson, Morgens. 1979. "The Dynamics of European Party Systems: Changing Patterns of Electoral Volatility." *European Journal of Political Research* 7 (1): 1–26.

Pereira, João, and Carlos Shenga. 2005. "Strengthening Parliamentary Democracy in SADC Countries: Mozambique Country Report." Pretoria: South African Institute of International Affairs.

Petrovic, Vukasin. 2012. "The Perilous State of Freedom in Sub-Saharan Africa." *Freedom at Issue,* February 3. http://www.freedomhouse.org/blog/perilous -state-freedom-sub-saharan-africa.

Pierre, Jon, ed. 2000. *Debating Governance.* Oxford: Oxford University Press.

Polity IV Project. 2008. *Political Regime Characteristics and Transitions, 1800– 2007.* www.systemicpeace.org/polity/polity4.htm.

Popkin, Samuel. 1994. *The Reasoning Voter: Communication and Persuasion in Presidential Campaigns.* Chicago: University of Chicago Press.

Posner, Daniel. 1995. "Malawi's New Dawn." *Journal of Democracy* 6 (1): 131– 145.

———. 2004. "Measuring Ethnic Fractionalization in Africa." *American Journal of Political Science* 48 (4): 849–863.

———. 2005. *Institutions and Ethnic Politics in Africa.* New York: Cambridge University Press.

Posner, Daniel, and David Simon. 2002. "Economic Conditions and Incumbent Support in Africa's New Democracies: Evidence from Zambia." *Comparative Political Studies* 35 (3): 313–336.

Posner, Daniel, and Daniel Young. 2007. "The Institutionalization of Political Power in Africa." *Journal of Democracy* 18 (3): 126–140.

Powell, G. Bingham. 1980. "Voting Turnout in Thirty Democracies: Partisan, Legal, and Socio-Economic Influences." In Richard Rose (ed.), *Electoral Participation: A Comparative Analysis.* Beverly Hills: Sage, 5–34.

———. 2000. *Elections as Instruments of Democracy.* New Haven: Yale University Press.

Price, Simon, and David Sanders. 1995. "Economic Expectations and Voting Intentions in the UK, 1979–1987: A Pooled Cross-Section Approach." *Political Studies* 43: 451–471.

Przeworski, Adam, Michael Alvarez, José Antonio Cheibub, and Fernando Limongi. 2000. *Democracy and Development: Political Institutions and Well-Being in the World, 1950–1990.* New York: Cambridge University Press.

Puddington, Arch. 2010. "The Erosion Accelerates: The 2009 Freedom House Survey." *Journal of Democracy* 21 (2): 136–150.

———. 2012. "The Arab Uprisings and Their Global Repercussions." In Freedom House, *Freedom in the World 2012.* http://www.freedomhouse.org/article/freedom -world-2012-arab-uprisings-and-their-global-repercussions.

Putnam, Robert. 1993. *Making Democracy Work.* Princeton: Princeton University Press.

Rabe-Hesketh, Sophia, and Anders Skrondal. 2008. *Multilevel and Longitudinal Modeling Using STATA.* College Station, TX: STATA Press.

Rabushka, Alvin, and Kenneth Shepsle. 1972. *Politics in Plural Societies: A Theory of Political Instability.* Columbus, OH: Merrill.

Radelet, Steven. 2010. *Emerging Africa: How 17 Countries Are Leading the Way.* Washington, DC: Center for Global Development.

Ramsayer, J. Mark, and Frances Rosenbluth. 1993. *Japan's Political Marketplace.* Cambridge: Harvard University Press.

Raudenbush, Stephen, and Anthony Bryk. 2002. *Hierarchical Linear Models: Applications and Data Analysis Methods.* Beverly Hills: Sage.

Reilly, Benjamin. 1997. "The Alternative Vote and Ethnic Accommodation: New Evidence from Papua New Guinea." *Electoral Studies* 16 (1): 1–12.

———. 2001. *Democracy in Divided Societies: Electoral Engineering for Conflict Management.* New York: Cambridge University Press.

Reilly, Benjamin, and Andrew Reynolds. 1998. *Electoral Systems and Conflict in Divided Societies*. Washington, DC: National Academy Press.

Reno, William. 2011. *Warfare in Independent Africa*. New York: Cambridge University Press.

Resnick, Danielle, and Daniela Casale. 2011. "Political Participation of Africa's Youth: Turnout, Partisanship, and Protest." *Afrobarometer Working Paper* no. 136. http://www.afrobarometer.org/files/documents/working_papers/Afropaper No136.pdf.

Reynolds, Andrew, ed. 1994. *Election '94 South Africa: The Campaigns, Results, and Future Prospects*. New York: St. Martin's.

———. 1999. *Electoral Systems and Democratization in Southern Africa*. Oxford: Oxford University Press.

———, ed. 2002. *The Architecture of Democracy: Constitutional Design, Conflict Management, and Democracy*. Oxford: Oxford University Press.

Reynolds, Andrew, and Ben Reilly, eds. 1997. *The International IDEA Handbook on Electoral System Design*. Stockholm: International IDEA.

Richardson, Bradley, and Paul Beck. 2006. "The Flow of Information: Personal Discussants, the Media, and Partisans." In Richard Gunther, José Ramón Montero, and H. J. Puhle (eds.), *Democracy, Intermediations, and Voting on Four Continents*. Oxford: Oxford University Press.

Riker, William, and Peter Ordeshook. 1968. "A Theory of the Calculus of Voting." *American Political Science Review* 62 (1): 25–42.

Robinson, James, and Thierry Verdier. 2002. "The Political Economy of Clientelism." Discussion Paper no. 3205. Washington, DC: Center for Economic and Policy Research.

Rodrik, Dani. 2004. "Getting Institutions Right." Unpublished paper. Cambridge: Harvard University, April.

Rose, Richard, ed. 1974. *Electoral Behavior: A Comparative Handbook*. New York: Free Press.

Rose, Richard, William Mishler, and Christian Haerpfer. 1998. *Democracy and Its Alternatives*. Baltimore: Johns Hopkins University Press.

Rose, Richard, and Doh Chull Shin. 2001. "Democratization Backwards: The Problem of Third-Wave Democracies." *British Journal of Political Science* 31: 331–354.

Rose, Richard, and Derek Urwin. 1970. "Persistence and Change in Western Party Systems Since 1945." *Political Studies* 18: 287–319.

Rosenbaum, P. R., and D. B. Rubin. 1985. "Constructing a Control Group Using Multivariate Matched Sampling Methods That Incorporate the Propensity Score." *American Statistician* 39 (1–2): 33–38.

Rotberg, Robert, ed. 2004. *When States Fail: Causes and Consequences*. Princeton: Princeton University Press.

———. 2007. "Nigeria: Elections and Continuing Challenges." Special Report no. 27. New York: Council on Foreign Relations, April.

Rotberg, Robert, and Rachel Gisselquist. 2008. *Strengthening African Governance: Results and Rankings, 2008*. Cambridge, MA: Ibrahim Index of African Governance, October.

Rustow, Dankwart. 1970. "Transitions to Democracy: Towards a Dynamic Model." *Comparative Politics* 2 (3): 337–363.

Saideman, S. M., D. J. Lanoue, M. Campenni, and S. Stanton. 2002. "Democratization, Political Institutions, and Ethnic Conflict: A Pooled Time-Series Analysis, 1985–1998." *Comparative Political Studies* 35 (1): 103–129.

Salih, Mohamed, and John Markakis, eds. 1998. *Ethnicity and the State in Eastern Africa*. Uppsala: Scandinavian Institute of African Studies.

Salih, Mohamed, and Per Nordlund. 2007. *Political Parties in Africa: Challenges for Sustained Multiparty Democracy*. Stockholm: International IDEA.

Sall, Babaly, Zeric Kay Smith, and Mady Dansokho. 2004. "Liberalisme, patrimonialisme ou autoritarisme attenue: Variations autour de la democratie Senegalaise." *Afrobarometer Working Paper* no. 36. http://www.afrobarometer.org/files/documents/working_papers/AfropaperNo36.pdf.

Sartori, Giovanni. 1997. *Comparative Constitutional Engineering: An Inquiry into Structures, Incentives, and Outcomes*. London: Macmillan.

Scarritt, James, S. M. McMillan, and Shaheen Mozaffar. 2001. "The Interaction Between Democracy and Ethnopolitical Protest and Rebellion in Africa." *Comparative Political Studies* 34 (7): 800–827.

Scarritt, James, and Shaheen Mozaffar. 1999. "The Specification of Ethnic Cleavages and Ethnopolitical Groups for the Analysis of Democratic Competition in Contemporary Africa." *Nationalism and Ethnic Politics* 5 (1): 82–117.

Schacter, Mark. 2001. "When Accountability Fails: A Framework for Diagnosis and Action." *Isuma: Canadian Journal of Policy Research* 2 (2): 1–9. www.isuma.net/v02n02/schacter/schacter_e.shtml.

Schaffer, Frederic. 1998. *Democracy in Translation: Understanding Politics in an Unfamiliar Culture*. Ithaca: Cornell University Press.

———, ed. 2007. *Elections for Sale: The Causes and Consequences of Vote Buying*. Boulder: Lynne Rienner.

Schedler, Andreas. 1999. "Conceptualizing Accountability." In Andreas Schedler, Larry Diamond, and Marc F. Plattner (eds.), *The Self-Restraining State: Power and Accountability in New Democracies*. Boulder: Lynne Rienner, 13–28.

———. 2006. *Electoral Authoritarianism: The Dynamics of Unfree Competition*. Boulder: Lynne Rienner.

Schumpeter, Joseph. 1942. *Capitalism, Socialism, and Democracy*. London: Allen and Unwin.

Scott, James. 1985. *Weapons of the Weak: Everyday Forms of Peasant Resistance*. New Haven: Yale University Press.

Severino, Jean-Michel, and Oliver Ray. 2012. *Africa's Moment*. Cambridge: Polity.

Shenga, Carlos. 2007. "Commitment to Democracy in Mozambique: Performance Evaluations and Levels and Sources of Information." Master's thesis. Cape Town: University of Cape Town.

Shi, Tianjian. 1999. "Voting and Nonvoting in China: Voting Behavior in Plebiscitary and Limited-Choice Elections." *Journal of Politics* 61 (4): 1115–1139.

Shively, Phillips. 1980. "The Nature of Party Identification: A Review of Recent Developments." In John Pierce and John Sullivan (eds.), *The Electorate Reconsidered*. Beverley Hills: Sage, 219–236.

Shugart, Matthew, and Daniel Nielsen. 1999. "Constitutional Change in Colombia: Policy Adjustment Through Institutional Change." *Comparative Political Studies* 32 (3): 313–341.

Shugart, Matthew, and Martin Wattenberg, eds. 2000. *Mixed-Member Electoral Systems: The Best of Both Worlds?* Oxford: Oxford University Press.

Sisk, Timothy, and Andrew Reynolds, eds. 1998. *Elections and Conflict Management in Africa*. Washington, DC: US Institute of Peace.

Sklar, Richard, Ebere Onwudiwe, and Darren Kew. 2006. "Nigeria: Completing Obasanjo's Legacy." *Journal of Democracy* 17 (3): 100–115.

Smith, Daniel. 2002. "Consolidating Democracy: The Structural Underpinnings of Ghana's 2000 elections." *Journal of Modern African Studies* 40 (4): 621–650.

Smulovitz, Catalina, and Enrique Peruzzotti. 2000. "Societal Accountability in Latin America." *Journal of Democracy* 11 (4): 147–158.

———. 2003. "Societal and Horizontal Controls: Two Cases of a Fruitful Relationship." In Scott Mainwaring and Christopher Welna (eds.), *Democratic Accountability in Latin America*. Oxford: Oxford University Press, 309–331.

Snyder, Jack. 2000. *From Voting to Violence: Democratization and Nationalist Conflict*. New York: Norton.

Steenbergen, Marco, and Bradford Jones. 2002. "Modeling Multilevel Data Structures." *American Journal of Political Science* 46 (1): 218–237.

Stokes, Susan. 2005. "Perverse Accountability: A Formal Model of Machine Politics with Evidence from Argentina." *American Political Science Review* 99 (3): 315–325.

———. 2007. "Is Vote Buying Undemocratic?" In Frederic Schaffer (ed.), *Elections for Sale: The Causes and Consequences of Vote Buying*. Boulder: Lynne Rienner, 81–99.

Takougang, J. 1996. "The 1992 Multiparty Elections in Cameroon: Prospects for Democracy and Democratization." *Journal of Asian and African Studies* 31 (1–2): 52–65.

Taras, Raymond, and Rajat Ganguly. 1998. *Understanding Ethnic Conflict*. New York: Longman.

Taylor, Ian. 2002. "The New Partnership for Africa's Development and the Zimbabwe Elections: Implications and Prospects for the Future." *African Affairs* 101 (404): 403–412.

Thomassen, Jacques. 1976. "Party Identification as a Cross-National Concept: Its Meaning in the Netherlands." In Ian Budge, Ivor Crewe, and Dennis Farlie (eds.), *Party Identification and Beyond*. London: Wiley, 63–79.

Throup, David, and Charles Hornsby. 1998. *Multi-Party Politics in Kenya: The Kenyatta and Moi States and the Triumph of the System in the 1992 Election*. Oxford: James Currey.

Transition Monitoring Group. 2007. *An Election Programmed to Fail*. Preliminary Report on the Presidential and National Assembly Elections. Lagos, April 21.

Transparency International. 2000–2011, annual. *Corruption Perception Index*. http://cpi.transparency.org/cpi2011/results.

Tripp, Aili Mari. 2010. *Museveni's Uganda: Paradoxes of Power in a Hybrid Regime*. Boulder: Lynne Rienner.

Tsebelis, George. 2002. *Veto Players: How Institutions Work*. Princeton: Princeton University Press.

Tufte, E. R. 1978. *Political Control of the Economy*. Princeton: Princeton University Press.

Tullock, Gordon. 1967. *Toward a Mathematics of Politics*. Ann Arbor: University of Michigan Press.

Tyler, Tom. 1989. *Why People Obey the Law: Procedural Justice, Legitimacy, and Compliance*. New Haven: Yale University Press.

Tyler, Tom, Jonathan Casper, and Bonnie Fisher. 1989. "Maintaining Allegiance Toward Political Authorities: The Role of Prior Attitudes and the Use of Fair Procedures." *American Journal of Political Science* 33 (3): 629–652.

USAID (US Agency for International Development). 2010. "Conducting a Democracy and Governance Assessment: A Framework for Strategy Development." Draft. Washington, DC.

van de Walle, Nicolas. 2003. "Presidentialism and Clientelism in Africa's Emerging Party Systems." *Journal of Modern African Studies* 41 (2): 297–319.

———. 2007. "Meet the New Boss, Same As the Old Boss? The Evolution of Political Clientelism in Africa." In Herbert Kitschelt and Steven Wilkinson (eds.), *Patrons, Clients, and Policies: Patterns of Democratic Accountability and Political Competition.* New York: Cambridge University Press, 50–67.

Vicente, Pedro. 2008. "Is Vote Buying Effective? Evidence from a Field Experiment in West Africa." Oxford: Oxford University, Center for the Study of African Economies, March.

Villalón, Leonardo, and Peter von Doepp, eds. 2005. *The Fate of Africa's Democratic Experiments: Elites and Institutions.* Bloomington: Indiana University Press.

Wang, Chin-Shou, and Charles Kurzman. 2007. "The Logistics: How to Buy Votes." In Frederic Schaffer (ed.), *Elections for Sale: The Causes and Consequences of Vote Buying.* Boulder: Lynne Rienner, 61–79.

Wantchekon, Leonard. 2003. "Clientelism and Voting Behavior: Evidence from a Field Experiment in Benin." *World Politics* 55 (2): 399–422.

Weatherford, Stephen. 1992. "Measuring Political Legitimacy." *American Political Science Review* 86 (1): 149–166.

Were, J. 2011. "How Museveni Gained 10 Percent and Besigye Lost It." *The Independent* (Kampala), February 26.

Whitfield, Lindsay. 2009. "'Change for the Better in Ghana': Party Competition, Institutionalization, and Alternation in Ghana's 2008 Elections." *African Affairs* 108 (433): 621–641.

Wilkinson, Steven. 2006. *Votes and Violence: Electoral Competition and Ethnic Riots in India.* New York: Cambridge University Press.

Wolf, Thomas, Carolyn Logan, and Jeremiah Owiti. 2004. "A New Dawn? Popular Optimism in Kenya After the Transition." *Afrobarometer Working Paper* no. 33. http://www.afrobarometer.org/files/documents/working_papers/AfropaperNo33.pdf.

Wolfinger, Raymond. 1965. "The Development and Persistence of Ethnic Voting." *American Political Science Review* 59 (4): 896–908.

World Bank. 2004. *World Development Report 2004: Making Services Work for Poor People.* Washington, DC.

———. 2007. *Database for Political Institutions 2006.* Washington, DC.

———. 2008. *World Development Indicators.* Washington, DC.

Yadav, Yogendra. 2000. "Understanding the Second Democratic Upsurge: Trends of Bahujan Participation in Electoral Politics in the 1990s." In Francine Frankel, Zoya Hasa, Rajeev Bhargava, and Balveer Arora (eds.), *Transforming India: Social and Political Dynamics of Democracy.* Oxford: Oxford University Press, 120–145.

Yakobson, Alexander. 1995. "Secret Ballot and Its Effects in the Late Roman Republic." *Hermes* 123: 426–442.

Youde, Jeremy. 2005. "Economics and Government Popularity in Ghana." *Electoral Studies* 24 (1): 1–16.

Young, Crawford. 1965. *Politics in the Congo.* Princeton: Princeton University Press.

———. 1976. *The Politics of Cultural Pluralism.* Madison: University of Wisconsin Press.

Young, Daniel. 2008. "Is Clientelism at Work in African Elections? A Study of Voting Behavior in Kenya and Zambia." *Afrobarometer Working Paper* no. 106.

http://www.afrobarometer.org/files/documents/working_papers/AfropaperNo
106.pdf.
———. 2009. "Support You Can Count On: Ethnicity, Partisanship, and Retrospective Voting in Africa." *Afrobarometer Working Paper* no. 115. http://www
.afrobarometer.org/files/documents/working_papers/AfropaperNo115.pdf.

The Contributors

Ravi Bhavnani is associate professor in the Department of International Relations and Political Science at the Graduate Institute of International and Development Studies in Geneva, Switzerland.

Michael Bratton is University Distinguished Professor of political science and African studies at Michigan State University, and a senior adviser for the Afrobarometer.

Tse-Hsin Chen is a postdoctoral research fellow at the Institute of Political Science, Academia Sinica, in Taipei, Taiwan.

Wonbin Cho is assistant professor in the Department of Political Science and Diplomacy at Sungkyunkwan University in Seoul, Korea.

Jeffrey Conroy-Krutz is assistant professor in the Department of Political Science at Michigan State University.

Benn Eifert is head of quantitative research for Overland Advisors in San Francisco.

Ari Greenberg is acting director of the Open Government Partnership in Washington, D.C.

Eric Kramon is a predoctoral fellow at the Center on Democracy, Development, and the Rule of Law at Stanford University, and a PhD candidate in political science at the University of California–Los Angeles.

Carolyn Logan is assistant professor in the Department of Political Science at Michigan State University, and deputy director for the Afrobarometer.

Robert Mattes is a professor in the Department of Political Studies at the University of Cape Town, director of the university's Democracy in Africa Research Unit at the Centre for Social Science Research, and a senior adviser for the Afrobarometer.

Edward Miguel is professor of economics at the University of California–Berkeley.

Devra Moehler is assistant professor in the Annenberg School for Communication at the University of Pennsylvania.

Pippa Norris is a professor in the John F. Kennedy School of Government at Harvard University.

Daniel Posner is Total Professor on contemporary Africa in the Department of Political Science at the Massachusetts Institute of Technology.

Carlos Shenga is a PhD candidate in political studies at the University of Cape Town, and a national investigator in Mozambique for the Afrobarometer.

Index

About the Book

How do individual Africans view competitive elections? How do they behave at election time? What are the implications of new forms of popular participation for citizenship and democracy? Drawing on a decade of research from the cross-national Afrobarometer project, the authors of this seminal collection explore the emerging role of mass politics in Africa's fledgling democracies.

Michael Bratton is University Distinguished Professor of political science and African studies at Michigan State University. He also serves as a senior adviser for the Afrobarometer.